The Best Man Who Ever Served The Crown?

The Best Man Who Ever Served The Crown?

A Life of Donald McLean

Ray Fargher

Victoria University Press

VICTORIA UNIVERSITY PRESS
Victoria University of Wellington
PO Box 600 Wellington

First published 2007

National Library of New Zealand Cataloguing-in-Publication Data

Fargher, R. W. S. (Raymond Watson Shaw), 1920-
The best man who ever served the Crown? : a life of Donald McLean / Ray Fargher.
Includes bibliographical references and index.
ISBN 978-0-86473-560-7
1. McLean, Donald, Sir, 1820-1877. 2. Statesmen—New Zealand—Biography. 3. Maori (New Zealand people)—Government relations. 4. Maori (New Zealand people)—Land tenure.
5. New Zealand—Politics and government—19th century.
6. New Zealand—History—1840-1876. I. Title.
993.022092—dc 22

Published with the assistance of The History Group of the Ministry for Culture and Heritage

Printed by Printlink, Wellington
Typeset by Ahi Text Solutions, Wellington

To Phoebe Meikle mentor and friend

Contents

Illustrations

Tareha Te Moananui
Carnell Collection, Alexander Turnbull Library G- 19389-1/1

The Cottage at Maraekakaho, built between 1862 and 1869
Author's collection

Christopher William Richmond
S P Andrew Collection, Alexander Turnbull Library G- 13502-1/1

J. D. Ormond
General Assembly Library Collection, Alexander Turnbull Library F- 156-35mm -E

Archibald McLean
Collection of Hawke's Bay Cultural Trust – Hawke's Bay Museum

Donald McLean c. 1870
Alexander Turnbull Library 1/2-103970-F

McLean residence at Napier, 1870s
Collection of Hawke's Bay Cultural Trust – Hawke's Bay Museum

McLean's grave, Napier Cemetery
Collection of Hawke's Bay Cultural Trust – Hawke's Bay Museum

Maps

Acknowledgments

I acknowledge the support and encouragement of the late Phoebe Meikle without which I would not have been persuaded to begin and to persevere with the task.

I am grateful to Bill Renwick who read several drafts and offered helpful and detailed comment shaped by his clarity of thought, and to Alan Ward who read the first draft and by his response persuaded me to review my approach to McLean's activities. I could not have had a more helpful editor than Andrew Mason who encouraged me to focus the flow of the narrative and by asking questions encouraged me to clarify my approach to telling the story of McLean's life and work.

I am grateful to many who read and commented on sections of my first draft – Michael King, Phoebe Meikle, Judy McDonald, Hayden Riggs, Christine Cole Catley and members of her Wellington Writers Group. My thanks to Angela Ballara and Barry Rigby who made time to check the final draft for historical inaccuracies and to offer helpful comments. Any errors that remain are my responsibility.

Many people gave me the opportunity for stimulating and informative discussions on McLean the man and on nineteenth-century New Zealand history. My thanks to Angela Ballara, James Belich, Judith Binney, Peter Boag, Dean Cowie, Paul Goldsmith, Moana Jackson, Danny Keenan, Don Loveridge, Vincent O'Malley, Claudia Orange, Barry Rigby, Te Ahukaramu Charles Royal, Keith Sorrenson and Alan Ward.

Peter Matheson, John Murray and Michael Grimshaw offered guidance on McLean's religious belief. Vincent O'Sullivan and Harry Ricketts shared with me their thoughts on the role of a biographer.

My thanks to students Jim McNicholas and Hayden Riggs for additional research and to Miria Simpson and Charles Royal for translations of Maori letters.

My thanks to John Huria for his meticulous editing of the final draft and to Fergus Barrowman of Victoria University Press for his support in the publication of this book.

I acknowledge the help of the staff of National Archives, the librarians of the Hawkes Bay and Taranaki museums and, in particular, David Colquhoun and the staff of of the Manuscript Room of the Alexander Turnbull Library, always helpful, friendly and competent over the years of my research.

Abbreviations

AJHR	*Appendix to the Journal of the House of Representatives*
ATL	Alexander Turnbull Library
GBPP	*Great Britain Parliamentary Papers*
NA	National Archives
NZPD	*New Zealand Parliamentary Debates*

Introduction

Donald McLean has so far not received the attention he deserves from biographers. The manuscript collection of his papers in the Alexander Turnbull Library has been an essential source for historians for more than sixty years. But there has been a general feeling among historians and biographers that though the lives of other leading nineteenth-century public figures were a manageable project, Donald McLean's life was not. The more than twenty metres of shelving of his papers in the Alexander Turnbull Library are a daunting prospect for a prospective biographer.

It is scarcely surprising, then, that few attempts have been made to write about McLean 'from the inside'. James Cowan published a full-scale biography in 1940. Although he had access to all McLean's papers the result was a sketchy and uncritical narrative. My unpublished MA thesis, written in 1947, examined McLean's work as the Government's chief land purchase officer in the 1850s. Alan Ward gives valuable insights into McLean's public life in *A Show of Justice* (1974) and in his essay on McLean in the *Dictionary of New Zealand Biography*. The present work seeks to fill a biographical gap by placing Donald McLean at the heart of his own story.

What drove McLean? To understand, we must look to his formative years. His early upbringing in a Highland gentry family of Presbyterian faith imbued him with a strong sense of family obligation as well as deeply held religious beliefs. Separated from his parents as a child, he was brought up in Scottish manses and accustomed to daily prayer and bible readings. McLean saw himself as called by God to a high purpose and believed that he was guided by Divine Providence. It was one further step to convince himself that he could not be wrong. McLean believed that if you were obedient to God you would prosper. His Scots upbringing demanded that a man must work hard in his calling. To waste time was a deadly sin. The pursuit of wealth was morally sanctioned, therefore, provided it was accompanied by a sober, industrious life. Like other young men who came to New Zealand in the early years of the colony McLean was 'on the make', eager to acquire wealth. His association with Crown land purchases enabled him to amass a lucrative landed estate of his own. Moreover, he was fortunate to gain powerful patrons in the Colonial Secretary, Andrew Sinclair, and Governors Grey and Gore Browne.

Pragmatism marked McLean's response in his dealings with Maori. He insisted that he purchased their land for the Crown only with their 'free and intelligent consent', yet to secure a sale he was prepared to engineer that consent and exclude some iwi or hapu who held customary rights.

McLean was fiercely motivated; in any enterprise which he undertook he had to be in control and he had to succeed. Friends became his enemies, if, like Henry Russell, Colonel Whitmore and Sir George Grey, they opposed or thwarted his plans. Within his family he demanded obedience from his wife, and his brothers and sisters came under his censure.

McLean was a man who walked alone. Always secretive, he did not confide his motives to paper either in official communications or in personal letters. He kept his thoughts to himself and did things in his own time and in his own way. This reticence presents a problem for his biographer seeking to analyse the motives for McLean's actions. From 1846 till his wife's death in 1852 he did keep a personal diary that revealed some of his innermost thoughts on his courtship and marriage. Even there he refrained from any comment on his mentor and master, Governor Grey.

In his role as government land purchase agent McLean discovered another motivation. He saw himself as the benefactor of the early pioneers, the man who was making it possible for them to build a better Britain on the other side of the world.

Equating Christianity with British civilisation, he saw himself as a standard bearer of British imperialism with a duty to raise Maori from their barbarous state. In these views, no matter how we regard them today, he displayed the ethnocentrism and paternalism typical of the Victorian age. He saw himself as a mentor guiding and elevating Maori. Like his fellow colonists, he believed that assimilation would be for their benefit. Unlike many of them, he maintained that Maori were a virile and intelligent race that would survive the impact of a superior civilisation. He was, however, prepared to wait for Maori to decide when assimilation should take place.

During the 1850s McLean's responsibilities broadened to include the Crown's management of its relations with Maori as well as the purchase of their land. In 1856, when the colony was granted responsible government, settler politicians pressed for the right to include Maori affairs within the scope of their self-governing responsibilities. McLean's role as the chief administrator in Maori affairs became a flashpoint of controversy. In carrying out Governor Gore Browne's policies for the administration of native affairs, which the 1852 constitution had expressly placed under the Governor's authority, McLean found himself under siege in the political struggle between the Governor and his ministers that lasted throughout Gore Browne's term.

By the time his career as a government official had ended with his forced resignation in 1861, McLean had established himself as one of the landed elite of Hawkes Bay in his own right and was himself a fount of patronage for members of his own family and for those who acted as agents in political and land-purchase matters. His obsession for control led him to monitor the activities of his siblings and to censure any departure from frugality and hard work. During the years McLean spent acquiring Maori land for the Crown he had many opportunities to purchase land for himself and he took some of them. At his death his landed estate in Hawkes Bay had a value which expressed in today's terms was worth more than $25 million. These private property dealings were to be the subject of personal attacks during his years as a member of the General Assembly.

With his Maraekakaho estate as his base McLean immediately made his mark as a leading provincial politician. As Provincial Superintendent and the Government Agent for the East Coast during the Pai Marire incursion and Te Kooti's depredations, McLean was in the thick of negotiations between the Crown, hapu and iwi. His autocratic tendencies again came to the fore and in 1868, in another battle of wills, he was dismissed as Government Agent.

At that time McLean was the member for Napier and becoming quite a force in Parliament. He had a reputation as one of the few men in the colony who understood Maori and could deal with them. He had had become convinced that policies of repression and land confiscation had failed. Te Kooti had to be hunted down, but the colony needed a period of disengagement between Maori and settler. As Native Minister almost continuously between 1869 and 1876 he successfully managed that disengagement. He was probably the only politician who could have achieved agreement between Maori and Pakeha. It was in part a pragmatic response: he recognised that the prosperity of the colony and his fellow pastoralists depended on peace.

After the wars of the 1860s, more than any other man, he sought peace and a measure of reconciliation. He withstood settler pressure to punish Maori further. In attempting to reconcile the settlers' demand for land to the Maori desire to retain independence, McLean failed to satisfy either. He was ahead of his contemporaries in his thinking on the place of Maori in a colonial society. From the time he entered the House of Representatives in 1867, McLean advocated limited self-government for Maori including a national council of chiefs. Although this would have left him in control as Native Minister, it was to his credit that he persevered in urging measures unpopular in a settler parliament. But in the last resort, if he had to choose between Maori and settler, McLean would stand alongside the settlers, especially when his own financial interests were at stake.

McLean's influence depended on his personal character and the relationships he formed with the rangatira (leaders). His failure to establish adequate legislative and administrative structures to govern those relationships resulted in a vacuum after his death, to the disadvantage of Maori. His successors as Native Minister lacked both his patience and subtlety and a concern for a people attempting to adjust to assimilation.

When he was appointed Sub-Protector of Aborigines in 1844, in his youthful enthusiasm McLean dedicated himself to work for the benefit of both Maori and Pakeha. As the years went by he had to accept that settler demands and Maori interests could not always be reconciled. Always pragmatic, he would ultimately bow to settler intransigence. For example, in 1856 he proposed Maori representation in Parliament, in 1867 he argued for eight Maori members in the House and in 1872 he proposed a limited measure of Maori self-government, but in each case he withdrew when faced with settler opposition. Given a dominant settler parliament that was not willing to spend money on or to share power with Maori, he was prepared to settle for what was feasible in admitting Maori to a limited share in the country's legislative and administrative structures within the context of settler supremacy. At the same time, whatever his intentions, McLean had an influential role in implementing policies that, before the end of the nineteenth century, were to lead to the political, economic and cultural marginalisation of the Maori people within what had been their own country.

Chapter 1
The Scottish Diaspora

Donald McLean was one of many Scots who, in the nineteenth century, migrated to British settlement colonies in Canada, Australia and New Zealand as well as to the United States, India, Latin America and Japan. In this they were following the path set by their forebears up to a century earlier, who had fought overseas in Britain's imperial wars.

Until the Act of Union in 1707, Scotland had been a sovereign kingdom. After the union, Scottish nobility followed the centre of authority to London. Samuel Johnson remarked that the noblest prospect a Scotsman ever saw was the high road to England. With the defeat of the Jacobite rising in support of Bonnie Prince Charlie in 1745, the Highland chieftains, who had fought on the Jacobite side, were eager to rehabilitate themselves with the Crown and regain their forfeited estates. They raised Highland regiments from their own clansmen and sent them to fight overseas for the British Empire against the American colonists or against Napoleon's armies in Europe. The Scottish regiments became the 'cannon fodder of imperial war'.[1]

While preserving their nationality, the Scots were prepared to accept loss of statehood in exchange for a satisfying and profitable role in the dynamic expansion of the British Empire. Sir Walter Scott in his novels could express a pride in Scottish tradition alongside an unquestioning loyalty to the United Kingdom. Donald McLean was descended from a Highland clan who had fought for Bonnie Prince Charlie and had seen the Highland Scots, an indigenous people, subjugated by English imperial might. A century later, McLean would display a fervent and unquestioning loyalty to that same imperial power, embodied in the person of Queen Victoria, and would advocate force to suppress any move by another indigenous people, the Maori, to retain their independence. The Scots overseas, accustomed at home to exercising more power over their tenants than the English, were 'more prone to take a strong line in suppressing colonial disorder and more unapologetic in devising new and more efficient forms of centralised control'.[2] Indeed, as James Belich has remarked, two Highland Scots were to ensure the dominance of a white settlement colony in New Zealand: Donald McLean, by buying up Maori land; and General Duncan Cameron, by military conquest of the Maori.[3]

During the nineteenth century, the combination of rural depopulation and urban growth caused the Scots to emigrate in large numbers. They migrated overseas when they felt the opportunities to be better than their prospects in Scotland. Overseas, the Scots adapted readily, willing to take risks and face challenges, while retaining their distinctive religious and educational practices.

They took with them their religious faith, evangelical in its unquestioning adherence to the Bible as the infallible word of God and in a belief in personal salvation through Christ. In nineteenth-century Scotland, Presbyterian Church ministers were important figures. They saw Scotland as another Israel and its proud, stiff-necked inhabitants as a second chosen people of the Lord. 'The commands of the Church were assumed by churchmen to be the standards which the population strove to follow in their daily behaviour, and the message of salvation that they preached from pulpit and tract was the frame in which people saw the drama of their lives.'[4] In 1843 came the Disruption. Forty per cent of the Church of Scotland ministers, led by the Revd Thomas Chalmers, walked out of the General Assembly to form the Free Church of Scotland, thereby surrendering their churches, manses and stipends. The issue was patronage: who was to appoint the minister – the congregation, or the noble patron whose right was set out in English law? The Free Church proclaimed that the right of the people and the law of Christ prevailed over English statute. This view was brought to New Zealand in 1848, after the General Assembly of the Free Church gave approval to Captain William Cargill and the Revd Thomas Burns to found a Free Church settlement at Otago. These men also brought with them Chalmers' social vision: a society that accepted a laissez-faire economy, rejected democracy in favour of the 'divine origins of a hierarchy where rich and poor had their obligations and their place', and upheld the 'prime responsibility of the individual for his own material well-being and spiritual health'. For Chalmers, the wealthy had a responsibility for personal philanthropy – to give freely of their time and money to the community. Andrew Carnegie, who had emigrated to the United States, in 1848 declared that 'the gospel of wealth but echoes Christ's world'.[5] These beliefs were apparent in Donald McLean's ambition both to get on in this world and, through personal salvation, to enter into the next world.

McLean was one of many Scots who became prominent in early New Zealand. Of the first Auckland entrepreneurs, John Logan Campbell and his partner, William Brown, were of Scottish descent, as was Thomas Morrin. Later, in Otago, the commercial and industrial world was dominated by Scottish immigrants who were active in banking, commerce, manufacturing, engineering, breweries, and woollen, flour and paper mills. Scots abroad maintained commercial links with Scotland, with Scottish banks providing capital for the development of the Australasian colonies. Scottish emigrants would employ only fellow Scots as McLean did with his Highland shepherds and managers in Otago and Hawkes Bay. He frequently received letters from Scotland seeking his help in enabling friends and relatives to find employment in New Zealand. In the development of the pastoral lands of the North and South Islands, Scottish runholders were also prominent. In Hawkes Bay, where McLean had his Maraekakaho run, a quarter of the runholders were Scots although they made up only 11 per cent of the population.[6]

The distinctive educational practices of Scotland, including a belief in education as a basic civil right, were also part of the baggage that Scottish settlers brought with them. Adam Smith argued that 'a man without the proper use of intellectual faculties' was 'mutilated and deformed' in an essential part of human nature: 'The stimulus of education widened the intellectual horizon and gave the tools to make the best of opportunities.'[7] Scottish people took pride in their schools and universities, which they held were in advance of anything in England. In the eighteenth century, Edinburgh and Glasgow universities were the centre of the Scottish Enlightenment. The Scots possessed a zeal for education not found among the working class in other European countries. Their provision for education enabled most working-class children to gain basic literary skills and a small number of boys to go on to more advanced study.

In Argyll, where Donald McLean attended three parish schools, seven out of ten children received an elementary education. Parish schools were controlled by the minister and kirk session, but the teacher's salary was met by a tax on landlords and tenants. The Bible was the only book for reading available in most schools. Parish schools taught both Gaelic and English. Although Highlanders spoke Gaelic, they realised that their children would need to read and speak English if they were to make their way in the world outside the Highlands.

The Scottish commitment to educational excellence and to equality of educational opportunity influenced the New Zealand pattern. The early state secondary schools were modelled on the Scottish grammar school rather than the English public school. Otago University, founded in 1869, was the first in New Zealand, as Otago Girls' High School was the first girls' school, established in 1871.

Donald McLean's family was of the gentry on Tiree, an isle of the Inner Hebrides, and linked to McLean of Ardgour. They had connections with the Campbells and Macdonalds. Donald's great-grandmother married a Campbell of Scanadale, while his grandfather took as his wife a Campbell of Dunstaffnage, a collateral branch of the Argyll family. The link with the Macdonalds went back to an earlier age when Macdonald, the Lord of the Isles, placed his son and heir in the household of McLean of Ardgour before conquering his foes. In gratitude he took one of McLean's sons, saying that he would make his fortune, and finally married him to one of his daughters. Donald McLean's family links with the gentry were recalled on his death in 1877. The *Hawke's Bay Herald* noted that Sir Donald McLean was the eighth member of his family on whom a knighthood had been conferred and that, on his mother's side, the McColls were connected by intermarriage to several noble and distinguished Scottish families. There was also a strong military tradition in the family. McLean's maternal grandfather, a Campbell and a baronet, served in the army, and among the Macdonalds there was a general and a captain from Glencoe. Two uncles, Charles and Donald, both saw service in the West Indies and died of fever.

Three generations of McLeans held a farm at Kilmaluag on Tiree as tacksmen to the Duke of Argyll. A tack was the term applied to a lease in Scotland and a tacksman, in usage restricted to the Highlands, was one who made a customary payment levied by a feudal superior. The tacksman, a close relative of the clan chief, was allotted a large block of land to oversee and was obliged to appear with his armed followers at the chief's bidding. By the early nineteenth century the tacksman ranked high in social status. He paid rent to his chief and either farmed the land himself or lived off the rental income from land that he sublet to crofters.

In Scotland, by the start of the nineteenth century there had been a significant population increase. This can be attributed to medical advances – for example, vaccination against smallpox, which had been killing a sixth of the population – and to the introduction of a new crop, the potato. In the Hebrides the pressure of population on resources had reduced people to subsistence level. On Tiree, home of the McLeans, the population grew from 1500 to 4450 between 1755 and 1831. Starvation threatened. Early in the nineteenth century, the landowners began to dispense with tacksmen, whom they saw as 'nothing but parasites interposed between a proprietor and his working tenants to suck up rents'.[8] When prices fell after 1815 with the end of the Napoleonic Wars, the landowners, hungry for money, failed to reduce their rents and, by breaking up the blocks allotted to their tacksmen, found they could place more people on the land, thus easing population pressure and ensuring themselves increased rents.

Population pressure in the Scottish Highlands became an incentive for migration. The region lacked the coal resources that enabled the Lowlands to absorb the increase within its rising industrial strength, which was based on the rapid development of a huge industrial complex centred on Glasgow, soon to become the second city of the British Empire. For a time the consequences of population growth in the Highlands were delayed by the introduction of the potato crop and an increase in cash income through short-term migration to the Lowlands for seasonal employment, together with growth in the production of goods for export – for example, cattle, and kelp (the rich alkaline ash remaining after kelp was burnt was needed for the production of soap, glass and linen). The old social structure of chieftains and retainers using traditional farming methods could no longer be maintained in the face of a growing population, yet Highland society was slow to accept the need for change. There was no coal to establish an industrial base. In the long term sheep farming was naturally best suited to the Highland economy. Indeed, there was no option; to continue the old agrarian practices would have destroyed any chance of economic survival by requiring the importation of food. The introduction of pastoral farming, however, meant less demand for labour. The alternatives became stark: either feed people through imports of grain, or bring about emigration. The noble landlords decided to clear the people and replace them with sheep. Already, of course, they had dispensed with their tacksmen, the natural leaders who might have provided the entrepreneurial element for a new commercial economy. It was in this context that Donald McLean sailed from Oban in the Scottish Highlands in July 1838, never to return.

Donald McLean was born on 25 October 1820, on the Isle of Tiree, the fourth of nine children of John McLean and Margaret McColl. Tiree is an island of the Inner Hebrides, twelve miles long and six miles wide. It has a mild climate tempered by a persistent wind so that today windsurfers gather from all over Britain to surf on Lake Bhasapol; while the thatched roofs of the old crofters' cottages are held down by steel cables and there is not a tree to be seen on the island. The soil is fertile and its Gaelic name, 'The Land of Corn', comes from the time when it supplied grain to the monks of the fifteenth-century monastery on the nearby Isle of Iona.

John McLean, Donald's father, inherited the farm at Kilmaluag when the lease had three years to run. Donald's aunt, Annabella McLean, believed that the tack was not renewed because John had intervened when one Colin McColl quarrelled with the Duke of Argyll's factor. This incident was more likely used as a pretext by the duke for the action he had already intended to take: to increase his income from rents by dividing the farm into small crofts. John was dispossessed of Kilmaluag by 1824.[9] When Annabella visited Tiree in 1852, she was sorry to see the house 'with only the walls standing to remind of all that they once possessed'.[10] John McLean's removal from Kilmaluag seems to have led to financial hardship and to his consequent departure from Tiree to Argyll on the mainland. Nothing is known about his life thereafter. His daughters, as they grew up, were destined for a bleak existence as lady companions in the homes of the gentry. Annabella nagged her nephews, including Donald, to contribute money to help their sisters to survive.

Little is known of Donald McLean's formative years in Scotland. The only sources are a few letters from his aunt in response to his inquiries about his family, and newspaper articles in New Zealand and Scotland at the time of his death, conveying conflicting accounts of his youthful years in the Highlands – stating incorrectly, for example, that he could scarcely read or write when he arrived in New Zealand.[11] While living at the manse of the local minister, the young Donald attended elementary parish schools at Craignish, Melfort and Luing, on the shores of Loch Melfort in Argyll, where he would have learnt basic literary skills.

At about the age of twelve, Donald went to live with his bachelor uncle and guardian, the Revd Donald McColl, minister in the Church of Scotland at Kingairloch on the west side of Loch Linnhe. After the Disruption in 1843, McColl's conservative outlook kept him in the Church of Scotland. He accepted the offer of the parish of Glenorchy from his patron, the Marquis of Breadalbane. McLean's education continued with private tuition from his uncle. He studied history, literature and divinity in preparation for the ministry, but it seems that he had no interest in entering that or any other profession. Later in life he expressed to his wife, Susan, a preference for open-air life in the country over the social round of the town. Donald's two elder brothers also left home as young men: Archibald for a seafaring life and Alexander to learn farming.

McLean's separation from his parents and his siblings at a young age and his isolation in the austere regime of the Presbyterian manse of his bachelor uncle no doubt contributed to the shaping of the man. He had been taught to repress emotion, yet was grateful when Maori rangatira displayed their regard and middle-aged women, like Helen Wilson, indulged their motherly instincts. Likewise, this early separation from family developed his self-reliance and readiness to make a new life in a faraway colony.

In McLean's papers there is only one letter from his parents, and that is addressed to his elder brother Archy. In later years, though he spoke of or corresponded with friends and relatives in Scotland, McLean never referred to his parents or his boyhood there. More significantly, nowhere in his diaries does McLean mention his parents. His father appears to have died before 1840 and his mother before 1844, the year in which he began to keep a diary. Was it that, like Dickens and Kipling, he felt bitter that his parents had abandoned him when they sent him away from home to be brought up in the manses of Presbyterian ministers?

After McLean left Scotland, he continued to correspond with his uncle and guardian until the latter's death in the 1860s. Neither showed affection. Topics were limited to inquiries and news about relatives, with McLean recounting at length his success as an official and his uncle, who remained in the Church of Scotland, commenting obsequiously on his association with his patron.

A photo taken at the time McLean left Scotland shows, by his dress and bearing, that this was no working-class lad but a young gentleman born to rule. In 1838 he had been invited by relatives to accompany them to New South Wales. There he gained practical experience in sheep farming. His employer then sent him to take charge of a new out-station near Bathurst. The eighteen year old found himself in charge of shepherds, bullock drivers, stockmen and carpenters. In writing of his experiences to Provost Lumsden of Glasgow, McLean described his men as 'a reckless bunch of transports' [convicts] whom he 'had difficulty in managing'.[12] This venture was abandoned and McLean returned to Sydney, where he heard most favourable reports of New Zealand as a country attractive to young adventurers. Through a New South Wales relative, McLean was appointed New Zealand agent for the Sydney merchants of Abercrombie and Co., who sent him to New Zealand at the beginning of 1840 to look after their interests. Aged nineteen and penniless, he landed in the Bay of Islands a day or two after Captain William Hobson arrived in HMS *Herald* on 29 January 1840. In later years he looked back to this moment. He had no idea what his future might be, 'although like most young men of my age my buoyant spirits anticipated bright prospects. But it never entered my head that the Treaty of Waitangi, which was being entered into at that time between Capt. Hobson and the New Zealand rangatira could in any way influence my career ... how thankful I should feel that my fate has been so successful. Few have done so well of the persons who came to New Zealand in that period.'[13]

Donald McColl, with avuncular interest, referred to a letter from 'his good friend Mr. Sinclair' (Andrew Sinclair, a naval surgeon and fellow Scot), who had 'acted the part of a friend and indeed of a father towards Donald and ... he had got him a good appointment in New Zealand to which colony young Donald was about to sail'. He noted that Abercrombie and Co. allowed McLean a good salary and a comfortable home but 'he must take some time if the Almighty spares him before he can assist his poor mother and family much but I am sure he is anxious to do all he can and that as soon as he can manage to aid them'.[14] Abercrombie and Co. was engaged in the timber trade, as well as mining copper on Great Barrier Island and rendering down the ore for shipment from Tryphena.

The earliest documentation of McLean's presence in New Zealand is a rudimentary commercial note dated 17 September 1841 and stating, 'Three months after date I promise to Daniel [*sic*] McLean, or order, the sum of Fifteen pounds in pork or other New Zealand produce Signed Robert B ...'

Shortly after this, McLean left Abercrombie and Co. and, with two other young men, all without experience or capital but with youthful optimism and some burden of debt, attempted to acquire rights from Maori to cut timber, and to buy a block of land at Motunau (probably near Whitianga in the Thames–Coromandel area). Their next employment was with a trader, John McLeod, sailing a schooner in the Hauraki Gulf and the Firth of Thames. By 1843 McLean was sailing a cutter from the Firth of Thames around Coromandel to the Bay of Plenty coast, on one trip taking on board several canoe-loads of 'brimston' (sulphur) from Whale Island near Whakatane, transporting Maori produce, pigs and potatoes, together with nails, tar, pitch, paint and tobacco, as well as passengers, both Maori and European.[15] To carry on his trading activities McLean had to become fluent in Maori. No doubt it helped that he was already bilingual, speaking both Gaelic and English.

One of his young business associates, an Irishman named J. H. Townsend, developed a friendship with McLean that continued through correspondence for years after he had returned to Ireland – a curious contrast between the ebullient and reckless Irishman and the cautious Scot. In February 1845, after McLean had become a government official, Townsend wrote from Adelaide to tell him of the failure of their enterprises. A stand of timber turned out to be a mile from the beach and contained only six trees; their association with McLeod had also been unprofitable. Townsend wrote that 'McLeod and Mootonow [Motunau] are deplorable – the duty off tobacco has certainly hurt the old ass and losses reflect mismanagement with gifts for women have left the poor old man badly off – my heart pities him but his dishonesty and his old foul tongue will ever have him as he is'. McLean should be thankful that he got out of the 'Mootonow' partnership with McLeod: 'the story of his being short of two thousand pounds in managing the branch of the bank at Campbelltown is true. I pity the poor old fellow but by Jove when men do dishonest things they must suffer for it.'[16]

The other young associate, John McLean, told Donald McLean in December 1844 that Townsend had had to leave New Zealand for Adelaide 'having behaved exceeding ill and taken to his old habit of drinking'. He had attempted to run off with the vessel *Marora*, belonging to McLeod, but was pursued and picked up near Browns Island, a few miles from Auckland. Writing from Adelaide, Townsend asked Donald McLean to tell no one of his intention to return to New Zealand and cheerfully insisted that 'people who now doubtless think me an unprincipled fellow or in plain words a damned rogue will have cause to alter their opinion'.[17]

After his return to Ireland around 1846, Townsend, who claimed to come from a leading influential family, married 'as respectably as my family entitled me' and became a county magistrate like his forebears. His letters to McLean recall youthful exhilaration in facing the challenge of the sea and of 'the old trials we have passed through together and the many squalls we have weathered'. In 1854 Townsend wrote of his vivid memories of the Sandspit Passage (between Pakihi (Sandspit Island) and the mainland at the entrance to the Firth of Thames), 'casting anchor in a gale of wind and passing a sleepless night'. He was sure that he could 'still steer a boat blindfold' from the Soldiers Point past Browns Island and down to Waiheke or the Sandspit Passage.

His letters also contain coy references to the attractions of Maori women. 'Old fellow how are you getting on and how do you and the Tangata Maori *not a word about the wahines* agree? ... neither do I forget the Coromandel harbour with all its beauties both natural and living ... How goes on the Maoris never forgetting the wahines, I mean the ones I knew.'[18]

In the early years of the New Zealand colony many migrants were young men with little or no money, looking for adventure and easily attracted by the charms of young Maori women. In recounting their adventures, the possibilities of fornicating their way around Maori pa loomed large. In 1846 James Grindell, later to become one of McLean's officials, objected to the missionary influence on the Maori since 'before these wretches took to psalm singing a man could get a pig and a woman at every place free but now it is just the reverse'.[19] Donald McLean, as well as Townsend, hinted at such activities. In a letter to an earlier companion, Charles Morison, by then living 'in the bush of New Holland' (New South Wales), he wished that Morison might come to stay at New Plymouth for five or six months as, now that he was a government official, he had 'a beautiful cottage, a black servant and thank God all the necessities of life with the very best society in the place ... of course there must not be a word now a days about native lassies as Protector that is all forgot and past' – he crossed out 'and so much the better'.[20]

In his early years McLean was often in debt. The money he earned from his trading ventures was insufficient for his needs. His response to financial difficulties revealed a characteristic that would prevail throughout his life: a tendency to procrastinate. The 1844 letter from John McLean, his companion with Townsend, reminded Donald of his debt and that as soon as possible he should forward a remittance for £18 8s 6d. John also informed him that there appeared to be no prospect of getting Ngatai or other Maori to pay even one shilling of their respective accounts. The only remedy, he said, was to try to get Ngatai at Motunau to repay him in land 'and this I have no doubt you could easily manage to arrange from your official situation' (Donald McLean was by then Sub-Protector of Aborigines). He asked Donald to send him the deed they signed with Ngati Maru, a Hauraki tribe, regarding their claim on part of the land at Motunau which they had agreed to concede for two guns. Maori had approached him twice talking of payment and 'I beg to impress on you the necessity to have these matters closed without delay'.[21] Charles Morison wrote from Sydney in 1844 to remind McLean that he still owed him £11 8s 9d. Morison was still waiting in 1847, and pleaded that he was 'not worth a shilling except for the little stock I have ... so for God's sake my dear fellow remit what you can'.[22] Payment did not arrive until 1854.

McLean continued to procrastinate over payment of debts even after he held a 'lucrative appointment' as Inspector of Police. In 1847 P. Abercrombie, a son of the Sydney merchant, wrote complaining that McLean had not replied to a letter requesting him to remit a balance owing, £20, as he was very hard up. Two months later Abercrombie wrote that McLean may have had an excuse for not remitting the money previously but surely he had had an opportunity since then. If McLean did not remit the sum either in full or in part he would take him to court.[23] Years later, in 1858, Abercrombie wrote from Melbourne that 'I have been turning over some old papers ... there seems to be standing in my books against yourself a balance of 67 pounds ... I remember your promising to remit but could get nothing but silver. As there are banks in your part of the world that can be easily overcome, but whether you remit or not let me have a long letter from you and tell me all the news from this part ... I'm worse than when I left New Zealand and now scarcely able to keep my head above water.'[24]

Chapter 2
Apprentice Years: Sub-Protector of Aborigines

In January 1844 Donald McLean found gainful employment through his patron, Dr Andrew Sinclair, who had become New Zealand's Colonial Secretary. He recommended McLean for a post in the Department of the Protector of Aborigines. McLean took care to cultivate his relationship with Sinclair, expressing his gratification that his patron was satisfied with his performance. He hoped that 'I may at all times continue to meet the approbation of my superiors in office, more especially yourself to whom I am indebted for many acts of kindness independent of the appointment I hold'.[1] On taking up his appointment as head of the Native Land Purchase Department a decade later in 1854, McLean spent three or four months in Sinclair's house and noted that he 'continues his unbounded kindness towards me'.[2] Their close association lasted until Sinclair's retirement in 1856.

The office of Protector of Aborigines reflected the influence of the humanitarian movement that had its greatest triumph with the abolition of slavery in 1833. The humanitarians drew their strength from their deeply held religious beliefs. Evangelicalism became a leaven inside all the churches. Evangelicals were marked by their piety and a belief that individual salvation could come only by faith. Within the Anglican Church, the evangelical Clapham Sect numbered Lord Glenelg, Secretary of State for the Colonies in the 1830s, Dandeson Coates, Secretary of the Church Missionary Society and Sir James Stephen, Permanent Under-Secretary at the Colonial Office, among its influential supporters. Stephen was the man who really ruled Britain's colonies for nearly twenty-five years. Evangelicalism stirred the social conscience of the nation, which was aroused to protect indigenous peoples from the onslaught of European civilisation and to rescue the 'heathen' from eternal damnation. The conviction that the end of the world was near and a belief in post-millennialism – the rule of Christ on earth – gave urgency to the mission to convert the heathen. New Zealand's first Protector of Aborigines was George Clarke, a member of the Church Missionary Society.

The instructions of Glenelg's successor, the Marquis of Normanby, to Hobson in 1839 embodied a cardinal principle of British colonial policy of the time: the obligation to protect the rights of indigenous peoples. The race-relations issue loomed large in the administration of Britain's colonies. At the Colonial Office, Sir James Stephen wished to protect indigenous peoples from the effects of the rapid introduction of European civilisation, but he was also committed to granting self-government to British colonists. Normanby's instructions to Hobson struggled to reconcile these aims.

The British Government at first considered that the benefits accruing to Britain would not compensate for the injury done to the Maori, 'whose title to the soil and to the sovereignty of New Zealand'[3] was indisputable and had been recognised by the Government. Normanby said that, while the British Government still held to that opinion, circumstances beyond its control had compelled it to alter course though 'with extreme reluctance'.[4] Normanby accepted that New Zealand would become a settlement colony. Unless the settlers were restrained by laws and institutions they would make war on 'uncivilised tribes until they disappeared as happened when brought into contact with emigrants from the nations of Christendom'.[5] Britain had acknowledged New Zealand's 1835 Declaration of Independence, a decision of doubtful validity since it consisted of numerous tribes incapable of acting in concert. Nevertheless, that recognition was 'binding on the faith of the British Crown'.[6]

Normanby therefore instructed Hobson to appoint an official to 'watch over the interests of the aborigines as their Protector' and to control land purchases, which should be conducted with 'sincerity, justice and good faith'.[7] Moreover, Maori should not be allowed to enter into contracts in which they 'might be ignorant or unintentional authors of injuries to themselves'.[8] The Crown should not buy land that was essential for Maori to keep for themselves. Any land bought should be limited to areas that Maori could give up without serious inconvenience.[9]

On joining the Department of the Protector of Aborigines on 1 April 1844, McLean was posted to the Auckland office to gain a knowledge of his duties and to act as Maori interpreter for the Chief Magistrate, using the language skills he had developed as a trader. In May, Hobson's successor, Governor Robert FitzRoy, sent him to resolve disputes among local Maori arising from the sale of land at Waiheke. At a gathering of 600 Maori on the west bank of the Thames, McLean assured the rangatira that the Governor would not sanction the sale of any lands they occupied without their approval, and got them to agree to define their boundaries. The Colonial Secretary's Office noted that the Governor 'highly approved the arrangement concluded by McLean ... and the successful conduct of an affair that had been the subject of much discussion and negotiation'.[10] In June George Clarke, the Chief Protector, sent McLean to negotiate with the Hauraki tribe Ngati Paoa over the island of Pakihi near Waiheke in the Hauraki Gulf. Ngati Paoa had complained that the purchase was not complete without its consent.

Donald McLean was appointed Sub-Protector for Taranaki the following month, at the age of twenty-three. On 8 July, Clarke instructed McLean to leave for New Plymouth and 'hasten to allay the excitement of feeling and to preserve the peace',[11] as Maori and European had become agitated over land disputes there.

The Chief Protector gave McLean detailed instructions on the principles to be observed in the discharge of his duties.[12] (See Appendix 1.) McLean was to watch over 'the interests of Her Majesty's Aboriginal Subjects protecting persons and their property and advance the social and moral improvement'. Disputes among Maori should be settled with the help of the rangatira in accordance with their customs. In cases of 'continued obstinacy', compulsory measures should taken in accordance with the recently issued Native Exemption Ordinance which provided that Maori offenders could be arrested only by their own tribal rangatira and be imprisoned only for criminal cases involving rape or murder, and not for civil offences. With the assistance of the rangatira, McLean should encourage Maori to bring their grievances to him, taking account of their customs which helped to preserve their society. War and cannibalism must cease, however, or Maori would be punished. Maori should be assured that the Governor would protect their property and no land would be taken except that which they were willing to alienate. Allowances should be made for both Europeans and Maori in their 'little disputes' owing to their ignorance of each other's language and bearing in mind the tendency of Europeans to tyrannise 'where there is a difference in the shade of skin'. An honourable union between the races should be encouraged. McLean should also make himself acquainted with every passing event and inform Clarke of every important event affecting either Maori or European. As well, he should send a half-yearly report with statistics on increase or decrease of the population.

Clarke's instructions to McLean, though revealing a paternalism similar to Normanby's instructions to Hobson, showed a concern to avoid overturning Maori customs too abruptly and a desire to help Maori to take part in the new European society. Clarke, in his evangelical zeal, identified British civilisation as an integral part of the Christian message brought to the heathen. As a Christian missionary, Clarke believed all men to be sinners and therefore equal in the eyes of God. Nevertheless, his religious belief and his ethnocentrism led him to hold that Maori beliefs and customs were so degrading as to require his advising McLean: 'By your elevated character elevate theirs. Never descend to their standard but raise them to yours.'

Although only four years had elapsed since the signing of the Treaty of Waitangi, Clarke's instructions made no specific reference to its provisions. He stressed the Crown's responsibility to protect the rights and property of Maori against potential European exploitation. He also suggested some practical precautions for the Sub-Protector to adopt in assessing approaches made to him by Maori and colonist.

McLean's territory, the Western Division of the North Island, stretched north to lakes Taupo and Rotorua and south to Wanganui. He was based at the infant settlement of New Plymouth, established less than three years earlier. McLean's instructions required him to make an annual visit to all inhabited parts of his district. To cover his vast territory, McLean travelled 20 to 30 miles in a day, sometimes by horse, sometimes on foot, in all some 800 miles before his return to New Plymouth. In the absence of roads, travel inland to reach lakes Taupo and Rotorua meant following Maori trails through rugged hill country and dense bush, fording fast-flowing rivers and then travelling across the open tussock land of the Volcanic Plateau. McLean depended on his Maori guides on these journeys. Travel, whether through the bush or along the coast, was exhausting and sometimes dangerous; his youth and powerful physique – McLean was over six feet tall and strongly built – were an invaluable asset. In 1845, for instance, travelling along the coast near Mokau, some of McLean's party nearly drowned in foaming surf; indeed, they believed that his servant had been lost. Fortunately the servant arrived at camp that night having struggled up a cliff face. Rain poured down incessantly, but they managed to pitch a tent and light a fire. McLean divided his meagre rations of food with the party and invited them to share in the shelter of his tent where they spent an uncomfortable night. So strongly did the rain flow through the tent that they struck the tent and set off at early dawn.

His party generally consisted of Maori acting as guides and porters together with his 'black servant', William, 'my good and faithful Sambo', who each night pitched McLean's tent, laid out his dry clothes, water to wash and lit a candle so that the 'feeling is as if you are dressing for dinner at home'. However, McLean also doubted the loyalty of his servant. His diary once recorded: 'Up at daybreak, roused Wm. to his work though some curious fears have once or twice entered my heart that my poor faithful Sambo will yet prove otherwise and even perhaps end his master's life. Still I cannot help thinking this is the Devil's delusion to cause my suspicion ... or else a warning from my Maker. Be this as it may let me not destroy my servant's character by even suspecting him.'[13]

In his annual journeys through his district McLean dealt with problems arising from contact between settler and Maori and with conflicts between

Maori custom and British law. He was made aware of the concerns expressed by rangatira over perceived threats to their rangatiratanga (authority) and their unease at the continuing pressure to sell their land. As Sub-Protector and as a representative of the British Crown, the young McLean found himself responsible for mediating among Maori tribes and arbitrating between Maori and settlers; he had to deal with Maori old enough to be his father or grandfather. In carrying out his duties, apart from his mana as the Crown's representative, his most valuable attribute was a fluency in the Maori language. McLean's diary entries recording his dealings with both Maori and settlers leave an impression of a maturity of experience rapidly acquired in the five years since he left Scotland. To the natural self-confidence of any young man, McLean brought also a self-righteous assurance in his ability to handle men and situations – an attribute on which he continued to congratulate himself throughout his official career. That he could win the confidence of the Maori rangatira suggests a gravity of demeanour not common among young men.

Clarke also monitored the progress of his young recruit. His letters offered advice and guidance. 'You will need patience and forbearance towards both Europeans and natives; it will be your duty to give the one race a better opinion of the other. Yours is a mission of peace.'[14] Four months later he was pleased that McLean was continuing to gain the confidence of both Maori and settler: 'upright and honest principles' would always win respect. McLean must strive to dispense 'even-handed justice to both races giving the most ignorant the most favourable consideration'. Clarke observed that Europeans offended Maori through ignorance of their feelings and customs and 'the Natives do the same to the Europeans'. McLean should point this out to both races so that they would be better prepared to 'amicably settle their little differences'. The future prosperity of the country, he believed, depended on 'the mutual good feelings of both races'.[15]

He insisted that McLean be 'firm with the natives' when they were being 'unreasonable with the Europeans'. Maori had been cutting and clearing timber from land that they had sold to the Crown. He instructed McLean to prevent any encroachment or cultivation on that land, to unite with the police magistrate and seek the help of the rangatira. 'Failing these means the sooner you can have a force to put a stop to it the better. I would not purchase another acre of land until the natives agree to remove every annoyance.'[16]

Difficulties provoked by disputed purchases increased during the mid-1840s. Clarke advised McLean to refrain from further purchase activities, nor mix himself up with land purchases as he saw a conflict of interest with his duties as an officer of the Protectorate. Clarke had never been comfortable with his conflicting protector and purchase roles. Finally in 1845 FitzRoy relieved the Protectorate of its purchase responsibilities.

Clarke did instruct McLean to give advice to both settlers and Maori, showing the latter 'how much they injure themselves by becoming unreasonable. It is only by a good feeling between the two races that prosperity can accompany their efforts.' McLean had sought advice on dealing with disputes where Maori women had left their husbands. Clarke confessed that he knew of no remedy, especially as many marriages were enforced with members of a conquering tribe and the women's wish to return to their friends and families was understandable. Where marriage grew out of mutual attachment there would be less running away. Meanwhile, trouble would continue until 'we can raise the moral conditions of the natives'. Clarke also required detailed reports: 'Little things should be noted by you as well as great things. Important inferences can often be deduced from small matters.' In turn, he approved of McLean's reports, sending extracts to the Secretary of State for the Colonies. In September 1845, for instance, Clarke noted: 'Your account of your interview with Te Heuheu (the powerful Ngati Tuwharetoa leader Te Heuheu Tukino II) was much in character and your quiet settlement of the little difficulties both among rival tribes and thoughtless Europeans will tend to make your services very acceptable to all parties.'[17]

Clarke most certainly did not approve of McLean's being in debt. McLean's patron, Andrew Sinclair, wrote that there was a warrant against him for a small debt which he had left unsettled and asked McLean to authorise him to pay it on his behalf in the meantime, 'as such a thing remaining unsettled will look ill in a Government officer'.[18] Clarke followed with his own reprimand.

> I was only just in time to keep you out of trouble and to maintain the character of our department. The case I allude to endangered your appointment, also an execution was about being forwarded to apprehend you for a paltry sum of money due to 'Allerton'. I have taken upon me to pay the sum and expenses thereon amounting in all to ten pounds three shillings. There was no alternative. I was necessitated either to do that or spoil your usefulness. I have done it and hope you will approve of it and authorise Dr. Sinclair to reserve that sum out of your salary. I hope in future you will be very careful of these matters.

He had consulted with Sinclair, who offered to pay the money there and then.[19]

Later, Sinclair wrote again that people were coming to him demanding money owed by McLean. He asked McLean to have someone else draw his salary and to make payments on his behalf. Although Sinclair would be glad to do what he could for McLean at all times, he did not like to have anything to do with money matters and 'particularly to have strangers asking me for money which I don't owe and as if I were under an obligation to them'. He added that he did not blame McLean as he was perhaps unaware that government officers 'are only on half salary at present and you might suppose that I have sufficient funds of yours in my hand'.[20] In fact Governor FitzRoy was insolvent in 1845.

At New Plymouth a difficult situation had arisen from the decision of Land Claims Commissioner William Spain to award the New Zealand Company the 60,000 acres it claimed to have purchased there despite tribal opposition. On a visit to New Plymouth in August 1844 Governor FitzRoy, unhappy with this decision, which could not be enforced against tribal opposition, instructed McLean to find out the extent of the land claimed by the company and what areas were disputed by the tribes.

In his report to FitzRoy in November McLean assessed tribal land claims around New Plymouth. At Waitara the principal owners Te Ati Awa, after a disastrous conflict with the musket-equipped Waikato tribes in the 1830s, had escaped to Kapiti, Nelson and Port Nicholson. In 1842–1844 many had returned to Taranaki, but McLean believed that with the principal owners absent it was not advisable to enter into the question of their individual boundaries. At Mangaraka the rangatira Te Waitere Katatore, an opponent of land sales and 'much complained of by the settlers', claimed some 1300 acres, though some Maori acknowledged being paid for land in that neighbourhood. McLean noted, however, that he had had assurances of friendship from most influential rangatira and that, since the Governor's visit, the rangatira showed much better feeling both among themselves and towards Europeans.[21] McLean also had his first encounter with Wiremu Kingi Te Rangitake, who stated that the land on which the Devon Hotel stood in the centre of New Plymouth was his, as well as land occupied by buildings as far as the crossroad north and the river bank south. The son of another rangatira claimed the land occupied by the houses of the surveyor and the New Zealand Company agent. McLean told them that he wished to have an account of all their different claims before the Governor arrived on his next visit.

Within the tribes there was disagreement about selling land.[22] In his diary McLean summarised the feelings of those within the area surveyed by the New Zealand Company in and around New Plymouth.[23] He had set out to counter their views. He told Ngamotu Maori (at today's port of New Plymouth) that the Europeans would not remain if they were not allowed more land and that it was in their own interest to have Europeans living among them in peace and quietness. McLean's interpretation of his instructions, derived from Article Two of the Treaty of Waitangi – that Maori be assured that none of their land would be taken from them against their will – was to pursue a policy of persuasion. Nevertheless, he actively persuaded Maori to part with their land.

> I am not here to beg of you to give up your land. I ask you to do so considering it will be for your own benefit. I trust if the Governor wishes you to give land you will comply with his request. He will do you justice and I hope you will esteem the many acts of kindness he confers on you and all the natives. Neither will he discontinue those good acts when he finds you are deserving of them.[24]

McLean understood the importance of gift exchange in Maori society and was already giving presents to encourage behaviour he approved of. On one occasion, after he had spent a day listening to a principal rangatira reciting the names of his forefathers, thereby establishing his claim to the land, the rangatira said that he was a seller of land and that the Europeans would occupy all his land. McLean gave then him 'a small present having found him well disposed to Europeans'. When Katatore brought him a pig as payment for a blanket given to him, McLean gave him a further blanket and tobacco 'to encourage him to frequent my home so that I might prevent his future annoyance by gaining some influence over him'.[25]

When Governor FitzRoy returned to New Plymouth on 8 November 1844 he met the principal rangatira to find out what land they wished to sell. The following day his meeting with a large group of Maori went on into the night. He declined to see them again until they had made up their minds to sell.[26]

On 30 November 1844, McLean told Clarke that he had obtained the signatures of the majority of Ngamotu Maori to the deed of transfer for a block of 3500 acres, to be known as the Fitzroy block. The gathering held to arrange this agreed that the goods should be divided into twenty-one equal shares, one for each hapu. One old woman caused dissatisfaction by secreting some of the property allotted to one hapu. There followed 'a general grasp for everything within reach. They fell on the Jersey cattle, the strongest party getting the largest number much to the dissatisfaction of the weaker and unsuccessful ones ... The scrambly scene was a source of great amusement to onlookers ... and had the appearance of an irregular cattle fair.' He intended to give money to those who had not received a fair share of the goods. The confusion had arisen because McLean neglected to follow Maori protocol when gifting, which required the rangatira to determine the allocation.

Crown purchase transfer deeds provided for native reserves to be retained by Maori within the land sold. McLean, along with representatives of the tribes, would walk around the boundaries and identify the land set aside. Accompanied by Frederic Carrington, the surveyor, and Chillman, clerk to the New Zealand Company, McLean began to lay out the reserves at New Plymouth. Some Maori complained that the land was not sufficient, but McLean reported that he had made every reasonable allowance for them.

★

As Sub-Protector, McLean also had to intervene in far-off disputes among Maori. In early January 1845, John Skevington, the Wesleyan missionary, sent word to warn McLean that there would be strife between the South Taranaki and Taupo tribes. The Ngati Tuwharetoa rangatira Te Heuheu had come south to seek satisfaction for an earlier defeat in battle. Skevington and Richard Taylor, the Anglican missionary at Wanganui, were attempting to mediate between the Taupo iwi, Ngati Tuwharetoa, and the South Taranaki iwi, Ngati Ruanui and Nga Rauru. Maori at New Plymouth, considering whether to go to the assistance of their besieged relatives, approached McLean for advice, About midnight on 6 January, McLean was aroused from sleep by some sixty members of the Puketapu hapu of Te Ati Awa calling out for him to assist their Taranaki kin. He did not answer until he had prepared his response; he advised them to go in peace and said that, as he was shortly travelling to Wanganui himself, he would join them there. Puketapu replied that they wished to travel with him but McLean refused, as he intended to take the longer route along the coast. He asked them to wait for him at Waimate in South Taranaki. By 4.30 a.m., having prepared his baggage and provisions, he was writing to the Chief Protector to inform him of his journey and his intention to meet with Tuwharetoa.

The Anglican missionary, the Revd William Boland from New Plymouth, accompanied McLean. They were joined by Maori from every settlement through which they passed, ready to assist their South Taranaki kin. McLean observed:

> The party moved with great regularity and good order; the whole scene having the appearance of a funeral procession in Great Britain accompanied by a Revd. Gentleman appropriately dressed in his black coat and white neckcloth to perform the religious ceremonies attended on scenes of death rather than people who had known nothing of religion or civilisation a few years past moving onwards to what they expected would be a scene of defensive warfare. It raised many happy thoughts in my mind to think how great a change had been effected amongst the New Zealanders within the last few years.[27]

The Maori party did not move as quickly as McLean wished, however, as it included old and feeble men who had been great warriors in their day and whose advice would be important in guiding their younger and less-experienced followers. McLean, intent on mediating between the tribes, went on ahead, explaining that he wanted to meet Te Heuheu's party as soon as possible and to learn their intentions so that he would be better able to advise the Taranaki

Maori. They agreed, saying that they placed themselves entirely in his hands. McLean pressed on. After some difficulty he persuaded local Maori to provide food for his party – 'a good supply of tutu wine and potatoes'. Members of his own party were so tired that McLean had to carry his own tent on his back until it was too dark to go farther. When they camped by a small stream, his party was so afraid of an attack that they hid in the fern and bushes near McLean's tent.

On arrival at Ihupuku Pa at Wanganui on 11 January 1845, they were met by a band of armed Maori described by McLean as expecting the enemy and 'behaving in a threatening manner'. He did not acknowledge this as merely the wero, the customary challenge to test the newcomers' intentions. On recognising him, McLean said, their demeanour changed and he was welcomed. The missionaries Taylor and Skevington told him that the tribes were likely to come to terms without fighting. Although McLean had a high regard for Taylor, whose views on dealing with Maori agreed with his own, he tended to attribute his various successes at Wanganui to his own influence. Yet it was Taylor who lived among the tribes and who had from time to time kept the peace before the arrival of McLean. Indeed, it seems that on this occasion a solution that allowed Te Heuheu to return north without losing mana arose from the combined efforts of Major Richmond, Bishop Selwyn, the two Sub-Protectors, Forsaith and McLean, and Skevington and Taylor.[28]

McLean remained at Wanganui to talk with Tuwharetoa. Some of these had reproached Taylor, saying that in a sermon he had called Te Heuheu a slave and that Iwikau, his brother, had been on the point of cutting him down. The missionary responded that he was grieved they should repeat what they knew to be false. Taylor and Skevington had a long interview with Te Heuheu. Taylor described how the rangatira, on being told that the wicked would be cast into Hell, said that he 'would have a fight with God first, that he would take Waitotara and he would soon make all the natives give up their faith'. Taylor 'could not listen to his boasting and blasphemous language without thinking of Sennacherib and I feel the Lord will manifest his power in bringing to naught all the evil devices of this poor benighted savage'.[29] McLean took a different, admiring view, later noting that Te Heuheu was 'the very pride and boast of New Zealand's chieftains'.[30]

The most frequent occasion for disputes between settler and Maori was damage done by settlers' cattle to unfenced crops cultivated by Maori. McLean, taking a police constable with him, would visit the place, assess the damage and award compensation – for example, £1 10s for the loss of forty bushels of potatoes. Sometimes Maori disputed the compensation. At Mangaraka, the rangatira Katatore demanded a payment of 50s for damage to his potato plantation by settlers' cattle. As McLean considered this demand unreasonable,

Katatore asked for £1 but the settlers would not pay more than 10s, which Katatore rejected. When rangatira placed an aukati on certain roads, McLean had to persuade them that this should not hinder Europeans in their journeys. Another cause of friction was interference on land occupied by settlers. One settler called McLean in because Maori were preventing him from ploughing his land. McLean ordered them off the land and 'reasoned with them as to their rash conduct ... they expressed themselves satisfied at my reasoning ... and promised they should not behave so badly in the future and expressed regret that they had caused me to be dissatisfied with them'.[31]

With his powerful physique McLean's strength soon impressed Taranaki Maori. When four men robbed a store, McLean tracked them and seized one by throwing him to the ground. Local Maori thought him 'a great fighting man' and eagerly followed his example, capturing two more.[32]

Inability to communicate because of language barriers led to misunderstandings. When a Maori dropped his knife, a settler's child picked it up and refused to hand it back. The Maori then took a pot belonging to the settler, who followed, struck him and took the pot back, whereupon the Maori took up an empty gun to frighten the settler. The settler complained to the police magistrate. McLean recommended a friendly settlement, gave the Maori some tobacco and warned the settlers against such treatment towards the Maori.

The problem of reconciling Maori custom and British law concerned McLean as he sought to elicit a Maori response to his exposition of British justice. On 28 April 1845, a group of Mokau rangatira wanted to know the Government's attitude towards murder following the recent killing of a local woman. McLean replied that the Crown would not tolerate such an offence. He asked the rangatira to consider whether murder of an unprotected female was consistent with their own laws and customs. Their response was that generally murder met with their disapproval, but as the woman was a slave captured in battle by her husband, they considered he had 'despotic rule over all her actions'. McLean told the rangatira that he would have no dealings with this murderer, who was present in the gathering, as his conscience would upbraid him if he did not by every means in his power condemn such a horrible deed. His diary recorded that the rangatira accepted his view, assuring him that they would remember his words.[33]

A few days earlier at Ingariri Pa, near Awakino in North Taranaki, McLean found that the Maori wanted Europeans to settle among them, either as insurance against a return of the Waikato tribes or to improve their trading opportunities. He took the opportunity to rebuke them for their ill treatment of Europeans already living among them and of travellers passing through their territory. They acknowledged this, but pointed out that they too had been ill-treated by the Europeans. McLean noted in his diary that it was 'very evident that such has too frequently been the case'.[34] He assured them that he would be their friend while the local missionary urged them to apply to McLean for redress as their protector. McLean reported to Clarke that by 1845 the Maori understood that they could rely on him to protect them if they made known their complaints and that there was no need for them to retaliate against innocent parties.

McLean was on his way to Kawhia in late 1845. Writing to Clarke from there, he apologised for being outside his district. He explained that as he could not confer with Clarke as frequently as he wished, he found great benefit from the advice and guidance of the Revd John Whitely, the local Kawhia Wesleyan missionary. McLean responded to Clarke's comments about settlers' criticism of the Protectorate Office that abounded in 1845.

> I cannot but feel for the sad calumny that is frequently thrown at the Protectorate and in striving to do their best for all it is really disheartening to meet with such unfounded censure but as the present is not a time for relaxation or dissent I suppose we must meet these difficulties with patience mindfull [*sic*] that there is one supreme being to whom we have to account for all our actions is reflection of itself by which if we are guided in the performance of our duties will cause us to be regardless of the slander of man.[35]

The inquiring mind of the young Scot eagerly recorded impressions of his new country in his diary – weather, landscape (including amateurish pencil sketches), flora and fauna, as well as observations on the Maori that would form the basis of his official reports. On one journey, when his party pitched his tent where he had a view of several villages, he observed that 'the regularity and decorum with the Sabbath is kept in the most secluded villages of a race of people whose simplicity and frugal mode of living corresponds in some respects with the humbler classes of our Scottish community ... the former are only emerging from a [indecipherable] and state of barbarism'.[36]

On the North Island's central plateau his diary recorded 'a heavy oppressive day over volcanic remains of burnt cinders and lava which is the governing characteristic of this part of the country'. Later, he came 'into the finest plain of land I have seen in the country resembling those of Bathurst in New South Wales with the river Waitakaruru running down the centre. The soil is as rich and fertile of a red and dark sandy loam with occasional swamps and covered with grass of a coarse description.' At Lake Taupo he noted the presence of kokopu, the largest fish found in the lake, some a foot long but on average seven to nine inches. 'When there is a constant wind from the south west for a few days they are driven on the shore in the surf which makes as great a noise as if it were a sea beach.'[37] On a previous visit McLean had visited hot springs, which he described as the most wonderful phenomenon of nature. Haunted by his Presbyterian upbringing, however, he went on to contemplate how

> a great trembling, rumbling sound is heard underneath as if the earth was going to open up and receive the traveller who is on the surface into the everlasting gulf of perdition ... No person could see this place without feeling intensely the awful end of a miserable sinner when committed to his last home and may God in his providence prepare us all for such a serious change.[38]

This description was written at Taupo in May 1845 where McLean learnt from Te Heuheu that Governor FitzRoy had sent Edward Shortland, Sub-Protector at Maketu in the Bay of Plenty, to inquire about Te Heuheu's position on the war in the north led by Hone Heke. Te Heuheu had responded that he did not advocate any aggressive action. Hone Heke's Ngapuhi had killed many of his friends, but he would not retaliate against them and would allow them to fight their own battle. He intended to consult with Waikato and other tribes about their dead relatives.

> He then entered into a disquisition on the strength of the natives – and fully displayed the martial bearing of a New Zealand chief when declaiming on warlike operations. His deportment portraying both dignity and determination which could not fail having an affect [*sic*] on all whom he might address. With a powerful but harsh voice he thus commenced: 'The New Zealanders are all a chieftain race. They will not be subdued by Europeans. From their infancy they have been skilled in war'. Heke's opinion was that the flagstaff was intended to enslave the natives and deprive them of their lands – that he had been told by an American trader who he named Te Hu and also by Rev W Williams which I told him would have been inconsistent with that gentleman but he still persisted that he had said so. He said that Mokou or Rangihaeata was also ready to create a similar disaffection at Pt Nicholson.
>
> Iwikau, his brother, then spoke. 'The Govt. are doing the natives a deal of injury trying to take our lands from us. I am greatly opposed to them and Heke is right in asserting his independence'. That he was suspicious of their movements from their first arrival at the Bay of Islands where he was when Capt. Hobson landed and was received with intense suspicion by all the Ngapuhi natives of that district. That the jealousy and suspicion then being entertained was the natural and long expected realisation of the disasters which were now taking place. That many who were parties to the Weyatagu [Waitangi] treaty had been persuaded by them and their missionaries. Whilst many councils were held amongst natives and Europeans that placed them on their guard as to the result of their negotiations which they then pretended would not be of a final character. He

> could then foresee as well as all other deserving chiefs who also held their own councils that the Govt. were usurping a right over their lands, chieftainship and property of which they would never make voluntary concession. 'We have not received these rights at your hands but has been our inheritance from the earliest times! We shall never submit to the ... measures you have used at Port Jackson and other parts of the world. How is it McLean? That all Europeans with whom I converse are opposed to the measures of the Govt.' A long argument ensued between the chiefs and myself which attracted the attention of a great number of the natives sitting around us.[39]

Iwikau maintained that the Treaty had deprived rangatira of their mana, lessening them in the eyes of their people. From the government that resulted he benefited not at all. He preferred traders who brought blankets and tobacco but interfered with neither his rights nor his land. Iwikau asserted that 'these traders and all Europeans were a bad race of people addicted to theft and falsehood otherwise they would not require the use of so many locks to their doors and boxes'.

McLean was disturbed at Iwikau's trenchant criticism of Europeans. This had come about, he believed, because the Taupo region had never before been visited by any government agent who, 'by his respectable bearing and conduct', would have encouraged different sentiments. He told Iwikau that, wherever there was a large body of Europeans, British laws must be introduced. These laws were intended to afford equal protection 'to you and to me'. The Governor, McLean continued, was a chief from his own country who deserved the respect of both races. He had not 'the most distant thought' of seizing their territory. His aim was to benefit Maori by making Maori and European one people. McLean promised Iwikau that his people would never be dispossessed of their Taupo lakes, forest and land without their free consent.[40]

The two rangatira reflected a growing concern among Maori that the Governor's actions, as shown by the imposition of customs duties, insistence on the Crown's pre-emptive right to buy land and attempts to impose British law, represented an unwarranted interference with Maori custom and a threat to the independent status of rangatira. At the same time intertribal rivalries prevented support of Heke in his stand for rangatiratanga. Historians, who once put Heke's 'rebellion' down to economic motives – loss of trade following imposition of customs and removal of the capital to Auckland – now stress its defence of customary authority. In the 1840s McLean had identified this motive for Heke's actions, a view that he noted had become widespread throughout the interior of the North Island. He had no doubt about the appropriate response: for 'the sake of British ascendancy ... a trial of strength should take place between the two physically'.[41] Even in his early years McLean held that

British sovereignty must be asserted, by force if necessary.

Te Heuheu was conciliatory, affirming his wish to preserve peace. He always stood by his friends, he said, and had saved Te Rauparaha when the latter was driven from his land and home by the Ngati Maniapoto. Te Heuheu hoped that the Governor would make peace with Heke once he had avenged those killed by Heke.

McLean sought his views on the earlier situation at Wanganui. Te Heuheu replied that Nga Rauru Maori had treated his name lightly. Although the Waikato would not rest until they had gained satisfaction for certain offences, he for his part would forgive them. He urged McLean to caution them against persisting in such conduct and to tell them that, if Waikato again offended Tuwharetoa, they would find him more determined than ever. He had no ill will against Europeans and reminded McLean that he had promised to respect their property.

McLean's paternalism may have led him to treat the Maori people as children, but when dealing with a rangatira like Te Heuheu he did not insult him by treating him as an inferior. His approach was that of equals. Beyond the proper observance of Maori protocol and acknowledgement of the rangatira's mana, he showed respect for the human dignity of the individual. With Te Heuheu, McLean also respected the rangatira's predominant status, and his wisdom and knowledge of other tribes.

Three days later, on a Sunday in May 1845, Iwikau approached McLean's camp. Accompanied by twenty of his people, he was on his way to see a grazier named Gotty who, he complained, had robbed him of his pigs. McLean forbade him to proceed, saying that Iwikau as McLean's host must acknowledge him and that they both should observe the day as Sunday and each should tell the other something of their customs. McLean was taking the opportunity to draw on Iwikau's knowledge. Iwikau demurred but decided to stay, though he withdrew while McLean and his Maori party had prayers and catechism. Next morning the neighbouring hapu, having learnt that Iwikau was on his way to seek satisfaction for his pigs, became alarmed at the approach of this fiery rangatira. Along with their Pakeha they loaded their firearms, determined to resist. Fortunately, McLean arrived first, ordered them to put away their guns and to receive Iwikau peacefully. He gave the same advice to the grazier Gotty.

When Iwikau arrived, McLean made the rangatira and the grazier sit down and put their respective cases to him. 'They both looked infuriated with each other ... I could hardly reconcile them to the decorum necessary for such an investigation.' After some questioning McLean decided that Gotty had deceived Iwikau. As the 'complications of the case might trouble a Lord Elton' (then Lord Chancellor), let alone someone so little versed in the law as himself, he thought reparation the best solution. After much argument the value of the pigs was agreed on and forty pounds of tobacco handed over to a delighted Iwikau. McLean recorded that satisfaction reigned. He accepted the hapu's compliments, saying that they would be doubly welcome if they supplied Iwikau and himself and his followers with a supply of food. 'This caused laughter, a continuation of speeches and shaking of hands.' This is an early instance of McLean's exercising 'a bit of blarney' and some cultural skill to relax the tension and complete a successful negotiation.[42]

In October 1845 McLean again set out from New Plymouth for Taupo, this time by way of Wanganui. Along the way he again found the tribes fortifying their pa, fearing attacks by Tuwharetoa when they should have been busy planting their crops. Maori interpretations of Christianity also concerned him; some were seeing the Almighty and his angels and stating that they were able to baptise in the name of the Holy Spirit. He was 'grieved to find this sad state of religious fanaticism originating from a false impression of the doctrine of repentance' and urged them to talk to their clergyman. After a dangerous journey along the beach near high tide, McLean arrived at Wanganui, where he stayed with Dr Peter Wilson. At dinner that night he drank 'some of the finest wine that was ever produced at table – a 55 year old wine from Cyprus'. The following day the Revd Taylor attempted to extract McLean's tooth, but after many severe tugs he failed, the instrument being too large.

From Wanganui, McLean travelled north to Taupo to meet Te Heuheu, who by this time thought that Heke would be more than a match for the Europeans. Te Heuheu warned McLean that Taupo and Rotorua tribes were prepared to attack Ihupuku Pa at Wanganui to test its strength and to obtain satisfaction for their relatives killed at an engagement at Patoka. Ngati Pikiao from the Rotorua area had sent Te Heuheu a basket of cartridges as a token of their willingness to attack, but he fired off all the cartridges as evidence of his desire for peace, which so far had been maintained by his efforts. At the same time he could not entirely suppress the desire for war among other tribes, who were anticipating a Heke victory in the North. This fuelled excitement throughout the North Island. Taking heed of Te Heuheu's warning, McLean feared a return to the innumerable feuds and grievances that had been dormant for some years. As the consequences would be serious for European settlements, he decided to visit as many of the rangatira as he could to dissuade them from war.

McLean continued north, camping by Lake Rotokawa near Taupo. He noted that the water required the addition of carbonate of soda as it contained quantities of 'sulphuric acid and alum'. After crossing lakes Tarawera and Okareka he arrived at Te Ngae near Rotorua, home of the missionary Thomas Chapman, where he met the Sub-Protector, Edward Shortland, who told him of the arrival of Major Grey, lately Governor of

South Australia, to be Governor of New Zealand.

Accompanied by the missionaries Chapman and Taylor, McLean met with local Te Arawa rangatira, who assured them that the few who desired war had little influence. They were worried and eager to know whether the new Governor would be for war or for peace, but feared that he would incline to the former. This would arouse the tribes who were waiting only to see the outcome of Heke's war. The presence at the gathering of some who had returned from aiding Heke at the Bay of Islands worried McLean, as their 'very untrue version of the engagements' showed that they were 'striving to excite bitter disputes against our cause'. At Maketu on the Bay of Plenty the old rangatira Pukuatua was 'sensible and well disposed' and wished to see the Taupo and West Coast people make peace. After the next harvest a large body would march from Taupo to Ihupuku to conclude a peace, and go on as far as Kapiti.[43]

At Ohinemutu, McLean found that young Maori children knew their English alphabet and a few words of English, and could count from one to a hundred with ease. All this, he believed, was to the credit of Chapman. McLean found the rangatira, Horokai, friendly and felt that he had removed any fears about the Government's intentions. When McLean moved north from Rotorua, however, he found the tribes showing support for Heke. They told him that all the Ngapuhi were about to join him in his next engagement, that Heke was urging all the tribes on the coast to prevent any further landings by Europeans, and that Te Rauparaha was ready to begin a war against the Pakeha. Returning south, McLean learnt from the rangatira Taonui that the Waikato would oppose Heke if he came near Auckland or touched a flagstaff there. There were rumours that Te Rauparaha was planning an attack on Wellington and the southern settlements, but Taonui said that he and Te Heuheu desired to protect all Europeans rather than upsetting the peace and tranquillity of the island.

In the first decade of the colony, governors were aware that the security of the small areas of European settlement depended on Maori goodwill. Unlike McLean, few settlers acknowledged that this would require an effort to understand the culture of the indigenous people among whom they had settled. When war broke out in the north with Heke, it was only the reluctance of tribes in other parts of the North Island to join him that averted a concerted attack on the scattered European settlements, which would have threatened the development of the colony.

Early in 1846 the Chief Protector told McLean that the new Governor intended to remodel the Protectorate Office and that, after 31 March, two officers only would be required.[44] Clarke indicated that McLean's claim on the Government would be borne in mind if opportunities arose of making appointments to native schools or other institutions.[45] As McLean prepared to relinquish his post, Taranaki Maori came to say goodbye 'to their Matua or Father as they term me tho I do not admire the term'. He hoped that the goodwill he had striven to promote towards all Europeans would continue.

Grey in fact abolished the Protectorate altogether. This was unfortunate, as sub-protectors had done much to deflect conflict between settler and Maori and had built up an understanding of the intricacies of Maori land tenure. The Protectorate had been responsive to Maori viewpoints and its subsequent absence had serious consequences. Henceforth, there would be nobody within government capable of assessing the impact of government policy on Maori interests.[46]

The new Governor's motives were mixed. Grey's objective was assimilation of the two 'races', a key element of which was to move quickly to bring Maori under British law. Grey saw the office of Protector of Aborigines as an impediment to this. He felt that, through this department with a missionary as its head, the missionaries were exercising a political role incompatible with their religious functions. The missionaries, for their part, having persuaded the Maori to sign the Treaty, regarded themselves as the guardians of the rights established at Waitangi, a role disliked by most settlers. Grey was aware that abolishing the Protectorate would establish his popularity with the settlers. But he was also pursuing a personal vendetta against Clarke and other missionaries for what he claimed was excessive greed and abuse of their position to acquire grants of land, and this no doubt strengthened his disposition to exercise sole control over native policy.

McLean, in giving up his position, reflected on his work as Sub-Protector

> with the greatest pleasure and satisfaction ... that, as far as I was able, my duties to God and man have been duly and strictly performed since I joined it and the series of successes that has attended my mission will be to myself reflection throughout my lifetime. Much as I regret the expectation of leaving New Plymouth, a place with a people that became so endeared to me and the native population who caused me so many anxious hours throughout the several eruptions in the islands ... but if my official connection is dissolved my own private feelings will ever I trust remain unaltered towards this place and people and the kind Providence that has so long watched over my several wants will not forsake me though I so often deserve his wrath and I hope that he may furnish sufficient for me in some part of the world.[47]

Unlike his superior, Clarke, who had antagonised settlers by his open support of Maori to ensure them the protection of the law against the settlers' pressure, McLean had been successful in convincing them of his impartiality between European and Maori. Leading settlers at New Plymouth, including the resident agent for the New Zealand Company, wrote to the Governor in praise of the manner in which McLean had discharged his duties. By his 'conciliatory conduct and strict impartiality' he had 'secured the respect of and friendly feeling of both races in this settlement' and that 'while acting in a spirit of justice to the Maori it was always in connexion with a natural feeling of sympathy for the defenceless position of the settlers'.[48] McLean was flattered but reminded himself that he should not 'let the vanities of this life be deemed of greater import to us than those of eternity'.[49]

Until his term expired in March 1846, McLean continued as Sub-Protector. He bought a mill for Wiremu Kingi and others, 'as it gives a great impetus to industry and other wheat growing exertions' on the understanding that Kingi would repay the Crown. McLean looked forward to the following year, when more Maori labour would be involved in harvesting with a corresponding reduction in European labour, and felt that every effort should be made to encourage Maori in such beneficial employment.

When McLean learnt that an attempt by the 'low labouring classes' of New Plymouth to rescue three of their number who were likely to be gaoled over a dispute with a mill owner was imminent, he became alarmed at the example that this would set for local Maori. The presence of troops, he felt, was needed to 'restrain the violent eruptions of feeling amongst the whites as well as the natives who are frequently so innocently blamed, nor will such formidable displays on the part of our countrymen have a good effect on them when they see the principal authorities slighted'.[50] McLean remained in town until the danger was over, determined to keep local Maori away from such a scene and to interfere if the magistrate, Captain King, was insulted.

By his even-handed approach, McLean succeeded in averting potential conflicts between settler and Maori in Taranaki and among Maori involved in intertribal disputes at Wanganui. His diary entries, if they represent events accurately, justify his smug satisfaction at his success as Sub-Protector. Certainly, he was scrupulous in recording opposition to his actions or the difficulties he confronted, though these appear to have heightened his satisfaction at the successful outcome of his endeavours. Like his later master, Sir George Grey, McLean displayed some skill in promoting his effectiveness as a government official. He cultivated the company of respectable settlers, disapproving of those low labouring classes and disreputable Europeans who lived among the Maori. In turn, the good-looking young Scot was flattered by the motherly attentions paid to him by the wives of important settlers such Dr Peter Wilson and Captain Campbell.

McLean was well aware of the defenceless situation of the tiny settlements at Wanganui and New Plymouth and that the colony's very existence depended on Maori goodwill. In New Zealand by 1846 there were some

12,000 colonists located in six settlements spread over 1000 miles and the Maori population was six or seven times larger. Prudence and expediency required that the tribes' consent be secured not only for the sale of land but in keeping law and order. Although settlers were concerned for their safety, many, by their open insensitivity towards Maori customs, did little to cultivate that union of European and Maori subjects extolled in Clarke's instructions to McLean.

In his first years as an agent of the British Crown, McLean developed approaches in his dealings with Maori that were to mark his future stewardship in the senior roles of Chief Native Land Purchase Commissioner and Native Secretary. He won the respect and confidence of both settler and Maori. This had eluded Governor FitzRoy, who openly charged the settlers with seeking the extermination of the native race and of obstructing the work of the missionaries. McLean never identified himself with FitzRoy's and Clarke's humanitarian position. If Maori and Pakeha were to live side by side in peace, he believed that the same measure of trust must be extended to settlers and Maori. Only in this way could a community embracing both races evolve.

When his position as Sub-Protector was coming to an end, in his diary he looked back on his life hitherto:

> The first reflection that naturally presents itself is my friends at home, my departure from them and neglect towards them, my career of disasters and pleasures in New South Wales, my disappointments, successes and reverses in New Zealand which I may hope prove a lesson through life. My unfortunate liberality, confidence in persons that ill deserved my favours and frequent instances of misconduct on my own part are severe feelings to contend against, but for all I freely forgive and would I may be as freely forgiven.
>
> Lastly comes my connection with Govt. which has now existed for two years this night. It commenced under many disadvantages and difficulties but amidst many staunch and disinterested friends who I believe really wished me prosperity and those who desired a closer alliance with me in my official career will not have, I trust, reason to cancel the impression they have formed. As I have before observed this is my second year in the Protectorate of arduous, odious, unenviable duties, but in my short career I have found them a pleasure. The spontaneous feelings of my heart are woven into its prosperity as far as the interests and social happiness and advancement of both races are concerned. I have ended my official career for the time being and may the Almighty whose aid and assistance I have all along received bless prosper and protect the numerous members of my charge. May he always continue to be the guide and counsel of those who have left their parent relying on his mercy to him.
>
> I this night before closing my eyelids humbly commit them and if destined to

> withdraw myself from amongst them may he in his Providence replace another better qualified for the full and efficient discharge. of these duties.[51]

This wish for the 'social happiness and advancement of both races' remained McLean's professed belief throughout his public life.

Chapter 3
Apprentice Years: Inspector of Police

McLean's appointment as Sub-Protector ended in March 1846. In April he received a letter from Governor Grey offering him the position of Inspector of Police in Taranaki with a salary of £200 a year and authorising him to raise a force of ten men and one sergeant at salaries of £1 5s per week. McLean hesitated. On the one hand, he would have a new and powerful patron. On the other, would such a change be appreciated by the Maori whose trust he had gained? On reflection, he decided that 'it would add to my influence over them and enable me better to secure their rights subsequent to their decision to sell'.[1] Having made his evaluation, he chose to attribute this to divine intervention, expressing pleasure that 'I might with extreme thankfulness to the Almighty acknowledge his providential gift of conferring on me a comfortable and lucrative appointment as inspector of police for this district. May his Providence guide me and support me in all my future proceedings that I may live to his Glory and honour.'[2] Such an air of sanctity was considered a desirable attribute in a public figure in the Victorian age. It was most marked in the life of W. E. Gladstone, perhaps the greatest British prime minister of the nineteenth century. His great rival, Benjamin Disraeli, took a more cynical view of public life: 'I have climbed,' he said, 'to the top of the greasy pole'. Disraeli once remarked that he was not upset if Gladstone was caught cheating at cards with a fifth ace up his sleeve, but he did object when Gladstone insisted that God had placed it there!

Given the overwhelming numerical superiority of the Maori in the colony's early years and the presence of a body of troops too small to guarantee protection for the settlers, the settlements' continued existence depended on Maori goodwill. Outside the small European settlements, the exercise of British law was almost unknown, apart from the infrequent appearance of officials such as McLean in his roles first as Sub-Protector and then as Inspector of Police and magistrate. A small number of resident magistrates, assisted by Maori assessors, were located in areas of European settlement. The handful of settlers who lived alongside Maori communities had to adjust to and accept their hosts' customs. Maori eagerness to acquire the tools of European technology, to extend their area of cultivated land, and so to participate in the new economy, resulted in their providing most of the crops needed to feed the recently established towns. Within the towns and their immediate environs, settler and Maori existed side by side in an uneasy interdependence based on economic necessity, sometimes marred by disputes and misunderstandings. They lived in different worlds and, with a few exceptions, neither really understood the other. Nevertheless, according to one historian, it 'worked well enough to make 1840–1860 the heyday of New Zealand race relations'.[3] On his arrival in New Zealand in 1846, Governor Grey, aware that his standing with the Colonial Office depended on his ability to deal with the Maori, set out to develop a comprehensive native policy. He identified McLean as suited to a key role in implementing his plan and, during Grey's first term of office, McLean aligned himself with the principles underlying Grey's actions. In his role as adviser to Grey's successor, Thomas Gore Browne, McLean was to maintain Grey's practice of using personal influence to carry out policy. After Grey went to South Africa in 1853, McLean would continue to write telling him of current developments in New Zealand.

Grey and McLean tried to gain a real understanding of Maori culture. Both preferred to operate through direct personal contact with the rangatira so as to win their confidence, respect and allegiance. Of all the nineteenth-century officials, Grey and McLean were the most successful in this objective. Grey was convinced that British law must quickly replace Maori custom to allow peaceful development of European settlement and to ensure the physical survival of the indigenous race. McLean shared his belief in assimilation. The future of the Maori, he believed, depended on their acceptance of Crown authority and their transformation into brown Pakeha, although as an official working in the field he was more conscious than Grey of the need for a longer period of transition.

As with other nineteenth-century administrators, Grey and McLean believed strongly that British civilisation was superior to those of indigenous peoples in other parts of the world, including the ancient civilisations of India and China. By the mid-nineteenth century the British felt comfortably superior, both technologically and morally, to other nations. Attitudes inculcated in Victorian public schoolboys prepared them to carry the white man's burden in ruling an empire that was intended to bring the benefits of civilisation to lesser breeds. Easy though it is to ridicule the unscientific judgements of those standard-bearers of the British flag – traders, missionaries, settlers and officials – and to deplore their ignorance of the diverse cultural values of indigenous peoples, in the mid-nineteenth century there were no anthropologists around to correct them.[4] While the superiority of European technology was unquestioned, the weakness of the ethnocentrism that accompanied it was a general refusal to find anything of value in the different culture of an indigenous people like the Maori.

The prevailing belief was that native races were destined to die out with the advance of European settlement. This belief was not confined to colonists. James Stephen of the Colonial Office, though a staunch advocate of the role of the British Government as a trustee, doubted whether the Maori would survive the nineteenth century. Wherever an indigenous people had been confronted by an influx of white settlers, the native people had ultimately declined, and it was assumed that this was the likely outcome in New Zealand. Indeed, by the 1850s some Maori rangatira were noting the decline in numbers in their own tribes and gave this as their reason for selling land and having white settlers live among them. McLean and Grey were in a minority in insisting that the Maori were a virile and intelligent race capable of adapting to the challenge of European civilisation and taking a significant role within a European society. The policy of assimilation would, they thought, be the key to Maori survival. They were unusual, moreover, in that they made an effort to understand the cultural values of the Maori and could empathise with aspects of that culture. They were, however, men of their time; they undervalued the indigenous culture just as they overrated the gifts of their own civilisation – whether the sanctity of the rule of British law or the sovereignty of the Queen.

The alternative concept of the 'noble savage' fenced off from all contact with civilisation could not survive in colonies of settlement. Maori themselves sought contact with Europeans and were eager to benefit from the new technology. Fields of wheat and flour mills flourished alongside traditional cultivations. Tribes who were in contact with Europeans became enthusiastic traders; by the 1850s they dominated the coastal shipping trade and were significant producers of exported goods. The younger rangatira became the modernisers. They selected and adapted, rather than adopted, elements of European culture. Maori Christianity combined Christian and traditional elements;[5] the Maori King movement was 'very much a Maori organisation not a copy of the English monarchy'.[6] In the first two decades of colonisation the argument was not over contact between colonists and Maori but over who was to make the decisions and control the extent of that contact. The idea of trusteeship acknowledged by the British Government and implicit in the terms of the Treaty of Waitangi was evident in the details of Grey's native policy. On the issue of Maori participation in the exercise of control at the national level, however, Grey was silent.

Grey's native policy encompassed the political, social and economic development of Maori in law and order, education, health, public works and land purchases.[7] Most important, as we shall see, was Grey's land-purchase policy, which was intended to ensure that the tribes had adequate reserves and that in return they would make their 'waste' or uncultivated lands available for Europeans to settle among them, thereby hastening the process of assimilation.

In 1846 Grey's first task was to suppress what he saw as rebellion against the Queen's sovereignty and to regain political control. At the same time, he assured the rangatira that the Government was committed to the terms of the Treaty and that he would not take their lands without their consent. He discarded FitzRoy's Native Exemption Ordinance, telling the rangatira that Maori and European were to be under equal laws and equal protection. Under the Resident Magistrates Courts Ordinance 1846 he continued something of FitzRoy's approach. Magistrates were appointed in populous Maori districts to exercise summary jurisdiction in civil and criminal cases and, to assist the magistrates, Maori assessors were appointed from among local rangatira. Although McLean preferred men who supported land selling and regarded them as government agents who were required to report on the state of their districts, the presence of the assessors and the influence they acquired with the magistrates made the proceedings of these courts appear to reflect the involvement of the local community in the law-enforcement process. By 1849 courts were operating at Russell, Auckland, Howick, New Plymouth, Wanganui, Waikanae, Wellington, Nelson, Akaroa and Dunedin.

To assist the courts a new force, the Armed Police, was established in 1846, growing within a year to 120–150 men, both European and Maori, at cost of £8000–£10,000 a year. The existence of police and courts was intended to encourage Maori to accept British law, but there were still significant limitations to that acceptance. Among Maori, adultery was regarded as a capital crime, slavery survived, utu allowed the injured party to exact retribution while tapu protected a rangatira from retaliation. Grey accepted the limitations. The law was applied only where Maori custom was not in conflict, nor did it extend effectively to remote inland districts. In general, courts operated successfully when they adjudicated between Maori and settler; they rarely punished serious Maori crime.

McLean's new position was the outcome of fresh measures by the Governor to encourage Maori acceptance of British law. Grey took up FitzRoy's use of Maori assessors to assist magistrates in dealing with cases involving disputes among Maori, but he did not provide for an annual salary, only payment for cases resulting in successful prosecutions. Maori convicted of theft could avoid gaol by paying into the court four times the value of the property stolen, this payment being used for compensating the victim. As Maori, particularly the rangatira, objected to gaol and would resist a court appearance, this measure made British law more acceptable and enforceable. Recruitment of a small number of Maori into a paramilitary police force was another measure. Grey viewed an armed police force as an essential element of coercion in 'assertion and preservation of British sovereignty, for the control of the turbulent, the protection of life, property and commerce and the security of the revenue which the country can at once yield'[8] Taranaki was the first region to have this new police force, and McLean its first inspector.

While visiting Wanganui before taking up his new post at New Plymouth, McLean said goodbye to one of the leading settlers, Captain Campbell, 'a friendly good-hearted man'. 'What seldom happens to me, the tears twinkled in my eyes and had I not Basil Taylor [Revd Richard Taylor's young son] with me, to whom I did not like to show my grief, I would have chosen a green hillock to have cried bitterly at the idea of parting with an old gentleman that I may never see again.'[9]

In May 1846, McLean learnt that the 'fine old chief' Te Heuheu had been killed by a landslide in his village on the shore of Lake Taupo. He regretted that

> the very pride and boast of New Zealand's chieftains is now gone nor will successive generations replace a more intelligent and well disposed man well versed in every tradition of his country people as well as the productions of the country for all of which from the largest tree to the smallest shrub he had some tradition or knowledge. He was a skilful botanist and knew the physical uses of many plants and herbs. Nor was he ignorant of the insects and birds of the country. What an irreparable loss to the Island. Would that I had half of his knowledge committed to paper. I would make a great sacrifice to obtain what I shall never have another opportunity of knowing. How sudden and awful are the works of the Almighty. Does not every day give us a convincing proof of the uncertainty of our existence.[10]

Te Heuheu's people believed that his death was the work of a taniwha over whom he had influence, but McLean hoped 'that the God of Gods has not forsaken him and that he is removed where superstition and heathenism are alike unknown'.[11] On another occasion, when farewelling an old white-haired pagan rangatira, McLean contemplated that they might meet up in a future existence. To accept that heaven might be open to unbelievers was unusually liberal for a devout Christian of that time.

On his arrival at New Plymouth in June, McLean enrolled nine men and one sergeant and marched his men into town to be sworn in by Captain Henry King, the resident magistrate. Grey advised McLean that, as Inspector of Police, his role would be to adjudicate disputes between Europeans and Maori and to ensure peace in his territory. McLean wrote to Major Durie at Wanganui for advice on managing his small force, and meantime drilled his men every day. His diary shows that for much of the year he was away from New Plymouth, travelling throughout his district; since he also held a magistrate's commission for New Munster, he was required to hear cases on his travels. (In 1848 New Zealand was divided into two provinces, New Ulster, north of a line from the mouth of the Patea River in North Taranaki, and New Munster, all land to the south.) As he became involved in land-purchase negotiations at Grey's direction, McLean's lengthy absences left control of the police detachment at New Plymouth to Sergeant Henry Halse. The sergeant's duties, as set out by McLean, were:

> 1 Night watch to walk about town and suburbs keeping eye on strange Native or European till satisfied of their intentions – note name and description of persons with whom they associate
>
> 2 Drill 9.30 – 11.30
>
> 2 – 4pm – drill with firearms
>
> 3 Cut firewood twice a week
>
> 4 Utmost cleanliness and regularity must be observed, bathing during warm weather encourage men to learn to swim
>
> 5 Parade 10 o'clock Sunday. Take names of those who are late
>
> 6 Assist in quelling differences between natives and Europeans – observing the strictest impartiality and moderating the extravagant ideas the natives are so apt to form of their damaged crops
>
> 7 Note and make known to me if any obstruction or annoyance is given to settlers especially those living beyond the Block
>
> 8 Any disobedience disorderly conduct or drunkenness by members of the force entered in red ink in the orderly book
>
> 9 Confidence I repose in you will be more fully established by the promptness and decision of your conduct under such contingencies as may arise that it is impossible for me to foresee
>
> 10 By strict and unswerving attention to your own duties with a kind and unassuming deportment towards the men you ensure their adherence to a punctual fulfilment of theirs[12]

McLean asked the Governor for replacement weapons as his police arms were inferior, for example, percussion caps were damaged and unfit for use. He suggested that the Governor inspect the equipment and judge how dangerous it would be to 'trust to either the arms or ammunition in case of any emergency'. When Grey made his first visit to Taranaki early in 1847, he inspected the police force and said that he was well satisfied with the bearing of the men and the arrangements for the barracks. He promised a better supply of arms. He told McLean that, when he was appointed, Grey was uncertain how well he would fulfil his duties, having had no prior experience,

> though he did not doubt my zeal from what he had heard of me. However, he was most happy to find that everything had been in such complete order – even better than his own force that he had thought so much of at Adelaide; that he was now so confident that he would think of enlarging the force ... I stated to His Excellency that I fully confessed my entire ignorance of conducting police duties when I first formed the service; and felt obliged for the handsome manner in which he conferred the appointment on me without at all knowing me personally.[13]

McLean had recruited two Maori among his nine men. By 1847 he had obtained Grey's approval to increase the proportion of Maori until Taranaki had the most bicultural police force in the colony. His recruits were younger rangatira, of whom Rawiri proved effective in mediating in disputes between Maori and settlers. In McLean's eyes, Rawiri was even more valuable in providing weekly intelligence summaries on the state of feelings among the tribes of the district.[14]

McLean's youth and physical strength were assets when carrying out his duties as Inspector of Police which demanded the same long and exhausting journeys as in his time as Sub-Protector. For example, on 5 January 1847 he left Wanganui to stay the night at nearby Kai Iwi. McLean left at 3.30 a.m. on the next day, travelled the sixteen miles to Patea by 8.15 a.m. As some of his men who had travelled twenty-seven miles were very tired, McLean went on to Waimate to stay the night with Revd William Woon, the Wesleyan missionary. Wet to the skin, McLean stripped off his clothes, had a good supper and retired to bed after prayers with the Woon family. On 8 January he rose at 3.30 a.m., donned his still-wet clothes and ate a slice of ham and bread with an onion. In pouring rain he got to Otumatua at midday. Having no dry clothes, he 'turned the natives out of the house and dried those I had on'. Leaving at 4.30 a.m. the following morning, he began a fifty-mile journey on an 'indifferent road', often covered with tall flax and tutu, crossing deep rivers flooded by mountain rains. For an hour he struggled to get his horse along a stony beach on the Taranaki coast. Accompanied by three of his policemen, he reached Tapuwai (Tapuae?) at nine in the evening. Arriving at Wairua at ten, McLean left his horse at a settler's house and walked into New Plymouth, arriving at one in the morning. He had some bread, cheese, brandy and water and then walked about to see if his police were on duty. Finding no one, he roused one policeman, who explained that it was Henshaw's watch. McLean found the man in bed and heard his explanation that, as he had been hard at work in the bush all day, he had been relieved by his sergeant. McLean then woke his friend Webster and lay down on the sofa to get a few hours' sleep.[15]

As magistrate, McLean took care to recruit, and to recommend as assessors, rangatira who commanded the respect of the tribes, or rather those that were 'friendly' – that is, willing to sell land. That he made extensive and effective use of these assessors was confirmed by his successor, G. S. Cooper, who reported that the authorities had derived most efficient assistance both from Maori enrolled in the police force and from Maori assessors in the difficult task of controlling and subjecting to the British law 'a race of warlike and hardy savages, greatly our superior in number and physical strength'. It seems that McLean had overcome Grey's objection to paying the assessors an annual salary, for Cooper noted that they had been regularly paid a small salary instead of the allowances usually given only when their assistance was required by resident magistrates. Cooper said that these assessors had more than once saved the New Plymouth settlement and the lives of individual settlers. In cases involving Maori and settlers, their decisions and advice had been respected and found to be just. They traced offenders and brought them to justice; they recovered settlers' property that had been retained, according to Maori custom, in disputes about cattle trespass. Moreover, their advice in land negotiations had 'always been faithfully and honestly given'.[16]

McLean's police sergeant, Henry Halse, a young man of similar age, differed markedly in social and educational background from other European members of the force. Halse had studied medicine in London before emigrating with his brother to New Plymouth. Unable to take up his New Zealand Company land, Halse welcomed the appointment. His fortnightly reports to McLean included items on the arrival and departure of ships, drunkenness among settlers, and complaints by settlers against Maori and vice versa. For example, in May 1848, Halse noted the arrival of two schooners, one of twelve tons from Waitara – Maori trade – and one, forty tons, from Wellington with a cargo of bricks and a single passenger, a mason from New South Wales. Two vessels sailed for Wellington with cargoes of flour, wheat, bran, maize, potatoes, turnips, onions and carrots. Two schooners sailed for Kawhia; one, which was involved in Maori trade, became stranded on leaving port. A boat that put out to the rescue found the crew drunk. Another small vessel that sailed for Kawhia contained a cargo of alcohol more than adequate for the small number of Europeans there: four cases of gin, one case of brandy, two kegs of tobacco together with half a ton of salt and a quarter of a ton of flour.

Drunkenness was a problem in the New Plymouth settlement. Halse reported that a settler and his son, aged nine, had been found in the street in a helpless state of intoxication, locked up and fined 5s with costs by the resident magistrate. His reports frequently referred to drunken incidents – for example, in 1851 he had been called out at 2.30 a.m. 'to suppress a drunken riot amongst some discharged soldiers of the 65th Regt'. He complained that 'the amount of drunkenness is positively dreadful'. Later, in a private letter to McLean, Halse admitted that he would prefer living among the tribes 'to being thrown in the way of the worst vices of those of my own colour who are infinitely below the scale of brute creation'.[17] This was a surprising admission, given Halse's low opinion of the Maori as expressed in an earlier letter to McLean. 'Never were my eyes so completely opened to the natives before. Institutions, Hospitals, Hostelerys, allowances, kindnesses and almost universal leniency will not change them. They are as wild and untameable as ever ... The sooner you return the better and curb your rebellious children before it is too late. They need a rough hand and a mouth the size of a cannon ball to bring them to obedience. Such was my opinion years ago and I have no occasion to alter it.'[18]

McLean took a different view, as we have seen, though there was one occasion when, rather than risk the appearance in court of a thief from an 'unruly' tribe (the Puketapu hapu) supported by a large number of his followers, he used his discretionary power to order 'a good horsewhipping'. McLean congratulated himself on delivering this rough justice, but how would he reconcile this to his commitment to even-handed justice? Although as a scion of the Scottish gentry he despised the English labouring class, would he have imposed that same punishment on a settler? McLean noted that King, the resident magistrate, 'will suppose that I have acted too rashly in this affair'. He was reassured, however. Captain King gave tacit approval: 'I cannot tell what I should say to you respecting the summary way you disposed of the case you describe, but I know that its result will have a better effect on the natives than legal punishment that might have been awarded him.'[19]

When he first moved to New Plymouth, McLean stayed with his friends, Dr Peter and Helen Wilson, whom he had known in Wanganui. Dr Wilson had become Superintendent of the Native Hospital at New Plymouth. Later, McLean built his house next to the Wilsons. Helen Wilson had a stepson but no children of her own, so young Donald McLean won her affection. In her letters she addressed him as 'My darling son' and ended 'Your old mother'. She introduced this lively young man to New Plymouth society and acted as his mentor. Responding to a letter from him, Helen Wilson remarked that she was 'not at all astonished to find that the Governor likes you, for you take good care, somehow or other, to make people like you, even when you destroy *their pet prickly pear plants* by leaping over their garden fence instead of going through their gate like a well-behaved lad'. This remark recalled their first encounter, though she assured him that he had 'won her heart even before breakfast was ended'. Like any mother she went on to scold McLean for his untidiness about the house. In response to his complaint about his landlady she remarked, 'As to the old lady being cross I am not astonished at that nor do I in truth think she was too highly paid when I call to mind the rummage *you* must have made in the house'.[20]

Where Maori and settlers lived in proximity, disputes and misunderstandings were common. The Governor and the settlers depended on Maori willingness to sell their land so that an ever increasing number of settlers could begin to make a living. Different farming practices were a major source of friction – for example, settlers fenced their crops but left their livestock free to graze; whereas Maori left their crops unfenced while leaving their horses, cattle, sheep and pigs to roam free. Settlers were alarmed and outraged when the Maori practices of muru (ritual plunder) and utu (reciprocity) were applied to parties not involved in the original dispute. Maori were offended and insulted by settler ignorance of or insensitivity towards their customs.

Examples of cases investigated by McLean's police included a Maori complaint against a settler for cattle trespass and non-payment for work done which was found not justified. A settler had five pigs stolen and a Maori was suspected of selling them to other settlers. Another settler reported that Maori were threatening to seize goods for non-payment of work done; Halse investigated, found the work unfinished and ordered them to complete it.

Taranaki settlers had problems in taking possession of land they had bought from the New Zealand Company. In 1841 Flight and Devenson bought seven sections from the company but by 1850 they had obtained possession of only one. They were angry that Governor FitzRoy would not agree to compensate them when he reversed Spain's decision to award 60,000 acres to the New Zealand Company. They complained that they had been 'left alone to suffer from the caprice of a mob of uncivilised men who had become emboldened to assurance and a tone of superiority showing itself in various acts of annoyance'. Where settlers had located themselves on land that had not been bought by the Crown, Maori regarded them as tenants-at-will and asserted that the Pakeha should share property freely with them.[21] Maori were asserting that the land was theirs and demanding the use of bullocks and carts. Settlers had to get permission and to pay a high price to cut firewood from the bush; tools were frequently borrowed and sometimes returned much damaged. One family of settlers were exasperated by Katatore, a local rangatira of Te Ati Awa who had stacked his wheat in their yard so that he could thrash it in their barn, while his wife came to make bread and bake it in their oven. Katatore had demanded to have a gown made for his wife and for flour to be provided to feast visitors to his pa. When his pigs trespassed and destroyed the settlers' potatoes, they drove them off with their dog, which attacked a pig. Katatore complained that the pig had died and, as the animal was sacred, demanded the dog's life as compensation under the Maori custom of utu. The settlers surrendered the dog and gave him two blankets to settle the affair. They protested: 'We have been compelled to purchase forbearance of the natives by giving leather belts, tobacco, food, fish hooks and other articles as well as drawing timber potatoes wheat etc. for them, they considering that we were sufficiently paid by their abstaining from any overt acts of annoyance.' The problems encountered by such settlers were one reason for McLean's opposition to settlers leasing land from Maori and therefore being subject to their 'capricious behaviour'.

Sergeant Halse drew McLean's attention to tensions in the New Plymouth settlement. Tamati Waka had told him that a Pakeha farm labourer had accidentally cut a Maori's leg. Misrepresenting the act as intentional, a taua (war party) was formed to plunder and burn the settler's house. However, when the cause of the injury was explained, the party dispersed after receiving utu from the settler. On another occasion, two Puketapu taua came into the town armed with guns and tomahawks to settle a dispute among themselves over the proceeds of rented houses, but, after discussion and criticism of bringing quarrels into a European settlement, the parties dispersed.

Halse expressed concern at Maori reluctance to submit to British law and their inclination to revert to their old customs if they disagreed with a magistrate's decision. He regarded Maori practice of utu as 'taking the law into their own hands' and 'presuming on their superior numbers ... This open contempt and defiance of the laws renders nugatory any attempt on the part of the Magistrates at adjudication between the two races ... I fear the long tried forbearance of the settlers is almost exhausted.' Halse was not optimistic over the prospect of assimilation. He wrote to McLean that 'the more I see of the native character, the clearer the conviction that the long talked of amalgamation and civilisation is not likely to take place during the time of anyone now living; and I question whether it will take place at all'.[22]

Although Grey had appointed McLean as Inspector of Police, he began to use him in a land-purchasing role, aware of his experience in investigating New Plymouth land claims for Governor FitzRoy in 1844. In 1846 he directed McLean to join Symonds, the Governor's Private Secretary, in settling the New Zealand Company's Wanganui land claim. In a dispatch to W. E. Gladstone, then Secretary of State for the Colonies, Grey noted that the land at Wanganui was originally purchased in 1840 by E. J. Wakefield. When Spain investigated the claim in 1844 he awarded some 40,000 acres to the New Zealand Company. He found that some Maori who had claims to the block had not been parties to the 1840 purchase and had refused to dispose of their interest. By 1845, when Grey visited Wanganui, he found the Maori ready to sell the whole block. However, when Symonds went to Wanganui, a new group of claimants had appeared, claiming a fifth of the block, and on inquiry the claim proved to be valid. Grey instructed Symonds to complete the purchase of 40,000 acres as the tribes were eager to accept the sum of £1000. Symonds was to make sure that they understood the boundaries of the block and to identify pa and cultivations reserved to the Maori by Spain's award, though he should try to persuade them to abandon some, those which might interfere with the settlers' pursuits. Symonds was instructed not to pay out any money until signatures had been obtained.[23] McLean was to assist Symonds to complete the purchase. According to McLean, it was he who conducted the negotiations with Symonds acting as an umpire between the parties. McLean was distracted by 'a good deal of bickering on the part of a few white people but not by any of the respectable settlers' except Dr Rees, 'whose storytelling had become a legend'. Rees alarmed Symonds with news that Maketu, an influential rangatira up the Whanganui River, would have nothing to do with the negotiations. McLean did not acknowledge that other up-river chiefs were also opposed to the negotiations. McLean's response was to walk to Maketu's pa and flatter him, saying that matters had not been fully discussed and thereby acknowledging the rangatira's right as a claimant. His diary noted that the chief was pleased that he was thought to be of sufficient importance to delay operations, 'but such is the vanity of New Zealanders that without a little blarney there is no getting on and good humoured leading does better than hard driving and gains numerous friends without enemies'.[24] This would not be the only time in negotiating that McLean used such tactics. Discussions went smoothly 'without any forcing or bribing on the part of Mr Symonds or myself' and he hoped to 'give the natives a full, honorable and just idea of what they are about to do'. However, when a rangatira approached McLean and agreed to part with his land and begged to 'get a little trifle to purchase rum I told him I did not encourage drinking but made a present of 2/6 with which he was well pleased'.[25]

McLean was surprised that the rangatira were uncertain of the boundaries and deplored the original negotiators' failure to establish these. The problem had been compounded because the purchase had been made from a rangatira who had only a nominal claim to the supposed block of land acquired by the New Zealand Company. McLean also criticised Commissioner Spain for failing to report that Ngati Apa from Rangitikei were claimants on the northern and southern boundaries to a considerable portion of the block. McLean told a meeting of Whanganui Maori that

> we were conferring an everlasting benefit on them by living amongst them. That

> money of which they were now about to receive a large portion was our greatest treasure that we wanted to have [no] underhand work but as clear and open as the sun shone overhead that their young men should go out with the surveyors to point out the boundaries that we did not wish to bind them to anything till they first saw openly what they were about that Mr Symonds was the principal Govt. agent for them to look up to that I as their Protector and adviser should wish them to take something that would increase and benefit them as payment for their valueless tracts of land they so foolishly set such store on that would be an example to all unruly tribes in their Island and their children after them to live in happiness amongst the English who could make them a great people.[26]

The gathering approved and agreed to send their young men to walk the boundaries with him. The following day McLean and his surveyors, accompanied by twenty local Maori, set out to determine the boundaries. Te Kanawa, running from hill to hill, 'managed with his natural quickness and good eyesight to lay down the boundary between the W[h]angaehu and Wanganui natives straight as a line could be drawn'. The subsequent deed of sale set out the exact boundaries in more precise detail than in some later deeds (see Appendix 2).

During these negotiations, McLean recorded in his diary conviction of 'the folly of confiding too much in the promises of any distinct tribes or parties but in dealing with them as any other race or people let even handed justice be our motto without which success in the general management of their affairs will never attend us. My determination is therefore, if not overruled, to carefully enquire into every individual claim minutely as far as lays in our power with a view to totally extinguishing all of them.'[27]

McLean believed that the Whanganui rangatira were eager for a speedy settlement of the land question so that they could depart for Te Heuheu's tangi at Taupo. It was 'astonishing to find what vast tracts of cultivated land the natives are parting with. It cannot be without regret on their part and it says a great deal for them to be so accommodating in their dealings.' On 4 June Symonds instructed McLean to break off negotiations over the Wanganui purchase as he feared Maori that would not honour the agreement after receiving payment and would demand larger reserves and more money. Symonds left Wanganui the following day to report to the Governor, despite McLean's plea to speak to the tribes before he left. 'I presume he has good reasons besides the exorbitant caprice of the natives to contend with.'[28]

McLean feared that they would never again agree to sell the land or allow the settlers to live in peace. He imputed unstated political motives for Symonds' decision apart from his doubts about Maori intentions. 'I dread to predict what the results of his policy may be. What are a 1000 pounds compared to the peace and safety of the settlers. There is no doubt if the British Government intend to rule supreme, they will ultimately claim the land.' McLean's immediate concern was for the settlers. 'My prayer is that God in heaven will protect the poor settlers who seem doomed to misery and misfortune, left weak and unprotected ... the seeds of discord may reap a bloody and unfortunate harvest ... would I have never seen Wanganui to be treated in this foolish manner.'

The rangatira, according to McLean, expressed anger and regret at Symond's departure after all the trouble he had taken in walking the boundaries. Pehi said that they were willing for the Europeans to remain but not to go onto the lands which had not been sold. Europeans should be ashamed in running off when Maori had relied on McLean's promise of payment. 'We are sorry your good words have come to naught as we did as you told us and obeyed your word as a person we all love.'[29] McLean congratulated himself that they were satisfied that he had no part in Symonds' decision. Whanganui rangatira wrote to Grey that they wished to complete the transaction since those who disputed the sale had no right to the land. They did not wish Symonds to return as he had 'acted like a child, disappearing in the night'. The Governor replied that he would send McLean alone in two months to reopen the question. When McLean went to Wanganui, however, negotiations had to be postponed because of threatening moves made by the up-river rangatira Ngapara and Mamaku. Grey reacted by sending 108 soldiers to garrison the town and protect the settlers.

Writing to the Revd Richard Taylor in April 1847, McLean remarked that he was anxious to get to Wanganui, where 'we have a most unruly set of natives to deal with; and my progress is very much retarded. But I trust that the despatch of a few Redcoats will bring them to terms; and that His Excellency will have them here before long. However averse I am to cruelty or oppression I certainly would advocate the application of the rod where it is absolutely deserved; unless the sight of it might keep subordination and good order.'[30] Here was the arrogant face of British imperialism. McLean in his youthful enthusiasm might dedicate himself to working for the benefit of both Maori and settler, but only as long as Maori remained subservient to their imperial rulers. McLean's pining for the 'Redcoats' to deal with an 'unruly set of natives' reflected his frustration, shared by Grey, that the imperial government had yet to establish that sovereignty which they believed had been ceded under the Treaty of Waitangi in return for certain obligations to protect Maori. McLean acknowledged that the Maori rangatira did not believe that they had surrendered independence by signing the Treaty.

In June 1847, McLean travelled up the Whanganui River to Pukehika (across from modern-day Jerusalem) where Taylor had organised a meeting of 1500 Maori. As magistrate, McLean inquired into various disputes and assisted the assessors to remedy them. There had been repeated thefts by Maori who had escaped the police and made their way to Pukehika. With the aid of the local rangatira, McLean apprehended the offenders and had them brought before him. The evidence showed that they had been encouraged in crime by a European named Joseph Bradford, who was in gaol on sheep-stealing charges. One rangatira, Hemi Nape, who had heard a rumour of a road being made through his country by way of Rangitikei to Taupo, expressed opposition to land sales. McLean noted that 'this with other idle rumours excited the jealousy of the Upper Wanganui natives which to a considerable extent I had the satisfaction of removing'.[31]

Back in Wanganui, McLean noted that 750 Maori attended Taylor's Sunday service, of whom 540 took communion. Taylor, whose mission station was at Putiki, opposite the Wanganui settlement, ensured that the lower-river Maori supported the settlers but their situation remained precarious even so. After lower Whanganui Maori captured those responsible for killing the Gilfillan family, they handed them over to the British, who hanged four out of the five. In May 'hostile natives' from the upper Whanganui blockaded the town. The rangatira Te Mamaku, who along with Te Pehi Turoa had been asserting claims to land and contesting any military presence there, insisted that his quarrel was with the soldiers and the Governor. He assured the settlers that they had nothing to fear as he recognised that their presence was advantageous for trade. A subsequent raid in an attempt to draw the soldiers out from their stockades led Grey to send reinforcements. After two indecisive skirmishes in June and July, the attackers dispersed. The settlers remained unhappy. One, J. Cameron, complained to McLean 'of the sad times the unlucky Wanganui settlers have of it now – between Maoris and Soldiers it is hard to exist – both parties seem determined to fleece us of all we possess, for what the former leave, the latter are sure to appropriate to their own purposes, the soldiers are most *incorrigible thieves*, there are 500 of them here now of the 58 and 65 Regts'. There had been a slight skirmish, Cameron reported, and four 'rebels' had been killed and thirty wounded. His house and those of five other settlers had been burned by the military after being plundered the previous day in broad daylight by sixty or seventy Maori. He complained that 300 soldiers made no attempt to protect the properties and 'indeed all we had might have been saved but I could never pursuade[*sic*] the old Captain [Campbell] to believe that the villains would prove so bold or that the *redcoats* would be such *poltroons* as to allow them if they did'.[32] As a result, he told McLean, settlers were leaving the settlement; Peter Wilson was one.

In 1848, when Grey directed McLean to resume negotiations on the

Wanganui land claim, McLean asked how he should deal with the up-river chief Te Mamaku who had taken a prominent part in the attack on Wanganui, and whether his claim on the New Zealand Company's block should be on the same basis as the rights of friendly Maori. In a shrewd appreciation, McLean assessed Te Mamaku's tribe, Ngati Rangi,[33] and Te Pehi Turoa's, Te Patutokotoko, located up-river near Pipiriki, as the most formidable and warlike on the Whanganui River. Not to recognise their claims would lead to endless difficulties if settlers tried to establish themselves on lands to which they had a claim.

Moreover, these rangatira would not consider themselves to be bound by their signatures to the agreement if their share of compensation was paid to other rangatira to be handed on to them. Conversely, to admit their claims and place them on the same footing as friendly Maori would be to give to tribes generally an impression that the Governor was acting out of fear and 'that those who have been most rebellious are treated with equal liberality and consideration as the most friendly'.[34] Lieutenant-Governor Eyre authorised McLean to treat with these up-river tribes as if they had not been engaged in rebellion against the Queen's authority.[35]

McLean considered that the delay in settling the Wanganui land question had made it more complicated, as numerous legitimate claimants were springing up. These included the Wanganui people, those of Putiki, the up-river rangatira Te Pehi and Te Mamaku, as well as Whangaehu and Kai Iwi Maori. All would need to be compensated 'to ensure any safety or secure possession to the unfortunate settlers who always suffer when there is any mismanagement or want of judgement displayed in settling matters for them'.[36]

During May 1848 McLean met the principal Wanganui claimants. He reported that the final adjustment of the Wanganui claim had been held up by a small number of Kai Iwi claimants who had 'enlarged and extended ideas of their rites [*sic*] to the land on which they had been established since Symonds had been there in 1846'. However, with the help of Whanganui Maori who appeared 'indignant at the pretensions of this party', he expected 'to reduce them a proper understanding'. He had persuaded the Kai Iwi claimants, who were Nga Rauru, to overcome their jealousy towards the Whanganui tribes and accept that a settlement of their claims would be the surest way to end their feuding and to encourage settlers to take up this land. Other tribes acknowledged by McLean at this time to have claims included Ngati Ruaka (lower river), Ngati Apa (east of river), Ngati Patutokotoko (upper river), Ngati Rangi, and Nga Rauru (west of river).[37]

As McLean travelled up the Whanganui River he found that Te Pehi Turoa and other rangatira who had taken part in fighting against the imperial troops were less enthusiastic about selling. Moreover, they objected to entering negotiations in concert with the Putiki Maori who had opposed them in the recent conflict. McLean overcame their reluctance. He attributed his success in persuading the tribes to unite in settling their claims to his announced intention of making a minute and public investigation of claims. This, he believed, persuaded many of the principal rangatira to moderate their 'exclusive ideas' and to admit that other members of their respective tribes had a right to compensation also.[38]

At three public meetings McLean sought the tribes' views. Their rangatira responded with animated speeches as they, in accordance with their own custom, 'cried, lamented and wept over their land which they now wished for ever to be given up to the Government'. McLean read over the deed and pointed out the boundaries of the reserves on the map.[39] On 26 May 1848 he negotiated the final deed (see Appendix 2). This was signed by eighty-three rangatira, among them those recently pardoned, and by three young boys brought forward at the request of the rangatira to be future evidence of the acts of their fathers. The following day a further 114 Maori signed. On 29 May the deed was read again to the assembled Maori to ensure their knowledge of the external boundaries, and another ten signatures were added. Rangatira expressed a wish that many Europeans would settle on these lands. Te Mawae stressed their commitment 'to fulfilling and forever remembering their present promises'. One thousand pounds arranged in ten bags of silver was paid as compensation for all outstanding claims. Twenty-two rangatira representing twenty-one hapu accepted amounts ranging from £10 to £90.

In McLean's opinion, permanent purchase of land was the only option under the pre-emptive provisions of Article Two of the Treaty. He did not contemplate any alternative, whether permissive occupation or leasing as envisaged by some rangatira. The Wanganui purchase, McLean's first major negotiation to be concluded, was his most satisfactory. He had been careful to conform with Maori custom. All the groups that had claims had been identified and involved in the negotiations. Agreement had been reached in the presence of all the hapu. The deed of sale set out the boundaries in great detail.

McLean apologised to Eyre for the delay in reporting his success. He had, he said, been stricken by a severe illness and for three days could not hold a pen in his hand – the first indication of the effects of a rheumatic fever that was to afflict him for the rest of his life. His mentor, Dr Andrew Sinclair, told him that the pains were not life-threatening and were probably brought on by stress. 'So therefore, if you have any remains of it still, pray study tranquillity, use flannel, live moderately and attend to your bowels.'[40]

In his official report McLean pointed out that the area, including Maori reserves, was 86,200 acres. Reserves estimated at 5450 acres were considerably less than Maori would have been entitled to under the New Zealand Company arrangements. However, valuable blocks of land, including one at Putiki Pa chosen by the tribes, would not have been available under Commissioner Spain's award. McLean argued that the current choice of land would compensate for the reduction in the total area.[41] He recorded in his diary, 'Land question settled. Natives in a good humour and everything satisfactory.'[42] His success established McLean's reputation as a negotiator with his superiors. Eyre acknowledged his 'zealous and able manner' in the conduct of negotiations. McLean noted that Eyre appeared satisfied 'but probably he might have felt it rather the reverse of pleasant that his own endeavours to effect what I had been sent for, were ineffectual. However be it as it may, duty and the McLean motto – "Virtue: Honest" shall be my rule of conduct however adverse such a course may be to some.' Governor Grey, in his report to the Secretary of State for the Colonies, Earl Grey, added his praise of McLean in achieving a 'satisfactory settlement of this complicated question'.

McLean wrote to his uncle in Scotland that he had recovered from a severe illness sustained during his settlement of the Wanganui land claim, 'but even if my life as an individual should be involved in bringing to satisfactory termination a question of such great public importance of how little consequence would it be compared to the benefits that present and future generations will derive from an amicable and conciliatory adjustment of the claims of so many powerful and hostile tribes as I had to negotiate with at Wanganui'. He rejoiced that many of his own countrymen 'who had been for years in suspense for their land in that settlement are now in peaceful and industrious possession and the settlers, the Government and the native tribes all unite in tendering me their good wishes for my services'.[43] Nevertheless, this purchase remains controversial due to an element of military coercion that paved the way to the purchase.

McLean remained even-handed in dispensing justice. He brought charges against a settler, Bayley, for infringement of a native reserve at Wanganui, both to restrain him and, for the good of the settlement, to make him a severe example to others who would maltreat Maori. Such actions raised allegations of McLean's bias against settlers. One, John Jackson, signing himself 'Land and Stockholder', wrote to Lieutenant-Governor Eyre complaining of the 'unrelenting conduct of Daniel [sic] McLean Esq. Police Magistrate during his sojourn at the town of Petre in the month of Aug 1850' (he first wrote 'Whanganui' rather than Petre then scored it out). He requested the Lieutenant-Governor to forward enclosed copies of his complaints to 'Sir George Grey, Governor-in-Chief and to the Right Honourable Lord Grey, Secretary for the Colonies. I further beg to say that I shall send copys [*sic*] of the same to the Members of Parliament for my own County.' Jackson made five allegations about McLean's conduct. The first was that he had authorised Maori at Putiki to destroy a number of houses, including two that belonged to Joseph Bradford. Bradford had had no chance to rescue his property or look after his mother and children as, at the time the houses were set on fire, he had been arrested on a charge of felony 'on which he was honourably acquitted there being no evidence to commit him'. Jackson had taken up Bradford's case as the latter was too poor to seek redress through a solicitor. Second, McLean had allowed bail to some Maori on the word of another Maori, whereupon they went to a settler's house 'for the purpose of committing a crime of murder on the said settler'. Two further complaints related to land transactions; McLean was alleged to have sold a 100-acre section to Maori for £40. This section, however, belonged to a settler living out in the country and had been sold without his knowledge. As a result, the settler for his own safety had to stop working on his section. On another occasion, McLean had laid claim to 150 acres which had been chosen by a settler to build a windmill to clean New Zealand flax and had demanded 200 per cent for the land, otherwise the settler would have to remove his mill. On arbitration, Robert Park, the New Zealand Company's surveyor, found against McLean. Despite this, McLean had persisted, thus causing a worthy settler to leave the colony. The fifth complaint related to supplying Maori with powder to shoot pigeons, whereon they killed the pigeons with spears and kept the powder for other purposes. Jackson claimed that McLean's actions as a magistrate had 'cast a gloomy aspect on the whole of the settlement and many are bent on leaving the settlement'.[44]

Jackson's allegations were referred to McLean, who drafted a reply from Ahuriri. On the destruction of Bradford's houses, McLean pointed out that these were Maori property situated on a native reserve and that Bradford's property had been removed by the police before the houses were burnt; further, these houses were used by Bradford to store stolen property and 'formed the nightly resort to the annoyance of some of the native rangatira and settlers of the dissolute debauched characters about the town'. Some Maori charged with felony told the magistrates that they had been encouraged to steal by Bradford, 'who is one of the remnants of a set of notorious scoundrels residing occasionally among interior tribes that have too long infested the neighbourhood of Whanganui escaping repeatedly deserved punishment'.

The second case was heard before three magistrates. The Maori were fined by the resident magistrate, security was given by their rangatira and fines paid.

The section of land that McLean selected for the Maori belonged to the New Zealand Company and was free of any claim. Later a settler named Williams told McLean that he had previously selected the same section. Park, the company's surveyor, had assured McLean that Williams was not pleased with the section and asked to be allowed to relinquish it.

On the fourth charge, McLean noted that Jackson was one of the settlers involved in the location of the flax mill. McLean had told Jackson and Gill that, if the site of their mill was within his selection, they could occupy it and pursue their flax dressing. When they indicated that they wished to lease or purchase that land, he proposed terms which they considered most liberal. Later they retracted, whereon McLean told them that they could have the land on any terms that Park might fix. This they declined. McLean then offered to make them a present of two acres if that was all they required for their flax dressing. They refused this offer too and 'as they were represented to me by respectable parties at Whanganui as troublesome and abusive characters who had no intention of going with their flax drying I would have no further communication with them'.

On the fifth charge, he said that a small quantity of powder had been given under written orders by police to Maori who had shown loyalty and good conduct. He had seen the dead birds and had accepted some.

McLean dismissed Jackson's complaints as arising 'from my having restrained certain impositions and proceeding of his at Whanganui which I need not mention in this communication' and added that respectable people at Whanganui regarded Jackson and his associate, Gill, as 'troublesome and abusive characters'.[45] Knowledge of Jackson's association with the radical Chartist movement in England would also not have endeared him to the conservative McLean.

As a young man McLean was sometimes troubled in spirit. Late in 1845 as he travelled with the Anglican missionary, Richard Taylor, he wrote in his diary, 'This day will be remembered by me throughout life as being one in which I opened the secret recesses of my heart and the various sins of my life and my Revd companion gave me the kindest and most friendly advice'.[46] A year later, at Christmas, he had 'thoughts of home flashing through my mind. How am I to forget my sweet native land and dearer friends I may never see again; but let me trust in the Almighty as my stronghold and my defence, hoping he may forgive the terrible sins of which I have, at one period of my life been guilty.'[47] No diary entry ever revealed the nature of these, whether sins of pride or of the flesh.

Again, in 1849 McLean confided in his diary:

> This is an eventful day in my life being the first time I have approached the Lord's Table to partake of the Holy Sacrament, but in doing so I was not so prepared as I should. Indeed my conscience loaded as it is with a multitude of sins, did not lead me to hope that I was a worthy partaker of the Holy Ordinance,

> and I may well now ask myself when I reflect on the solemn communion with a Saviour which that act affords a true Christian, why, O guilty sinner, did you presume to partake of the Lord's Supper without thy wedding garments on thy lamps being provided with oil why didst thou come forward with a heart loaded with sin and guilt? ... Oh it would be well for me to consider whether I have not deserved severe punishment by this unworthy coming to the Lord's Table ... if before thee oh my God I have sinned may I humbly ask forgiveness and implore merciful pardon ... My soul thou art not yet right in thine sight. How far then must thou be from thy Maker?[48]

In the nineteenth century the taking of communion in the Church of Scotland was reserved for special occasions, often only twice a year. In the Highlands only the old or very devout took communion – that is, until they believed themselves to be worthy to approach the Lord's table. McLean's concerns reflect his youthful uncertainty in such matters.

He had not intended to partake of the sacrament until he was invited to by Richard Taylor and his wife. Twelve months earlier, he recalled, he had asked Taylor to administer 'the Lord's Supper' when he had been very ill, 'doubtful whether I should be a long liver from the severity of my rheumatic attack'. McLean now found himself in the same place and in good health. He reflected, 'Remember oh my soul, that now more than ever, thou art placed in the hands of thy God, and to watch and to be vigilant for all your actions, that thou mayest be more fully prepared than thou wert to receive the Divine gifts of thy Almighty Sovereign whilst thou zealously attend to and perform the duties of thy earthly one'.

McLean had firm religious convictions, presumably fortified by his upbringing in Presbyterian manses. As an adult, his religion was manifest in the daily discipline of prayer and Bible reading. Unusually for his time, he shunned sectarian strife. On his frequent journeys he was content to worship alongside Anglicans, Wesleyans and Roman Catholics. Unlike the missionaries, who were revolted by what they saw as heathen practices among Maori, McLean could contemplate meeting in some future existence with a heathen chief like Te Heuheu. His religion was intensely personal, centred on his relationship with his God rather than his obligations to his fellow men and women. Most of all, his faith sustained him in a belief that, in all his actions, he was guided by Divine Providence. It was but a further step to the conviction that, under such guidance, he could not be wrong. In this he reflected the view that Providence had ordained that Britain should be the instrument of progress in the nineteenth century.

Family as well as spiritual problems demanded McLean's attention. His aunt, Annabella McLean, made plain her displeasure that Donald and his brother Alexander had never inquired about their orphaned sisters or even 'if they were living ... and I leave yourselves to judge whether that was acting the part of brothers or not. I dare say that you will not take this well but I consider it my duty ... to tell you so.' It seems that his sisters had been forced to seek employment as ladies-in-waiting or governesses in the houses of the gentry. McLean's indifference was contrasted with the action of his younger brother, John, who, by offering all his earnings as an apprentice seaman, gave his sisters what little money they had. Annabella went on to chastise Donald for believing that his sisters were qualified in music and 'nice handy work ... a girl obliged to work for her bread in a master's house is not allowed to look for any accomplishment at all but hard work'.[49]

McLean had his own financial problems, however. His failure to pay his debts, whether through procrastination or lack of money, resulted in threats of court proceedings. In 1847 he received a solicitor's letter on behalf of a Mr MacDonald demanding money owing to a Mrs Anderson for lodgings in Auckland in 1844. McLean's response was to offer £20 in the next quarter and hope that the solicitor would overlook any interest due 'as my present supply of cash is very limited'. He hoped that 'by fulfilment of my present promise you will not find it necessary to take further proceedings against me'. Help came from an unlikely source. The Revd Richard Taylor had told McLean that he had money to invest at 8 1/2 per cent. McLean offered to take £100 for one or two years and asked that the money be paid in Auckland either to Mr McDougall of Fort St or Mr McDonald of the Caledonian Hotel 'who will purchase some things and settle little matters for me in Auckland'.

Whatever McLean's response to his aunt's call for money, it is unlikely that any remittance was forthcoming in view of his debts. However, after three years on a salary derived from his 'lucrative appointment' as Inspector of Police, he was more optimistic about his financial future. 'God who feeds the ravens is bountifully bestowing his mercies which if some time longer continued will soon relieve me from pecuniary embarrassment that has greatly disturbed the tranquillity of mind I should otherwise enjoy.'[50]

Chapter 4
Apprentice Years: Early Land Purchases

Between 1846 and 1851, acting under instructions from Governor Grey, McLean bought for the Crown land totalling nearly 1 million acres in the southern half of the North Island. In Hawkes Bay, Ahuriri (265,000 acres), Waipukurau (279,000 acres) and Mohaka (86,000 acres); on the West Coast, Rangitikei (225,000 acres) and Wanganui (80,000 acres); in Taranaki, the smaller Grey, Omata, Tataraimaka and Bell blocks. This was a period when Maori were eager to sell land and to encourage settlers to bring trade, and McLean's purchases at this time were generally obtained with the free consent of all those who had a customary interest in the land. However, by the end of the twentieth century some of these purchases were to be the subject of claims before the Waitangi Tribunal.

Under the Treaty of Waitangi, the Governor had the sole right to buy land from Maori. At the same time he had a responsibility to protect Maori interests. To develop New Zealand as settlement colony, Grey set out to buy large blocks of land in advance of settlement at low prices with the intention of averting potential conflict between Maori and newly arrived colonists. The land thus acquired was to be sold to settlers at much higher prices, with the difference being used for opening up the land to settlement – for example, by building roads and bridges – and for buying more land. Grey therefore preferred large areas, from 100,000 to 300,000 acres.

During Grey's first term of office from 1846 to 1853 he decided where land was to be bought and determined the price to be offered. McLean was the official entrusted with carrying out the negotiations. His reports and his private letters to Grey were deferential in tone. Although he offered advice and made suggestions, at times he sought Grey's presence at negotiations and it is clear that he waited on the Governor's instructions. McLean's excuses to Maori that he could not exceed the price set by the Governor were genuine. Only on one occasion, the sale of the Waipukurau block, did he exceed his instructions by offering a higher price, because he thought the time was propitious to win the tribe's consent.

The complexities of Maori land tenure were beyond the previous experience of European officials and settlers accustomed to the principle of individual land ownership. Maori land ownership centred primarily on the hapu (sub-tribe).[1] Customary interest was based on ancestral claims together with continuous occupation, and sometimes on conquest and subsequent occupation. Land was held collectively by hapu though it might be cultivated individually. The rangatira of the hapu was not a feudal lord: he did not own the land but he was the leader who expressed the consensus of his people. All land was owned, but there were disputed territories often claimed by more than one hapu. Boundaries were not precisely defined, though they took account of natural features. Another complication was that the lands of a major hapu were not necessarily contiguous; they could be interspersed with those of other hapu. Land tenure was further complicated in that more than one tribe might claim an interest in the same piece of land. Such claims were usually dealt with by negotiation, and occasionally by warfare.

The British concept of land ownership centred on property; the Maori concept on a relationship between people. The important elements in determining ownership were the whanau (the extended family) and the hapu. As hapu grew or diminished or reformed land boundaries were fluid and subject to continuous change. Sometimes sharing of resources among hapu led to overlapping boundaries, and a continuous, stable boundary encompassing the entire territory of a hapu was unknown. 'Instead there was a constant process of adjustment to accommodate births, deaths, marriages, adoptions, alliances, migrations, wars and a host of related matters.'[2] The absence of a continuous boundary caused difficulties when determining the exact area to be sold, though some natural features were identified.

More than most officials, McLean grasped the complexities of Maori land tenure and appreciated that British law could not apply. He was aware that before 1840 Maori had no concept of the sale of land. Early land sales in Northland were seen as 'tuku whenua' – a permissive and temporary occupation of the land by Pakeha. Within a decade of the signing of the Treaty of Waitangi, rangatira were coming to accept that the exchange of land for money meant a permanent separation. McLean emphasised this in drafting the standard preamble to a deed of sale:

> Now we have fully considered wept over and bid adieu to this land inherited by us from our forefathers with all its rivers lakes waters streams trees stones grass plains forests good places and bad and everything either above or below the soil and all and everything connected with the said land we have fully and entirely given up under the shining sun of the present day as a lasting possession to Victoria the Queen of England and to all her successors for ever
>
> And in witness of our assent to all the conditions of this paper have hereto subscribed our names and marks ...

Settlers, however, insisted that Maori land rights existed only over the land that Maori actually cultivated. The rest was seen as 'waste' land. McLean took a different view:

> That the natives have acquired right to such an unlimited extent of country as was found conducive to their subsistence should at once be admitted by any unprejudiced person and this would include the whole uninhabited country excepting the islands of the South that appear to have been a considerable time depopulated as if to open a country to our overgrown population in Britain ...

The system was complex.

> There was a great deal said to and fro as to their individual claims which by any person understanding what passed would be a conclusive argument against the speculative theories of native rights to property who stating that individual claims do not exist others even go so far as to believe they have no rights except on the lands they actually cultivate.[3]

McLean accepted that no individual had a clear title to land that was not entangled with the general right of the clan or tribe and often with the claims of other tribes who might have migrated from the area.

When a meeting was convened to discuss the possibility of a sale, McLean, in determining rightful claimants to a block, allowed all those who had claims 'to freely participate without distinction of rank or race', as both had been 'too much overrated' in land negotiations. He held that a rangatira had no exclusive rights apart from what he claimed in common with other members of the tribe, and that any leading role he took in disposing of the land was due entirely to the admission by his people of his right to take part in its disposal.[4]

> In war, in council, in politics and in the internal management of certain discipline among his followers, from whom, if not a man of independent spirit and high virtue, he will be desirous of courting goodwill and co-operation in his plans that are generally if of any moment, decided in common council with the tribe – the old men and warriors taking precedence or having the most weight in consultations. It is true, however, when a Chief has great sway, he is in a greater measure despotic, and does not confine himself within the prescribed bounds that a chief, by custom, is supposed to do.[5]

A rangatira's mana could influence a decision, but, when he spoke, it was to express the consensus of the people.

As an example of the intricacies of a claim, McLean noted that even forest trees were claimed by individual owners. He considered that most claims were based on a right of inheritance, though they could also be derived through conquest; this must, however, have been consolidated by permanent occupation – that is, by 'building pas, making tracts of actual cultivation, or exacting a yearly tribute from the remnants of the original owners'.[6] For example, in the purchase of the Manawatu block the rights of the original owners, Ngati Apa and Rangitane, had to be considered first, followed by the permissive occupation of an interior portion granted by them to their allied tribe, Ngai Te Upokoiri from Heretaunga in Hawkes Bay. Next came Te Rauparaha's and Te Rangihaeata's Ngati Toa right of conquest, and finally the occupation of the lower part of the Manawatu River by the powerful Ngati Raukawa, originally from Waikato.[7]

The attributes that made McLean successful in negotiations were, first, his fluency in Maori. Rangatira were confident that what they said would be correctly understood and that, conversely, when McLean spoke he was accurately conveying his thoughts. The second was linked to the first: his understanding of and adherence to Maori protocol, together with a respect for the human dignity of individual rangatira. A third factor was his patience; he understood the importance of taihoa – of waiting to achieve consensus. Last, he set out to win friends by flattery – as he put it, 'a little bit of blarney goes a long way'.[8]

Between 1847 and 1850 McLean's initial Crown purchases were in Taranaki, Rangitikei and Manawatu, while the purchase of the Wanganui block was also completed. Governor Grey's intention was to establish a strategic corridor along the West Coast to link Port Nicholson with the infant settlements of Wanganui and New Plymouth. First, though, Grey used the increased military force available to him to quell the Maori resistance in the Bay of Islands that had defied Governor FitzRoy. He then dealt with resistance in the Hutt–Porirua area where the Ngati Toa rangatira Te Rangihaeata and Te Rauparaha were opposing extension of the settlement north of Port Nicholson. Grey forced Te Rangihaeata to retreat and he captured Te Rauparaha. Although evidence for Te Rauparaha's direct involvement in the fighting was doubtful, Grey kept him a prisoner without trial first on the *Calliope* and then in a cottage in the Auckland domain for nearly a year. He did not allow him to return home to Waikanae until January 1848.

During Grey's first term, McLean's land-purchasing tactics did secure sufficient land in advance of demand for settlement. Because early purchases were made in the presence of and with the consent of all the rangatira and their hapu who had an interest in the land offered for sale outside Wanganui, they were not challenged at that time. The eagerness of Maori to have European settlers living in their midst was a powerful factor in the success of land purchases during this period. As well as enhancing opportunities for trade, land sales enhanced the mana of the tribe and secured a reciprocal alliance with the Governor against the threat of hostile tribes. For example, in the Rangitikei Ngati Apa sought protection from the more powerful Ngati Toa and Ngati Raukawa. It should not be thought that consent to sell was originally unanimous, but days of debate at tribal meetings and the shrewdness, patience and increasing mana of McLean as principal negotiator generally produced a remarkable transformation.

Intertribal feuding was evident throughout the Taranaki region. The earlier invasion by Waikato, the exile of Te Ati Awa and their subsequent return had all destabilised relationships among hapu and iwi. Moreover, the decline in population, including the loss of elders, led to confusion over existing boundaries and increased pressure on a smaller number of people to defend their existing resources. In McLean's eyes, Taranaki, with its original occupiers dead and the remnant unable to use or occupy the land, should not be allowed to lie waste. He believed that the rangatira's authority had been eroded and that there was no longer a dominant chief, only several rangatira of hapu. Even before their conquest and dismemberment as a tribe, he asserted that, 'Te Ati Awa were proverbial for being exceedingly quarrelsome'. Rangatira had little influence, nor could they command obedience to check internecine feuds. He described Te Ati Awa as a number of families who acted independently of one another except in time of war, and thought that their landed rights were held in 'an equally independent manner'.[9] The impressions McLean acquired during his time in Taranaki in the 1840s conditioned his approach to land-purchase negotiations during the 1850s. For him, the Taranaki tribes remained a troublesome, quarrelsome lot.

In Taranaki Grey sought to buy land at Waitara in the north, and around and to the south of New Plymouth. To obtain the land he wanted in Taranaki, Grey had first to address the problem arising from Governor FitzRoy's reversal of Commissioner Spain's award of land to the New Zealand Company there. W. E. Gladstone, then Secretary of State for the Colonies, having read FitzRoy's dispatch informing him of this decision, wrote to Grey expressing his 'great surprise and regret' that FitzRoy had failed to offer him a full report on the course he had pursued or the reasons that led him to that decision. He instructed Grey to give full effect to Spain's award, 'unless, indeed, which I hardly think probable, you may have seen reason to believe that the reversal of the Commissioner's judgement was a wise and just measure'.[10]

In 1847 Grey directed McLean to make every effort to acquire this land.

Where tribes were located within this area, equal or greater portions would have to be bought outside. As FitzRoy's promises had induced the tribes to return to their land, Grey wanted to ensure sufficient reserves for the tribes' present and future needs and to take the remaining portion for the settlers. Some 60,000 to 70,000 acres were to be offered to the New Zealand Company but McLean was not to pay more than 1s 6d per acre, the average price to be less. Grey stressed the need for the greatest economy.

Ownership of the land at Waitara was to prove particularly problematic. Waitara Maori did not consider themselves empowered to negotiate without the consent of several absentee rangatira then residing at Kapiti, whose people had customary rights over the greater portion of the land. In the 1820s the Waikato tribe had attacked and driven Te Ati Awa from Waitara. Most of the tribe had migrated to Kapiti and to the northern tip of the South Island. After 1840, Te Ati Awa began to return to their ancestral lands in Taranaki. In his preliminary investigation of Te Ati Awa claims, McLean noted that they had earlier claimed land as far north as the Awakino River but had to abandon this in the face of repeated attacks by Ngati Maniapoto and Waikato. Ngati Maniapoto were cultivating land as far south as Urenui in North Taranaki, a situation that could lead to another war if all the Te Ati Awa returned to Waitara. Although Te Ati Awa acknowledged their conquest by Waikato, McLean told Grey that Waitara was the land sought by Waikato and that they did not wish to occupy land south of the Sugar Loaves Islands.

When McLean reported to the Colonial Secretary in February 1847, he forwarded letters from those who wanted to sell and those who wanted to retain their land, noting that William King (Wiremu Kingi Te Rangitake) 'the chief of Waikanae' wished to return and live at Waitara with his followers.[11] Wiremu Kingi wrote that he and his people, because of their 'great regard' for the Europeans, had supported the settlers and fought against Te Rangihaeata when he threatened the Wellington settlement. Kingi continued:

> Friend McLean you do not write to me. Do not think that we are influenced by any other reason no there is but one law with the Queen and the Governor.
>
> Friend McLean my love is great for my land at Waitara the land of my forefathers and parents. Do not listen to what people say respecting it [meaning the sale of it] You know Hurataonga [Heretaunga [in the Hutt] was the land that occasioned Rangihaeata's fighting and therefore be thoughtful.
>
> Friend McLean all the people here are fond of their land at Waitara and when we have done with Rangihaeata's troubles we will think of going. If Rangihaeata persists in fighting a war against us we and the Europeans will fight with Rangihaeata.[12]

Ihaia, a Wesleyan teacher who favoured selling land, wrote to McLean that a large meeting held at Waitara with some hundred men and forty women present had determined that they could not accept Wiremu Kingi's claim to a 'single footstep' of the land. 'Friend they are wrong in claiming land here we shall soon show you a list of our forefathers that you may see who does own. Friend do not listen to the words of some persons as they are taking my karakas and they are also dissatisfied at my having cattle and the Europeans being so kind to me … so do not heed what these people have to say. Listen to us we are willing to sell our land.'[13]

Governor Grey made his initial visit to Taranaki in February 1847, meeting with Ngamotu and other local Maori at the Devon Hotel in New Plymouth. McLean described how the rangatira were taken into the long room with the doors left open so that the remainder seated on the grass outside could hear what was going on. Grey, speaking through his interpreter, explained his intentions to Wi Tako, a Ngamotu rangatira who had migrated with his people to Wellington in 1832 following the Waikato invasion. He invited the rangatira to convey these thoughts to the meeting, as 'many of them were savages and could not comprehend what was for their good'. As Commissioner Spain had awarded the land to the Europeans, Grey intended that settlers should continue to live on the land they had occupied and warned that they were not to be molested. However, Spain's award notwithstanding, he considered promises made by FitzRoy as binding, for 'the words of a Governor were sacred and not to be broken'. Grey would retain ample lands as reserves for the tribes; what they did not require he would purchase for the settlers' use. As the lands reserved would increase so much in value, he would allow the tribes to dispose of part of this land but advised them that they should always retain a sufficient quantity for themselves and their children. Any Maori who opposed his views, which were most favourable to their interests, he maintained, would have the validity of their claims strictly investigated and, should these be invalid, they would be excluded from all privileges the Governor was offering. The seeds of subsequent Maori opposition to land alienation were sown at this meeting, and McLean was to be involved in the consequences of this opposition.

The rangatira resisted Grey's terms. Pohorama said that FitzRoy's agreement was the only one he intended to keep. Grey replied that Pohorama had no right to the land as he had disposed of it while others were absent. He accused him of causing of all the trouble that followed, and that the only amends he could make would be to assist in getting the matter settled. Eruera spoke to the same effect as Pohorama and drew a similar reply from the Governor. Te Puni and other Wellington-based Ati Awa claimed that they had not received payment for land they had sold to the Governor. Grey promised that Te Puni should be paid for his interest in the land purchased by FitzRoy, as well as keeping a good reserve for him. The only support came from the rangatira Rawiri and Te Waka, who said that they were disposed at all times to favour the Europeans. Wiremu Kingi Te Rangitake also opposed any sale of land at Waitara without his sanction and his presence. There were many absentee owners and no permanent sale could be effected without them. Grey, however, would not delay operations on Kingi's account. He told Kingi and others to nominate agents to select the lands that they wished to have reserved.

On the following day Grey had more success with the Taranaki tribe when they offered to sell land at Tataraimaka to the south of New Plymouth He instructed McLean to negotiate without delay. McLean concluded the purchase of 4000 acres at Tataraimaka for £210 in May and of 12,000 acres at Omata between Tapuae and New Plymouth for £434. Fourteen of the Waitara Maori, led by Ihaia, also came to offer their land for sale. Ihaia had previously written to McLean giving his reasons. 'It is through the Europeans that we have returned to our lands. With your assistance we have pacified Taonui and the land remains in peace. Therefore it is not right that there should be strife about the land and now I consent that the European should have the land when the Govt. comes. But when you get home from Wanganui there will come natives from here to oppose the sale; but do not listen to them but write to us that you may go and talk the matter at your place.'[14]

No immediate arrangements were made. At the next meeting forty or sixty Puketapu Maori, led by Raniera, Katatore and Warana, 'offered determined opposition to part with an inch of land'. McLean reported that Grey repeated his threat that, unless they accepted his arrangements, he would question and investigate the validity of their claims. His arrangements were for their good, Grey pointed out; they would be wise to settle while they had the chance. They should remember that at one time they were driven from their land and 'they had better not run the risk of this being repeated; that he was not to be tossed about from place to place as they thought proper' but would adhere to his own plans. McLean commented in his journal: 'The natives did not much relish the Governor's speech and set off home.'[15] Grey's negotiating stance was to take an extreme position at the initial discussions. If he found resistance, he devised a line of retreat, which he would present in his dispatch to the Colonial Office as a masterly change of tactic.

Before he left New Plymouth Grey, accompanied by McLean, assured the New Zealand Company representatives that they would receive 60,000 or 70,000 acres, excluding reserves. Grey instructed McLean to put Wicksteed, the New Zealand Company agent in New Plymouth, in possession of the southern block at Tataraimaka and other lands as he acquired them and to have the land surveyed to meet the settlers' needs. He told the New Zealand Company representative, Colonel William Wakefield, that sections would be opened for the immediate use of settlers in the lands to be purchased first. On the following days Grey and McLean met with Wakefield and Wicksteed to discuss the location of native reserves, which had been scattered throughout the block to assist in amalgamation of the races. Grey thought it 'highly imprudent' that not one section had been reserved beside the Waitara River and proposed that Maori retain the north-east bank. McLean agreed.[16]

Grey confirmed his instructions in writing. McLean was to reserve sufficient land for the tribes' present and future needs and to purchase the remaining portion of the district for Europeans. 'Natives who refuse to assent to this arrangement must distinctly understand that the Govt. does not admit that they are the true owners of the land they have recently thought proper to occupy.'[17] In all matters of importance McLean was to consult with Captain King, the resident magistrate, and acquaint him with the steps he proposed to take.

Writing to the Governor's private secretary, McLean assured him that Grey's visit had given confidence to the settlers and 'quite paralysed the natives'. The survey of native reserves was almost complete and the tribes seemed 'perfectly' satisfied with the 'ample provision' made for them, including 'a nice sea frontage of 80 acres and 300 of good bush and fern land some distance back'. Puketapu, the large hapu resident east of New Plymouth that opposed land sales, however, were, McLean complained:

> as bad as ever; and will not be better till there are plenty of Redjackets to keep them in subordination. They are well termed by Symonds 'a blackguardly republic', where all pretend to exercise authority without having any influence to maintain it. I believe they intend opposing our crossing the Waiwhakaiho River with the boundary; but it is not likely we shall seek their permission when prepared to go there; as I conceive they are advancing claims to larger territory than they ever possessed in that neighbourhood.

A month later McLean protested that Puketapu continued to be 'most troublesome', refusing to comply with any of the Governor's terms for the settlement of the land question. They had been harrying settlers to make them leave the lands they had been occupying and cease farming outside the block. McLean did not mention that this land had not yet been purchased by the Crown.[18]

McLean reconnoitred the country around Moturoa or Ngamotu near New Plymouth to ascertain the extent of Maori cultivations. He decided that reserves of 700 acres out of a 7000-acre block would be adequate if divided into three portions for the separate hapu. In reviewing the advantages and disadvantages of having Maori interspersed among settlers and of ensuring sufficient land for their present and future needs, he concluded in favour of having a friendly tribe among the settlers. One advantage would be to check the exorbitant cost of labour brought about by the scarcity of European labourers, as Maori were prepared to unload and load cargo at cheaper rates.

As McLean rode out of New Plymouth early one April evening on his way to Umuroa he reflected on the quiet beauty of the countryside with its rolling bush-covered slopes. Taranaki mountain towered above the plain and the 'still and silent ocean'. The ocean's marked changes were 'proof of its great Creator'. His thoughts turned to the land's potential. Surely the Almighty never intended such a bountiful land should be left to lie waste with its original inhabitants dead and gone and the survivors unable to occupy or use the country.[19] For all his understanding of the Maori economy with its cultivating, hunting and gathering of the products of forest, river and sea, McLean dismissed this as a primitive economy, destined to give way before the superior technology of the Europeans. For him, God had kept New Zealand pure and undefiled until in his bounty he would give it to the settlers to be a land flowing with milk and honey for ever.

At Umuroa, McLean met with the Taranaki tribe, whose rangatira, Hori Kingi, he referred to as 'George King, a handsome open-countenanced stately man who is a great favourite of mine'.[20] McLean told the gathering that he was prepared to buy land near the town. The tribe responded that they had initiated the offer and would agree to sell because they wanted Europeans to have the land from Tapuae to the town so that 'the Puketapu tribe who continued their deadly enemies should be driven from there in consequence; that they were squatters on the land and that they should retain it no longer ... Old Paul of Warea says "I love the pakeha but hate the Puketapu Maoris. They are my old enemies and still continue treacherous and deceitful".'

McLean was also concerned for the safety of the Taranaki settlers, dependent on a handful of police and an untrained militia. His anxiety was relieved by the coastal tribes' offer at Umuroa to assist if he got into any difficulty with the 'notorious Puketapu'. Their assurance that they would never unite with Puketapu 'but would sooner die alongside the Europeans than even remain neutral' was acknowledged as 'a blessing from Divine Providence who clears our paths in the darkest and most intricate times'. McLean found it convenient to exploit intertribal feuds. He admitted to himself that, though it appeared inconsistent that

> I should not soften and smooth down feelings of hatred and animosity I must always look to the safety of the English which is only secured by the inter-tribe feuds. Had we indeed the power and preponderance of numbers on our side, I should be the first to conciliate and extinguish the feuds and reconcile

> old grievances that they should not make their appearance among the rising generation. It is of paramount importance in the present crisis to keep up a friendly feeling with this powerful tribe, who I begin to think are firmer in their allegiance than mercenary allies of any kind are found to be.[21]

Like other colonial administrators he recognised the necessity to secure the collaboration of a section of the indigenous people to maintain imperial control without the constant use of force.

McLean, who held a poor opinion of English labourers as a class, rejoiced at their vulnerability at New Plymouth as they, 'not unlike the Puketapus with their land, thought they could stick out for high wages and make a grand thing of the Government Survey'. However, he engaged a Maori party to go with the surveyor Frederic Carrington on the southern survey.

Later that month Taranaki iwi agreed to sell part of their land. At a meeting with McLean at Tapuwae there was not a dissenting voice among 170 present. Puketapu, however, continuing their determined opposition, stopped a survey party on the south-west side of the Waiwhakaiho River. One of their elders, Paul, and his followers broke away, however, and offered to sell their land, though McLean noted that it was of no great extent. Reporting to the Colonial Secretary, he said that, because of Puketapu's troublesome conduct, he and Captain King had decided to appoint one of the friendly rangatira as a policeman to keep watch on their activities.

McLean also had to deal with the absentee Taranaki claimants. The first public meeting was held at Government House in Wellington on 8 April 1847. It began with a quarrel between Te Aro Maori and Motutara's party about land between Herekawe and the Sugar Loaves (off Moturoa). McLean noted that the Governor did not appear to be alarmed 'by their clubbing and fighting which ended by the interference of Wiremu Tako, Kemp and myself', and that this squabble was 'only what was customary with our Taranaki rabble at their meetings'. Even at this early stage McLean was irritated by his inability to negotiate extensive land purchases in Taranaki. However, by 12 April he had settled with Ngamotu Maori for the balance of £100 due on the Fitzroy block since 1844, and had paid one instalment of £130 out of £390 to purchase the Grey block (9970 acres), which surrounded the Fitzroy block. McLean congratulated himself on reaching a settlement of the Fitzroy block with the absentee owners, a 'troublesome and formidable tribe' (Taranaki?), for the comparatively small sum of 2s 1/2d an acre when Taranaki land, taking the New Zealand Company's payment into consideration, cost 2s or more an acre. He believed that the importance of the agreement lay not just in gaining title to the land, but in settling claims by absentee owners who would otherwise have returned to the district to 'give annoyance'. He was satisfied that his stay in Wellington had given him insight into Maori claims in Taranaki and prompted many who would not otherwise have done so to offer their land for sale. The readiness of the rangatira to use their newly acquired writing skills in corresponding on this subject drew his favourable comment.

In December 1848 McLean, assisted by the resident magistrate and the New Zealand Company's agent, Dillon Bell, completed the purchase of the Bell block of 1500 acres in the Puketapu district for £200. With the money, Puketapu bought twenty-two heifers and steers and horses and a cask of tobacco. McLean cautioned Grey that, although the land had been sold, Puketapu attitudes made it imprudent to immediately locate settlers on it. He recommended waiting until there was a large European population and a greater readiness on the part of Puketapu to settle the 'long standing and perplexing land question'. There were signs that some of the 'more obstinate' rangatira were beginning to revise their stance. If Grey was prepared to wait, a successful outcome was more likely.[22] Not until 1850 did Puketapu finally consent to the settlers' occupation of this block. King chided McLean for his 'liberality' towards absentee Maori owners who had claimed payment for their rights to land in the block. In his view, the sum was too big and would arouse some jealousy among other resident Maori. Meanwhile, McLean's friends would welcome his return to Taranaki as 'we have more darkies already than we desire and would willingly dispense with every addition to the number of that colour'.[23]

McLean asked the Governor for money to build a road towards Mt Egmont through land bought from Ngamotu and Taranaki Maori. Settlers had found the land more fertile as they moved into the interior. 'This beautiful district in the neighbourhood of the most peaceable Te Ati Awa tribes promises to become numerously inhabited by an industrious and persevering class of settler.' The road would help to consolidate the settlement rather than having settlers scattered over a district where many Maori were still hostile to the extension of settlement. Given the large numbers of absentee Maori who were now returning to New Plymouth, another advantage would be their employment in making the road.[24]

McLean's diary recorded his satisfaction at his successful land-purchase negotiations [with Taranaki and Ngamotu Maori] and that his decisions were for the good of Maori and settler alike:

> ... may I not humbly acknowledge the aid of a kind and good Providence, in the conduct of these purchases and transactions, which have so satisfactorily terminated. May He still guide me to act with equity, justice, and full consideration for the various interests I have to recognise and satisfy: and lean on that only true

> aid and support that will strengthen me in this life; and afford me sure protection in a future eternity ...
>
> Two papers received from Uncle Donald, Letters, Land Accounts, and native supplies with Capt. King.
>
> On the whole this has been a tolerably busy day ...
>
> On Thee, my God, my only hope, –
> My rest, my aid, my strength secure;
> Do I this night in comfort rest,
> Confiding in the Arm of Right,
> That will not cause me to depart
> From religious virtue's happy path;
> Howe'er beguiled my heart may be,
> Oh, let me ever trust in Thee;
> That I may not forgotten be,
> Or left to follow one but Thee.
>
> Such is the excessive pride and vanity of man, that anything composed or produced by him, is, in his own estimation, considered as eminently superior to what it may, or is even entitled to be thought by others; who, from impartial judgment would deem our attempts an assumptive arrogance to perpetuate; although tacit approbation, proceeding from our erroneous and ill-founded ideas, of our being such immaculate objects in self-esteem ... Unworthy one, humble and abase thyself; aspire to nothing beyond thy reach or sphere; leave thy talents to improve and become developed by application and study; and never put too strong reliance on thy own insufficient powers, which are the laughing-stock of those who know thy vanity; and that Ecclesiastics says, – 'All under the sun is vanity'.[25]

In November 1847 McLean made preliminary arrangements to buy land on the north-eastern side of the Waitara River. He gathered information on individual claims and cultivations that would enable negotiations to continue when the planting of crops had finished. But the difficulty perceived by McLean was that those resident at Waikanae might not approve of land sales. This difficulty might be overcome, he thought, if the Governor would authorise negotiations to compensate absentee owners. Of those who had submitted their claims for investigation, about a third of the Waitara population were prepared to agree to the Governor's proposals without reference to the absentee owners. McLean and his surveyor, in company with local Maori, had walked over their lands on the northern side. He concluded that the land-sellers' claims were so intermingled with those opposing a sale as to be scarcely accessible.[26] But McLean was confident that he could win over the opposition.

By December 1847 Grey had decided that it would be dangerous to push ahead against opposition. He directed McLean to suspend all land-purchase proceedings in Taranaki immediately while he was in negotiation with the New Zealand Company. This was to be done in such a way as not to arouse alarm among the tribes. McLean responded that he had halted all surveying and other operations and that 'every precaution shall be adopted to prevent unnecessary sensation amongst the natives'.[27]

In 1848 Grey set out his plan to deal with Waitara. He proposed that all Maori claimants south of Ngamotu and Waitara, with the exception of some Puketapu, be induced to abandon their claims on the south bank and locate themselves north of the Waitara River. South-west bank Maori were to abandon their cultivations over a period of years and move to the north-east bank. Those who would soon return from Kapiti would also settle on the north-east bank and give up all claims to the south-west bank. To secure agreement, the Governor would admit their claims north-east of the Waitara and pay compensation, recognise and permit disposal of claims at Waikanae and Totara together with compensation, survey village sites and ensure that the amount of compensation would be spent on securing 'their permanent advancement in civilisation and prosperity'. His intention was to secure a strong and friendly tribe and to provide a good line of defence for the New Plymouth settlement. The proposal would also open up fertile land for settlement and provide a river port superior to the open roadstead at New Plymouth.

McLean observed that it was the missionaries who had persuaded the Waikato tribes to give up their right to retain Waitara. As a result Te Ati Awa had come to assume 'the exclusive rights to the soil as if forgetful of the clemency of the conquerors but gratitude being a quality so generally remote from emancipists who have been subjected to the ruthless tyrant's rule why should we in barbarous New Zealand look for its realisation'.[28]

On his way north at Waikanae on 15 March 1848 McLean met Wiremu Kingi who was anxious about his land at Waitara and asked if McLean had come to stop him from returning. He vowed that he would go with 'the first fair wind' to the land of his fathers and would not part with any of it to the Europeans. The rangatira Ihaia, along with Matiu and Hemana, spoke in support of McLean's mission. Ihaia told the gathering that he wished to be guided by McLean. 'He has kept peace abroad among other tribes wherever he has travelled. He has done more to promote peace than all of us put together could do. He is my parent. Let him be a parent to all of us. Who is to pop up or over my parent standing in the midst of you?' McLean did not conceal his satisfaction at this speech. 'Although I have always a strong aversion to write whatever appears favourable to myself, I think the simple speech of a friendly, unsophisticated native may without impropriety be inserted in my private journal.'[29] He was deceiving himself: his journal contains many entries recording others' approval of his conduct.

McLean reported to Lieutenant-Governor Eyre that Wiremu Kingi and his party not only were firmly opposed to giving up the south-west bank of the Waitara to settlers, but were urging other tribes returning to unite in building a large pa at Aorangi, the site of the original fortification on the south-west bank. As Ngati Ruanui and Taranaki had no connection with Waitara, McLean believed that their only object could be to join Kingi in preventing settlers gaining any land there. With the help of Ihaia and Matiu, a younger brother of Wiremu Kingi, McLean was trying to dissuade the other tribes from joining with Wiremu Kingi. He noted that the 'unusually sulky manner exhibited by William King suggested he would accede to no reasonable terms' while he had support from other tribes.

When instructed by Lieutenant-Governor Eyre to give priority to settling the Waitara issue, McLean had warned that if Te Ati Awa were encouraged to sell their land at Kapiti they would return to Taranaki and oppose land sales there on the ground that, having been persuaded to sell their land in the south, they had a right to their original possessions in Taranaki, especially Waitara, 'to which they have such an unalienable attachment'.[30]

Early in April 1848 McLean called a meeting at New Plymouth that was attended by 500 Maori. At this meeting McLean traversed events from the time of Commissioner Spain's award. When the tribes were ready to treat the Governor's proposals with respect he would make them known. He warned that it was not from weakness, as they thought, but from a desire to preserve and improve the race that Maori were uniformly 'treated with such kind forbearance and consideration by the Governors of the country'. McLean reassured Taranaki iwi and Puketapu that Europeans were not seeking to gain their lands, as they were doing at Waitara, and urged these tribes to return to their own lands. Several rangatira declared that they were ready to sell the Puketapu and Waitara lands that they did not need.

Wiremu Kingi, angered at their attitude, exclaimed,

> My fathers and friends, why treat me in this manner? Why not speak this way before, when our old men were alive to advise on this subject? Now that I am in the canoe to leave here you sell the land to which I was retiring, from under my feet ... My land! My land! I will not give up my land till I am first dragged by the hair and put in gaol![31]

Kingi's supporters said that they would 'sooner lose their lives than part with their land; that food would not grow on the payment they would receive for it; Europeans were not strong enough to take it; and they should rather have their throats cut than let the "Pakehas" or white men have the favoured land of their ancestors'.

Wiremu Kingi did offer to sell a small portion of Waitara, but McLean refused to negotiate unless he gave up the south-west bank and occupied the north-east bank. The following day, Kingi came to talk to McLean 'in a more subdued and friendly manner', asking to see the map again and to have a talk about Waitara. McLean reported that Kingi now found the Government's proposals 'very good', though he would have difficulty in agreeing to them immediately. Those who had come with him from Kapiti would accuse him of betraying them, after he had promised to locate them on the south-west bank, while those of his own tribe who had no land on the north-east bank would still feel strongly attached to their original land and would not want to occupy other tribes' land. McLean believed that he had had an assurance from Kingi that, once he arrived at Waitara, he would use his influence to sell the south bank, though Kingi had stressed that no land could be bought until the tribe was unanimous, otherwise there would be disputes. It seems that Kingi was trying to avoid a confrontation by hinting that the decision not to sell might be reconsidered at some future time. McLean, eager to carry out Governor Grey's instructions, grasped at this as a definite promise. McLean had failed to buy this land on the south-west bank. Grey believed that, because of his failure, McLean thereafter held a grudge against Wiremu Kingi.[32]

Grey had asked McLean how to prevent Te Ati Awa living at Waikanae from returning to Taranaki. McLean replied that the journey would take ten days and, as they would probably stop near Wanganui, their canoes could be seized then. In 1848, however, Wiremu Kingi and 587 of his people set off from Waikanae in a fleet of forty-four canoes and other vessels, arriving in Taranaki without opposition. Owing to some misunderstanding, Lieutenant-Governor Eyre countermanded Grey's instructions to send a naval vessel to intercept them.[33]

After Te Rauparaha had been released by Grey in 1848, he visited Waikanae, affirming friendship for the tribes there and offering to be their rangatira since Wiremu Kingi had left for Taranaki. He had been advising them not to sell their land to Europeans nor allow roads through their district. McLean believed that Waikanae Maori were not impressed, as they had previously experienced Te Rauparaha's insincerity. He noted that Te Rauparaha's influence over the warlike tribes of the interior as well as on the south coast had been lost as a consequence of his imprisonment. McLean visited Otaki where Te Rauparaha assured him that peace would prevail as the Maori were frightened that the Governor's steamboat and troops would overtake them before they could combine. He offered to give early information of the tribes' 'bad intentions and designs' to the Government. He said that the Maori would be less troublesome if they lived in towns with respectable Europeans connected with the Government and able to talk in Maori. He asked for such a town at Otaki.

McLean also noted that Otaki Maori were busy erecting a church like the one being built under the Revd Octavius Hadfield's direction at Waikanae. McLean thought it 'most gratifying to witness various indications of improvement ... and the spirit of emulation that exists among the tribe (of the most cunning and crafty chief of the Islands) as to who shall have the neatest wooden cottage and dairy and the most comfortable entertainment for strangers'.[34]

Te Rauparaha's influence had declined, McLean believed. He had not been able to persuade Ngati Raukawa to take up arms. The tribes had seen the progressive benefits of association with the Pakeha. McLean thought that Te Rauparaha, 'having lost caste with his own people' wanted to support his dignity by appearing friendly with Europeans, as his experience of imprisonment had made him fear and respect them. There were, he said, few rangatira more capable of giving correct information on the general state and disposition of the tribes. McLean described Te Rauparaha as:

> an old chief notorious for treachery, deceit and every skilful artifice that enables him to seduce his hitherto blind followers, [he] is a man low in stature, not exceeding 5ft. 3 or 4 ins; sharp countenance, quick eye and artful look. Indeed his countenance, although it has nothing in it of peculiar interest, fully indicates that he is a man of considerable ingenuity and quick perception ...[35]

Unhappy that the Taranaki tribes' opposition was thwarting McLean's attempts to secure large tracts of land for settlement, Governor Grey directed him to look to the Rangitikei. In 1847 McLean had encountered opposition there both from Ngati Toa under Te Rangihaeata and from Te Heuheu. Iwikau, Te Heuheu's brother, had written to McLean in December 1848 to warn him and the Governor not to consider buying land there. Iwikau reminded him of the strife over land at Port Nicholson and the Hutt Valley. All these lands were 'given up as payment for Te Rauparaha. These are the lands for him to live on ... Let this land alone for McLean unless our talk be wrong unless mine is so and Te Whero Whero and the Governors is wrong. Listen to the word he Rangihaeata is lamenting his land. There are only two places for him to reside on. And if these are striven for he will rise again.' He went on to condemn Ngati Apa for derogatory comments they had made, saying, 'Do not listen to the Maoris when they object to my words and to Mokau's [Te Rangihaeata's].

It is not for these people to dispose of my land. Originally the land was theirs – in these days it is Mokau's and Te Rauparaha's lands. This is my word if he lived in the sand in the water in the great sea it would be their land. The River is mine from Tongariro to Waikato. I am going to be near European food and clothing do not cut me off let me be near to the Governor and to the Europeans. That is all.'[36]

At Rangitikei settlers were eager to obtain land. Richard Taylor told McLean that these sheltered and watered pastures would feed the many thousands of cattle that were pouring in from New South Wales. McLean waited for more than a year before approaching the tribes. In January 1849 he accompanied Lieutenant-Governor Eyre on a visit to Manawatu. After breakfasting in Eyre's tent at 5.30 a.m., they started off for Te Rewarewa in heavy rain. Losing their way on the bad road, they wandered through a raupo swamp up to their knees in water. The Lieutenant-Governor was dressed in a tartan plaid and plaid trousers – a suitable dress for such an excursion, thought McLean, though 'they were not so becoming for him to wear as they should be for me'. Later in the morning Eyre addressed a meeting of 600 Maori. He came as a visitor, he said, and not to talk about their land. However, if they desired to dispose of lands they did not need for their own use, McLean was empowered to negotiate. McLean told them that he intended to proceed with the Rangitikei purchase so they could not say that he did it without their knowledge. The Ngati Raukawa rangatira, Taratoa, opposed all land sales, whether at Rangitikei or Manawatu, saying he should 'clasp the land in his arms and not part with it'. Other rangatira spoke in a similar strain, according to McLean, under the influence of Te Rangihaeata, who strongly opposed the introduction of settlers.[37]

By February McLean found the tribes more disposed to sell. A cautious approach had been justified, as 'time must be allowed to the natives when negotiating with them for land which is so dear an object to them that they will never part with it hurriedly or immaturely – at least not part with it in satisfactory manner. I am now paving my way well and step boldly where I could not a month ago lay my foot without causing suspicion or jealousy as to my movement.'[38] He found Taratoa, and all the Maori on the Rangitikei River, now decidedly less opposed to the sale. He noted that, if he found opposition to selling in Manawatu, he would treat with the rangatira separately and by this means bring the majority to terms. This tactic foreshadowed his approach in Hawkes Bay in the later 1850s. McLean was aware that rangatira were eager to advance the welfare of their tribes by the trade that would accompany the appearance of settlers in their district. He could exploit their anxiety to maintain their mana lest they fall behind others in taking part in this new economy.

When Ngati Raukawa met McLean at Awahou in March, he managed to overcome their opposition to the sale of land south of the Whangaehu River. McLean had heard that Te Rangihaeata had been saying that he would attack Ngati Apa, 'destroying them as he would a fish floating in a canoe before it received a death blow from the fisherman'. When he met Te Rangihaeata, however, McLean believed that he had come to accept that Europeans were justified in the purchase. Taratoa remained uncertain. McLean considered Ngati Apa to be the 'hereditary possessors of the district' but Rangihaeata and others were claiming a right of conquest. Rangihaeata said that he wanted to keep Rangitikei as a place of refuge if he was compelled to retreat from the British forces.

McLean had invited the eighteen-year-old John Davies Ormond, private secretary to Lieutenant-Governor Eyre, to accompany him on his Rangitikei land-purchase expedition in 1849. Ormond wrote an eyewitness account of the negotiations. After the resident owners, Ngati Apa, had offered to sell, the various tribes met to discuss the proposal. About 4000 Maori were present. Those advocating the sale arranged themselves in one group, with the non-sellers, chiefly Ngati Raukawa and Te Ati Awa, opposing them across the meeting ground. Every morning they assembled in this fashion to greet McLean, who displayed throughout 'marvellous tact, patience and bearing'. His counsel was always to 'let everything be well considered'. Each evening, rangatira would come to McLean's tent for a korero that went on late into the night until McLean would snuff out a guttering candle as a signal for them to depart. After almost a week gone by, McLean told Ormond not to depart because a change was coming. That afternoon, the Whanganui people declared that the best way to settle the different claims of ownership would be to sell to the Government, whereupon with Ngati Raukawa and Te Ati Awa they crossed over to the selling party, whose numbers had been steadily increasing throughout the week. Finally Te Rauparaha and most of Ngati Toa gave their consent, leaving Te Rangihaeata alone, opposing and furiously denouncing Te Rauparaha's desertion.[39]

The meeting acknowledged Ngati Apa's right to sell as far south as the Rangitikei River. Ngati Raukawa insisted they retain the south bank of the Rangitikei so as to keep all the country between Porirua and Whangaehu in Maori hands. When McLean reported to Governor Grey, he pointed out that not only had the Rangitikei district been acquired but this had been done with the consent of a powerful tribe [Ngati Raukawa?] that was hitherto opposed and one that had been in contact with Wairarapa people and other tribes similarly opposed. This purchase had weakened the combined opposition and had demonstrated that the Government had proper regard 'for the present and future prosperity of the tribe with whom it was in treaty'.[40] However, one of the major issues with McLean's negotiations with Ngati Apa was his determination to buy one large block. This meant that many hapu did not obtain separate reserves and had to shift inland.

McLean congratulated himself on having broken through a 'combination' set up to make a stand against giving up more land. More than once McLean used the term 'combination' in referring to Maori attempts to unite in resisting further land sales and the Crown's attempt to thwart such co-operation. He used it in the context of the Combination Acts, introduced during the Napoleonic Wars to suppress trade union and revolutionary agitation. McLean saw Maori attempts to unite against land sales in the light of this English legislation.

To conclude the purchase of the Rangitikei block, in May 1849 McLean met Ngati Apa on the military parade ground at Wanganui to sign the deed of transfer. He was accompanied by officers of the 65th Regiment, two justices of the peace, the New Zealand Company's surveyor Robert Park, several settlers and rangatira of other tribes.[41] McLean called on anyone who wished to speak to do so before the deed was signed. According to McLean, various rangatira declared their firm resolve to part with their land and to take advantage of European settlement among them. McLean read over the deed of sale. All consented except two, who sought to retain some large reserves which they had applied for previously but which McLean had not been willing to grant, for he considered that they had ample reserves. When the deed was read a second time, consent was unanimous. The two who had dissented revealed that their motive had been to secure as much money as possible 'before holding the pen'.

Next day the assembly gathered before a tent, Maori arranging themselves in their hapu in the order in which they should be paid. The deed was read again and signatures taken. Some rangatira exhorted their tribes to fulfil their engagements, to look to the Governor as their guardian and Europeans as their friends, while others declared that they need not speak, as the tangi for their land was the best evidence of their favourable intentions. After the tribes were asked, in turn, if they understood the nature of the agreement, the first payment of £1000 was divided into 100 equal bags; one each was allotted to eighty-six hapu, with the remaining fourteen bags to be handed to the major rangatira. The remaining purchase money, £1500, was to be paid in three equal instalments on 15 May each year.

In the Rangitikei purchase, on Grey's instructions, McLean had acted as the agent for the New Zealand Company. By 1849 the company was in financial difficulties and could not find the money to make the second payment. This delay concerned McLean, especially as discontented tribes had prevented settlers from occupying land at Turakina. To tell Maori that the Government was unable to meet the payment would only alienate them – indeed, they might well argue that the settlers paid their rent more punctually. McLean felt that Maori should not be disadvantaged by the New Zealand Company's inability to fulfil its financial obligations. The result was that William Fox, the company's agent, approached Eyre to ask that McLean cease negotiations on behalf of the company and that his employment as a special commissioner buying land for the company be terminated. Fox, however, said that he was satisfied with McLean's exertions and zeal when employed by the company. Relations between Grey and the company had become strained, Grey feeling that he was being blackmailed into finding money to complete payments on land the company had purchased. By 1850, however, the New Zealand Company had decided to close down its operations and to surrender its charter.

Although he knew that it would be a tedious and difficult task in winter and less expensive if postponed until summer McLean decided that the survey of the interior boundary of the Rangitikei block should proceed. It was begun on 24 July and completed by 10 August 1849. Where practicable, it had been directed along ridges and other prominent features. He thought it advisable that the boundary line and the native reserves within the block be shown distinctly on the plan before a Crown grant was issued to the New Zealand Company.[42] That this plan was not available to Maori who signed the deed in May 1849 suggests they may not have fully understood the boundaries of the purchase and the 'ample' nature of their reserves.

In May 1849 McLean learnt that some young rangatira, including Te Rauparaha's son Tamihana, had drawn up an agreement that neither they nor their descendants should ever dispose of their lands to Europeans except by annual leases for cattle grazing. 'They talked of having the document printed and with a view to more sacred observance of their promise therein contained to have copies affixed to their New Testaments.'[43] This decision is perhaps the earliest sign of what was to develop into the King movement.

The extent of the Rangitikei purchase inland alarmed the rangatira Te Oti Pohe, whose Otara followers McLean described as outcasts from Taupo and other tribes.[44] McLean believed that the rangatira could not establish any claim to this land nor give any reason for his opposition other than the increasing possession of land by Europeans and the prospect of inland tribes being dispossessed of all their land. McLean dismissed his fears 'as unfounded as his claims appeared to be'. In his diary he wrote:

> An eventful day for Rangitikei and one which I have every cause to be thankful for having succeeded in retiring Pohe and his party to Otara after their demonstration of obstinacy to establish themselves at Porewa. Pohe seemed much

> amused at my requesting him to provide hua huas for me when I went to his place at Otara, for ordering my enemy in the Land Question to prepare a feast for me struck them all with astonishment ... It is to the Almighty and to Him alone that I am truly and sincerely indebted for the success of the present day.

The Rangitikei purchase completed, McLean, as the Crown's representative and accompanied by Richard Taylor, travelled up the Whanganui River to visit the interior tribes. He noted how the 'sun pierced through the mist and reflected on the splashing of our paddles as each canoe in front was pressing up against the force of the fresh. Our own natives eagerly singing their shrill canoe songs and happily consoling themselves of arriving in good time to Hikurangi.' Hori Kingi, the Putiki rangatira, had the Union Jack flying on his canoe and his greenstone mere, the marker of chieftainship, in his belt to indicate, according to McLean, that while he respected the emblem of the Queen's sovereignty he did not neglect his own emblem of Maori nationality. McLean accepted that British rule was confined to the coastal settlements and that the tribes of the interior would regard a Maori emblem with greater favour than that of any foreign sovereignty. 'How necessary it must be to see these natives and to conciliate their regard and esteem for our beloved sovereign and how proud I should feel at being esteemed with a commission as Her Majesty's servant on this occasion when in company also with an ambassador of the most high of our heavenly King.'[45] At Pukehika, a large clay-walled church had been built at Patearero Pa. To McLean this signified the Maori desire to turn away from tribal warfare. If only there were more zealous missionaries like Taylor, he reflected, there would less chance of conflict. He regretted that there was only one missionary where four were needed to cover the district effectively. He thought that a missionary should be stationed at Pipiriki, where Maori were 'becoming impregnated with ideas of roman catholicism which its zealous missionaries will rapidly promote in a field where the natives are in that incipient state of transition from heathenism that leaves the mind ready to grasp at the most alluring description of religion that presents itself'.

Two days later the Highland sense of 'second sight' made McLean uneasy. Dreams had disturbed his sleep, 'but how far they may be considered of import or not I have not yet decided so fully as I should wish, that they are sometimes premonitions of subsequent events has been more than once obvious to me'.[46] McLean had a slight accident, drawing blood when he knocked his head against the pole of a house. When the Maori saw the wound the next morning they showed anxiety, asking whether they should knock down the post, house and all as utu for the injury or whether, in accordance with custom, he should claim the land or whether they should heave a post and dig some ground to designate the spot where the accident befell him.

Following the success of the Wanganui and Rangitikei negotiations, Eyre urged McLean to buy land in Manawatu. McLean refused to be hustled. He insisted that he should delay until the tribes had been reconciled to the sale of the Rangitikei block. In his letters to Eyre he emphasised that it would need time before Te Rangihaeata and the other rangatira were prepared to negotiate a further land sale. For this reason he had incurred a little expense to send Te Rangihaeata a small present to remove any soreness he may have felt for the loss of Rangitikei. Two months later Eyre harried McLean to return to Manawatu without delay and resume negotiations. Again McLean procrastinated. It would be unwise to try to buy land in Manawatu so soon after the Rangitikei purchase, he said. Although small areas could be secured without the acquiescence of the several conflicting parties, the cost of occupying 'such precious and debatable ground' might be many times the cost of the purchase. Such considerations made him, he said, 'weigh carefully and examine every step that I take in negotiating for land with such a revengeful and easily excited race'.[47]

The Manawatu negotiations also brought out missionary opposition to the ongoing purchase of Maori land. McLean believed that, through the intervention of the Revd Octavius Hadfield, tribes who had intended to sell land had reverted to opposition. In 1851 he complained that the Anglican Church was the only religious body that opposed the Governor's land-purchase policy. At Waikanae, for example, local Maori led by their Anglican Maori teacher had opposed sales. McLean found it 'most disagreeable' to find that any Anglican clergy should be most opposed to the operations of the Government, while almost invariably the clergy of every other persuasion supported the Government.[48]

At Wanganui at the end of 1849 McLean noted the dawn of the new year 'with all the beauty and splendour that the sun of the southern hemisphere displays when it ushers out of the womb of the eastern horizon'. Even as he rejoiced in the sun's rays he was troubled that he was not truly thankful to the Almighty. How easy it was 'to forsake the paths of virtue and religion and go on with the rolling tide of time increasing the evil dispositions of nature in our onward course. May heaven grant amidst all the changes and perplexities I may never forsake the paths of rectitude and truth.' His diary entry ended on a more worldly note: 'Breakfasted at Captain Campbell's – old man's milk [whisky] being handed round in accordance with the old Highland custom before and after breakfast.'[49]

★

McLean's diaries contain detailed descriptions of landscape and people, whether it be of a Maori pa or of the activities of his own Maori servants who accompanied him on his journeys. For example, in March 1850 McLean travelled to Mokau, in northern Taranaki, having been told that the tribe there were eager to sell land at Awakino. On his journeys he conformed to the Highland custom of refraining from travel on a Sunday. His diary recorded a stay at a Maori pa.

> Nothing can exceed the misery of being closed in an uncomfortable native pah on Sunday where there are squawking children ... The dogs, pigs and other tame, impertinent, half-petted, half-starved animals use every freedom with your house, food and peace, added to which the natives get around you in idle groups and leave you unable to do a single thing with any degree of pleasure. [McLean liked to spend his Sundays in serious reading.] If you walk about a train of idle, well-disposed boys follow you and watch your every step and gesture with as much eagerness as if you were a wild show or some thing to be looked on with astonishment and great surprise. If you go to a steep hilly place they will run before you skipping and romping like young kids on the very steepest places they can meet.[50]

On the return journey to New Plymouth the next day, the party left at three in the morning and had to wade through the surf. 'After getting through the first rollers I stripped off to save my watch and got on pretty well. William [his servant] fared rather badly being too short for the high breakers that threatened every moment to sweep us off our feet.'[51]

At the end of April, McLean set out for Wanganui and Wellington. He enjoyed his Maori party's company at a campsite.

> The notes of the kaka, tui and smaller birds in the forest, the shining of the sun, and the murmur of the Mangohewa stream give an air of grandeur to the scenery where we are encamped. There is something very pleasant in encamping with Maoris. All are engaged, some lighting fires, others breaking wood, others getting fern for a bed and pitching a tent, some seated by the fire comfortably smoking their pipes, while the rest are lying down, fatigued, to await the opening of the food oven; or employed mending their clothes after the tearing of the bush. The young boys are delighted that the day's journey is over. They eye the oven with the anxious look that hunger occasions ... there is a native just on his way with two large pieces of nikau which would feed three men ... Hinau berries are most plentiful. The oven also is being opened, containing a large quantity of Haori or wild mushroom. This with pure water from a stream would of itself be a good hermit's feast ... Eels and kokopu are found in the river.[52]

Travelling up the Waitara River, he camped at Te Iringa with Ngati Maru, described by McLean as a branch of Ngati Ruanui. There he congratulated himself on 'edifying the natives as best I can on historical matters and the advantages of submitting to the law instead of as usual relying on main force; giving them illustrations on the advance we have made in the Highlands from doing so, also giving them hints about the Reformation and other historical matters, which seem to interest them very much'.[53]

In April 1850 Governor Grey, impressed by his protégé's effectiveness as a land-purchase negotiator, decided to offer McLean a fulltime role. On 19 April, while at New Plymouth, McLean received by overland mail his commission from Grey, dated 5 April. As was his custom, he invoked divine aid in the discharge of his responsibilities, then continued:

> May my acknowledgement to God for this preferment be duly solemnised by some act of charitable or religious offering to ease the mind partly of the debt it owes its Maker – say – five pounds for the Rev. R. Taylor's reading desk and one or two acts of a similar nature ... To the Governor-in-Chief, Sir George Grey, to the Colonists and to the Aborigines for their united appreciation of my services I feel most seriously indebted and never shall I refrain from doing them all the good service that lies in my power and as far as my humble merits go, I shall endeavour in all my proceedings to stand by their welfare and that of their posterity more than my own aggrandisement or the ephemeral applause of the transient present.[54]

Grey's acknowledgement of McLean's worth may have lessened his feeling of insecurity as a government servant subject to the whims of patronage. McLean confided in his diary one month later, 'who knows when my duties are finished I may some day be told we require you not. Past services are not considered in this Colony and however much you have done for its advancement does not give entitlement to you to any remuneration beyond the scanty pay you received while in the service.' His strong sense of duty and his loyalty to his sovereign, however, led him to reflect that 'I have a presentiment that I shall die in the service therefore let me devote my time, health and life freely to it. My labour shall not be lost on a large portion of the community whose prosperity I am striving to promote. If my heart was right with my maker my worldly cares would not weigh too heavily on my overburdened mind.'[55]

As McLean was spending more of his time in land-purchase negotiations in Hawkes Bay, in June 1851 Grey required him to decide whether he should continue to live at Taranaki on his pay as Inspector of Police or become a general Land Purchase Commissioner at a guinea a day plus expenses. McLean, conscious that his future depended entirely on the Governor's patronage, said that he would accept whatever the Governor wished. Grey responded that it was for McLean to decide. However, if he continued as a commissioner, he would establish claims on the Government and, when land purchases ceased, would be eligible for another appointment as he 'had done a great deal for the country, more than any other man in it'.[56] The Governor then appointed McLean a Land Purchase Commissioner on an annual salary of £400, though he would continue to act as Inspector of Police without pay.

In 1851 Sergeant Halse warned McLean that settlers were complaining at the long and frequent absences of their Inspector of Police and were calling for another officer in his stead. Grey's demands on McLean to conduct land-purchase negotiations in Hawkes Bay resulted in his absence from New Plymouth for more than a year in 1851; but it was not until 1852 that G. S. Cooper was appointed in his place as Inspector. Halse also told McLean that the settlement was in a state where any slight incident might excite serious consequences. A military force of some strength was needed, as the presence of a small force would not gain respect.

McLean elaborated on this tension when he advised the Governor that Taranaki was in a disturbed state following the 'wanton' activities of two settlers, Henwood and Conn, who had shot and wounded a Maori's horse, but that there was not enough evidence to bring them to trial. 'I regret very much that reckless Europeans should act with such indiscretion in a settlement where the natives are so easily excited ... I have sent instructions to the police to use the utmost vigilance in detecting and apprehending future offenders.' The Kawau or town Maori were the most friendly, but McLean doubted whether they could be relied on in the event of aggression from the 'avowedly more hostile' Puketapu. In McLean's eyes 'friendly' and 'hostile' became synonymous with land sellers and non-sellers. There was no doubt, he said, that recent events had led both settlers and Maori to look for military protection. Locating military pensioners where their service as labourers would be in constant demand would prove infinitely more acceptable to the settlers than regular troops.[57]

Thomas King, a prominent New Plymouth settler and a friend of McLean, likewise urged him to approach the Governor to provide a force to protect settlers and preserve law and order. McLean's proposal for military pensioners rather than troops would be of benefit, he acknowledged, but anything less than a force of 400 would be too small to quell the harassment to which the settlers had been subjected. King disapproved of McLean's intention to appoint more native police in place of the Europeans. This action would leave only one European policeman; of the remaining four police, two would be absent with the Inspector, a third fully occupied with duties in the service of the Harbour Department, and the last, Newton, 'attending to his own private pursuits without performing any duty'. King protested that it would be 'very ill-judged to place a defending force in the hands of uncivilised men'. A native policeman unaccompanied by a European would find it difficult to preserve order when confronted with the 'notorious and violent conduct of drunkards'; he would not be able to explain or make himself understood, which might lead to more serious results.[58]

Chapter 5
A Mania For Land Selling

By 1850, no longer the apprentice, Donald McLean had shaped a pattern of negotiation that enabled him to take advantage of initial Maori eagerness to sell land. His reputation was now established as New Zealand's most successful land-purchase official. Governor Grey set land-purchase policy and determined the location and extent of land to be bought after tribes wishing to offer it had approached Grey or McLean as they travelled about the country. McLean had no input into forming policy but was the trusted official dispatched to conduct the subsequent negotiations.

McLean's negotiations followed a clear pattern. Once an offer to sell a block of land was known, his first step was to summon a meeting of tribes who might claim any customary interest in the land. A surveyor was present to assist McLean and, in company with tribal representatives, they would traverse the boundaries of the proposed purchase, noting the claims of various tribes, defining natural features to act as boundary marks, and identifying reserves consisting of villages, cultivations and sacred places. When the meeting finally agreed to sell, often after days of lengthy argument, the question of price would be settled. Some months would elapse before the tribes assembled again to witness the signing of the deed of transfer – for example, nearly a year went by before the deeds of the three 1850 Hawkes Bay purchases were signed. At this time, tribes again had the opportunity to register a protest. After the deed was signed, McLean paid out the first instalment of the sale price. Additional payments as agreed were made in subsequent years. Payment by instalments was administratively convenient as colonial revenue was insufficient to cover all land-purchase commitments in any one year. Spreading this expenditure over several years enabled the Governor to buy a greater area of land, while withholding the full payment also kept the rangatira in line. McLean made oral promises but avoided spelling out the legal and practical consequences that Maori could no longer use the resources of the land that had been sold. Later, this led to a trail of dissatisfied sellers.

Once the tribes consented to sell, the question of price aroused a strenuous bargaining contest. Maori felt that they were receiving a paltry sum and but a temporary gain in exchange for their land – the very core of their way of life. Others raised storms of protest for the more mercenary reason that they hoped to obtain the highest possible price before putting pen to paper on the deed of sale. In negotiations McLean assisted the tribes to come to a decision by making a prominent display of the actual coins (he preferred clean and shiny ones).

The final step, after the deed had been signed and the first payment made, was to survey boundaries and to mark out reserves. With the Ahuriri, Waipukurau and Mohaka purchases pre-purchase surveys did occur. This survey task could be delayed, often for months, by the absence of any available surveyor. This was unfortunate, for delay resulted in friction between settlers and Maori over the extent of their respective properties. Not until two years after the signing of the deed of sale in August 1850, for instance, did McLean begin to cut the inland boundary of the Wanganui block, starting from the town.

This shortage of trained surveyors was a serious handicap at a time of expanding settlement. McLean's reports frequently referred to attempts to secure surveyors before buying new land or to hasten the survey and opening up for settlement of land recently acquired. Town sales, rural sales, native reserves, roads, old New Zealand Company surveys forever requiring redefinition of their boundaries – all demanded the work of a surveyor. Besides these activities, indoor work was always at hand; this included the production of working plans and records of plans and grants which had to keep pace with outdoor operations. Even by 1861 the Land Purchase Department had only three surveyors and one cadet. Although the services of other surveyors in the colony were used, the work remained in arrears. An attempt in the early 1860s to remedy the situation by diverting a company of the Royal Engineers to New Zealand was rejected by the British War Office, which regarded it as an attempt by the colonial government to obtain cheap employees to perform colonial duties.[1]

In 1848 the Canterbury Association's move to establish an Anglican settlement in New Zealand led Grey to buy land for that purpose. He instructed H. T. Kemp in 1849 to act on behalf of the New Zealand Company and to buy the whole of the Wairarapa Valley, apart from native reserves, and to extend purchases as far as possible north to the Ahuriri district (near present-day Napier). A sum of £5000 was available, to be paid in equal instalments of £1000. As a large European population would soon be located in the region, native reserves were to be clearly defined. Meanwhile, the Canterbury Association, mindful of the need for a good harbour, rejected Wairarapa in favour of Port Cooper (Lyttelton) in the South Island.

In 1849, Tareha and other Ngati Kahungunu rangatira, wanting white settlers in Ahuriri, had offered to sell land: 'Friend Governor Grey approve of this our request for White people for this our land and let them be Men of high principle or Gentlemen not people of the lower order – let them be good people – let them be the Colony of Missionaries who we have heard are coming out.'[2] Lieutenant-Governor Eyre forwarded their letters to William Fox, Principal Agent for the New Zealand Company, offering to begin negotiations with the rangatira.

The missionary William Colenso, who earlier had been asked to help the Governor, met with the rangatira, told them of the Governor's plans to buy land and advised them to talk the matter over among themselves. He saw himself as the guardian of Maori interests. 'Now I am asked to counsel you to sell all your lands to the Government; but I tell you candidly I cannot do so. I shall not now deviate from what I have always told you. Never to part with the whole of your Land and, when you part with any, be sure to have a good natural boundary between. Henceforth I shall not have a word to say on the Land Question.'[3]

When the New Zealand Company surrendered its charter in 1850, McLean, who replaced Kemp as the land-purchase officer, was instructed to go to Wairarapa with the least possible delay and renew negotiations. In August 1850 Te Hapuku and other Ngati Kahungunu rangatira offered to sell land in Ahuriri and Wairarapa. McLean's advice to Eyre was that such advances 'while they should not be too hastily acted upon neither should be entirely overlooked or neglected'. To succeed in buying extensive tracts of land he advocated 'a steady course of negotiation' that allowed time for discussion and for adjusting conflicting claims as well as creating the most favourable opportunity for making a purchase. Time was needed to 'neutralise' the opposition of tribes making a stand against land sales.[4] This was McLean's interpretation of Normanby's requirement that land be bought only with the free consent of the Maori.

Grey directed Eyre to make every effort to complete the purchase of the Manawatu and Wairarapa districts. However, he thought that trying to buy land in the Ahuriri district first would facilitate later purchases in Wairarapa. Even though Grey's 1846 Native Land Purchase Ordinance had made leasing of Maori land illegal, the practice had continued in Wairarapa, frustrating his attempts to buy land there. Maori enjoyed the benefits of substantial annual rentals and were reluctant to sell. If the Crown could buy land in Hawkes Bay, the prospect of freehold land would attract the Wairarapa squatters north or so the Governor believed. He would then be able to threaten Wairarapa Maori that he would enforce the ordinance prohibiting leasing so that they would lose their Pakeha unless they agreed to sell to the Crown. McLean was authorised to institute proceedings against lease-holding settlers or 'squatters' under the Native Land Purchase Ordinance. Grey knew the rangatira would be reluctant to sell as long as there was the opportunity to lease their land to settlers.

In November 1850 McLean had several meetings with Grey in Wellington. He had completed his final report on the inland boundaries of the Rangitikei and Wanganui land purchases and also briefed the Governor on recent disturbances in Taranaki, as well as discussing the native hospital at Wanganui and translating letters in Maori for the Governor. Grey regretted that McLean's official accounts submitted for expenditure incurred had not been paid. He blamed others, implying that, because of an order he gave regarding expenditure, officials had withheld these payments to annoy the Governor. However, when McLean was ready to leave for Hawkes Bay he found that the accounts were still unpaid, there being no money in Treasury.

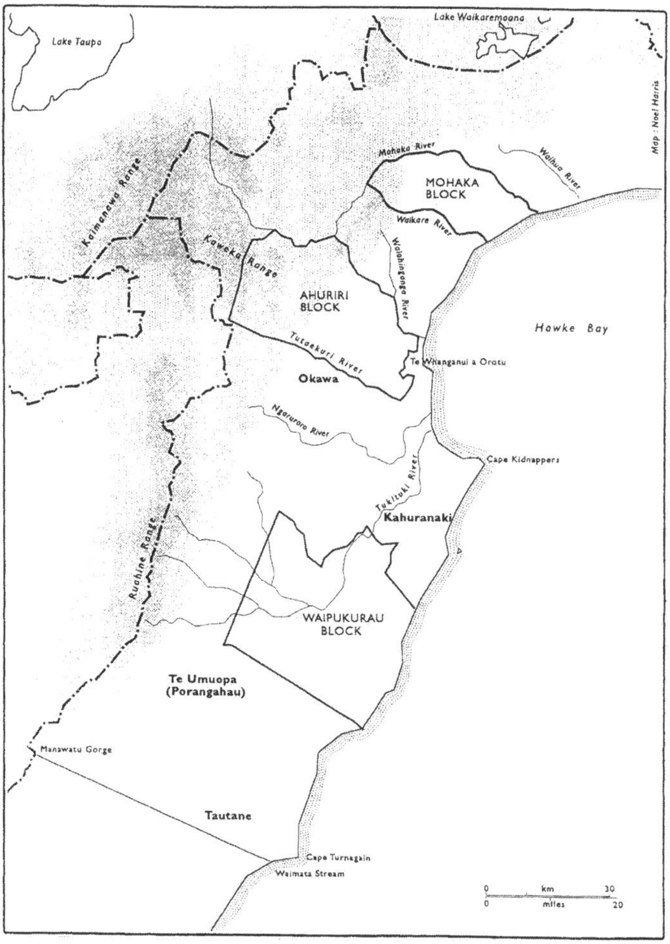

Map 1. Secret Deals: Crown Purchase Issues, 1850–1862

Before going to Hawkes Bay, in December McLean travelled up the Rangitikei River. Near Apiti he described the scenery as 'wild alpine country with white foaming rapids and streams rolling down the hills with such violent force as if they would resist the efforts of men to pass them'. His Maori party, having emptied the canoe of baggage, were in the

> white foaming surf of a mountain torrent poling up with savage fury while others are up to the armpits quite naked hauling with their might against the stream and screaming wildly for victory ... the last canoe now comes, beautiful my heartys – pull and she goes – heave my jolly boys. Now back for the loads – you have all conquered the water's furious rage. Well-done boys! Well-done New Zealanders! In your own mountain glens you are a fine, animated, happy, cheerful, persevering race. Far would it be from me to wish that the blessings of civilisation should extinguish your race as I extinguish your claims to these wild mountain ranges of your ancestors.[5]

Between December 1850 and April 1851, McLean was in Hawkes Bay negotiating the purchase of land at Waipukurau, Ahuriri and Mohaka to fulfil Grey's policy of buying large blocks of land in advance of settler demand. Arriving at Waipukurau, McLean confided in his diary:

> How important or otherwise this day may prove to the interests of New Zealand only the Almighty foresees and let me humbly in his name, the great author of the universe, proceed to the very important duties that lay before me. Without his aid how poor and insignificant could be my best efforts. Throwing myself entirely on his gracious providence I will earnestly endeavour to do my best for the welfare of the both races of the important and interesting tribe to whom I am now being introduced. May heaven prosper them and those of my own country who may come to live among them.[6]

As some hapu had not yet arrived for the meeting to debate the sale of land, McLean spent the day moving around, as he believed much could be done by 'seeing the different hapu and conversing, laughing and instructing them at the same time'. After Ngati Kahungunu had assembled, the following day was spent in discussion. McLean was accompanied by a party of Ngai Te Upokoiri from Manawatu who had interests in Heretaunga (today's Hastings). On the journey he had coached them in arguments in favour of selling. Discussions continued for some days. McLean described Matiu, a teacher who had been opposing the sale, as standing 'in a very desolate manner like the pelican in the wilderness – the majority look on with some indifference on his opposition. He has now got up to speak in favour of selling his land and welcoming me to the place – a wonderful change in one night.' On the following day Ngati

Kahungunu again met with McLean, saying that they were prepared to sell a small portion of their country initially and indicating that they were disposed to having Europeans settle among them. He was encouraged by this response, 'the women particularly favourable always a good omen of success in such undertakings'.

McLean was much impressed with Te Hapuku, the Ngati Te Whatu-i-apiti rangatira. He later made a record of Te Hapuku's speech, though he felt it had 'lost force even in the short time from 14 to 25 Dec. a deal of its richness and figurative beauty. The dignified step and determined countenance of the man with his clear voice and looks of a chief induced me to think most highly of him more so than I have of any chief I have met for many a day.'[7] Welcoming McLean and Ngai Te Upokoiri, Te Hapuku indicated his willingness to sell while complaining of settler pressure for haste: 'Is the land such a light trifle that it does not pain my right side to part with it? We shall do with the land as we the proprietors of it think proper only give us a time to think about it.'[8]

Having gained nominal consent to the sale of land at Waipukurau, McLean went on to Te Aute, where the local hapu offered to sell land. McLean declined to negotiate, saying that as 'the mania for land-selling had only struck them, they had better consider the matter well and express their final determination' when they all assembled at Ahuriri.[9]

McLean intended to check the spread of illegal leasing from Wairarapa into Hawkes Bay, as this would hamper his land-purchase negotiations. He gave Henry Tiffen notice to remove his sheep from land he had leased. His intention was to convince the rangatira that, if they persisted in leasing land, the Government would prevent Europeans from coming to settle among them. Alexander Alexander, one of the early Ahuriri settlers, had negotiated with Ngati Hinepare for a run of 12,000 acres and bought sheep to graze on the property. On McLean's advice that he would be infringing the Native Land Purchase Ordinance, he did not proceed. When he heard in 1851 that McLean had bought the block for the Crown, he wrote to his fellow Scot asking the Government to issue him a licence to occupy the block for twenty-one years.

McLean spent a night at Colenso's mission station at Awapuni – a bleak, swampy site beside the sea. On another occasion he noted: 'The surf had a heavy droning sonorous sound as if its rage would overflow the land.'[10] Colenso advised him that the rangatira Te Hapuku, Te Moananui, Tareha and Puhara had the greatest influence in the area and nothing of importance could be effected without their consent.[11]

On 20 December some 500 Maori gathered to meet McLean outside the trader Ankatell's house on the Western Spit (now Westshore) at Ahuriri. Tareha told McLean that they had been discussing the sale of land for long enough and were ready to sell. 'Welcome to your land! The water is ours, the land you see before you is yours.'[12] The 'water' was Te Whanganui-a-Orotu, the Ahuriri lagoon. McLean did not record his response, though later he argued that Maori had not excluded it from the sale. In writing up his 'arrears journal', McLean confided that he could not record the speeches of 20 December 'owing to the confused statements the Natives gave me'.[13] It was unusual for McLean to admit that he could not follow the nature of a discussion with Maori. The talking went on. According to the rangatira E Waka, there was still a moa living in the mountains included in the purchase, an area he wished to reserve. McLean's response was to 'laugh him out of such an absurd idea', although he had heard a tradition that one still existed on the East Coast.[14]

The rangatira invited McLean to go with them to identify the boundary of the purchase and to point out their reserves. These, he noted, seemed to be increasing, but 'I will give them their tether to see how far they will go then I shall bring them to reason afterwards and hold them to what they agreed to have at the public meeting'.[15] That Ngati Kahungunu might wish to keep this land for 'their present and future needs' and to enable them to participate as partners in the new colonial economy did not seem to enter into McLean's calculations. He saw the splendid land of the Ahuriri Plain as 'destined by nature to be a great field for British enterprise and industry'. He had been impressed by its potential and estimated that it contained '1,000,000 acres of splendid land immediately available for colonisation'. He longed for the day when he would have the means to acquire 10,000 acres of these plains which he thought were not to be compared in beauty to anything he had seen in New Zealand or Australia. In ten years he expected the wool exports to amount to £50,000. 'It is in reality the country for the fleece', he later wrote.[16]

The following Sunday prompted McLean to regret that his Sundays were 'not as well spent as they should be. The train of reflection which a Christian should pursue are frequently interrupted by matters of shadowy importance compared with the great end of man.'[17] On Christmas Day 1850, having caught up with his journal entries, McLean enjoyed a dinner sent by Colenso – a fine rooster and rice pudding along with a glass of Madeira. His party felt that it was really Christmas, although 'we had not old man's milk or the roast beef and plum pudding of old England'. As the day ended, McLean, then aged twenty-nine, reflected whether he should ever see another Christmas Day, and on his soul

> in its frail tenement of clay progressing to its state of final or rather earthly dissolution ... Man think of thyself, know thyself, and consider what a frail creature thou art. Remember that destiny is in the hands of an impartial judge with whom you must not trifle. Call to mind that all that is essentially dear to you for eternity is at stake and oh prepare thy wicked heart to appear before

> the Great Redeemer who suffers that you might obtain redemption for your numerous sins. Purify your heart of its accumulating vices, reduce your pride, place your reliance on God and he will not forsake you in time of need and trouble ... Examine yourself and enquire strictly if you have performed your duty honestly to God and to man and when assured that you have as far as lies in you done so, go to rest in the name of the heavenly maker ...[18]

His diary entry ended with thoughts of his friends and relatives enjoying a happy Christmas in Scotland.

The last day of the year brought forth McLean's familiar musings on his relationship with his Maker. His concern was for the future of his soul in eternity. His religious and spiritual feelings had been on the decline, yet the Almighty had granted him success in his public efforts. He feared his heart was not right in the sight of God:

> Oh keep me in thy fear O Lord, and learn me to pray that all my thoughts prepared may be for that most awful day when man the image here below no more can plead delay or rest his idleness and guilt on tottering forms of clay which summonsed from their mouldy earth shall tremble and reform like infant Penitence before the rod of full grown man...
>
> Give me but grace to know my way that I from justice never stray nor from the ways of God that I thy righteousness and truth may ever uphold that when my worldly race is run I may find favour with the Lord.[19]

On New Year's Day McLean wished that the coming year might be 'attended with the Almighty's blessing on my efforts for the good of the country in which I live and for the welfare of those who may hereafter resort to it'. He believed that he had been called by God for this purpose. And then to business. He approached Karaitiana Takamoana about buying the heads of Ahuriri (Mataruahou (Scinde Island) and Te Taha (the Western Spit)), which were essential to control the harbour entrance, 'as the place would be an awkward purchase without it'.[20] Karaitiana appeared willing to sell but, as McLean noted, Tareha and Torotoro, the principal owners, proved unresponsive. McLean persisted, going to Awatoto to speak to Tareha. In March his diary recorded: 'held a long korero with Tareha about the purchase of Ahuriri Island [Mataruahou] and; the price paid for land at Taranaki of which he had a great idea which I moderated by telling him the exact truth which is always the test'.[21]

McLean also spent some time with William Colenso, in McLean's eyes 'a straightforward excellent man' from whom he could learn much. McLean tended to emphasise the excitable nature of the Maori. He did not appreciate the essential drama of debate on the stage of the marae and that the more important the topic, the greater was the vehemence of exposition to do it justice. As

Colenso told him of the treatment he had received at the hands of the Ahuriri rangatira Tareha, Te Moananui and Takamoana, with their 'obstinacy and violent passions', he responded: 'How careful I must be in dealing with these people and how bitter they are and how far they will carry their malignant passions when once excited.' He deplored 'the contradictory, changeable and evil disposition of the natives'.[22] Colenso, feeling himself isolated, was eager to cultivate the friendship of such an influential official. McLean, for his part, might have been less impressed by Colenso's assessment of the Maori character had he detected that it was the missionary's confrontational style and determination to make the rangatiras' authority subordinate to his own that had provoked excitable responses. Only a few weeks before, Colenso had come into physical conflict with some of the leading rangatira.[23]

McLean encouraged rangatira to consult with him. Paora, 'a quiet sensible young man, well disposed to the English', had travelled from Mohaka to Ahuriri and was eager for McLean to visit his place to talk about buying land. McLean observed: 'It is satisfactory to find the chiefs coming in from such distances to see me and consult me about their land; and their confidence in me should prompt me at all times to watch over their interests as if they were my own.'[24] Te Moananui had warned McLean that the Ngati Tuwharetoa rangatira, Iwikau, was opposed to land sales, and in particular to the location of the inland boundary of the proposed Ahuriri block above the Titiokura saddle. Ngati Hineuru, who were associated with Ngati Tuwharetoa, were disputing this boundary. McLean decided to write to Iwikau to tell him, in case of future opposition, that he was buying land at Ahuriri.[25]

McLean avoided haste in these negotiations. He spent six weeks in February–March travelling north to Wairoa and on to Poverty Bay, returning by way of Mahia Peninsula. As he went, he secured offers to sell land and discharged his duties as a magistrate, even though he was outside the New Munster boundary of his commission. The flats at Wairoa he found rich and fertile and the tribes eager to sell. McLean was cautious, however. He preferred to buy on one side of the river only, leaving the other for the tribes. He explained that Europeans' sheep and cattle would destroy their crops and be a source of trouble. If they were all agreed to sell, they should fix their asking price and the boundaries of the block, after which he would consider the price to be paid. Although the south bank could also be purchased 'to deprive them of more, however anxious they are to sell, would be unjust to them as they are a very numerous tribe about 2000'.[26]

McLean and his party of Maori bearers then journeyed overland from Wairoa to Poverty Bay, first by canoe up the Wairoa River. Progress was slow; five miles by late afternoon. McLean was philosophical.

> I was more amused than annoyed as a stranger would be, at our slow movements

> in starting. There was so much talk, adjusting, going ashore for paddles and things forgotten; all ordering and none acting; that before we moved from the bank a full hour was spent. And almost always in these large canoes this is the case with the natives before they start. They go slowly; then more rapidly; then a race full speed. Then almost suddenly to a full-stop of another half an hour before they move. Thus the day is spent in alternative intervals of idleness, landing and eating at each other's village, and going at railway speed when urged by any sudden impulse to do so.[27]

Leaving the river, the party travelled over poor, steep hill country until they descended to the fertile Poverty Bay flats. McLean noted that ninety-six Europeans had developed a substantial trade out of the port at the small settlement of Turanganui (today's Gisborne). He suggested that the port could be improved if rocks at the entrance were blasted away. One hundred acres of cultivated land exported to Auckland 11,000 bushels of wheat, 3000 bushels of maize, sixteen tons of potatoes, and ten tons of onions along with twenty-seven tons of pork.

McLean addressed the assembled rangatira at Poverty Bay, explaining that he did not have the authority to buy their land but he would listen to their views. At Turanganui, a meeting over the sale of land for the site of a township showed that the hapu was divided. McLean decided not to pursue the matter. In his capacity as magistrate, McLean had the rangatira Rawiri act as an assessor in two cases. In future cases of differences between Maori and Europeans, he instructed him to write to the Governor. He summonsed a European to appear before him to answer a charge of having sold gunpowder to a Maori. After hearing evidence, McLean fined the guilty party £20 and ordered the powder canisters to be shipped to Auckland. He swore in a settler as a special constable to search premises for 'munitions of war' and offered a £5 reward to any native who would inform against the future sale of gunpowder in the belief that these measures would put a stop to further such activity. McLean's visit highlighted the intermittent presence of any official able to implement Grey's intention to establish British law throughout the island.

On his return journey south, McLean visited Mahia, where some 140 Europeans and 200 Maori earned their living by whaling at Table Cape, with twelve whaling stations and twenty-six boats. Resident whalers complained that whaling ships from Hobart, America and other places were preventing whales from coming into Hawke Bay, thus materially injuring the shore-whaling parties. They asked McLean to urge the Governor to make laws to protect their interests by, for example, controlling the number of boats to be employed and rules to stop each boat trying to seize the whales, thereby driving them from the bay.

At Ahuriri, McLean confronted what he saw as jealousy among the rangatira and struggled to get Te Moananui, who showed resentment towards Te Hapuku, to cooperate with the other rangatira. Both rangatira favoured selling land but were caught up in boundary disputes. When McLean met up with Colenso at Patangata, he learnt that he too had advised Te Moananui to cooperate. He welcomed Colenso's assistance, describing him as 'a zealous, conscientious man and an excellent devoted missionary well entitled to support from the Government'. McLean also complained that he had a severe headache and 'the natives talking all night does not improve it'.[28] Te Hapuku and Te Moananui both came to see McLean, Te Moananui complaining that Te Hapuku was opposing his intention to sell but that, when it was Te Hapuku's turn to sell land, he did not welcome other rangatira intervening. Te Moananui warned McLean that Te Hapuku and his hapu did not have a customary interest in the block under negotiation. He was becoming disturbed that McLean was slighting his mana by giving preference to Te Hapuku. McLean's reaction was that 'it is a difficult thing to unite a party of natives to agree to any subject in which their jealousies of each other are concerned'.[29] Although Te Hapuku did not rank above other rangatira in Hawkes Bay, McLean chose him as his agent to conduct negotiations over land there. Te Moananui, Tareha and Puhara felt that their mana had been diminished. McLean's preference was unwise, and unease among the Ngati Kahungunu rangatira was to grow until it led to intratribal war. McLean, however, was so impressed by Te Hapuku's personal qualities that he wrongly came to identify him as the paramount rangatira of the East Coast from Turanga to Wairarapa. 'Hapuku is acting precisely as I have instructed him; that is, he goes about negotiating and arranging with his tribe for the sale of more land, and today he tells me that has obtained a very large, splendid district including the best grazing land at Heretaunga.'[30] Encouraged by McLean, Te Hapuku offered to sell land as far south as Wairarapa. Through his having Ngati Kahungunu affiliations, Te Hapuku had an interest in land there, but his authority to offer to sell land was confined to his own hapu, Ngati Te Whatu-i-apiti. Nevertheless, he assured McLean: 'I will not have two ways respecting the land it will all be sold to you on to Wairarapa which place you the Europeans have already paid for us yearly rents and my "Rangatira wenua" or chieftain land is for the first time transferred to you therefore I wish to have a great payment to commence with that I may meet with less difficulty in purchasing the rest of the country with you.' McLean thought him 'an exceedingly well informed chief more so than most I have met in the island'.[31]

However, on his return to Ahuriri in late March, McLean became agitated when he received a letter from Colenso saying that he had had reports that McLean in his negotiations over Ahuriri had been departing from his intention to listen to dissenting views and to buy only land that the tribes did not require. McLean, ever-sensitive to criticism, reacted quickly. Colenso should have checked before accepting these assertions: 'Justice and fair play to the Sovereign I serve, all her subjects of every race shall be my motto as it always has been, let others say what they will.'[32] McLean rode off immediately to rebuke Colenso, accompanied by 'his entourage of leading chiefs, surveyors and others, forty in all'. He convinced Colenso that he had been misinformed: never would he take land without the full consent of the rightful owners.[33] McLean did not say that 'full consent' was obtained only after he persisted in overcoming resistance from reluctant owners.

McLean's party moved south at the end of March to continue negotiations for Te Hapuku's land – the Waipukurau block. In the evening around the camp fire, Te Hapuku and McLean made 'speeches in favour of selling, settling other opposition, never interfering with European land and treating the English well [which] were kept on till midnight, much to the enjoyment of our party, who have a great thirst for listening to speeches and criticising them afterwards'. At one point in the survey, local Maori began to quarrel and threaten to withhold portions of land within the boundary. McLean used his skill as a mediator to overcome their opposition, urging them to reconcile their differences, to unite to settle the land question and not to engender feelings that might lead to future strife among their own and European children. Europeans were a numerous race, he warned, and 'To oppose them would be folly, but to act mildly and quietly would be the surest means of obtaining their wishes and of securing their rights without infringement of any kind; that our laws were powerful to protect them in their just rights.'[34] McLean sought to avert racial strife and keep the peace, but Maori had to accept a subordinate role.

At Ruataniwha, during negotiations for the Waipukurau block, McLean complained that his party had 'been compelled to listen to a very long korero about ancestors and claimants' by Apiata, the main spokesman, 'and a very long winded one … who called and named every man, woman and child at Manawatu, Wairarapa, the Middle Island, Waikato, Taupo, Maketu, Bay of Islands, Tauranga, Turanga, ake, not forgetting the Ngatiraukawas, Ngatiapa, Whanganui and all the people he could think of. This speech tried my patience, was loudly applauded by the natives, and of course I put my displeasure, unperceived in my pocket, and whenever he stopped I did not give any others an opportunity to figure off in the same manner; although … one or two others made an attempt.'[35] This speech was undoubtedly intended to establish Apiata's claim over the land under offer and to point out that many different groups had rights at Waipukurau, although McLean preferred to describe it as Te Hapuku's block.

Although familiar with the intricacies of Maori customary land rights,

McLean put the responsibility on the rangatira to settle among themselves what he termed their 'little differences' about boundaries, reserves and other questions. Te Hapuku supported him, advising his peers to give up 'small dissensions of every kind'. To hasten negotiations, McLean set out to simplify the complexities of customary land rights. He wanted to deal with only one body of claimants. He told the assembly at Waipukurau that Hoani Waikato should combine with Te Hapuku as their lands adjoined. It would be difficult and expensive for him to ascertain the extent of Hoani's claim. They should unite in making one sale as well as reducing their asking price.[36]

The tribes having agreed on boundaries and reserves for the Waipukurau block of 300,000 acres, negotiations began over the price. McLean offered £3000. Te Hapuku pointed out that people in Wairarapa were receiving £3000 every year for leasing their land. The tribe countered with twenty separate notes, all demanding £20,000. McLean found the speakers unanimous in agreeing to part with their land, 'land for which they had fought and lost hundreds of their people; a land abounding with all description of native food, land sought after by all the tribes of the Ngapuhi, Waikato, Ngatipaoa, Ngatiraukawa and others without gaining possession of it'. Speakers demanded: 'Let the price for your "tapu" land be what we ask for it! Do not reduce it. This is the first time the land on this side of the island has been offered to the Queen. Let your dealings be liberal and we shall give you all the land you require from us. Nothing will be withheld from you ...' A 'violent Ngapuhi rangatira named Wiremu' (from Poverty Bay) advised the gathering to ask a high price, arguing that when the Europeans got the land they would sell it at a great price but would give nothing to the original Maori owners. He had taken part in land sales and knew what was required. They should keep their land rather than give it away for nothing. During this speech McLean and the surveyors retired to a tent, where they dined while Wiremu 'was edifying the tribes with his superior skill in obtaining large "utu" for the land'.

Believing that his people's future prosperity lay in land sales,[37] Te Hapuku appealed to McLean, 'for his people were ebbing while the white man was flowing'. Therefore, they welcomed the strangers to fill the land. 'Why should it be idle? Let it have English smoke, English fires, English houses and English fences!' As they faced the prospect of their subordination, they feared that they were surrendering their old way of life for an uncertain place in the new order. Te Hapuku continued: 'Let your price be handsome! What is a thousand pounds among my people? It will not be a pound for each of them. When I thought of that last night, I felt keenly for the transfer of the land of my fathers and grandfathers.' The rangatira reflected Maori feelings – feelings that were to strengthen as more and more land was sold – that they had sold their birthright and that little remained. 'I turn you over my greatest wealth, a wealth that never fails or reduces, and you offer only this small sum that will not burden the hands of my children or clothe my old women or slaves.'[38]

McLean replied that it was not in his power to accede to their 'exorbitant expectations'; he would, however, talk to Governor Grey, to whom he was responsible. He did not explain that the British Government's policy required the Governor to use the profit from the resale of Maori land – his main source of revenue – to fund the development of the colony. The price offered to Maori therefore had to be far less than the value of the land once it was opened for settlement. McLean resorted to another justification. They should realise, he argued, that the land, once in government hands, would increase in value as money would be spent on roads, bridges, and so on, and settlers would come to live among them, bringing their wealth with them, and enrich Maori by doing so. Was it any wonder that the Governor sold the land to settlers at a higher price? Maori did not have the resources to bring people onto the land. Rather than leaving the land to lie idle, Maori should transfer their land to those who would turn it to better account.

McLean insisted that the land was worth only £1000 – a large sum, he claimed – but he would go further than he had ever done before and offer another £1000 in the following year and a third instalment of £1000 in the year after. Most seemed 'thunderstruck at the small amount'. As the meeting broke up Te Hapuku handed over a note asking for £7000–8000. McLean increased his offer to £4800. Te Hapuku had to accept. McLean confided in his diary his concern that, contrary his instructions, he had offered a higher price without consulting the Governor, but hoped that Grey would approve, as the natives would be offended if, after all their trouble, nothing was decided.[39]

On 5 April 1851, he noted that this day marked the anniversary of his appointments as Sub-Protector of Aborigines in 1844, Inspector of Police in 1846 and Land Commissioner in 1850. He went on:

> To a reflecting mind these anniversaries should be accompanied with a due acknowledgement of the Almighty's providence in blessing my efforts to perform my duties, and I should also thank the Almighty for bestowing such blessings upon me ... and let my mind be strongly imbued with feelings of justice to my fellow creatures of both races. May the same God who upholds me also uphold the natives; and cause my efforts to acquire their country, to prove an eventual and present benefit to their race and all their posterity. They are certainly a most manly, interesting people whose extinction or oppression I should regret, and whose improvement I shall always regard with equal interest as my own – although I cannot carry all the plans for their welfare that I can foresee would be of great advantage to them.[40]

In McLean's eyes there was no contradiction between his efforts to acquire Maori land and his intention to devote himself to the improvement of the race!

Negotiations for the Ahuriri block ended in reluctant agreement on the price in May 1851. Here McLean departed from his earlier practice of allowing ample time for debate and consensus to emerge. He met with the rangatira alone. Tareha and the other rangatira asked for £4500; McLean responded that the surveyor's value was only £500, and that it was poor land producing nothing of value. This was in fact the 'splendid land' which McLean coveted as a future pastoralist and of which he had told the Governor that it was capable of producing wool exports worth £50,000 a year! Although McLean's instructions did not allow him to fix the terms of payment without reference to the Governor he felt that with such 'a fickle people' he should name a price: £1500. The rangatira 'almost left the ground with disgust at the smallness of the price'. He told them coolly that his power to grant prices for land was limited and that he could not and would not exceed that price. After some excited discussion among the rangatira, McLean got up to leave. He knew that Te Hapuku had enhanced his mana by the recent sale of the Waipukurau block. The rangatira present were conscious that in turn their mana would be diminished if they failed to negotiate a sale with the Governor's right-hand man. McLean's tactic worked. The rangatira stopped him, saying they would agree to his price. Their capitulation, despite their dissatisfaction, also reflected their eagerness to have European settlers among them to trade with. After they had agreed to sell, they wrote to Grey pointing out that their agreement arose from their desire to have a town with Pakeha settlers among them and urging haste. They were signalling their wish for an ongoing relationship for the mutual benefit of Maori and Pakeha.

McLean congratulated himself that 'a question which will contribute greatly to the welfare of this island has been satisfactorily settled ... Thank God for his aid and guidance in this matter.'[41] McLean saw the 'welfare of the island' only in terms of benefit to the settlers; that Maori would be adversely affected did not appear to count. He seemed unaware of his hypocrisy in invoking God's help in using dubious negotiating tactics.

Ten days after leaving Ahuriri, McLean reached Paekakariki. Leaving at 6 a.m. he rode into Wellington six hours later. He then called on the Governor to report on his success in buying land in Hawkes Bay.

In October 1851 McLean returned to Hawkes Bay to complete the sale of the Waipukurau block. After leaving Wellington, he travelled along the rugged coastline past Cape Palliser and up the Wairarapa coast to Castlepoint and on to Porangahau. His party included Maori servants (to look after the camping gear and supplies), the surveyor de Pelichet, Williamson (a copying clerk from the Land Purchase Department), and a contingent of Wellington Te Ati Awa with their rangatira, Wi Tako, who were to act as advocates for land selling. Williamson, whose horse was carrying bags with £2000 in gold sovereigns, plunged in over his head when riding through a swamp. The horse 'set off at full gallop with the treasure' and was recaptured only after an hour and a half's delay. McLean was furious: 'I would feign have horsewhipped the fellow for his stupidity.' He thought him a man of little judgement or sense. As a copying clerk he was 'a drawback rather than any assistance and as destitute of politeness as the most common clown'.[42]

McLean stopped overnight at the homes of Wairarapa runholders. While staying at Bidwill's run, one of McLean's party, an old Dane, stole a cap from one of Bidwill's men. McLean dismissed him, 'the fellow declaring his innocence in his broken English in the most imploring terms but all to no effect, how apt we are to be imposed upon by the scum of the earth that float about with such plausible appeals to our feelings and with such false pretensions and claims to our sympathy – often have I now been imposed upon by such characters of whom I shall be more guarded in the future'.[43] There seems to have been some unrecorded incident of deception in McLean's early years; as more than once he referred to occasions when he had been taken advantage of.

At Purvis Russell's run in Whangaimoana McLean attended a gathering where he took the opportunity to display the bags of sovereigns for Maori to handle. He warned prospective runholders against taking up new runs on illegal Maori leases and, where occupation had been recent, ordered them to remove their flocks. Further north in Hawkes Bay, he met up with Donald Gollan who was already running sheep, including some of McLean's, although purchase negotiations for his run were not yet complete. When McLean met with local Maori he was encouraged to find that they were ready to sell a block covering eighty miles of coast from Castlepoint north and extending inland to the Tararua and Ruahine ranges.

Before the tribes assembled to sign the deed of sale for the Waipukurau block McLean spent an evening with Te Hapuku, suggesting that as the Governor had agreed to pay the price he had asked for his land (albeit after McLean had made him reduce the price from £20,000 to £4800), in return he should give the Governor an additional tract of land. McLean did not note Te Hapuku's response but recorded that 'I went on to explain to him how land acquired its value and kept up the conversation till 12 or 1 in the morning'.[44]

The tribes gathered for the signing at the end of October 1851. McLean waited for Te Hapuku to assemble the participants, break them up into their hapu, each headed by its rangatira, and record the names of each hapu. McLean would not allow Maori to make a claim as a member of more than one hapu – another example of his intention to simplify negotiations. So busy were the Maori with the erection of temporary shelters that no business could be done for the first two days. Later they mustered in their hapu while McLean took delivery of their claims. The following day he called up and examined the papers of the different hapu. He accepted Hoani Waikato's claim to be independent of Te Hapuku, marked the block out on the map and proposed a sum of £300 for it. Te Hapuku countered with £360 to which McLean agreed. Each hapu involved received £8. Afterwards he went over the deed of Te Hapuku's block with the hapu and divided the balance in equal portions of £9. McLean, supported by Te Hapuku, proposed a payment of £100 to the Wairarapa rangatira to satisfy all their claims. Another considerable sum was paid to the Ngai Te Upokoiri rangatira of Manawatu for their interest in the block.

McLean read the deed to the assembly of 600 men, women and children, and showed them a map of the district with reserves marked, carrying the map about so that all could see it. The reserves amounted to 4378 acres, considerably larger than for Ahuriri block of comparable size. There were 377 signatures to the deed as well as witnesses. As McLean believed there was 'some confusion', he again checked the 191 hapu involved. (McLean was following his usual practice of sorting people into hapu to suit his purpose of purchasing from manageable units rather than the reality on the ground.) Each hapu would receive £9. The money was counted in the presence of the rangatira 'including Hapuku, Moananui, Paraone, Ropata, Maike, Te Harawira, Morena, Te Wakapapaka, Wereta Te Kawekairangi, Puhara, the Queen and others whom I invited into the house to discuss the best method of division'. In observing Maori protocol by inviting the rangatira to decide, McLean showed that he had learnt his lesson from the shambles over the Wanganui payment in 1849.

McLean was satisfied that the distribution had gone off well. Te Hapuku 'as usual, behaved admirably, acting quite with the generosity and dignity of a chief throughout the whole proceeding … The natives behaved with unusual quietness and decorum and in the evening there was less apparent dissatisfaction among the natives than I have witnessed at any similar meeting. Certainly the sum they received was handsome and much more becoming to the Government to pay them well than to have after difficulties and dissatisfaction.'[45] McLean was impressed that £1800 could be distributed among the hapu without any squabbling when he and the few Europeans present were entirely at the mercy of what had been a 'turbulent savage tribe'.[46]

In November McLean moved north to Ahuriri, where he was joined by other Europeans. This he found disagreeable as he could not separate himself from them. Some were needed as witnesses but, apart from the surveyors

Robert Park and de Pelichet and the local settlers Captain Thomas and young Henry Tiffen, he wished the others were elsewhere. 'We can have neither food nor comfort while surrounded by such strangers and stragglers as fall in with a person in the bush and stick to him like a burr.'[47]

McLean was sensitive to criticism that he was taking advantage of the rangatira. Tareha and other rangatira had been reluctant to include Mataruahou and Te Taha (Westshore Spit) in the sale. Over the sale of Mataruahou, Colenso had advised the tribes to have a clause inserted in the deed giving them free rights to have their vessels enter and leave the harbour, 'besides such hints as would no doubt be to their advantage'. This aroused a tetchy response from McLean that 'it does not appear to me essential that the natives require such advice when they are in treaty with the British Government'.[48] He resented any suggestion that he had neglected to safeguard Maori interests. He again discussed boundaries with Tareha and Te Moananui and persuaded them to reduce what they wanted as reserves on Mataruahou, observing that 'they were very reasonable much more so than during my former visit. Wi Tako seems to give them very good advice.' Two days later McLean went with Park and Tareha to fix the Mataruahou boundaries. On the next day, 14 November, the draft deed of the Ahuriri block of 265,000 acres was submitted to the tribes. At first they objected to a reserve of only 500 acres at Puketitiri (north of Napier) when they had asked for several thousand acres. However, 'after some long talking and very proper enquiries and arguments I got through the several clauses of the deed'.[49] There were still problems, especially from the Tangoio people, who were 'a very troublesome lot to deal with, more so than any of the rest', though McLean attributed their discontent over their share to not having been fully consulted during the first stages of negotiations.

The total area of reserves in the Ahuriri block amounted to about 1 per cent of the land. Reserves were either land remaining in Maori title or Maori land held under Crown title. There were four different categories, intended to meet Maori needs: first, land excluded as being the site of existing habitations; second, lands that were important resources – bush areas, lagoons and canoe landing-places, and lands for more modern uses, such as whaling stations and pastoral grazing land; third, lands reserved because of their historical and spiritual significance, such as wahi tapu, urupa and old battle sites; lastly, Crown grants to rangatira.[50]

Although Article Two of the Treaty stated that Maori land could be sold only with their free consent, McLean often overrode Maori requests for the extent of reserves, usually insisting on smaller areas. Governor Grey did not have a specific policy, and McLean made arbitrary decisions about the extent of reserves on the basis of their potential value for settler use. The Waipukurau and Ahuriri blocks were of similar size but the reserves were 4738 acres and

2475 acres respectively. Even after the establishment of the Land Purchase Department in 1854, there appeared to be no specific guidelines available for district commissioners.

On 17 November 1851 the tribes assembled to sign the Ahuriri deed. Before the meeting the Europeans had lunch, McLean noting that the women – Mrs Villiers, Mrs McKane and Mrs Fraser – ate with their children, and before their men, 'to show the natives we paid deference and respect to females; forming a great contrast to themselves in those respects ... Mr. Alexander [a local settler] and some whalers from different stations were present. The day was magnificent; a fine bright sky and shining sun, with happy countenances, plenty of food, a ship hoisting her Union Jack in the offing, boats and canoes racing, natives quiet in demeanour and everything combining under the direction of Providence to bring to a happy issue my labours at Ahuriri.'[51]

McLean made a long opening speech to the assembled tribes, explaining the nature of the deed and 'expressing a hope that it would be the means, as they were on the decline, of uniting them with a stronger power, that would, under the mild dispensation of our laws, befriend and protect them.' He read over the deed and showed the boundaries on the map. The rangatira assented. Three hundred signed the deed, including some children that they might be witnesses to future generations. One thousand pounds was counted in the presence of the principal rangatira and handed over to the hapu in nine lots; seven lots of £100 and one each of £150 to the Tangoio hapu and to the rangatira Oneone (Tareha's father).[52] McLean noted that the sellers, having distributed their money, were busy the following day spending it on clothes and other necessities.

Following the sale McLean spent much of the week dealing with court cases, native disputes, settling accounts, 'getting the house across the water put to rights', writing to Wellington and 'looking after copies and translations and deeds'.[53]

Regarding McLean's conduct in negotiating the purchase of the Ahuriri block, the Waitangi Tribunal in its report on Te Whanganui-a-Orotu concluded that it was 'hard to escape the conclusion that McLean deliberately remained silent on the future ownership and control of the harbour so as not to prejudice the success of his land purchase negotiations'.[54] This view is supported by McLean's irritation at Colenso's intervention. It is unlikely that the rangatira would have agreed to include the harbour, given their reluctance to sell Mataruahou. Nevertheless, in 1851 neither party seemed to see the ownership of the lagoon as an issue. It is surprising that the rangatira do not appear to have mentioned the concerns raised by Colenso in any of their meetings with McLean, who usually recorded any opposition. They appear to have accepted the section in the deed of sale which provided for a landing-place for their canoes and protection for their customary fishing activities as recognition of their ownership of the harbour. McLean, for his part, assumed the inner harbour to be an arm of the sea belonging to the Crown under English common law, much as Wellington Harbour or the Waitemata in Auckland were. Shipping was already using the harbour at Corunna Bay and Onepoto Gully at the western end of Mataruahou. In 1851 McLean's proposals for small reclamations around Mataruahou left almost the entire inner harbour available for Maori to continue their customary fishing activities. He could not have been to expected to foresee the extent of the early twentieth-century reclamation of Napier South or the outcome of the 1931 earthquake in converting a lagoon into land seven feet above high tide, which would lead to the question of ownership of thousands of acres of potential farmland.

There is no record of McLean raising the ownership of the inner harbour with the rangatira, nor of the rangatira referring to this matter again after Tareha's initial statement in 1850 that 'the land is yours, the water is ours'. However, in his early land purchases McLean set out to ensure that there could be no cause for future dispute over the nature and extent of the boundaries. In his report on the Ahuriri purchase he noted that 'the lands have been accurately surveyed, outside boundaries, and boundaries of Reserves carefully defined, leaving no possible doubt or future cause of difference, on which, hitherto, have occasioned so many disputes'.[55] McLean's confidence was misplaced. Maori continued to believe that the lagoon and its islands had been reserved.[56]

There was a sequel to the purchase of the Ahuriri block. When McLean bought the Tutaekuri block in 1855, comprising 6000 acres of lagoon and swampy mudflats, a third was held to be inside the Ahuriri lagoon's boundaries. Did this represent an acknowledgement that the lagoon had not been included in the 1851 purchase? Or did McLean consider that he was extending the Ahuriri purchase to include a further part of the lagoon? In 1875 H. K. Taiaroa, Member of the House of Representatives for Southern Maori, raised the question of land reclamation being in breach of the right to fisheries contained in the Treaty of Waitangi. McLean gave an emphatic reply. When lands were ceded to the Crown, all rights connected with them also were ceded. These included rivers and streams and whatever was on or under the surface of the land. All deeds of sale included such a clause. He denied any Treaty breach, saying that the Government had 'carefully preserved the rights of the Natives'.[57]

When appearing before the Native Affairs Committee inquiring into the Ahuriri purchase in 1875, McLean gave a politician's answer. Maori had asked for the reservation of their pipi and fish but he did 'not recollect that they said anything about the sea at that time'. His statement was correct. He did not go on to say that in 1850 Tareha had said 'the land is yours, the water is ours'. Nor did he draw attention to Tareha's claim for compensation in 1861 over land that was being reclaimed. This land Tareha regarded as his property and as having been under the sea when he sold the Ahuriri block. G. S. Cooper told McLean that Tareha had not raised the issue again, so he hoped that he had convinced him he was wrong.[58] Earlier, Cooper had warned McLean that the Ahuriri block would yet cause trouble. He wished that 'we would dare bounce them I should say rather threaten them with condign punishment feeling assured we were able to inflict it. But I suppose we must "wait a little longer".'[59]

In his negotiations McLean frequently turned to the theme of 'worthless' Maori land and the benefits that would accrue to Maori from transformation of the countryside with the presence of British settlers. Sometimes the rangatira inquired, with devastating logic, why Europeans sought so eagerly after their 'worthless' lands. When McLean informed the Ahuriri tribes that their land was very poor land, they replied that it was not poor in their eyes and even if it did not please the Pakeha, it did for their pigs, rats and birds. McLean's remarks were part of his bargaining technique, for he knew that the land was valuable for all the requirements of the Maori economy since their arrival in New Zealand. The implication was that, as the Maori did not command the necessary resources, they should stand aside and allow the white settlers with their superior civilisation to transform the land. McLean set out his vision for New Zealand in a letter to his wife, Susan, when he was concluding the Ahuriri purchase. One day, he promised he would take her to Hawkes Bay to visit the scene of his operations and to recall what took place. She would see 'instead of a waste wilderness, cottages with their smiling cheerful inhabitants gratefully acknowledging the advantages they and their smiling redfaced healthy urchins may derive from the early pioneer of the land of their adoption but it is to the Almighty we have to acknowledge all thankfulness for these innumerable blessings that He in His wisdom bestows on the wicked children of men. How little do we deserve his great and wonderful mercies.'[60] It seems that McLean saw himself as the 'early pioneer' responsible for this Arcadian vision of a better Britain even if he felt compelled to attribute it to the intervention of the Almighty.

McLean completed the sale of the Mohaka block (85,000 acres) for £800 on 5 December 1851. In contrast to his other negotiations that year, McLean had earlier spent little time in discussion of boundaries, just one day in January and again in March. Having explained the boundaries the previous day, McLean read out the deed of sale, handed around the map and elaborated on the reasons for and advantages of extending payment over a number of years. After discussion with the rangatira, it was agreed to divide the payment, £100 each going to Waikare and Mohaka hapu. Bad weather delayed McLean's departure, but this brought an offer of additional land from Waikare to Moeangiangi which would secure a good road from there to Tangoio.

Before returning to Ahuriri, McLean made a brief overnight visit to Mahia. On 8 December he rose at 3 a.m., heard a number of cases involving disputes among whalers, had completed these by 5 a.m. and left by sea for Ahuriri at 5.45 a.m. He hoped 'the adjustment of these cases will have a good effect in these outlandish parts and demonstrate to both races the supremacy of English law and the necessity of its dictates being complied with'.[61]

Back at Ahuriri, McLean had talks about buying land between the Waikare and Wai-o-Hinganga rivers that would link up with the Ahuriri block. In making his way back to Wellington along the coast, he talked to two rangatira at Porangahau about selling land at Akitio and Tautane. At Mataikona, just north of Castlepoint, a large group discussed the sale of their land. As there were still some differences, McLean asked them to have further talks among themselves and to get their rangatira to write and tell him the result.

When he returned to Wellington in late December, McLean briefed Grey on the success of his Hawkes Bay negotiations. Delighted with the East Coast situation, the Governor instructed McLean to prepare reports to send to the Colonial Office in London.

Chapter 6
Courtship and Marriage

From time to time, McLean's land-purchase duties took him to Wellington. His diary entries for December 1848 show that he was becoming a frequent visitor to the house of Robert Strang, a Lowland Scot who was Registrar of the Supreme Court. McLean's purpose, though not recorded, was undoubtedly to seek the company of Strang's daughter, Susan Douglas Strang. On Christmas Day he spent the evening at the Strangs after taking part in the Highland sports on Thorndon flat. The games, which included throwing the hammer and wrestling, were conducted with great good humour, the team led by McLean and Lieutenant Gordon defeating that of Bethune and MacDonald. As a young man Donald McLean delighted in his physical prowess and was known to leap on a table and dance a Highland fling. The games having ended, the participants hoisted McLean onto their shoulders and, with bagpipes playing, marched off to Barrett's Hotel where he shouted whisky for the gathering and exhorted them not to forget their country nor their loyalty as Highlanders. As he made his way to the Strangs, he met Sir George Grey and recounted this incident. Grey replied that McLean was owed this tribute for what he had done for the settlers at Wanganui. McLean, however, insisted that it was given solely in recognition of his standing as a Highlander.

Nevertheless, in his own eyes, McLean was well satisfied with his contribution. He reflected that it had fallen to his lot to be concerned 'in such pursuits as may have a considerable influence on the prospects and happiness of people yet unborn and who may be inhabiting the lands I am now negotiating for years after I am mouldering in the dust'.[1] This belief that future generations would give thanks for his endeavours would motivate McLean in his years of government service.

McLean's duties meant infrequent visits to Wellington, so most of his courtship had to be carried on by correspondence. During 1849 McLean and Susan had reached an understanding but he wished this to be private and warded off inquiries.

> From what Mamma [Susan's mother] says it would seem that you are somewhat unhappy or rendered so probably by idle gossiping insinuations which I believe

> are too frequently practised on young girls in your situation. Let such not disturb you in the slightest. Keep yourself cheerful and happy and if I can be permitted as your senior by a few years to use a little dictation I should say reject with your usual prudence and discernment all approaches of familiarity with your feelings except what is sanctioned by your Father and Mother whose kind parental care is ever alive to the interests of their dutiful and affectionate child. May your regard and esteem for them never be alienated by any change that takes place during your existence.

McLean regretted that his work at Wanganui had delayed his return to Wellington longer than expected

> so much so that you will under Mamma's tuition have become perfect in playing the 'Dalhousie March' and ever so many Scotch marches and tunes besides ... There are frequent enquiries made respecting you but to speak candidly I have never openly acknowledged the understanding existing between us, on the contrary from a naturally silent disposition I have rather concealed my intentions than otherwise, conceiving it desirable on your behalf as well as my own to observe a certain delicacy on such matters. Moreover I have been under some apprehension that our anticipations might not be so happily realised as we should wish.

Although he intended to tell her of his work, he felt that there was not much to interest a young lady. His occupations were 'limited to rambles among the interior tribes and amusements, to some happy evenings at the mess of the detachment of the 65th [Regiment] stationed here, also some agreeable hours with the settlers one or two of whom are from my own part of the Highlands'.[2]

During 1850, despite the understanding of their relationship, McLean and Susan maintained formal methods of address that slowly gave way with an increasing acknowledgement of mutual affection. Susan began her letters 'My Dear Mr McLean', and ended, 'believe me my dear Mr McLean, Yours very sincerely, Susan Douglas Strang'; likewise McLean – 'believe me I remain, Ever yours sincerely, Donald McLean'. By the end of the year they had moved to – 'My dear Donald' and 'My darling Susan', while Donald playfully admonished his 'little pussy' and 'little slave'.

He began to share his thoughts, though not yet his feelings about her:

> I am much happier when in the country than at Wellington, here you can enjoy the beauties of nature with intense delight ... I looked over the beautiful plain of the Rangitikei and fancied to myself what abundant mercies were provided for man by his Creator ... Cottages are springing up here in all directions, beef mutton milk and cheese are plentiful where last year you would get nothing but a few

> potatoes wild pigeons and eels to eat ... every few miles the axe of the industrious woodsman startles you from some train of thought with which the stillness of the scene might overwhelm you. I am sorry for it but it is a great failing of mine that I sometimes as I am told ride off full gallop without answering a question to anyone who may be speaking to me but upon my word this may appear affectation although it really is not for I am sorry to say after all that I am not by any means a deep thinker ... I am very anxious to hear what your amusements books employments thoughts wonderings and little changes or disappointments have been since I left These should all be candidly communicated inasmuch as they are now of more concern to me than at any previous time ...[3]

This vision of the settlers' transformation of the landscape and his contribution in preparing the way was to become a recurring theme with McLean.

Donald approved of Susan's gardening: 'it is such a delightful healthy occupation what can be more pleasing to a young lady than indulging in those simple recreations that refresh the mind and generate sentiments of thankfulness and love towards a beneficent Creator who bestows so many blessings on his unworthy creatures ...'

Susan hoped in return that when he next returned to Wellington, he would spend longer than a month. Donald replied that the longer he was away, the more fondly and more frequently did he think of her. His concern was that she should 'lay in a good stock of religious and historical knowledge, as

> it will be of infinite advantage and great pleasure to us both through life. I regard external accomplishments as altogether subordinate to the careful improvement of the mind which should be nourished with as much system and regularity as we provide wholesome food for our bodily sustenance. What is more delightful than to read and converse over what we read by a nice clear winter fireside when we are relieved of the cares of the day.[4]

Susan was responsive. He was pleased with her diligence in reading, though he expected to be told of her views on the books she read and of the characters contained in them. 'I expect to hear more from you respecting McCauley's [*sic*] history than your opinion that he thinks too highly of Oliver Cromwell.' He was glad that she had gone to a ball. 'I hate going to balls and dances, they are so very tiresome and stupid. However Susan I am really glad that you went and I trust you will always attend such places when it is agreeable to yourself to do so.'

No capital, and sometimes in debt during his first ten years – that was young Donald McLean's situation after he arrived in New Zealand in 1840. Like many of his contemporaries he was a young gentleman on the make. His official salary as Inspector of Police, £400 a year, was his sole source of income, but he set out to make his fortune. He soon acquired property, 200 acres at Wanganui and a house and land at New Plymouth next to his friends, the Wilsons. By 1851 his assets, including loans to Europeans and Maori, amounted to £1706; his debts were £210.[5] He was now in a position to marry. Donald and Susan announced their engagement. Within ten years he was to value his estate at £24,979.

Writing to him in May 1851, Susan regretted that since they had become engaged, his duties had kept him away from her. Three months later, on 28 August, the marriage of Donald McLean and Susan Douglas Strang took place in Wellington at the Presbyterian Church, followed by the wedding party at the Strangs' house, Dalmuir Hill, on The Terrace. They spent their fortnight's honeymoon in a cottage at Taita. After a brief five weeks of married life, Donald departed to continue his land-purchase negotiations, writing to his wife:

> I trust your crying fit did not last long after I left; feel assured Pussy that I cannot help feeling the extreme affection you evince towards me and I sincerely trust that I shall ever prove equally dutiful to you however cold I may at times appear. Here I am darling where we spent such a truly happy fortnight[6]... the time we spent together was the happiest I ever enjoyed since I left home ... I could write you a very long letter puss although we are but a few hours separated were I to indulge my feeling ... tell Papa to supply you with whatever money you require, get a new bonnet and summer dress for yourself ... write me often, do not above all things neglect your duty to God under every little trial place your reliance on Him who is alone able to comfort and support you and to whose care and protection I now my dearest wife commend ... You may rest assured I shall not be longer absent than I can possibly help – so you must sleep sound tomorrow night, read some amusing books or get through your favourite Charlemagne or any other you fancy but be sure not to think of the nonsense I often bothered you with when dressing that hair of yours instead of rather thinking of what you read.[7]

At the end of September Donald noted that, although he had made no diary entry for over three months, this period had embraced a 'very important epoch in my life – the most important circumstance being that I have got married and enjoyed five weeks of extreme happiness with a wife that promises to be kind, faithful and affectionate. Indeed she is all that I could desire and I wish that Heaven's blessings may attend us both ... Poor thing she cried bitterly when I parted with her but duty must be attended to and its stern demands complied with to the sacrifice of all other feelings.'[8] McLean put official duties before family obligations. Much later, his work prevented him from meeting his sisters when they arrived in New Zealand. Likewise, work prevented him from travelling to say goodbye to his son when he left to go to school in England.

Marriage released Donald's emotions. Within a week he was writing to Susan from Bidwill's Wairarapa station:

> I cannot allow any opportunity to pass without expressing to you how much happier I now feel than I did before we were married, my heart is now firmly fixed on an object it loves and I have reason to hope that through life you will have frequent opportunities of proving that my regard for you is not of such an ordinary or transient nature as to occasion any neglect for happiness and welfare, sincerely do I trust that our marriage will be one of lasting happiness to both of us as long as it is the Almighty's pleasure to spare our lives in the enjoyment of each other's company.
>
> There are plenty of nice books here and strange to say I read over all I see about love, marriage etc. than I did before I became wedded myself there is a sort of enchantment about the feeling that renders me more cheerful than during our courtship days and happier probably, excepting that I often feel for poor Mamma's illness, than I have been at any other period of my life. You may think it strange my feeling so happy without you, but when I feel that you are thinking of me and when I feel that I am not idle but actually engaged with my duties, my mind gets a degree of repose that I never enjoy in the fictitious employment and society of a town, let it be ever so small. The life of a person in the country where he can rise early as I did this morning with a clear brilliant sky and keen appetite at 7 for breakfast is certainly not to be compared to late rising late going to bed, late parties, that neither improve the mind or the body but frequently disturb the peace of the one and destroy the health of the other.[9]

Donald continued to dwell on this theme. He made plain his wish to leave their cottage on The Terrace in Wellington and to settle somewhere in the country. He asked Susan to consider whether they should live permanently at Wellington or at Ahuriri, where the climate was beautiful. He was undecided, as much would depend on the state of her mother's health. He went on to link the country life to the worship of his Maker:

> Here you can have sweet lonely communion with your Maker and behold his works on every side you turn from the clear running stream that affords you refreshment to the trees of the forest that give you warmth and shelter down to the minutest shrub and plant that you tread; all these are objects of a great Parent's care, and shall we then if we confide in His mercy be overlooked or neglected. No my dearest while we firmly rely and trust on God we need never be afraid wherever we are or however desolate our state that he will forsake us, and truly are those whose trust and confidence is in the God of their creation.

> I think that even the most minute and trifling incidents of life are regulated by him and that even the slightest terms of good fortune that may accidentally attend us, are not the effect of an accident so much as of his Paternal mercy and care, shall we not then consider it our first and most important duty to dedicate and sanctify ourselves to that God whose mercies we so richly experienced.[10]

As Donald moved on to Hawkes Bay from Wairarapa, his letters conveyed his awakening love for Susan. 'I never had the slightest idea before our marriage that I should be so constantly thinking of you at all hours morning noon and night ... notwithstanding thinking and desire to be with you I feel much easier and happier than ever before our engagement that caused so much foolish speculation and gossip to our acquaintances and which frequently gave us both considerable annoyance more especially as little pussy seemed very cross when told that her highland lad should never turn again.'[11] Five days later Donald told Susan that he had bought twenty volumes of Allison's *Europe* for their amusement during the long winter months, 'just exactly the kind of reading you are so fond of, deep reasoning and extensive knowledge conveyed in a most agreeable and pleasing style'. Meantime, Susan flattered him, assuring him that, indeed, 'darling you have quite spoiled me you are too indulgent and pet me too much, I trust however I shall repay your love by being through life an affectionate and dutiful wife. I feel that I can never do enough for you.'

Susan remained in Donald's thoughts as he went about his work. His diary entries, written late in the night, record his concern.

> I wish I could get an opportunity of writing to her. I am sure, poor pussy, she must be anxious about my long silence and absence. However, she is under the protection of a greater and higher Power than is on Earth. How comfortable the feeling of being married to one whom I love so sincerely; and whose habits and affectionate disposition so entirely meets my approbation. I wish she may be long preserved; and if it is God's will that I may also be spared to enjoy her company. But this I leave in the hands of that God who has given life and existence; and Who has bountifully and graciously prepared my path. To Him and to Him only be the thanks.[12]

The next evening, after the successful signing of the Ahuriri deed, Donald reflected that 'Another day is past and gone, and Susan my pet is left alone to Him who ever hears her prayer … may his gracious love prepare us for that last awful day when we before Him must repair … Oh! take her Father in thy care. She is more to me than I can say.'

The closing months of 1851 were a time of distress for Susan; she had a miscarriage, and her mother was seriously ill. Susan moved from her new home on The Terrace to the Strang's house to nurse her mother until she died.

Donald's response came from the strength of his religious belief:

> I think there is nothing on earth my dearest Douglas that gives so much tranquillity and ease of mind as putting our trust in Providence, it is wonderful how it brightens our path and removes our saddest apprehensions last night I was perplexed with grief and sorrow on your and Mamma's account, today I feel wonderfully relieved from all my anxiety, first I prayed to Him who alone can alleviate the affliction and distress of our affectionate mother and the 121st Psalm for the 27th morning of the month opened to me, 'I will lift mine eyes to the hills: from whence cometh my help – My help even cometh from the Lord who made heaven and earth.' Read the Psalm through dearest it is a most beautiful one and particularly applicable to you at present. It is to God who shall preserve thy going out and thy coming in from this time forth for evermore that I now commend you ...[13]

His wife was to him 'everything in the world', yet the happiness of his marriage troubled him. He confessed, 'I find you are in my thoughts as I wake in the morning instead of the Almighty who has given me and you all and every blessing that I enjoy'.[14] Had he and Susan become so engrossed in each other that they had neglected their religious duties? Was Susan's miscarriage a sign of the Almighty's displeasure? On reflection he assured himself that 'the Almighty will not be displeased with over affection to any creature of his own formation that He has made one with myself'.[15] One Sunday, Donald confided in his diary that 'I do not know whether I have spent the day well or not and now I should have a double inducement to spend God's day in a holy manner. The evils I commit are shared by my dear partner and ever affectionate and thoughtful wife if I do wrong; and that the Almighty in his power and justice chastises me of course my wife must suffer as she is now one and the same as myself.'[16] Poor Susan! A Victorian wife could expect no life apart from that of her husband.[17]

In 1852 Donald was to spend six months of his married life away from Wellington. Writing to Susan from Porirua Barracks in January, he urged that, with the fine weather, she should plunge in the water and out again and when she got home to take care not to lace her stays too tightly: 'remember your promise yesterday pussy and do not foolishly persist in injuring yourself from a most foolish desire to appear small waisted and genteel, nothing is more ridiculous and ill judged therefore give it up'. He told her that he was extremely concerned and urged her to muster up all her resolution and courage and avoid those 'disagreeable fits'. She was to consider her diet, take a cup of tea and some bread at 5.30 a.m. and go for a bathe. She was to be very careful 'until I get you to work as a dairy maid, then I am sure you will be quite as healthy as I am. I feel as if the Porirua air possesses some magical qualities for I feel quite different already from what I have been in Wellington.'[18] Two days later he returned to this concern. He wished Susan to stay with her father, 'especially as you may have a return of those foolish fits that you occasionally indulge in. I mean the hysterics, the fainting of course you cannot avoid poor thing.' Possibly Susan's 'disagreeable fits' were her reaction to McLean's constant admonitions.

He chided Susan for giving way to constant grief over the recent death of her mother. They would meet in heaven and therefore she should envy her mother's happy state: 'do not murmur against the Almighty's fixed decrees we are at his disposal and not our own, the life we enjoy is terminated at his pleasure and patient resignation to whatever befalls indicates a proper Christian spirit'.[19]

In May, writing from Rangitikei, he hoped soon to return and clasp her in his arms again. 'I feel every hour I am separated as long as I used to feel a week before our marriage. Nevertheless, he expressed his disapproval at her 'fretful changes of temper' and trusted that she would never give her

> devoted husband any cause however slight to be displeased with her only imagine how painful it is to be absent from you and how often I must suffer cold wet and various hardships for my pussy's sake remember that you are everything to me and that I cannot help feeling any appearance of ingratitude on your part not my pet that I accuse you of such but that it is just as well as the thought struck me to warn that I expect to be loved with equal devotion and self-denial as I experience on your account and never to leave me as you did on that foolish night the remembrance of which and some of the circumstances still rush through my heart in a painful manner.[20]

It seems that they had a quarrel and Susan had rushed off to her father's house.

McLean spent most of July and August in Taranaki. As Susan was again pregnant he declined invitations to dinners and parties. He had no pleasure in them without her company, he said, although he did accept invitations from his old friends Captain King and Helen Wilson. He again took Susan to task. Helen Wilson had been annoyed that Susan had not written to her, as etiquette required. Her neglect would not raise her in the estimation of his friends, while her failure to reply to his patron, Dr Sinclair, could not be excused. He urged her not to procrastinate, otherwise they both might have occasion to regret it. McLean monitored her social life and warned that, now she was married, she should look to

> the best and most respectable members of society for examples for your guidance. I have often felt that your inclinations to associate more intimately with persons of doubtful position in society than with those of more genuine and respectable

> description and the sooner you change your sentiments on this subject the better ... I do sincerely trust no imprudent acts or conduct of yours will cause it to be an unhappy life either ... nothing delights me more than to see a good and amiable wife who anticipates her husband's wishes and calmly undergoes every trial to make him happy. Few wives my dear pussy are more attentive and fond than you are...[21]

He went on to reiterate his love: 'I feel dull and lonely without you indeed the longer I am absent the more intense my love for you becomes.' Susan dwelt on the physical expression of their love. 'I hope I shall dream again as I did the other night that my darling had come home. I dreamt that I was sitting with my arms around your neck and kissing you.'[22]

She was disappointed to hear from her father that Donald could not leave Taranaki for several weeks, writing 'how I hate the name of that horrible place I am sure that it has caused me more vexation and annoyance than I can tell ... it really is dreadful to think you are going to be away so long I have now given up all hope of seeing you before my troubles begin'. McLean wrote from New Plymouth to assure her that he would not delay an hour longer than duty required but that he had been busy getting the police records ready to hand over to his successor, G. S. Cooper. He found Taranaki society much improved by people of a 'very superior class', though his old friend Helen Wilson still took the lead in society despite the wealth and respectability of many of the newcomers. In her he saw a suitable model for his wife. 'She is not unlike you in some of her ways making due allowance for being old and grey headed ... She is a lady and a woman who has seen much of the world and yet at her advanced years you would be surprised how much she anticipates every wish of the doctor's and how devoted she is to him whoever is there she will not in any way neglect "Don Pedro" as I call him.'[23]

Donald, ever secretive about his relations with Susan, wrote that he had not mentioned her pregnancy to Helen Wilson. Although he was pleased that Robert Strang was so attentive to his daughter, his only fear was that 'you are being spoilt for the bush with too much care and petting. I do not intend to continue it so you must look out when I get to Ahuriri as I shall intend to work you a little more than you do at present.'[24]

Donald returned to his theme of country life in a later letter to Susan, remarking that 'I have greater hopes than ever of your making a "gude wife" for the bush and you may even arrive at the wonderful distinction of being a highly accomplished dairy maid when decorated in your short gown and grey petticoat with sleeves tucked up and fat arms slappering away among cream, cheese, butter and all the other niceties of the dairy – do not laugh at this because I intend it in reality'.[25] There was potential for future conflict as Susan, a high-spirited young woman, much preferred the social life of Wellington to the quiet of the country. As a dutiful wife, however, she would be expected to be obedient to her husband's wishes.

On their first wedding anniversary, Susan wrote to Donald that she trusted their love would grow every year. 'I know my dearest love that I have your entire affection and I am sure it will be my own fault if I lose it. The longer I am your wife the more my affection for you increases. I have not a single wish or hope that is not connected with my dear husband.'[26] In early September 1852 Donald returned to Wellington. His happiness was shattered when his young wife died in giving birth to a son on 7 November. Donald's religion obliged him to accept this tragedy with stoic resignation, but his grief broke through in his lament.

> You are gone to the world of spirits my own dear Douglas; and left me to mourn thy loss when I can share death with thee then happy shall be my lot ... But thou hast left a pledge of affection which I must not now neglect; and O may his mother's affection be renewed in this little prise [sic] I have got. May his Heavenly Father protect as mother he has got none ... Thou art still in my presence, my Susan, but alas in its lifeless form ... and soon shall that same be taken from me to mix with the kindred worms.[27]

A year after Susan's death he wrote in his diary:

> It has been the will of Heaven that my mild sweet unoffending Susan should be taken to her final home. But even at this moment I must not repine. God knows better than I do how to dispose of his creatures. He gives and He takes away; and blessed forever be his name. O that my heart could henceforth join in holy aspirations of thankfulness to the Almighty for his endless blessings; and enable me to join in Heaven, when it pleases the Lord to take me thence to her who is now in the enjoyment of Heavenly bliss; and may my heavenly Father bless, protect and nourish and establish in the fear and love of God, my young son Douglas; that he may be a blessing to all his friends and relatives; and that he may be blessed and sanctified in his generation.[28]

Donald left his baby son Douglas in the care of his grandfather, Robert Strang. Later, when Donald was stationed in Auckland, Douglas went to stay there with the Revd and Mrs Kingdon, whom Donald had known during his time in New Plymouth.

During 1853, Donald wrote to his uncle, that he had been 'constantly from home, either negotiating with the tribes for land, paying instalments due on former purchases or settling disputes among them'. He was worried about his sisters but could not see his way clear to bring them out to New Zealand. He still intended to go home and bring them back but he did not want them to come until he was able to provide for them. Meanwhile, he trusted his uncle would look after them, assuring him that a sum of £400 was available for their needs.[29]

McLean never loved again, retreating to the lonely life of a widower. He ceased to keep a personal diary that recorded his thoughts. As a Highlander, McLean was capable of strong feelings, and it was fear of emotion rather than an absence of feeling or coldness of spirit led to this withdrawal. He was immensely fond of his son. While normally a poor correspondent, he wrote frequently to young Douglas – though even in these letters, like many Victorian fathers, he suppressed any open affection. Generally, it is in a man's friendships and his loves that his innermost feelings are revealed but, apart from his letters to Susan, McLean kept his own counsel. Although J. D. Ormond claimed that McLean made friends with everyone, this was a political tactic. McLean had very few close personal friends. In his first years in New Zealand there was Townsend, the young Anglo-Irishman; Peter and Helen Wilson at New Plymouth were old enough to be his parents; F. E. Maning, the Native Land Court judge, corresponded regularly and at length. Ormond claimed McLean as his oldest friend, but for McLean their relationship was more one of mutual self-interest; each could help the other to advance his career. Among his brothers and sisters only towards his youngest sister, Annabella, did he show any real affection.

From time to time McLean, who was thirty-one when his wife died, contemplated marrying 'some amiable woman of property'. His uncle advised him to postpone this until he revisited Scotland, as he would find a more suitable bride there. In 1861 he talked of delaying a planned visit to Scotland because he had 'a hope that I cannot easily banish that Miss Lully might not be indifferent to my wishes'. It is not known who Miss Lully was, but in the event nothing came of this courtship. Hannah Richardson, who was to marry Ormond, was unimpressed by McLean's advances: 'He is everybody's favourite, but I saw nothing particularly pleasing in him, he is very plain looking.' His flattery she found 'most unpleasant ... if he means what he says I think little of his judgement, if he does not mean it the flattery is too great'.[30] On this occasion it seems that McLean's skilful use of a 'bit of blarney' that had captivated Maori and Pakeha had failed to impress.

Chapter 7
'If There is No Land a Man Cannot Live'

Between 1851 and 1861 the European population of New Zealand increased dramatically from 26,000 to 99,000, overtaking a Maori population estimated at 60,000. No longer did settlers feel dependent on Maori goodwill, while McLean felt the subsequent settler pressure for land. This was at a time when the tribes had completed their first sales with the intention of achieving a positive interaction with the new Pakeha economy. By the mid-1850s, however, the rangatira, alarmed at the numbers of European settlers and concerned at the erosion of their independence, were wary of parting with more of their land. Governor Grey had to reconcile conflicting requirements: in the Treaty of Waitangi the Crown had a responsibility to protect Maori interests, but at the same time the Crown had accepted that New Zealand would become a settlement colony. Moreover, the British taxpayer objected to spending money on colonies and the Governor was expected to finance his administration out of the sale of land.

Like the Governor, McLean assumed that the acquisition of Maori land was necessary and desirable. His task was to identify the appropriate groups that had the right to sell. He saw no alternative and rejected any Maori notion of something less than permanent alienation, such as permissive occupation or leasing. Grey and McLean opposed leasing Maori land on two grounds: one practical, that Maori would cease to offer land for sale; and one cultural, that no European should be subject to the control of a Maori.

After 1851 McLean was struggling to buy land. Faced with growing opposition in the North Island, he departed from his earlier practice of open negotiations to obtain the consent of all those who had customary rights. He began to cut corners. He would make a first payment to those willing to sell but made no move to survey or occupy the land while he tried to negotiate his way around the remaining opposition.

Although McLean spent some time travelling around the southern half of the North Island in 1852, the amount of land purchased was less than in previous years. Success in Taranaki still eluded him. Several Taranaki tribes – Taranaki, Ngati Ruanui and Nga Rauru – had developed a substantial trade with the settlers at Wanganui and New Plymouth and they did not need to sell land to encourage settlers into their midst.[1] Taranaki settler pressure on the Governor to buy more land, however, heightened tensions between those hapu who were in favour of selling and those opposed – tensions compounded by long-standing quarrels. Attempts to buy land so divided Maori that consequent skirmishing threatened to spill over onto lands already occupied by settlers and led to confrontations between armed parties within the town of New Plymouth. An offer to sell land often arose from a rangatira's wish to assert a superior claim, thereby increasing his mana at the expense of other claimants. Conflict resulted, sometimes converting rangatira who opposed land sales into coming forward with offers to sell land. This generated more unrest in Taranaki than in other parts of the island. For instance, Katatore, an opponent of land sales, could turn around and offer to sell land to discredit the mana of another rangatira. In 1851, to assert his mana, he offered to sell land between New Plymouth and Waitara. McLean was reluctant to accept, as the sale would certainly be disputed.

Although G. S. Cooper had replaced him as Inspector of Police in Taranaki in 1852, McLean still kept contact with his settler friends there, while difficult land-purchase negotiations by Cooper required his intervention from time to time. On 29 June 1852 McLean set off for Taranaki at Grey's instructions to buy more land for settlement. Strong opposition to land sales remained, though he was encouraged to find that they were prepared to discuss the subject 'with more deliberation and frankness than they had hitherto been in the habit of doing'. Two rangatira, Parata Te Huia and Te Tuki, following a dispute with Katatore, had offered to sell an extensive Puketapu tract of land. At the same time these two, who along with Katatore had been leading opponents of the occupation of the Bell block, accepted £30 as compensation for their claims to that land. McLean thought that no objection remained to the whole of Bell block now being handed over to settlers, subject to the condition laid down by the Governor that the settlers in locating themselves must accept responsibility for any quarrels with the local Maori. In August McLean reported progress to Andrew Sinclair as Colonial Secretary.[2] Taranaki suffered, he wrote, from a constant influx of absentee claimants from other parts of the island. They generally opposed land sales, making it difficult to extinguish their titles. Among the factors hampering land purchases, he identified the large Maori population of the district, 'their jealous consideration' of the interests of absentee claimants, the high land prices paid by Europeans and noted by Maori, and the limited reserves the Government had been able to make out of the small purchases made. To overcome these difficulties more liberal arrangements were needed. McLean proposed that the 7000 acres between the Mangaraka and Waiongana rivers should be reserved for Maori, as the Puketapu hapu were greatly attached to this area. This proposal would remove their opposition to selling the remaining portion. He recommended that they should receive a price higher than the 1s 6d he was authorised to pay.

It was here that McLean tried a new tactic in attempting to acquire land. He set out to negotiate a purchase first from those willing to sell, but made no move to complete the purchase or to survey the land until he had the agreement of the remaining claimants who had been initially opposed to it. Previously in Taranaki in the 1840s and with the 1851 Hawkes Bay purchases, he had been careful to gain the consent of all claimants to the land under offer before starting to negotiate the sale. The success of this new tactic encouraged him to use it also in the Wairarapa and Hawkes Bay purchases of the later 1850s.

At New Plymouth, McLean also intervened on behalf of town Maori who had been prevented from making improvements to their pa by settlers' threats of legal proceedings. He told Cooper that, with the New Zealand Company agent's permission, the land in question had been given to the Maori in exchange for town land they had occupied, although it had never been surveyed. Indeed, when the Waikato tribes threatened to attack it, the settlers had assisted in fortifying the pa. Moreover, the tribes were entitled to this land under Governor FitzRoy's arrangements. McLean advised Cooper, along with the resident magistrate and the Commissioner of Crown Lands, to arrange a plan of the boundaries and ensure that the Maori remained in occupation.[3]

Attempts to buy land around New Plymouth brought more opposition. Honiara Te Puni, a Te Ati Awa rangatira living in Wellington and a friend of Grey's, appealed to the Governor over the sale of land north of the Waiwhakaiho River:

> I have a word to say to you and McLean. What is the extent of your love for me? It is not right that another person should talk about my land. It would be different had I formerly seen that the father of these people resided and planted on these lands. My thought is that the land is man's parent. If there is no land a man cannot live.
>
> Listen this is not a proper proceeding. It is a wrong one. If you pay money to these natives where is the land for that money?
>
> ... My wish is let the boundary remain at Waerengapoka on to the boundary post at the sea. Let not this boundary be altered or broken.[4]

McLean minuted this letter for the Governor's attention. The sale of this block had been agreed to by the majority of resident Maori as well as absentee claimants. McLean thought it obvious that Te Puni was opposing the sale because he intended to return there himself. It would be unjust to the majority of the claimants as well as to settlers much in need of land, he advised, if Te Puni were to block the sale. He recommended that the Governor separately define the claims of Te Puni and his followers so that the majority of claimants could sell without interfering with Te Puni's interest. This advice was significant, as it foreshadowed by seven years a similar solution at Waitara, when Wiremu Kingi opposed the sale of Te Teira's block. In 1859, when McLean denied that this purchase represented a change of policy, he may have recalled his handling of Te Puni's interest as justification for his statement.

The measure of control exercised by Grey is reflected in a letter McLean sent from Taranaki expressing concern at the absence of instructions 'as to the means and views Your Excellency entertains of such purchases'. Something had to be done to put the settlers in possession of more land as soon as possible, he said, and he awaited Grey's instructions. McLean also asked for the money to be available in advance, as he had found in negotiating that a greater impression could be made 'if we actually exhibit a sum for their acceptance, the knowledge of its being at hand when discussing a sale has sometimes a talismanic effect'.[5] Hence McLean's desire for clean and shining gold coins!

In 1852 Cooper found himself confronted with growing opposition. Some tribes were willing to sell land but were dissatisfied with the price offered by the Governor. They would prefer to sell direct to the settlers. Parata Te Huia told Cooper that, once he had been paid for the land he had already sold, his dealings with the Governor would cease:

> He does not like his [the Governor's] price for the land. It is a bad price. It will be better to put a stop to his purchase of land, because the payment is wrong. It is a bad payment to the Maoris. But he receives a large payment from the Europeans. Where is the good of this thought – that it should be large to you and small to us. This is like the story in the Scripture about Annanais and his wife who kept back a portion of the payment of their land. This is just like you.[6]

Settlers were offering £2 10s for farmland and £1 10s for bush land. The Governor would only pay 5s or 2s 6d per acre.

Cooper, well coached by McLean, replied that he was sorry that Parata would cease to sell land to the Governor. He chided Parata for listening to 'foolish pakeha' who were trying to lead their young men astray. They would not pay the price they promised. Even if they did he asked:

> would they return any portion of the land to you as the Governor does; or would they expend any of the money in roads, in bridges, in Hospitals, in Schools, in

> sending out more Europeans to cultivate the land; and to buy more afterwards; and to bring cattle, horses, sheep, carts, ploughs, machines, blankets, tobacco and the thousand things of the Pakeha.

These were the real payments for the land, Cooper maintained. The money paid at the time of purchase was but a small matter. However, it was the Maori's land and they could refuse to sell it to the Governor. He threatened that, if the settlers did buy from them, 'the Governor may perhaps have a word for them'.[7]

Cooper's personality and lack of judgement alienated both settler and Maori. Aware of continuing unrest in his district, he looked to his patron to come to his rescue.

> I am really ashamed to bother you with such long and troublesome letters but you know what a difficult position I am in and were it not for your kindness and the good feeling which exists between us, I do not know how I should get on at all. I depend on you to explain everything Sir George may require to know and I know you will do it in such a way as to keep me as clear as possible of blame in his eyes.[8]

Cooper had been private secretary to Governor Grey, but the evident interest that he and Lady Grey displayed in each other apparently led the Governor to exile the young man to a post far away from Government House.[9] Cooper was still uneasily aware that the attraction between Lady Grey and him had been the reason for his departure. Grey was not vindictive, however, and thought Cooper a promising young officer and indeed he was right, for Cooper was later to become Colonial Secretary.

As head of the Land Purchase Department, McLean monitored the work of his subordinate officers and gave them his support, though most lacked his skill and patience as a negotiator. Cooper's progress on the negotiations for the Waiongana, however, met with McLean's approval. He told Cooper in March 1854 that the Puketapu owners had been 'supporters of an obstinate opposition which is now breaking up but which you must continue still to watch with anxious care'. McLean praised the rangatira Rawiri Waiana, 'our well tried old friend through whom alone we have a footing in the Puketapu district'.[10]

A few months later, Cooper's impetuous actions precipitated conflict. When Rawiri and Paora offered to sell land inland from the Bell block, Cooper accepted and asked them to cut the boundaries. As these two rangatira set out with twenty-three unarmed men, they met Katatore, supported by twenty armed followers. Katatore gave them several warnings to desist and then opened fire, killing four and wounding others, including Rawiri, who died in hospital. Flight, the resident magistrate, the Revd Hanson Turton, W. Halse and Dr

Peter Wilson, Superintendent of the Native Hospital, all wrote to McLean. Their reluctant consensus was that the Europeans must avoid interfering in what they believed to be a tribal quarrel. Intervention could turn it into a land question, and the Government did not have sufficient forces to deal with opposition.

Wilson told McLean that his 'old friend' Rawiri had died of wounds. He had secured a lock of the rangatira's hair and arranged with his widow to hand over the rangatira's greenstone mere to McLean. Rawiri's funeral took place on the disputed land despite opposition; over 100 of Rawiri's supporters were present. Cooper, Henry Halse and Wilson stood by as the Wesleyan missionary Hanson Turton read the funeral service. Rawiri's pall was Wilson's tartan plaid of the 42nd Regiment, 'so he had the colour of a gallant corps to cover him and his friends were gratified therewith'.[11] Halse reflected settler opinion when he described Rawiri as a 'firm friend of the Government and Europeans'. Although acknowledging that neutrality was the only safe option, he felt that the 'friends of the murdered have perhaps this claim on the Govt; that they fell in an effort to procure us some land'.[12] Turton told McLean that Cooper should not have insisted on cutting the boundary line of disputed land when it was plain that some of the rightful claimants were opposed and that Katatore would fight, nor should Cooper have encouraged Rawiri to overcome Katatore's objections by a trial of strength. Turton regretted that Cooper had ever been allowed to have any involvement with Maori affairs. Although a clever young man and good at office routine, he was unsuited to work among Maori because he could not control his temper. 'They say he stamps and swears in the presence of the natives if at all discomposed by them and drives them away in great anger.' He behaved in the same arrogant manner with the settlers, bringing himself into 'great dislike with all parties'. Turton believed that, if Cooper had not been restrained by the other magistrates, he would have rushed headlong into strife with Katatore.[13] Two days later, Turton wrote again to McLean saying that, although he had managed to prevent vengeance being taken on the murderers, the Puketapu hapu were determined on reprisals. They had laid a tapu on the beach and highway while they lay in wait to cut off any stragglers. Katatore, for his part, was planning to join forces with Wiremu Kingi and Arapata Watatiri for an attack on Puketapu. As subsequent strife would affect the out-settlers, Turton urged McLean to return to Taranaki. He also suggested that he deal with the resident claimants by buying up their claims on the map without requiring them to survey the boundary in person, and to leave the land unoccupied until the claims of Katatore's party had been purchased.

Meanwhile, Cooper had been monitoring letters from Ngati Ruanui on the land question. He confessed to McLean that he had intercepted and opened letters, taken copies and then forwarded them on as they contained nothing that could cause mischief. He intended to continue this practice so he could be forewarned of trouble, and urged McLean to be on his guard against alluding to any knowledge of these letters when talking to the tribe.[14]

More intertribal fighting broke out in December, the issue this time being adultery. Ngati Ruanui invaded Ihaia's pa; casualties totalled eleven killed and fifteen to twenty wounded. Halse warned McLean to be prepared for further disturbances as the tribes were always armed, believing this to be their only protection. Meanwhile, he complained, they were not producing for themselves or providing labour for settlers. Halse asserted that the tribes considered themselves neglected by the Government; the absence of any official appointed over them meant that they kept their complaints, wishes and wants to themselves.

Maori unrest was not limited to Taranaki. In March 1853 skirmishing between Ngati Apa and Ngati Rangatahi, and Ngati Raukawa led Grey to send McLean to Manawatu to settle these differences and take steps to ensure the settlers' safety. McLean found the disturbances serious enough to stay on until the district was in a peaceable state. He recommended to the Colonial Secretary that, in a district that had a large population of various tribes, there should be another officer, besides the resident magistrate, with responsibility for seeing that Maori grievances were redressed promptly. Many differences arose from misunderstanding rather than intentional injustice on the part of either race. 'I feel that, when tribes like these have surrendered their lands to the Crown, their improvement and the nature of their relations with the Europeans should be an object of continued solicitude and care on the part of the Government.'[15] McLean might have pointed out that the role proposed for this officer had been a major component of the work of sub-protectors until Grey abolished their department in 1846.

In August 1853 Cooper wrote from New Plymouth that Maori had offered all the land from Piki Para to the top of Mount Taranaki – a third of the mountain and its spurs. 'The great thing is of course the "whaka noa" for Taranaki. They say they have for the first time given Taranaki to the Pakeha.' Cooper was optimistic that this sale could be the key to acquiring the whole district.[16]

The arrival of further shiploads of immigrants at New Plymouth increased the pressure to buy land. Taranaki settlers wanted the Governor to take up land north of the Waiwhakaiho River for the new arrivals, as without it there was no alternative but to take up bush land without road access. More than 120 new settlers remained in New Plymouth living on their capital. Possession of the Waiwhakaiho purchase had been held up by questions about reserves and disputed titles. Cooper maintained that he could buy more land if he had the money. Henry Halse suggested to McLean that, 'as you are referee on all native matters from your authority and experience', he should arrange funds that could be easily and promptly paid by the province under any arrangement the Governor might direct. Halse saw changes at New Plymouth. 'The place seems to be taking a start. Hundreds upon hundreds are preparing to join us and all we want is land, which will pay for itself handsomely. The people who come are not of a class to be sent into the forest, and besides they will not go.' To hasten McLean's return to Taranaki Halse assured him that he had got 'some excellent wines expressly for your coming!'[17]

For most of 1853, in fact, McLean's attention was fully engaged elsewhere – mainly in Wairarapa where illegal leasing of Maori land for grazing had been an ongoing problem. In 1851 he had congratulated himself that his successful land purchases in Hawkes Bay, combined with the liberal regulations proposed for depasturing stock on Crown lands, would set back unauthorised grazing on Maori lands in Wairarapa. His self-congratulations were premature, however, as illegal leasing continued. McLean found it difficult to convince the tribes that leasing should be replaced by a more permanent arrangement. Hawkes Bay Maori, when urged to sell land, pointed out how much better off and wiser were the Wairarapa tribes, who collected over a thousand pounds every year from the lease of their lands, while they themselves were offered only a few thousand pounds as final payment. In Hawkes Bay McLean ordered one runholder who had leased land from Maori to depart, 'or else land selling is at an end'. In McLean's eyes this was one of the evils of the system of leasing; another was that it encouraged Maori 'cupidity'. For Maori, leasing was more profitable, with its rents and opportunities for trade with European settlers. Once leasing was prohibited, if they needed money they had no option but to sell if they were to keep European settlers among them.

McLean thought that the prime evil of the leasing system was its insecurity. Europeans who leased land were held by Maori to be tenants on sufferance in their homes and were liable to be evicted without notice in the event of a quarrel between Maori and settlers. That settlers should be subordinated to the supervision of Maori landlords was repugnant to McLean's belief in the superiority of British civilisation over the indigenous culture. He never contemplated the option of a legal lease with safeguards for both parties that might have offered settlers the security they sought. By making leasing illegal, Crown policy was to force Maori to sell their land to get the capital they needed to compete in the Pakeha economy.

McLean advised Grey that the renting system had such a hold on the Wairarapa tribes that it would be difficult to persuade them to abandon it. The Government, however, as well as committed to upholding the law, was pledged to tribes who had already sold their land, to put an end to this system. McLean gave specific examples of the 'evils' it produced. At Mr Kelly's house, Maori looked on him as a mere tenant on sufferance to be ejected at any moment. One of Kelly's servants was attacked when he tried to stop a local Maori taking food from the kitchen. At Mr Gillies' station, having cautioned local Maori not to break his mill, Gillies found himself violently attacked and knocked down by the rangatira Ngatuere Tawhao, who ordered Gillies and his family to move off the property that night with his goods and chattels, leaving the house for Ngatuere's occupation. These frequent quarrels, in McLean's view, would generate bad feelings for which the natives might eventually suffer, while 'in the meantime with a few exceptions the settlers are obliged to put up with insults and use the most humiliating forbearance on their part not only towards the rangatira but to every insignificant member of their tribe, or otherwise subject themselves to the loss of all their improvements and property, the result of many years of hard labour and toil'. McLean did take some action to overcome the problems of illegal leasing by negotiating to buy the homestead blocks of the squatters.

Maori were aware that leasing of Maori land was illegal under the Native Land Purchase Ordinance; they also saw the law being broken with impunity. The Governor was faced with a problem. On the one hand, firm action against illegal leasing would mean for Maori loss of rent and the opportunity to trade with the settlers. On the other hand, to legalise leasing of Maori lands would have meant a decline in land sales to the Crown. Grey and McLean opposed leasing because it competed with their plans to purchase lands ahead of the needs of settlement. They wanted to buy at a low cost of 1s to 2s an acre when there was little demand and resell these lands to settlers at a higher price to finance the colonial government. Land sales were to be the main source of revenue. Grey therefore tried to suppress leaseholding but he was only partly successful. In the Wairarapa he had to tolerate it: the original squatters were allowed to remain, though McLean enforced the ordinance against new arrivals. Where tribes disputed the ownership of land and a sale could not be concluded, both parties would resort to leasing to gain money and to maintain their claim to the land.

Te Hapuku was still involved in negotiations, as he had an interest in land leased to settlers in Wairarapa, for which he received a share of the rent. The importance of his collaboration is shown in his letter to McLean:

> [W]e have your letter and your thoughts; and we are greatly pleased with them.

> You have given to us as thoughts for us that is for me. I shall adopt them in carrying out our joint work; as I was the first to invite you to Heretaunga that I might see your ways, that is the ways and customs of the European ... Yes it is quite right that the root of the tree and its branches should fall and be in one direction by one axe; and if one tree falls let it all fall with the branches.

At the end of March 1853, Te Hapuku, at McLean's request, went to Castlepoint to negotiate for land, accompanied by Hori Niania, writing that 'when the talk is straight I will come home'. He asked that both Park and de Pelichet be available to survey the boundaries, otherwise the work would be prolonged by two or three months. It would not be right for him or for the owners of the land to settle the amount of the payment. McLean should be present, 'that our words may be the same. But if you say we are to name the payment then give me some guide of light to go by that it may be straight.' Te Hapuku also urged McLean to check the leasing of land in Wairarapa. He wanted the squatters expelled so 'that the natives there may experience poverty and that you may have the whole leaves and branches of our tree and that we may live in a state of light and peace'.[18] The resulting settler demand for land in Hawkes Bay would enhance Te Hapuku's prospects of favourable sales and thereby his mana. His influence among other Maori impressed Purvis Russell, a Hawkes Bay pastoralist. 'I have never been very sensible of the prestige of rank but I am unable to conceal from myself a certain ascendancy which this noble savage has obtained from me. My inability to clothe my ideas in powerful Maori of course precludes me from combatting successfully the crude but powerful arguments which he makes use of at our casual meetings.'[19]

McLean's 1853 reports, noting tribal disputes and the insecurity of the small settlements, balanced Grey's over-optimistic assessments. Reporting to the Colonial Office before his departure from New Zealand, Grey affirmed that both races already formed one harmonious community and were 'insensibly forming one people'. Certainly, the early 1850s were a time of increasing prosperity for the colony – a prosperity in which the tribes shared as they adapted to and participated in the economic development of the North Island. British law was confined to the small European coastal settlements that depended on trade with Maori. It was misleading, however, to leave the British Government with the impression that all Maori accepted Grey's 'amalgamation'. Increasing numbers of settlers and Grey's expansive land purchases were making the rangatira uneasy.

In his diary McLean was frank in his approbation or criticism of the conduct and character of those with whom he associated, whether missionaries, rangatira or settlers. About the governors with whom he served, however, he refrained from comment, perhaps because his continued employment depended entirely on their patronage. Governor Grey was McLean's mentor, and McLean expressed his appreciation: 'I shall always esteem it an act of great condescension and kindness on the part of Your Excellency to have proposed my health as you have done at a public dinner at Wellington. It is one of those circumstances that I may have occasion to look back on in future years with infinite satisfaction.'[20] After Grey went to South Africa, McLean as Chief Native Land Purchase Commissioner continued his policies. He looked on Grey as his friend and corresponded with him in South Africa. Grey reciprocated with his public acknowledgement of McLean's contribution to the settlement of the colony. In his diary McLean thought that the future town in Hawkes Bay should be named Georgetown or Greytown in honour of the Governor.

McLean and Grey had much in common. Both were young; in 1846 McLean was twenty-five and Grey thirty-three. Both initially won the confidence and respect of the Maori rangatira, not only by their fluency in Maori, but also by their understanding of Maori customs and protocol and by the courteous treatment they accorded rangatira. At the same time they were zealous standard-bearers of British imperialism, convinced of the innate superiority of British civilisation and believing that they had a responsibility to undertake a civilising mission. A genuine concern for the well-being of the Maori and for their future in a colony of expanding European settlement led Grey to advocate a policy of assimilation. McLean, as the official working in the field, was more keenly aware of the problems involved in implementing such a shift. Later in the 1850s, as Native Secretary, he was to express the view that Maori should be allowed to continue to conduct their affairs according to their own customs, and that the Government should wait for years, if necessary, for an approach from the rangatira when they wished to be brought under English law.

Both men were autocratic in temperament and found it unpalatable to have to cooperate with others in a system of responsible government. Neither could ever be wrong: Grey because he was confident in his own ability; McLean because he was guided by Divine Providence. Grey, in his later years in the New Zealand Parliament, however, became more radical in his approach to issues such as land holding and the parliamentary franchise. McLean, whose family had ranked among the Scottish gentry and who was to become a member of the pastoral land-owning class, despised the labouring class and feared their evident and potential capability to resort to riotous behaviour.

Both men could be devious. Grey, in his dispatches to the Colonial Office, and McLean, in reporting to the Governor, tailored their reports to impress their respective masters with their skilful handing of their responsibilities.

Dispatches and reports that stressed the extent of Maori unrest and the danger to the settlers would be followed by accounts of how eloquent persuasion and effective action had won over the tribes and restored peace and prosperity to the colony. Grey composed his dispatches with an eye to winning Colonial Office support for his actions. One historian wrote of Grey's technique that

> he could generalise and insinuate with an ease and subtlety of phrase that created irresistible impressions, yet on analysis he will usually be found to have said far less than he has implied, and the long detailed enclosures to his main despatches – which were printed in small type in the Blue Books and must have often been passed unread – contain evidence which qualifies his broader statements, and to which if challenged he could refer and claim strict veracity. It was the hardest thing in the world to catch Grey telling a downright lie, but no one was more adept at telling the truth in such a way that it was almost certain to be misunderstood.[21]

McLean was adroit at writing dispatches and reports that presented himself and his activities in a most favourable light. When it suited, Grey ignored instructions from London. McLean, however, was always loyal to his patrons, Governor Grey and later Governor Gore Browne. Unlike many of their fellow colonists, Grey and McLean believed that Maori were a virile and intelligent race that would survive the impact of European civilisation so long as they were guided and controlled by men like themselves. Maori came to trust and finally to mistrust both men. Grey and McLean exercised their authority through personal influence based on their status and their personal charm. This was reinforced by material rewards to 'loyal' rangatira – pensions, gifts of livestock and agricultural machinery, appointment as assessors, and so on. Critics condemned this as a 'flour and sugar policy'. The weakness of their personal rule was that they did not set up legislative and administrative structures to allow their work to continue after their departure from office.

The impending departure of Governor Grey at the end of 1853 led McLean to write to him at length expressing his concern that it might lead to changes in native policy.[22] He could not conceal his anxiety about how 'the faith of the Crown' would be observed in land purchases once Grey left the colony, as the next governor might not 'enter into the spirit or nature of these engagements' as Grey had. Discounting both the flattery of the subordinate to his patron and McLean's anxiety over his future employment, there remained a concern that, although McLean and Grey had worked in harmony, the next governor might not continue this co-operation, to the detriment both of Maori and of McLean's future advancement.

Land purchases had been carried on, McLean observed, without any systematic provision for funding. The new Constitution Act of 1852 made land purchases a first charge on land revenue but set out no specific provisions for its operation. McLean thought it wrong for such an important subject to be left to the discretion of the proposed General Assembly, as it would 'be foreign to their ideas and comprehension'. A land-purchase department should be established with its expenditure provided in the annual estimates, the money to be deducted from the general land revenue. Quarterly estimates of money allocated for land purchases would enable the head of the department to be answerable to the general government for the manner in which these moneys were expended. Such a provision, with guidance, would allow the head to decide whether to proceed or abstain from certain negotiations. Without proper funding arrangements, large sums of money would be needed to buy certain lands. Under a regulated system, 'the whole country could be acquired at a comparatively moderate outlay extending over a considerable period of time'. This land-purchase department should not be 'a mere contingent appendage of the Government, liable to be interfered with by every change of government'. Nothing was more ruinous than to check negotiations once begun. Maori became obstinate, and it would take years to induce them to change their attitude.

Many important purchases had been completed but there remained many millions of acres of the North Island to be acquired. While land purchases had been under Grey's personal direction, McLean had not sought for any such requirement, 'feeling assured that while I laboured for the public good, my acts would be confirmed by Your Excellency, but, as I like others, may soon regret Your Excellency's departure and friendly countenance and co-operation, I think no less a duty to the natives, the public and myself than is actually called to bring this subject to Your Excellency's consideration'.[23] McLean's advocacy was persuasive. Before Grey left New Zealand he approved the establishment of the Native Land Purchase Department, with McLean as Chief Native Land Purchase Commissioner.

In November 1853, a year after his wife's death, McLean reflected with satisfaction on his progress through life; thereafter he ceased to record his private thoughts.

> This little book that has journeyed so oft with me is now coming to a close. Something like life it has been to me; and it contains memo, scraps and sundry notes ... And what is life but a series of unconnected incidents, of reverses, of trials, afflictions, and disappointments; with here and there a happy sunshine in the midst of the wilderness ...
>
> Still I have no cause to complain. God has been merciful to me, much beyond my deserts. My daily wants have been supplied. Health I have enjoyed. My worldly affairs are in a prosperous state. My duties have been going on successfully in a greater or lesser degree. The natives continue their confidence

in me. The Government both General and Provincial, have expressed publicly their satisfaction at my proceedings. Each stage through the country indicated improvements towards which my efforts have contributed ... And why should I not thank the Great Spirit that has granted all these blessings ... [24]

Chapter 8
The Factotum Kicks and Rebels

> How I shall get on under the new system I do not yet know but probably not so well as hitherto. The people are now for having all the power in the hands of political demagogues of their own choosing. However I shall try it for a time and if it does not please me I shall say good morning to them and retire to the country to look after my own.[1]

Thus McLean reacted to the introduction of responsible government in 1856. The system of responsible government required the governor to act on the advice of his ministers, who were to be chosen by a premier who commanded the support of a majority of the members of the House of Representatives. McLean resented the prospect of being subject to ministerial supervision and for the next five years he frustrated attempts by ministers to bring him under their control.

Before Governor Grey left New Zealand in 1853 he ensured that the new provincial councils he had set up were operating, but left responsibility for the establishment of a General Assembly, consisting of an elected House of Representatives and a nominated Legislative Council, to his successor. In 1854 the Acting Governor, Colonel Robert Wynyard, confronted with Edward Gibbon Wakefield's resolution calling for responsible government, referred the matter to the Colonial Office. Having surrendered to similar settler pressure in Canada in 1846, the Colonial Office was reluctant to fight the battle again. With almost indecent alacrity, it directed Wynyard to implement responsible government.

In its second session in 1854 the House made financial provision for the operation of the Native Land Purchase Department with McLean as Chief Native Land Purchase Commissioner at a salary of £400 a year and £100 for travelling expenses. The head office consisted of two clerks and a secretary. In addition, there was provision for two district commissioners, £300 for presents to rangatira and £100 towards the expenses of the survey branch.[2] McLean's recommendation for a deputy commissioner to keep up the correspondence with the Government and Maori during the absence of the chief commissioner was deferred.

Ruins of the McLean home at Kilmaluag on the Isle of Tiree

Donald McLean, age seventeen

Donald McLean, c 1850s.

Susan Strang

Douglas McLean, with his grandfather Robert Strang

Governor George Grey

Governor Thomas Gore Browne

Wiremu Kingi Te Rangitake

Wiremu Tamihana Tarapipipi Te Waharoa

First Cottage at Maraekakaho

In outlining the work of the Native Land Purchase Department to the House of Representatives in 1854, McLean proposed to continue Grey's policy of buying land in advance of settler demand. Ample funds were needed, as the longer the purchase of land was delayed 'the more will be the expense and difficulty of acquiring it'. It was not sufficient, McLean said, to buy land to meet the immediate demand from existing settlers; additional land had to be bought to provide for the increasing number of immigrants from Britain, America and the neighbouring Australian colonies. Of the 28 million acres of the North Island not more than 4 million acres had been bought. In the South Island, a quarter of the land area, mainly in Nelson and Canterbury, would soon be available for settlement.

'No other subject has embarrassed the Government in its dealings with the Natives or retarded the progress of the colony so much as the adjustment of the Native land question', wrote McLean. Adequate support for the new department was essential, not only to avoid a repetition of past difficulties, but to enable the country to be opened up 'for steady and progressive colonisation'. To buy land from numerous tribes was a difficult matter, 'arising not only from the complicated nature of their claims, but from their jealousies of each other, their superstitious objection to the alienation of the lands of their ancestors'. District officers should be appointed to buy land and prepare their districts for the introduction of European settlers, particularly in Auckland, Waikato and Waipa, Mokau and Kawhia, Taranaki, Bay of Plenty and Wellington province. These officers, with fluency in the Maori language and an understanding of Maori customs, would be capable of settling disputes. Surveyors would be needed to mark off the external boundaries of land purchases and native reserves.[3]

The system of reserving land for Maori, operating since 1840, should continue, McLean believed. Lands reserved for Maori within areas sold to the Crown were for their own use and subsistence. There had been 'a distinct understanding that they should not at any time be called upon to alienate any land so reserved, it being considered essential for their own maintenance and welfare to retain them'. These were lands cultivated and occupied by Maori and generally large enough to provide for their present and future wants. McLean's paternalism was evident, however; Maori would not be trusted to look after their own land and instead local boards consisting of resident magistrates, missionaries and 'one or two intelligent Native chiefs' should administer the reserves for 'the social, industrial, religious and educational advancement of the natives'. Boards should not have the power to alienate any reserve except with the Governor's permission. In 1856 the Native Reserves Act provided for local boards of trustees, established with Maori consent, to administer reserves in the interests of Maori. In practice, however, the trustees, being usually local settlers, administered the reserves by letting them at cheap rentals. Dissatisfied at this outcome, the tribes would not agree to handing over more reserves to the trustees.[4]

McLean pointed out that the provision of large reserves within well-defined natural boundaries had greatly contributed to a good understanding between Maori and European settlers.[5] In his view a policy of inalienable reserves had a dual purpose: to ensure that Maori had land left for their use, and to generate goodwill towards the settlers.[6] When he gave instructions to District Commissioner Kemp to buy land in Northland in 1855, for example, McLean told him that all purchases were to be subject to 'ample reservations' for present and future Maori needs. If reserves were clearly identified by natural boundaries such as rivers, this would reduce the surveying costs as well as preventing disputes. He told Kemp 'to use the utmost care and discretion … as each officer will be held responsible for any difficulties or disturbances that may arise from any purchase in which he is engaged'.[7]

McLean's appointment as Chief Native Land Purchase Commissioner meant a move to Auckland. First, he stayed with Dr Andrew Sinclair, still Colonial Secretary, who, McLean told his uncle, 'continues unbounded in his kindness towards me'. He bought six acres in Hobson Bay in 'a pleasant genteel situation for a residence and close to the sea embracing what is so expected of a McLean to have the element near him on which to float of his own'.[8] He was thinking of his ancestors on the Isle of Tiree.

In 1855 McLean spent only four months at his head office in Auckland. The rest of the year, apart from a fortnight in Nelson, he was moving around the North Island, visiting Wellington, Ahuriri, Wanganui and Taranaki. In 1856, however, he remained for nine months in Auckland wrestling with the demands of ministers following the introduction of responsible government. He seemed more comfortable out in the field personally conducting negotiations than in managing his department from a desk in Auckland.

The new governor, Colonel Thomas Gore Browne, came from a family whose sons traditionally entered either the armed services or the church. One brother became Bishop of Tasmania, another was a Cambridge divinity don. When Gore Browne arrived in New Zealand in September 1855, his first task was to oversee the implementation of responsible government. When the newly elected House of Representatives assembled in April 1856 the first two ministries, those of Henry Sewell and William Fox, were quickly overthrown but that of Edward Stafford was to last from June 1856 till July 1861.

Gore Browne had very little guidance or precedent for his role under responsible government, though it seems that he had had some communication with Lord Elgin, who, as Governor, had overseen a similar transition in Canada in 1846. In his private letters to officials at the Colonial Office, as distinct from his official dispatches, Gore Browne set out his impression of the issues he faced and the difficulties to be overcome. Soon after his arrival he wrote that whether the colony would be governed by the provincial councils or by the General Assembly would be the vital question for the next session of the assembly. 'Many of the settlers … insatiably eager for land, desire to obtain it honestly if possible but if that is not possible still they desire to have it. Under this pressure the local authorities would be in a dilemma – inevitable war with the natives if they yield to the demands of the Europeans and continual battle with the latter if they resist them. He hoped to bring about a settlement of land claims and other disputes in the North Island but, if the provincial councils were given the power to deal with disputes between Maori and Europeans, 'we shall be involved in difficulties from which extrication will not be easy'. He ruefully commented to the Colonial Office: 'Sir George Grey's ability is indisputable but he gave up the reins just as the coach was starting. Since then the horses have run away, the servants have only thought how they could get safely off and it is left to me to get them into a steady pace. The task is not an easy one but I hope for the best and have no misgivings.'[9]

Gore Browne's arrival increased McLean's influence. Before determining his native policy, Gore Browne, a conscientious and intelligent official, sought the views of people, including missionaries, who had intimate associations with Maori. However, he was strongly Anglocentric. He made little attempt to learn to speak Maori and failed to develop that personal relationship with rangatira that had enabled Grey to establish the mana of the Governor as the Queen's representative. When a rangatira came to Government House to see the Governor, Gore Browne sent him off to McLean with a note saying that he could not understand a word the fellow was saying. Maori came to regard McLean as the intermediary with the mana; letters from rangatira began 'To the Governor and McLean'.

McLean soon gained the Governor's confidence. The two met frequently whenever McLean was in Auckland. No minutes were kept, but the Governor undoubtedly relied on McLean for first-hand briefings on the attitudes and activities of the North Island tribes. These meetings were often held over a working breakfast at Government House. The Governor's wife, Harriet Gore Browne, made Government House the centre of Auckland's political and cultural life. She succumbed to McLean's flattery, becoming a firm friend. She summoned McLean to dine at Government House, sometimes at short notice, and required his presence at her madrigal evenings where the political happenings of the General Assembly were the main topic for discussion.

As Chief Native Land Purchase Commissioner, and later Native Secretary,

McLean had close contact with the Governor. At first Gore Browne gave him a free hand in determining both the location of land to be bought and in settling the price, though purchases were still limited by the amount of government revenue available. 'Push on with your purchases and let me know at your leisure what purchases you have made and where', wrote the Governor. Yet, although he was prepared to delegate responsibility to McLean as a trusted official and to listen to and accept his advice as the expert on Maori matters, it was the Governor and not McLean who made the policy decisions.

In giving advice to the new Governor even before his arrival, McLean recommended that he make provision for not less than £50,000 a year to buy Maori land. He noted that this requirement was so obvious that he did not need to give reasons, but then went on to set them out. Colonisation of the North Island had been retarded by the unsettled state of the native land question, involving 'many of the early settlers in ruin besides entailing a debt of 286,000 pounds on the colony'. Although these difficulties had been overcome by buying Maori land, increasing numbers of immigrants meant there was still insufficient land to meet the demand, especially in Auckland province. When Maori were willing to sell, any check on acquiring land would retard the prosperity of the colony. As for the rangatira, their pride would be injured if the Governor did not take up an offer to sell. Recently McLean had had many approaches from rangatira eager to sell. If their offers were rejected, they might later from 'their fluctuating disposition' decline to sell. There were numerous instances of such happenings as well as difficulties arising from an inability to complete a purchase promptly. Sufficient funds should be available to buy land without delay while it could be obtained for a moderate price, rather than run a risk of not securing any land or having to pay an 'enormously high price' later.

In Auckland province 600,000 acres had been bought since 1854. Two purchases, Orakei and Waiuku, which had cost £6000, when sold to settlers would bring £50,000 or £60,000 for the Government, apart from the ongoing revenue arising from European settlement. Therefore, apart from the political importance, it was important for the Government to make funds available.

Despite the advantages of selling, McLean sensed that the rangatira were coming to recognise that they were giving up their independence, laws and customs and having to accept English law and authority. In districts where land had been sold, English law was respected, while elsewhere it was disregarded. The rangatira saw the sale of their land as 'an act of great national importance'.

Regulations introduced by Grey had reduced the price of land to 5s and 10s an acre, and McLean believed that this would benefit Taranaki Maori. When the Hua block (14,000 acres) was bought in 1853, it was agreed that £1000 out of £3000 of the sale price should be held back to buy land for the tribe in lieu of the extensive reserves usually provided; this seems to have been on McLean's initiative. Under the previous system, he argued, land set aside as a reserve allowed Maori a common right of cultivation and occupation, but no individual could 'alienate his claim or clearly define his right'. As a consequence, these reserves had been 'a fruitful source of quarrel and oppression'. Under his new proposal, each man would have an individual piece of land secured by a Crown grant that he could dispose of as he pleased, putting him 'in a position of security'. This was the first instance of individualisation of title, a practice that McLean was to promote in later years. He saw the benefits as a weakening of opposition to land sales and an 'increased eagerness to sell of those formerly well disposed to the Government'. At the same time, the living conditions of the Maori would improve as they exchanged their 'wretched hovels' in unhealthy pa for substantial houses built on their own land, and acquired the means to increase their livestock and extend their cultivations. Maori would gain a better knowledge of the value of money and in a very short time would be on an equal footing with the English settlers. Through their property they would qualify for the vote and 'thus in the course of time a tribe of wild and semi-barbarous savages will become a body of loyal, wealthy and valuable settlers'.[10] If this was indeed his intention, he failed to consider how far his acquisition of their land would deprive them of the very asset that would make them wealthy.

McLean did not spell out how far individualisation of title could have extended but seemed to envisage the rangatira joining the colonial landholding class. No official had a better understanding of Maori custom and the relationships among members of a tribe regarding land tenure, yet he was ready to overturn customary land rights, a key element in Maori life, in his belief that the only future for Maori lay in assimilation of the races.

Governor Gore Browne proposed to retain control of native affairs. He would listen to his ministers' advice on this subject but not necessarily act upon it and, where he disagreed, he would submit the matter to the Secretary of State for the Colonies. In these early years of self-government the Governor and his ministers had to develop a satisfactory working relationship. McLean, however, resented any ministerial intervention. Where he had responsibility he had to have complete control, therefore he supported the Governor's keeping control of Maori affairs. In response to a confidential request from the Governor, he set out his views. He opposed the management of native affairs by ministers, on the grounds that ministers as elected representatives were liable to be changed at frequent and uncertain intervals. He went on to argue that the 'feelings, habits of thought and customs of the natives should be carefully considered in any measures proposed for their Govt'. They would rather be governed by Crown representatives than by elected representatives whose 'precarious tenure of office' would not allow them, 'even if so disposed', to gain the confidence of the Maori, 'whose retrospective habits of thought and feudal attachment to their rangatira would not easily reconcile them to be governed by the representatives of English constituencies unacquainted with their wants, prejudices or requirements'. Her Majesty's representative by virtue of his office was regarded by Maori as their guardian. Ever since the objects of the British Government had been explained to them at the signing of the Treaty of Waitangi, they had looked to the Governor for 'redress of their real or imaginary grievances'. Any change in these relations, McLean argued, would arouse great mistrust.[11] McLean's official advice tended to reflect what he understood to be the Governor's position, though in this case it coincided with both his own appreciation of Maori needs and his distaste for the involvement of elected representatives, along with a determination to maintain the independence of his own growing empire.

By August 1856, however, the Governor's 'reserved powers' in native affairs had led to an impasse, with ministers complaining that McLean and F. D. Fenton, acting Native Secretary, had 'set up a little Empire of their own'. The Governor was adamant that he would not surrender control of native affairs. The ministers were 'equally resolved not go on with an *Imperium in Imperio;* a back stairs influence guiding or misguiding him upon this most important branch of Government'.[12] Ministers talked of resignation, but Gore Browne came up with an acceptable compromise. For administrative convenience, the Native Secretary's Office and the Land Purchase Department would be amalgamated and come under the general oversight of a Minister of Native Affairs. The personal rivalry between McLean and Fenton was so intense that the exasperated Governor declared that one of them would have to go. The pragmatic McLean believed that Maori could be controlled by establishing personal relationships and by gifts and pensions. Fenton worked from principles and urged the Government to take charge and set up new institutions to enable Maori to govern themselves. In the event it was Fenton who was removed. McLean would be Native Secretary as well as Chief Native Land Purchase Commissioner. He was to submit all correspondence with comments to the Native Minister, who would forward this with his additional comment to the Governor. Ministers accepted that the final say rested with the Governor but reassured themselves that, as the General Assembly would hold the purse strings, they retained control. McLean approached T. H. Smith to be his Assistant Native Secretary – his duties being to take charge of the office, keep the accounts and oversee the publication of the *Maori Messenger*, the government newspaper.[13] Although Smith was a scholar fluent in Maori, his personality made him unpopular with the rangatira. McLean, however, needed him to supplement the administrative skills in which he himself was deficient. He warned Smith that he was uncertain whether ministers would approve the appointment as there was a great disinclination to spend money on native affairs. For a time McLean had to pay Smith out of his own salary as Native Secretary.

Ministers had their suspicions of McLean. In August 1856 Sewell wrote: 'But now comes a new difficulty. How it will end I know not. The factotum Mr. McLean kicks and rebels. He does not like being put into harness, and so there threatens a new danger. But the Governor seems to hold stoutly to our side of the question; and I suppose it will end in McLean giving in.'[14] A month later he recorded that 'McLean accedes to the new regime'.

Conflict was soon renewed. The Governor had retained control of native affairs. McLean could now reconcile his reluctance to submit to political interference with Gore Browne's intention to exclude his ministers from that area of decision making. Within a few months McLean protested that it was 'most subversive of efficient control over the officers of this Department if they are encouraged by His Excellency's responsible advisers to go before ministers on subjects connected with the organisation of the Native Department, or in fact on any subject on which they may form different views in reference to the conduct of Native Affairs'. He was willing at all times, he said, to provide information for ministers but, if ministers insisted on a right to call in officers of his department, it would be 'a breach of official etiquette', and to do so without reference to the head of the department would result in 'dissatisfaction and disorder' in the department's working. He complained that subordinate officials had been in the habit of going to ministers to volunteer information without his knowledge or concurrence and he insisted that the Native Department should remain strictly non-political.[15]

McLean continued to resist attempts to bring his department under ministerial control. He complained to the Governor when the 1858–59 estimates appeared to place the Native Secretary's Office under the direct control of the Native Minister, as the Native Secretary had thus been made subordinate to the minister. McLean saw this as inconsistent with the relationship between the Governor and his responsible advisers in the management of native affairs.

When Fenton was appointed resident magistrate in the Waikato in 1857, he resumed his struggle with McLean. Smith, the Assistant Native Secretary, told McLean that Fenton had been complaining that the Native Office had failed to consult with him or to keep him informed of matters relating to his own district. Smith denied the charge. He condemned Fenton's conduct when the Governor had gone to Waikato to meet the runanga (Maori council) there, saying that Fenton had insisted on being present but had made no attempt either to acknowledge or to repudiate the role of the runanga, or to support the Governor's views.[16]

Fenton, who saw himself as the protégé of the Native Minister, C. W. Richmond, refused to communicate with the Governor through McLean as his departmental head. The Governor, believing that Fenton desired to supplant McLean, remarked that when Fenton was acting as Native Secretary, he had insisted that no correspondence should go to the minister until he had commented on it. Gore Browne thought it 'quite impossible' that a subordinate should be separated from his own department and allowed to correspond with the chief of another.[17] Once again McLean triumphed. Fenton was removed from his Waikato post in March 1858.

Although the decision to amalgamate the two offices was made for administrative convenience, it was justified as benefiting Maori, who had been confused about which department they should approach. This amalgamation, however, compounded a contradiction inherent in the articles of the Treaty of Waitangi that had confronted successive governors since 1840. Settler pressure demanded that the Governor negotiate to buy land at times and places when the best interests of Maori required that they retain their lands to compete effectively in the evolving colonial economy. McLean's role as trustee for the Maori people was in conflict with his responsibility to act as the purchaser of Maori land. Moreover, land purchases occupied most of his time.

Native policy was for the Governor to determine and for McLean to implement, although, as Gore Browne trusted McLean, he did have influence in forming policy. As Native Secretary, McLean adopted a 'taihoa' approach: he was prepared to leave Maori to operate under their own customs and to come over gradually to British practice in their own time. He did, however, foster an extension of the work of the resident magistrates. Men such as H. T. Clarke in the Bay of Plenty, James Clendon and W. B. White in the north, and James Mackay in Nelson had some success in resolving disputes.

Soon after his arrival, Gore Browne travelled extensively in the colony. On Maori affairs, he sought the opinion of well-known colonists, including Bishop Selwyn and the Chief Justice, William Martin. He sent this evidence to the Colonial Office, saying that the 'native question' caused him great uneasiness. Maori were becoming alarmed at the ever-increasing number of European settlers and conscious that 'they wax weak as we wax strong'. This feeling was the source of 'continual small disturbances'. Gore Browne said that he had always obtained redress but it had been by diplomacy rather than an acknowledged right (in this diplomacy the Governor relied on McLean): 'A state of chronic disease has been treated with anodynes.' Maori could not be 'improved' without instruction or education and this required money.

Ministers, jealous of his reserved powers, might refuse to provide the money and yet hold him responsible for the consequences. The time had come to secure the friendship of the rangatira and to educate their people.[18]

Gore Browne also set up a Board of Inquiry into Native Affairs to advise him on native policy. When McLean appeared before the board, he revealed his thinking on land-purchase policy. Maori were very divided on the sale of land, he acknowledged. The late Tuwharetoa rangatira Te Heuheu regarded the central interior of the North Island as sacred land never to be sold. Along the West Coast as far as Taranaki, except for Wanganui and Rangitikei, there was what McLean called a combination against selling land. On the East Coast, the Bay of Plenty and the inland Waikato, tribes had joined this movement. McLean attributed their opposition to a fear that the number of Europeans was increasing so rapidly that Maori would eventually be dispossessed. In selling their land they felt that they had surrendered their independence, and this feeling was strongest among those who had little contact with Europeans. Where land sales had taken place, Maori were prepared to sell more. These districts included the northern part of Auckland province, Thames and the West Coast between Kaipara and Mokau, except for Kawhia. From the North Cape as far as Tauranga, with certain exceptions, Maori were willing to sell. McLean believed that Maori were content with the present system as it offered 'ready money'. Payments were made by instalments over a period of years. The first, usually the largest, was divided among the general and more remote claimants, while the real owners received the subsequent payments. McLean recommended that the price paid should be increased, although, he explained, when Maori decided to sell price became a secondary consideration. In Auckland, the average was 1s an acre, in Wellington 4 1/2d an acre.

The operation of Maori land tenure, McLean told the board, was such that no individual had a clear title to land that was not entangled with the general interest of the tribe and often with the claims of other tribes who might have migrated from the area. The system was complex. The rule that applied to the purchase of one portion of land did not apply to another, so that 'A great deal must be left to the person purchasing'. McLean reiterated his wish that every Maori could get a Crown grant of land, any tribal claim having first been 'obliterated' by government purchase. Individual Crown grants would break up their 'confederations'. Maori should be encouraged to buy land from the Government in town and rural areas and government loans should help them to build houses.[19]

Not long after Gore Browne took office, McLean advised the Governor that he should not agree to any withdrawal of British troops stationed in the colony. Although there was no immediate threat to the settlements, any withdrawal could lead to 'serious disturbances'. Careful management could minimise difficulties but, with two 'dissimilar races', disputes and misunderstandings must be expected. The troops' presence would reduce the possibility of those 'mutual aggressions', the results of which, 'if once allowed to ripen into a war of the races, years of tranquillity would not be able to efface'. Maori were well aware of their superiority in numbers. They were well armed and skilful in the type of warfare suited to their country and 'fond of the excitement of war; and resort to it periodically among themselves on the slightest provocation'.

Careful management, in McLean's eyes, meant preventing Maori from uniting. If they were to unite, he argued, they would prove a dangerous enemy, but their internal feuds, mainly over land, had kept them separated. The tribes who lived beyond the limits of the colonial settlements would 'in the gradually strengthening feeling of nationality' sink their differences and 'resist the foreigners, not as disunited, but as a nation'. Withdrawing troops would threaten not only Europeans but also friendly tribes.[20] This was McLean's first recognition of the growing attraction of what would turn into the King movement.

While Gore Browne retained control of native affairs, he depended on his ministers to provide the money to implement his policies. He therefore had to carry his ministers with him. With settlers increasing rapidly in number and eager to acquire Maori land, he recognised that the potential for conflict would grow. He thought that Grey's assurances about a peaceful amalgamation of the two races 'had been far from reality. Either Grey had been carried away by his feelings when he spoke of them in the manner he did or things had changed in the interval since his departure.' Gore Browne regretted that many land titles, purchases and other matters, that were supposed to have been settled finally by his predecessor, remained undecided. He was soon complaining of having to fulfil Grey's past promises with inadequate means.

In reporting to the Colonial Office, Gore Browne contemplated the alternatives if arrangements with his ministers over control of Maori affairs proved unworkable. He could either hand control over to his ministers or govern Maori separately with a Crown commissioner, restricting the control of the General Assembly to the South Island and to certain areas adjoining the North Island settlements. On ministerial control, he said, 'unprejudiced men' were opposed to it. He also thought the option of a separate Maori district far from desirable if it was possible to do justice to Maori by other means. No doubt separate control would be best for Maori interests and would be acceptable to missionaries and many outlying settlers, but it would founder on the 'determined hostility' of the General Assembly. Under separation, most of the revenue contributed by Maori would be available for their improvement instead of being spent by and on English settlers – 'this the latter have doled out with the cold hand of charity and with great self-laudation'. Gore Browne felt that he could handle Europeans or Maori alone but that to combine such conflicting interests was demanding in the extreme – he believed he had one of the most arduous positions in Her Majesty's Service.[21]

When the General Assembly considered the 1856 estimates, the Governor asked for expenditure on native affairs in addition to the £7000 provided for education under the civil list. For presents and food he asked, no doubt on McLean's advice, for £300, 'far less than will meet the most urgent demand', but he was sure that members would see the 'judicious liability' of this matter. An additional sum of £600 was needed for pensions for those rangatira who had rendered important service to the Government, and £3000 for loans. In the past they had repaid their loans promptly while the property they acquired encouraged them in peaceful habits.

These proposals continued Grey's and McLean's approach of securing compliance through the exercise of personal influence. As Native Secretary, McLean was prepared to develop a structure of Maori self-rule at district level. He was less enthusiastic about any body that would involve rangatira in administration at national level unless he could continue to exercise control through personal influence. As Gore Browne developed his native policy in 1856, McLean responded with a detailed memo offering advice on key aspects: education, communications, the need for intelligence agents, individual titles and finance. Grey had decided that the sum set aside for native affairs should be spent on education. McLean criticised the effectiveness of the £7000 provided for this and delivered through Anglican, Roman Catholic and Wesleyan missions, and recommended the appointment of an education board or inspector to inquire into and report on reforms. These native schools were, he assessed, generally well conducted and the scholars making progress 'in the habits of cleanliness, industry and regularity'. The main obstacles he identified were a shortage of experienced teachers, and students unaccustomed to discipline who were irked by rules and constraints and supported by their parents, who saw restraint as 'degradation'. Nevertheless, he looked forward to the development of a national education system that would benefit Maori as much in 'agricultural and mechanics as of the domestic, moral and social duties'. Perhaps he was influenced by the model of the Scottish parish school of which he was a product. Tribes should be encouraged to support these schools by gifts of land and produce as well as a 'small annual donation'. He thought the 'diffusion of useful knowledge' was of such importance for the future of the Maori race that other denominations should not be excluded from mission schools and, when schools were set up for the settlers' children, they should be open on equal terms to Maori youngsters. Although McLean may have seen education as an instrument to convert Maori to European ways, his demand for equality of educational opportunity would have disconcerted many settlers.

'Bridle roads' were needed to open up the country and facilitate postal communications. The main route should go through the interior from Auckland by way of Waikato, Waipa, Taupo and Ahuriri, on through the 40 Mile Bush to Wairarapa and over the Rimutaka road, already formed, to Wellington. This route would open up the most fertile part of the Auckland province and would pass through the most open and accessible parts of the country. The alternative was to carry the overland mail by way of Taranaki to Wellington, thereby linking the settlements of Taranaki, Wanganui and Manawatu. The disadvantage was that this route did not open up suitable country and would have to follow the coastline, while the eighty miles between Kawhia and Taranaki was mountainous, heavily wooded and impassable except to foot travellers.

McLean valued the collection of authentic information on the state of the Maori tribes and recommended the appointment of 'political agents', especially in the densely populated parts of the North Island. The need was urgent, he said, because the missionary societies in England had begun to withdraw their people from New Zealand. The missionaries had a great influence among the Maori, 'naturally a religious race', and their departure would make the task of governing more difficult as Maori would again resort to wars that the missionaries' mediation had helped to avoid. McLean wanted the duties of a political agent to approximate to those of the missionaries. They should, however, have the powers of a resident magistrate to deal with disputes among Maori and to control Europeans who, in remote districts, thought they were beyond English law. The agents should provide summary redress for cattle trespass, as Maori had 'just reason' to complain when settlers' cattle were allowed to run at large, destroying crops – this practice formed one of their strongest objections to selling land to Europeans, according to McLean. Principal rangatira should be invited to take part in the adjudication of all cases, with small annuities to the most energetic. By this and other means, 'the institution of chieftainship now fast mouldering away, would be recognised and to some extent upheld thus affording a means of governing the tribes through the agency of their own rangatira which is evidently the most effective way of keeping them in check and ensuring their confidence and co-operation'. Each political agent should receive instructions suited to the 'peculiarities of the tribes and district to which he was appointed'. A few Maori policemen attached to each agent would assist him in his duties and help to suppress the sale of alcohol and arms – contraband goods. In addition, something dear to McLean, agents would be most valuable in providing intelligence reports on the activities and attitudes of local tribes. These spies would be his eyes and ears to give him advance warning of what Maori were thinking and doing.

McLean supported the idea of introducing individual titles to Maori land, but argued that the proposal by the Board of Inquiry into Native Affairs would not work as Maori would not agree to make the necessary mutual concessions. Their customs had no place for the transfer or exchange of land in perpetuity. Only recently had they come to understand the process of bargaining and selling that would enable the Crown to issue grants of land to individual rangatira. It was vital to provide for Maori to acquire land by purchase from the Government, as this would be 'the surest means of breaking their tribal confederacies and of inspiring greater confidence in that power from which their more secure and permanent tenure is derived'. McLean saw these tribal 'confederacies' as illegal combinations, similar to nineteenth-century trade unions in England. The process would take time but the certainty that they could obtain land to leave with an undisputed title to posterity would give them confidence in the system. In the meantime he thought a start could be better made in the South Island with its very small Maori population. This task could be done within eighteen months using a surveyor, a native commissioner and four labourers.

On finance, McLean, though aware of the General Assembly's reluctance to spend money on native affairs, insisted that ministers would have to find the money. Maori deserved financial help: they were not represented in the 'Councils of the Country' yet their numbers were double that of the colonists; they possessed five-sixths of the North Island and contributed a large portion of the colony's exports and revenue. The Government had to take these factors into account and acknowledge that measures adopted for 'the advancement of the natives in their transition state will in a great degree depend on their own happiness and industry as a race as well as the general prosperity of the Colony of New Zealand'.[22]

McLean's advice to the Governor made no reference to provision for Maori representation in the General Assembly. Three weeks previously, however, letters he exchanged with James Edward FitzGerald show that McLean contemplated placing rangatira on the electoral roll with a Crown grant as title to their lands. FitzGerald, despite his liberal views on race relations, dismissed the idea. Any proposal to place the entire Maori population on the electoral roll 'would awake the greatest alarm throughout the colony' and place the Governor in a most invidious position.[23] FitzGerald did not seem to consider that Article Three of the Treaty guaranteeing Maori the rights of British subjects required Maori representation. Eager not to alarm a leading member of the assembly, McLean replied that his main object in introducing Maori representation had been to use this as a way of 'raising them in the scale of civilisation' and bringing them under English laws and 'gradually and cautiously preparing them for the exercise of those political privileges which they should eventually enjoy'. Nothing had been further from his thoughts than to admit any political influence on the part of the Native Department, which should remain strictly non-political.[24] McLean accepted FitzGerald's advice that settler opposition to Maori representation would result in a constitutional crisis if he persisted in this proposal.[25] He omitted mentioning it in his advice to the Governor, though he did point out that Maori had no representation despite constituting the majority of the population and contributing extensively to the economy.

Anglican missionaries and pro-Maori officials were concerned at the adverse effects of a settler-controlled government on Maori, and looked to McLean, as Native Secretary for support. In February 1856, C. O. Davis, the Chief Government Interpreter, urged him to return to Auckland and take control of the Native Office. T. H. Smith, as the Acting Secretary, although an 'excellent Maori scholar, amiable and religious', lacked influence as Maori disliked him. Davis believed that McLean, on the other hand, was respected by Maori and had their confidence. He warned that 'there are not wanting those to take advantage of your absence and to try to injure you in various ways'. Officials with differing views were making the Native Department 'unsettled and unsatisfactory'.[26]

The Wanganui missionary, Richard Taylor, also sought McLean's support. He feared a widening breach between the two races unless the Governor intervened. Maori had no representation in government, had been denied their rights as British subjects and had gained 'nothing but deterioration by their alliance with us'. He thought it unreasonable that, at Wanganui, where they had sold all their surplus land, they could not lease any of their reserves to the settlers even 'with the consent of their true guardians the miss [missionaries] and how diametrically is this opposed to the Treaty of Waitangi'. The prosperity of the colony, however unwilling settlers were to acknowledge it, depended on the harmonious union of the two races, Taylor declared. He was sure that McLean, from his own observations, would support his concerns and convey them to the new Governor.[27]

Within a year Taylor wrote again, regretting that McLean had not yet visited Wanganui and reiterating his anxiety at the treatment of Maori. He was concerned that, with politicians in charge, the Treaty of Waitangi was being ignored. Pressure to sell had alarmed the rangatira, who feared that their mana would be lost along with their land. Taranaki tribes were about to unite in agreeing not sell land. As early as 1853 a meeting at Taiporohenui had led to a coalition of tribes opposed to the sale of further land, except for Nga Rauru at Waitotara. Tribes in Waikato, Kawhia, Mokau, Rotorua and Taupo had all given their adherence to 'this law of purupuru [pupuri] whenua [withholding of land from sale]'. Apart from Te Hapuku and the Whanganui–Rangitikei tribes, he was not aware of any who were sincerely attached to the British Government. Taylor attributed this attitude to government policy: 'we degrade the rangatira and they see it, they know if they part with their land they have parted with mana. As well we [have] given them no equivalent they lose their grade.' In Taylor's opinion something 'more substantial than a few occasional gifts was needed to attach the rangatira and to banish their suspicions' – an implied criticism of the policy introduced by Grey and followed by McLean. Provincial councils, Taylor asserted, were 'composed of settlers (in this part not of the most enlightened and educated portion) who carry anything but a good feeling towards Maori into Council'. Rangatira were being imprisoned and he was pained at the 'wanton and inconsiderate way of offending those who have been our greatest friends'.[28] He deplored the settlers' efforts

> to demoralise the natives by inducing them to drink and their success. Intoxication is daily becoming more general and the rising generation more debased. Every effort is made to induce the native to sell his land and yet he is treated as a dog and I very much fear the good feelings which have hitherto been entertained by the natives towards the Europeans will go away especially as we have some here on our bench who are ready on the slightest cause or misunderstanding to arrest and throw into jail the greatest chief.[29]

McLean respected Taylor but he did not extend that same regard to other Anglican missionaries. He accused them of persuading tribes to withhold their lands from sale when they had a moral obligation to support the Crown. Such was his animosity towards the Revd T. S. Grace at Taupo that in December 1856, he urged the Governor to approach the Church Missionary Society (CMS) in London to have him removed from the colony. He charged that Grace was using every means in his power to thwart government measures and to encourage the tribes not to sell their lands. He complained that Grace had been telling them that 'the whole of the Europeans are impostors; against whom he feels it his duty to preach most inflammable sermons and discourses'. As Grace was stationed in an area beyond European influence he would do great harm, McLean argued, submitting that the CMS could not be justified in employing a person 'whose object appears to be more to promote disaffection among the natives towards the English Government than to fulfil the Christian duties of his office'.[30] When Grace heard of McLean's action he demanded that the official substantiate his allegation. Grace rebutted the charges and convinced the CMS that he had opposed the King movement. The outcome was that Grace continued to minister to his congregation at Taupo. McLean, however, could be vindictive; he neither forgot nor forgave.

★

Before the first meeting of the General Assembly in 1856, McLean reported to the Governor on the extent of land-purchase operations throughout the country. In the South Island, he noted, with the exception of D'Urville Island, a dispute at Akaroa and 'certain reservations essential for the subsistence of the Natives the claims to that Island may now be considered as fully settled'.[31]

In the Bay of Islands, McLean estimated that 100,000 acres could be bought for some £6000. At Whangarei, 230,000 acres had been bought for £9900 between February 1853 and March 1856. A growing export trade in kauri gum and timber had enhanced the commercial importance of Northland and this, combined with the readiness of Te Rarawa, Ngapuhi and Ngati Whatua rangatira to sell land, made the region a desirable area for the extension of settlement.[32] Negotiations had begun with Te Aupouri and Te Rarawa rangatira to buy two blocks – Muriwhenua South (86,885 acres) and Whareama (13,555 acres) – at 4d an acre. McLean approved the price but told H. T. Kemp, the District Commissioner, to take 'the utmost care' in drafting the deed, as some of his previous deeds had been 'vague and therefore objectionable'. He offered a model deed that would be 'intelligible to and binding upon the Natives'.[33]

To gain further land close to the town of Auckland would need £5000, McLean estimated. Extensive areas of Thames, Piako and the Bay of Plenty could be bought if a land commissioner were stationed there. Land purchases were moving gradually towards Waikato and Waipa districts but, he advised, it would be a considerable time before any interior land would be sold as local Maori had been reluctant to sell even the homestead lands of the few Europeans who had been living there for many years.

Within Wellington province there were still 700,000 acres unpurchased at Ahuriri and Manawatu. Of these, 300,000 acres – part of the Ahuriri plains near the harbour mouth – might be bought in the next eighteen months if funds and survey assistance were available. McLean maintained that, as this land was suitable for agricultural and pastoral pursuits, funds should be available to complete the purchase when the Maori were ready to sell the land.[34] He did not mention his interest in acquiring some of this land for himself.

In Taranaki, only 60,000 acres had been purchased. McLean advised that, because of continued tribal feuding, there was no prospect of acquiring more land there. He did not point out that the origin of these feuds was increasing government pressure on Maori to sell land and that the conflict was between those wishing to sell and those wanting to retain their land. McLean noted that in 1847 and 1848 the Tataraimaka, Omata, Grey and Bell blocks had been acquired but from that time no further purchases had been possible until 1853, with the acquisition of the Waiwhakaiho block (17,000 acres) for £545 and the Hua block (14,000 acres) for £300. With the addition of the earlier Fitzroy block the estimated area was 61,770 acres at a cost of £7663. Two blocks –

Oakura (8000 acres) and Waiongana (10,000 acres) – were under negotiation, but 'powerful opposition' had been encountered. Success continued to elude McLean in Taranaki.

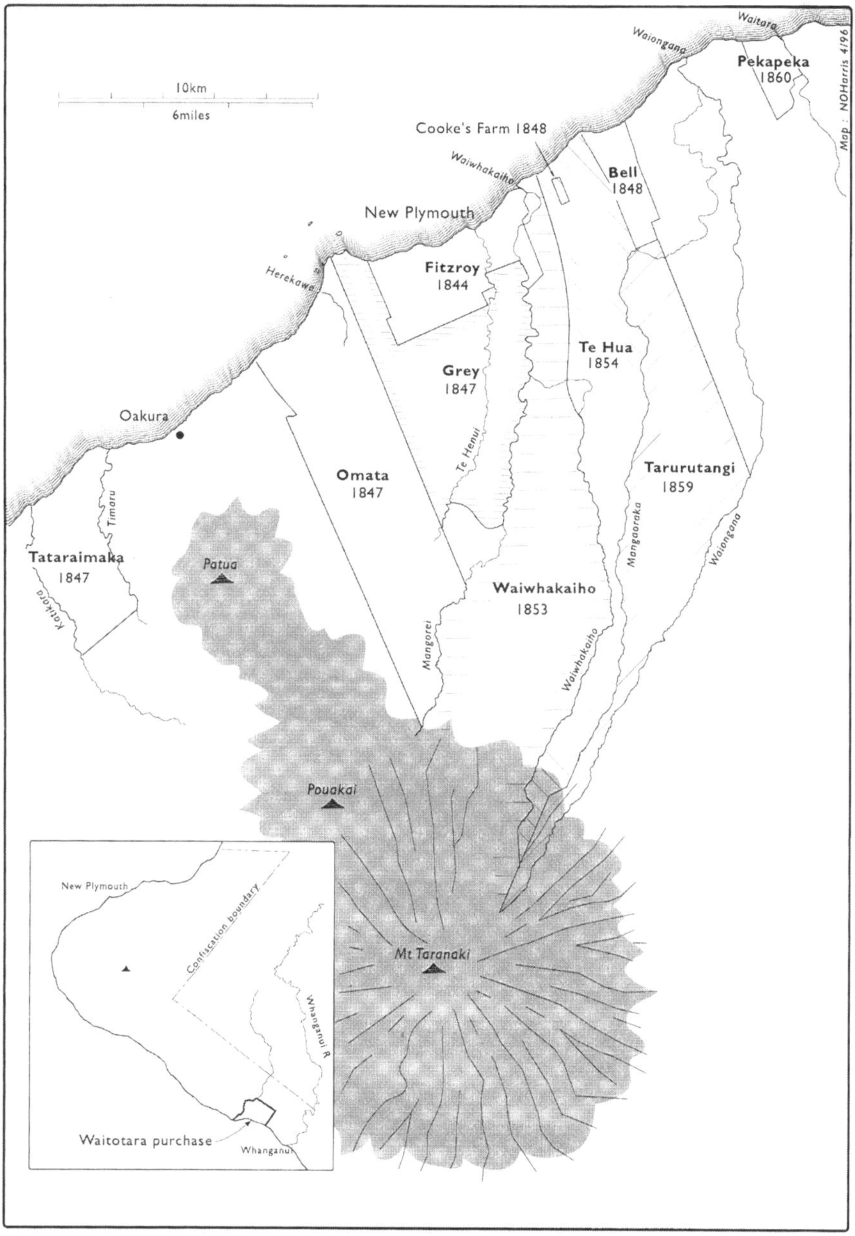

Map 2. Crown 'Purchases' 1844–1860

Chapter 9
Unbridled Power?

From 1856, as Chief Native Land Purchase Commissioner and Native Secretary, McLean had become de facto ruler of the North Island beyond the small European coastal settlements. With only an acting governor for two years from the departure of Governor Grey in 1853, McLean increased his influence, as he did when Governor Gore Browne arrived in 1855 having no knowledge of Maori customs. McLean was the visible presence of British imperialism. Among the rangatira McLean's mana was greater than that of any other Pakeha. He used the provision for contingency expenditure to make gifts of livestock, agricultural implements, flour mills and so on to rangatira to secure their loyalty. 'Friendly' rangatira who were prepared to sell land were rewarded with pensions. Governor Gore Browne set the policy, but he trusted McLean, listened to his advice and gave him a free hand to negotiate.

Ministers resented McLean's exercise of power even as they acknowledged the extent of his influence among Maori. Whenever there was a crisis, C. W. Richmond, the Native Minister, would approach the Governor to have McLean dispatched forthwith to keep the peace. Ministers, with their classical education, might have recalled the story of Philoctetes, rejected and exiled by the Greeks for the insufferable smell of his wound. As he possessed the invincible bow, however, they had to send for him if they were to have victory over the Trojans. Ministers might detest McLean, but they were uncomfortably aware that his influence among Maori was the difference between peace and war.

McLean's exercise of power infuriated many colonists. In a letter to C. W. Richmond in 1858, Francis Dillon Bell's antagonism towards McLean was evident. Bell, a member of the House of Representatives and a former land-claims commissioner, advocated ministerial responsibility in native affairs. The House would not vote money to McLean, he said, as members believed in neither the man nor his policy, though they acknowledged that his system had some advantages and that he was the best man to carry it out. Nevertheless, he considered that McLean was not indispensable; the House could govern the natives themselves without him. Bell continued: 'It's all very well to say "Trust the Governor" but trusting the Governor means trusting Donald McLean and we absolutely decline to do that.' Only if the Native Department was made answerable to the Native Minister, if the staff became government servants, 'not the confederates or enemies of one individual', and if the Governor consulted with the minister and no one else without the minister's knowledge, would Bell 'vote the money' for native affairs – and then liberally. He accepted that the Governor had an imperial power of veto on ministerial proposals, but members would never agree to the Governor's deciding how to spend the money as he liked, as in practice that meant that McLean decided.

Guarantees were needed before the House would vote the money, Bell said. He would want to know what policy the ministers would follow – 'whether you mean the Flour and Sugar Policy or Another System; whether Donald was to be Deus Ex.[in charge] or the Governor and you'. If what the House wanted overrode McLean's views, then Bell would vote the money provided it was spent on the advice of the Native Minister, as he thought Richmond was just as capable of governing the natives, he said. Bell's aversion to McLean was that 'he claims, he, to govern the Natives; "seul je ferai le bien de mes peuples." Whereas I say that the natives are to be governed by principles, pray to be governed by principle and care not for men – care no more for McLean than for me or any other man. I affirm that Allah is Great and McLean is not his Prophet.'[1] Bell did not understand the Maori world view whereas McLean did and used this understanding to establish his mana.

Bell apologised for 'this harping on Donald' but he reminded Richmond what he had often said about McLean:

> Admit his system and he is the man to carry it out. Also if you admit him give the *power*; it's not fair to encourage in that case Fenton and the rest of them to go in at him. He will certainly keep you in peace as well as anyone else and as certainly buy land; but he will keep the peace in his own way and buy what he likes: and he is entitled to be let alone: he is far too able a man and far too valuable if his system is necessary, to be interfered with by the Governor and people who don't know if 'kahore' means yes or no.[2]

Bell had misread the relationship between the Governor and McLean, however. Gore Browne was not McLean's puppet: he was in control and determined policy. And the introduction of responsible government had in fact curbed McLean's independence. Although the Governor reserved native affairs under imperial control, he had to ask for funds from an assembly that was prepared to advance money only for land purchases. McLean therefore had to take account of ministerial policy. Gore Browne stood by McLean. In a private letter to Gairdner at the Colonial Office he criticised the views of his Native Minister, Richmond: 'The meaning of the document is evident and the writer cannot disguise it viz., "that until I Deborah arose there was no prophet in Israel" and I and my colleagues are alone competent to manage native affairs. Mr. R [Richmond] is very able and is, I doubt not, a conscientious advocate of democracy, viewing an irresponsible official with instinctive dislike and considering a very indifferent settler preferable to the best man who ever served the Crown.' Gore Browne assured Gairdner that it would take 'an octavo volume' to refute Richmond's arguments in detail, hence he would confine himself to 'demolishing his strongest positions'. He defended McLean in these terms:

> The Native Sectry., a man of great experience, entirely trusted by Sir G. Grey and myself, is no match for Mr. Richmond whether in talking or writing but he falls on the only safe ground viz., his great experience and intimate knowledge of the native character. In these he is to be admitted to be unrivalled and in them Mr. Richmond is necessarily deficient. The former clings to facts, the latter to theories and as long as I am responsible it is needless to say that I cannot risk the peace of the country by allowing the latter to throw dust in my eyes.[3]

Despite their differing views, McLean and Richmond had to work together to resolve immediate problems. Continued illegal leasing of Maori land worried McLean. The problem had spread from Wairarapa to Hawkes Bay, he advised the Native Minister in April 1857. Land recently bought at Porangahau cost three times that paid for the adjacent block at Castlepoint. Leasing encouraged 'increased avarice' on the part of the tribes while the colony had to bear the expense of keeping a few settlers in possession of their illegally held runs. McLean identified two 'dangerous principles ... one that of encouraging native cupidity, the other that of permitting settlers to evade laws that interfere with their personal advancement thereby submitting laws enacted for the general weal to become subordinate to the interest of a few isolated runholders'.[4]

He recommended that the Government check this activity or it would be faced with a repetition of the Wairarapa squatting, with 'all the evils and expenses it entailed'. There would be a scramble for runs, with Maori joining with settlers in opposing land sales. The outcome would be an end to land purchases. Maori who had sold would regret their decision when they saw those who had held out obtaining large annual payments. The non-sellers were claiming greater mana for having English settlers altogether in their power and being free to order them off their run if they did not comply with their demands: 'in fact the whole system is so bad and degrading that no Englishman would long submit to it'.[5]

In August 1857, looking back on the first year of responsible government,

Gore Browne recalled his initial inability to influence his ministers' policies and the subsequent change in their relations until he was confident that their actions had come to reflect his own views.

> They pursued their own way regardless of my existence nor could the Assembly be induced to notice despatches from the C. Office unless it suited the humours of the moment. I felt that the only course was to do as one does with a runaway horse, viz., ride with a loose rein, keeping a firm seat and the eyes open. The plan succeeded; excitement passed and responsibility has had the effect of a ploughed field on a runaway horse. Mr. Stafford who was certainly the last man I should have selected as my adviser has become particularly courteous and indirectly my influence though unseen has not been unfelt for the whole council have become more or less converts to my views.[6]

During 1858 the Stafford Government introduced comprehensive measures to deal with the 'native question' by modifying British institutions to meet Maori needs. Successive governments were to grapple with the issue of how far Maori should be admitted to the legislative and administrative roles of government. Legislation passed that year included the Native District Courts Act which provided for judges to sit with Maori assessors and juries to enforce laws; the Native Schools Act continued to subsidise mission schools and to provide for Government inspection, and the Native Districts Regulations Act provided for local councils under a Pakeha chairman to make by-laws on matters of local importance.

Another bill, the Native Territorial Rights Bill prepared by C. W. Richmond, proposed Crown grants in individual title that could then be sold direct to settlers. The Governor and McLean opposed this bill and the Colonial Office was of a like mind. It disallowed the bill, believing that it promoted settlers' interests at the expense of the Maori race. Aggrieved settlers wrote to the Secretary of State for the Colonies in London to protest. They argued that Maori supported the bill. However T. H. Smith, McLean's Assistant Native Secretary, said that there was no general desire to exchange native title for one derived from the Crown, nor were Maori prepared for the introduction of any system of individualisation of title. He denied that existing land-purchase operations had 'notoriously failed', citing the extensive land area bought in the previous ten years. He also denied that the system had resulted in frequent disputes. He reiterated McLean's assertion that not one dispute had arisen out of the department's purchases. (He ignored the fighting between Te Hapuku and other Hawkes Bay rangatira over land sales or the most recent example of Te Teira's block at Waitara.) Many disputes he believed had been caused by individuals trying to buy land and these had had to be resolved by the department's officers. As European individuals could not buy land until the passing of the 1865 act it is difficult to determine what Smith was saying. The cause of these 'quarrels' had been a policy, encouraged by McLean, of clandestine sales by individual rangatira who ignored the rights of other owners, which had developed into shooting wars with many casualties. Smith claimed that Maori saw the advantages of having colonists settle on their land but preferred treating with the Government when they decided to sell.[7] In the debate neither ministers nor the Governor and his officials considered that there was a need to consult with the Maori rangatira or to invite their participation in drafting proposals that would so intimately affect their way of life and their future well-being. Ministers assumed that they knew what Maori were thinking and believed in their own good intentions. Gore Browne, McLean, Stafford, Sewell and Richmond all displayed the same paternalism towards Maori, though they might disagree not only over policy but also over control of that policy. McLean's opposition was not always to ministerial proposals, but often to who was to implement them.

The Native Territorial Rights Bill, however, proved more controversial. This proposed that the Governor-in-Council, that is, the Governor and his ministers, award Crown grants to Maori in individual title that could be sold direct to settlers. Richmond, the Native Minister, knew little about Maori land tenure and cared nothing for Maori culture. He echoed a common view in aiming to stamp out 'beastly communism' and to 'civilise' Maori – that is, to make them adopt British practices. He intended to award a Crown title to individual Maori owners who would then be free to sell their land to settlers, with a tax of 10s an acre to provide a land fund for the Government.

The Governor objected to ministerial interference in native affairs and, with McLean's support, reserved the Native Territorial Rights Bill for the consideration of the British Government. Gore Browne looked to the Colonial Office to support his recommendation to disallow the bill, advising that he be recalled if the British Government was not prepared to support him. 'By great forbearance, constant watchfulness and command of my own temper I have hitherto been able to uphold the influence of HM Govt. and retain the respect due to it by both settlers and natives but if it were supposed that I was not well supported at home I should be powerless with both and alike useless to HM Govt. and the Colony.'[8]

Richmond's plans also drew a response from McLean in the form of a draft memorandum. As Native Secretary he supported his Governor's intention to retain imperial control of native affairs. As head of the Native Land Purchase Department, it suited him to exclude ministerial control from the detailed operations of his department. Personally, he welcomed the continuation of the control he had exercised and the independence he had enjoyed in carrying out his responsibilities. He reacted to implied criticism of his stewardship by remarking that 'someone unacquainted with the colony would suppose that for the first time the difficulties of the native question were appreciated and successfully dealt with and that legislative measures proposed need only be implemented to smooth all difficulties'. He asserted that much had already been accomplished on behalf of Maori: schools and hospitals had been established (when in fact very few schools and hospitals had been established except in a few coastal locations), magistrates stationed in native districts with native assessors and a native police organised, Maori were employed on public works and given loans to help them buy ships, mills and so on, and individualisation of title had been introduced.

Ministers saw their duty as being 'to preserve and civilise these natives and to bring the aborigines as speedily as may be under British institutions', said McLean, but they underestimated the magnitude of the undertaking. It would be futile to pass legislation when insufficient resources were available to implement their proposals. Rather than new laws, the issue was how funds could be best used for developing existing institutions. If the ministers' aim was to make fundamental changes to the existing Maori social organisation, he maintained, they had to be prepared to spend money or their scheme would fail. Attempts to apply some untried theory that ended in failure would seriously harm Maori. McLean's caution made him argue for the status quo, for building on the basis already laid, for supporting and conciliating the rangatira and thus securing them to the Government. He warned that native policy 'should not be made the subject of experimental theorising or subservient to the ends of party politics'.[9]

McLean had drawn attention to the weakness in the ministers' 1858 legislation: that the settlers were not willing to spend money on helping Maori. Ministers, for their part, saw McLean's opposition as further indication of his reluctance to surrender control of his own empire. They resented his influence and would have rejoiced at his dismissal, yet they had to acknowledge that they could not do without him. No other official could so command the respect of the Maori or resolve their disputes.

McLean also condemned ministers for their failure to appreciate the relationship between the British Government and the Maori rangatira embodied in the Treaty of Waitangi. He spelt out this responsibility in a lucid exposition. The British Government, having acknowledged the independence of the Maori tribes, had entered into a treaty by which sovereignty was passed to Queen Victoria. Ministers were claiming powers in relation to Maori that had been vested in the Crown, and these had never been delegated. There was no need to assume these powers had been forced on the British Government. 'They had to be used for the benefit of Maori which the honour of Britain was pledged to protect.' McLean continued:

> With these powers certain obligations were associated. The treaty which cedes the one imposes the other. Justice and good faith demand that the former should not be delegated without a sufficient guarantee for the due recognition and honourable fulfilment of the latter. Such a guarantee would be wanting were these powers unconditionally delegated to the colonists who might interpret these obligations differently. The intelligent consent of the New Zealanders [Maori] as one party to the treaty upon which both are founded is also necessary before such a transfer could take place.
>
> The granting to the Colonists of a system of responsible government was an act of the Imperial Government to which the natives were in no way a party, and their relations with the latter in virtue of the treaty of Waitangi are not affected by it. All the acts of the Imperial Government affecting the interests of the natives have been done with the free and intelligent consent of the latter, who as an independent power entered into a treaty with the former, ceding certain rights upon specified conditions. Neither power can divest itself of the obligations contracted by that treaty except by mutual consent without a breach of National faith.

McLean pointed out that the British Government, in its dealings with Maori, had been opposed to the settlers' assumption of rights that might injure Maori interests. He reminded ministers that the 'extinction of the race as a consequence of the occupation of the country, or as the "alternative" of their union with the English settlers was never contemplated' and referred them to the Marquis of Normanby's instructions to Captain Hobson in 1839. The 1852 constitution granted self-government to settlers. The Crown, however, had kept relations with its Maori subjects as the domain of the Governor as the colonists' representatives might not consider themselves bound to protect the Maori or to fulfil the British Government's obligations. Although it might be argued that the true interests of Maori and colonists were identical, it did not follow that members of the House of Representatives, whose special duty lay with their European constituents, would always take the wider view. 'If true of the two races that their interests are one, how much more so of the Colonists as a whole; yet who would therefore be satisfied to allow a Government chosen by three of the provinces to legislate for the remaining three?'[10]

In his approach to the Treaty of Waitangi, McLean differed from most of his fellow colonists. He saw it as a covenant that could be changed only by the agreement of both parties. The Treaty that conferred sovereignty on the Queen also required certain obligations towards Maori. These he did not spell out, though from time to time he made statements that indicated his thinking. In any action affecting Maori, including the sale of their land, the Crown should proceed only with their 'free and intelligent consent' (nevertheless, after 1854, when McLean negotiated with Maori for land on behalf of the Crown, he regularly resorted to engineered consent to secure a purchase). For McLean the Crown was committed to even-handed justice towards both races, and had a duty to elevate Maori from their state of 'savagery' and to assimilate them into British civilisation, when they would have a share, though a subordinate one, in the legislative and administrative structures of government.

McLean and the governors he served were required by the British Government, through its commitment to the Treaty of Waitangi, both to protect the Maori and to acquire their land to settle an ever-increasing flow of colonists. These objectives became irreconcilable, and the Crown's representatives in New Zealand struggled to deal with the consequences. The issue of the Queen's sovereignty found McLean on the side of those who upheld the imposition of British imperial rule by force. After the wars of the 1860s, McLean came to see himself as the one man who could achieve a reconciliation with the disaffected tribes. Did he come to believe that he and he alone could save his country?

Yet Gore Browne and McLean were confronted with a fundamental dilemma if they retained control of native affairs. To implement his policy, the Governor needed money. Apart from £7000 set aside under the civil list, Gore Browne depended on a settler-dominated parliament that was unwilling to spend any money for Maori purposes apart from land purchases. As long as Maori remained a distinct and separate people, McLean argued, they needed the protection of the British Government; as they amalgamated with the colonists, however, distinctions of race should not be perpetuated. Every effort should be made to induce the Maori gradually to assimilate with the colonists and to exchange their customary rights to land for a Crown title. So long as they remained a distinct people, they should maintain their relations with a British Government morally bound to see that the Crown's obligations were honoured.

In another draft memorandum, McLean dispassionately analysed the two peoples' perceptions of the Treaty, saying that the Maori rangatira believed they had given permissive occupation for colonists to settle in New Zealand. 'None were aware, though there were various suspicions, that the Treaty could in any way interfere with the free and independent exercise of their rights, privileges and customs', whereas the British colonists believed that the Treaty conferred 'rights of sovereignty which the natives never practically understood or recognised. With few exceptions neither party fully comprehended their actual relative position as occupants of the same country.'[11]

McLean recognised that most Maori interpreted the Treaty relationship in a manner different from the British Government. Maori sovereignty was a concept that he could not accept. God had ordained that settlers must own the land where they had come to build a better Britain. To acknowledge the concept of permissive occupation would be to place the British in an inferior relationship to Maori; it would also halt land purchasing. Furthermore, settlers would be denied the increase in value of the land they farmed. Colonists had come to New Zealand as men on the make, eager to make their fortunes in this new Britain of the south. McLean was one such man. He might empathise with Maori and understand the obligations imposed by the Treaty, but he would not allow these to stand in the way of a successful career as a government official and as a member of the landed elite.

McLean certainly understood what it meant to Maori to be parted from the land of their ancestors. He wrote in his diary in 1853 as he was preparing for the vast Wairarapa purchases:

> No doubt to the New Zealander the small handful of gold he receives were it not attended with any other contingent advantage for his land appears very inadequate in his ideas for the sacrifices he makes in transferring the extensive tracts of his country – the land of his ancestors – to foreigners who have no feelings in common with his, to whom the hills and valleys where he performed many exploits, where his parents and children maybe ended their existence, where he may have had many a death struggle to maintain his rights, where he has chased the wild animals and birds of the forest and where he has a thousand associations into which a stranger to native character cannot enter ...[12]

In referring to the 'superstitious objection' of Maori to the alienation of their land, McLean seemed to grant their culture a positive significance. This was very different from the views of the missionaries who saw a Maori 'superstitious' system as primitive and evil, soon to be banished by the light of the Christian gospel. Nowhere did McLean define what he meant by superstition, but he seems to have anticipated twentieth-century anthropologists in equating it with the myths and mysteries that make up the fabric of an indigenous belief system. Brought up on the Gaelic myths of the Highlanders, he could understand the element of myth in Maori culture. In 1851 he had written 'Superstition is more essential to upholding the fabric of society than any other ingredient with which man is endowed'. He went on to quote from Edmond Burke's *Reflections on the French Revolution* on the subject of superstition: 'By an arbitrary act to offer sudden violence to their minds and feelings; forcibly to degrade from their state and condition and to stigmatise with shame and infamy that character and those customs which before had made the measure of their happiness and honour. If to this be added an expulsion from their habitation and a confiscation of all their goods, I am not sagacious enough to discover how this despotic sport made of the feelings, conscience, prejudice and properties of men can be discriminated from the rankest tyranny.'[13] How far did McLean link these thoughts with the situation of the Maori under British imperial rule?

McLean reflected on the changeable nature of the Maori character. 'There are places in the native mind that can only be compared to mental epidemics. At one time it is so strongly impregnated with superstitious beliefs, at another it yields to acquisitiveness. Afterwards it expands itself into a species of self-denial and profuse liberality to gain a name. Sometimes it relapses into extreme covetousness but it fails to realise steadiness or consistency of character; throughout every phase ambition associated with a desire to gain personal distinction is a most prominent feature.'[14] In his land-purchase negotiations McLean was prepared to exploit these traits. Yet he was ready to acknowledge that there was 'much to admire in the New Zealander, much that might be said in their favour from their generosity, fidelity and hospitality to Europeans. Their vices are few compared to their virtues and many of these have been introduced by our countrymen.'[15]

McLean's official assessment of the relationship between the Crown and Maori was supplemented by a personal view on race relations, expressed in 1866 when he had no responsibility for the conduct of native policy. He lamented that many of the colony's highly intelligent men held the most absurd views about the Maori and wasted time discussing crude theories on how to deal with the Maori race. One group thought that all that was needed to make Maori into loyal subjects was to enforce law and order. They overlooked the fact that time was needed for Maori to appreciate the law, as it had been in England. To force English law on a 'semi-barbarous people' was not the way to make English institutions respected. The wiser course was to leave Maori alone until they became convinced of the need for English law. The clergy, for their part, believed that religion alone would civilise the Maori. Legislators put their faith in abstract theories of law, others in an 'appeal to the sword'. No one seemed to arrive at a middle way, while everyone deprecated the intentions of any party that would not 'adopt one of their pet schemes'.

Few were prepared to inquire into the past history, religion and 'superstitious Beliefs' of a people to determine the principles on which to build 'a fabric of government'. McLean identified the English weakness: 'John Bull with all his love of justice' had 'too little regard for the feelings and motives of people differently constituted from himself' to arrive at the best means of governing a people like the Maori. At the same time, McLean observed, Maori were subject to the 'same passions and infirmities' as other members of the human family. They could be easily managed by those who had studied their character. McLean was prepared to use his understanding of Maori to manipulate them. Nevertheless, the pragmatic McLean was prepared to seek to reconcile two disparate cultures.[16] These statements, the diary entry of 1851, the official paper of 1858 and the private letter in 1866, give the clearest indication of the basis of McLean's approach to the handling of Maori–Pakeha relations in the colony. This view set him apart from the majority of the colonists. His later career as a politician was marked by his failure to convert his fellow colonists to supporting his policy.

Chapter 10
Later Land Purchases 1853–1859

McLean's early purchases in the 1840s, including Wanganui and his first Hawkes Bay purchases in 1851, were relatively satisfactory. Maori were eager to sell and at least some hapu with customary interest in the land were involved in the negotiations, though some hapu and rangatira were ignored. William Williams and Samuel Williams claimed that as long as Sir George Grey and Colonel Wynyard were in New Zealand, Maori felt that they had an appeal against unjust sales, but that with their departure they had been 'handed over the tender mercies of the Land Purchase Commissioner who almost entirely disregarded their remonstrances'.[1] Land-purchase commissioners were likened to 'stinging nettles and bayonets always pricking and goading them on to sell land'.[2] The rangatira complained that McLean's land-purchasing activities had changed and that they were being subjected to new tactics aimed at subverting opposition to land sales. Some purchases had been made in secret or, when ownership was disputed, commissioners had favoured claimants wishing to sell the land. Moreover, the authority of rangatira had been disregarded if they objected to selling land, while opposing factions had been left to fight it out. Archdeacon Octavius Hadfield in giving evidence before the House in 1860 criticised McLean, saying that he 'was guided by no fixed principles in acquiring the land; that sometimes he dealt with the conquerors, when they were inclined to sell, at other times with the conquered, sometimes with the leading rangatira, at others with an inferior one; that I had heard of instances in which an inferior member of the tribe had been dealt with'.[3]

To link changes in land-purchase methods to the substitution of McLean's influence for that of Grey was incorrect. McLean had pursued Grey's policy that purchases were to be openly negotiated and with the consent of all the claimants. So long as that policy secured land sufficient for settler needs, there would have been no reason for a switch to tactics that aroused resentment and opposition. The rapid increase in the number of colonists made McLean uneasy that relations between Maori and settler would quickly deteriorate if land was not available. Settlers would be left to sit idle, gazing at Maori land which in their eyes was 'waste' land – a view that would have been reinforced by his six years' association with Taranaki settlers. The need to buy land in advance of settler demand became urgent, and McLean and his commissioners were increasing the pressure on the tribes to sell. At the same time, rangatira were becoming more reluctant to sell. They were also alarmed that, with the ever-increasing number of settlers, Maori would soon be outnumbered.

McLean's response was to push ahead with land purchases but negotiating, sometimes in secret, with those willing to sell and then waiting till opposition subsided or he could manoeuvre his way round those opposed. The result was a series of untidy and incomplete transactions that led to delays in surveying the land, subsequent negotiations and further payments to other claimants.

The rapidly growing European population increased the pressure to keep land purchases ahead of settler demand. McLean believed that he had no alternative but to extinguish all claims that were likely to give 'any trouble or annoyance' and to make every effort to acquire more land to meet the constant demand.[4] In 1855 his efforts centred on Hawkes Bay and the Wairarapa. Negotiations were conducted either directly by McLean or by Cooper acting under instructions from McLean. Land was bought, either to allow for the development and extension of settlement or for pastoralists to expand their sheep and cattle runs.

An additional factor had been the establishment of the Land Purchase Department. Now he had the additional responsibility of supervising and delegating negotiations to his district commissioners of whom there were seven by 1860. Although he left them to conduct negotiations he required detailed reports on their progress. These district commissioners were often men of inadequate ability who lacked his negotiating skills; nor had they empathy with Maori rangatira. McLean, however, protected his district commissioners, defending them and condoning their weaknesses, and he seemed reluctant to discipline them; they in turn professed their gratitude for his support, as they were entirely dependent on him for their continued employment. For example, W. N. Searancke, the new District Commissioner for Wairarapa, was criticised for shouting and swearing at rangatira. When Searancke was under attack in the House of Representatives in 1860 he acknowledged to McLean that 'I have many kindnesses to thank you for and am willing to be guided by you in all things except personal attacks'.[5]

G. S. Cooper's lack of judgement in handling Maori in Taranaki had brought on armed conflict there. Despite this McLean continued to advance his protégé, having him transferred to his own department as Land Purchase Commissioner for Hawkes Bay–Wairarapa in 1854 where, as we shall see, he was involved in negotiations. In September 1855 McLean warned Cooper to comply with the new Governor's direction that in future negotiations he was 'to use every possible caution in cases where the title is disputed or a difference of opinion exists in the minds of the Native owners'. On no account were negotiations to begin until 'such differences had been amicably settled between the parties concerned'.[6] These instructions were justified, given Cooper's previous impetuous conduct in Taranaki. In the wider context of land-purchase policy and increasing Maori resistance, they were significant. The reference to the Governor's direction is puzzling. Gore Browne had been in the country less than a fortnight at that stage and had yet to acquire an understanding of the complexities of land purchases and of Maori custom. The instructions must have originated with McLean. Did he invoke the Governor's name merely to impress Cooper? Had he presented the Governor's direction as the future policy to be followed by all district commissioners? If so, why had he himself breached this policy in recent transactions when he brought rangatira to Wellington to negotiate the purchase of Hawkes Bay land, purchases that were to be disputed by some of the owners? More than most men McLean was capable of genuine self-deception, believing himself to be guided by Divine Providence. He did not appear to see any contradiction when he himself acted contrary to the instructions issued to his own staff. McLean instructed Cooper to pay instalments on earlier purchases in Wairarapa and to complete unfinished negotiations, but not to make any new purchases.[7] McLean himself, however, initiated advance payments to rangatira for new blocks including one while in Wellington in January 1856.

McLean continued to have cause to reprimand Cooper. In March 1856 he wrote that he was 'sadly vexed and annoyed' that Cooper had not forwarded the public accounts in his charge when he knew that they were needed before the House of Representatives assembled. 'I really am at a loss to know what you were doing all this time and certainly expected much more assistance from you than you are affording.' At great inconvenience, he said, he had dealt with numberless matters which Cooper should have seen to. He did not know why Cooper, with a horse at his disposal, had not ridden to Porangahau from Ahuriri, only two days' journey, while he, McLean, was 'slaving on foot morning noon and night in Nelson going round the boundaries of reserves. It did vex me not a little to find by your note that nothing whatever was done at Ahuriri, Porangahau, Wairarapa and elsewhere. But no doubt you will be able to explain the matter to me at Auckland. I have had my scold now.'[8] Cooper dispatched an injured reply forthwith, lamenting that, after receiving such official and private letters, he felt that he could expect no mercy when he reached Auckland. He would get everything in order to hand to head office. Then, 'if it so please His Excellency and yourself to dismiss me from the public service for disobedience of orders and for working to the best of my poor ability and weak judgement to prevent a Native war at Ahuriri, to open 100,000 acres to settlers and to arrange the Porangahau question, if I say, for taking these responsibilities on my shoulders and so missing the steamer I am to be relieved from all further trouble in Her Majesty's Service, why I must only try to survive the blow and earn a livelihood by shepherding or otherwise as best I can.'[9] He justified the delay by the need for caution rather than hasty action that could have ended in a 'second Taranaki business', his ill-considered action that resulted in an intertribal skirmish and the death of Rawiri.

Most of the South Island land had been bought before McLean became head of the Native Land Purchase Department in 1854. Governor Grey negotiated the Wairau purchase from Ngati Toa in 1847 on the grounds of possession by right of conquest. In 1848 he went to the South Island to negotiate with Ngai Tahu for the purchase of land south of Kaiapoi to Otago, excluding reserves, for £2000. He instructed Kemp to complete the negotiations for the purchase, but the reserves were never allocated.

In 1853, following Grey's instruction that no land could be bought in the northern half of the South Island without the agreement of the 'conquering chiefs' in the North Island, McLean bought the remaining claims of Ngati Toa in the Waipounamu purchase for £5000. Ngati Toa would receive £2000 immediately. The remaining £3000 was to be paid in instalments to 'conjoint' tribes 'Ngatiawa, Ngatikoata, Ngatirarua, Rangitane and Ngai Tahu'. It was agreed that Ngati Toa would meet with the South Island tribes in 1854 to decide how the £3000 would be divided and on the land to be reserved from the sale.[10] In December 1854 when McLean held a second meeting with Ngati Toa at Porirua and paid over the remaining purchase money, he extracted a promise that the Ngati Toa leaders would go with him to the South Island to influence the tribes to accept the purchase.

McLean first went to Taranaki in 1855 to offer to buy South Island land to which Te Ati Awa had no intention to return. He was successful, the signatures including that of Wiremu Kingi. In November McLean went to Waikanae and negotiated the sale of land round Tory Channel. All these negotiations involved non-residents that had some customary interest in the land and left the resident claimants at a disadvantage. Meantime, McLean had sent surveyors to the Sounds area to lay off reserves. Local Maori became more alarmed at this move, arguing that their consent must first be obtained.

In 1855–1856 McLean made payments and arranged reserves for Ngai Tahu and other South Island tribes, though he regarded the Waipounamu purchase as already settled by Kemp. McLean took the view that, unlike the North Island, where he believed the tribes had a valid claim to occupy all the land, the South Island was virtually unoccupied, although he did acknowledge unfinished business over Ngai Tahu reserves. Whereas in the North Island he cultivated the friendship of the leading rangatira, in the South Island he made little effort to become acquainted and often left negotiations to his district commissioners. McLean did not involve himself as directly in South Island land-purchase negotiations as he did in the North Island. When he did visit the South Island he had less time for negotiations and departed leaving unfinished business.

Not until November 1855 – and then at the prompting of the new Governor – did McLean meet with the Golden Bay and Tasman Bay rangatira. McLean held that the land had already been sold and that he was merely extinguishing outstanding claims, and he offered £600 for the rangatira ceding all their lands in the South Island.[11] In January 1856, McLean went to Marlborough to negotiate. He noted that the original Rangitane owners in the Wairau area had sought compensation as Ngati Toa conquerors (in about 1825) had not recognised their claims. McLean agreed that they had been overlooked. Rangitane Maori asked for £2000; McLean got them to accept £100 but with 'ample reserves'. The reserve block, ten miles long and two miles wide running from Te Wairau to Robin Hood Bay, contained only 40,000 acres of good land and was surrounded by swamp, useless for Europeans to farm. McLean considered that there was sufficient land to sustain the 120 Maori who lived there. 'Besides they are the chief cultivators of land here; and to stint them in their reserves would not only be unjust but very wrong as a matter either of policy or economy.'[12] The reserves when granted however, did not extend to the agreed area.

At Waikawa, six days later, Te Ati Awa and Puketapu offered land for sale. Witi Kau, principal rangatira of Tory Channel, asked for £6000 for land from the entrance to Waitiruru, a hill above Anakiwa. Puketapu asked for £3800 for Totaranui from its entrance, including Port Gore, to Waitiruru. Bargaining went on for three days until McLean took the principal rangatira aside and pointed out that their reserves would be large and contain some of the best land of a very poor, hilly region; therefore his price would not exceed £500. In fact the reserves when granted proved to be very small. The rangatira left, complaining that this sum would not amount to sixpence for each of them. McLean would not budge, saying that they could either accept or reject the offer. The following day a deputation of rangatira returned, prepared to accept £1000. Finally, they were forced to agree to McLean's terms. He saw this as an important and final settlement of the claims of Te Ati Awa to a part of the country that had many historical associations including the recent conquest of the original inhabitants by Te Rauparaha, Te Pehi and Te Ati Awa. Captain Cook had anchored there; it was a great resource for shipping, containing the finest harbour in the island, as well as the 'scenes of many revolting cruelties and cannibalism in older times'. McLean returned to his vision for

New Zealand: that 'its hills and dales become the future home of a great and glorious happy and contented people; who will treat with kind indulgence any of the aboriginal remnants who may reside among them and treat them with consideration; whose power although once a wild courageous race is diminishing almost as fast as the snows of the Kaikouras – with all their vices they have very redeeming qualities'.[13] While he saw himself as the benevolent protector of Maori, today the Waitangi Tribunal findings assess his role in a different light. The South Island purchases meant that the Government had acquired the land with its substantial resources at a cost of £6787 while Maori were left with small reserves inadequate for them to engage in any pastoral economy.

From the new purchases, including both sides of Pelorus Sound, McLean assessed that 35,000 acres would be available for sale at 10s an acre. There could be at least 68,000 acres out of a purchase comprising a quarter of the South Island, or 8 million acres, from which the Government could expect to realise £34,000 while total expenses were estimated at £21,500. This would leave a significant amount available for immigration, besides 'settling the native question' and acquiring mineral wealth estimated at £11,000. The outcome would be most important by 'securing the various bays and harbours in the Straits and Queen Charlotte Sound; and establishing without future difficulty with the native tribes the sway of British rule over the whole of the Island; and enabling more British colonists to find a home in many of the parts that will be thrown open; as well as in the various undiscovered tracts of land hereafter found in this part of the Island'. McLean recommended that Europeans who had bought land from Maori, and whose claims had been acknowledged by them and were not excessive, should have title granted without 'vexatious delay or heavy expenses'.[14]

Except for Nelson and Marlborough, McLean left negotiations to his district commissioners and rarely intervened in their negotiations especially with James Mackay, one of his more capable officers. In 1858, McLean instructed James Mackay to extinguish Ngai Tahu customary rights to the Kaikoura block of 2 million acres and the Arahura block of 7 million acres for £150 for each block.[15] Mackay managed to reduce Ngai Tahu's asking price down to £300 for the Kaikoura block and T. H. Kemp completed the purchase in March 1859, including 5575 acres in reserves. McLean seemed to view this land as waste land already belonging to the Crown by annexation of the South Island. This was followed by a payment to Poutini Ngai Tahu for their rights in the Arahura block, which had been neglected in the original 1848 purchase.

If McLean were to be judged on the outcome of these South Island and later Hawkes Bay purchases he would not be found to be an effective land purchase officer. Faced with growing settler demand for land and increasing

Maori reluctance to part with their land, McLean abandoned his practice of the 1840s and early Hawkes Bay purchases where, by and large, he had secured agreement to sell from all those with a customary interest with the land on offer and had ensured that the boundaries and reserves had been clearly defined.

In the 1850s McLean began negotiations with those prepared to sell, whether resident or non-resident, minor or major customary rights holders. The result was unfinished and untidy agreements; sometimes several payments for the same block of land had to be made over the years to satisfy the rightful claimants. Archdeacon Hadfield had condemned McLean's negotiating approach as guided by no fixed principles.

This change of policy was set out by McLean when he appeared before the Board of Inquiry into Native Affairs in 1856 when he said that the initial payment went to the general and more remote claimants and the subsequent payments to the real owners.[16] He did not say that this represented a change of policy or that he was negotiating first with a minority willing to sell.

McLean's land purchases in Hawkes Bay and Wairarapa between 1853 and 1859 show the changes in his approach and how these negotiations began to unravel. McLean had identified the region as the most fertile and attractive in the North Island and where he intended to buy land for himself – an additional incentive to press on with acquiring Maori land.

In 1853 land-purchase negotiations centred on the Wairarapa. McLean recommended to the Governor that operations should extend into the best grazing districts as this should eventually lead to possession of the entire plain. The country south of Hawkes Bay and east of the interior ranges was extensive, while the native population did not exceed 3000 or, he estimated, rather less than 1000 to each 1 million acres.[17] McLean's breakthrough in Wairarapa came when Ngati Kahungunu agreed to sell land on the coast. In June 1853 the deed of sale for the Castlepoint block (275,000 acres), bounded by the Waimata and Whareama rivers and inland by the Puketoi Range, was signed by some 300 Maori. The payment of £2500 was to be spread over three years. (Within four months McLean and James Kelham, a Wellington merchant, had arranged a Crown lease of 10,000 acres of this land at Akitio.)

McLean was fortunate that, following Colenso's conversion to dogged opposition to land sales, his influence over the East Coast tribes had diminished by recent events. Bishop Selwyn had suspended him from his duties after evidence of his adultery with a Maori woman, while a complaint of assault on a rangatira, Tipuna, over the custody of Colenso's half-caste child led McLean, in his capacity as magistrate, to charge, convict and fine Colenso.[18]

Not until his farewell visit to the East Coast late in 1853 did Governor

Grey begin wider negotiations with Ngati Kahungunu. Although Grey was credited with the success of purchases on the East Coast, it was McLean who had prepared the way. Grey landed at Palliser Bay and spent a week in Wairarapa, encouraging and receiving offers from rangatira to sell their lands, before moving on to Hawkes Bay. McLean was left to follow up and arrange the details of the sales, boundaries and payments. He journeyed with a 200- to 300-strong Maori escort, including Te Hapuku and other rangatira. Two packhorses carried the gold, from which he made small advances on the blocks of land offered to him each night – an operation described as McLean's 'potato planting'. As no deeds of sale had been signed, these payments might be held to be bribes as an inducement to sell.

Between June 1853 and January 1854, McLean made forty-one purchases totalling around 1.5 million acres in the Wairarapa at a cost of £23,547.[19] (See Appendix 5.) This so stretched the Crown's financial resources that the Governor had to make a personal loan of £2000 to enable the transactions to proceed. Recent research suggests that the initial surveyors' estimates were inaccurate – multiplying the length of the block in miles by the width and converting to acres.[20] Turton's Maori Deeds records that 2,038,099 acres were bought in Wairarapa for an average of 2¾d an acre. However, the whole Wairarapa region amounted to some 2 million acres and in 1854 some areas still remained in Maori ownership. Bagnall's estimate of 1,500,000 acres seems more valid.[21] In the absence of surveyors, McLean made the initial payment on a deed of sale that contained no exact definition of boundaries. He hoped that the survey would be completed before subsequent payments had to be made. The immediate consequence was that the Crown did not know the definite acreage of land that it had bought, while the Maori sellers could not identify the exact boundaries of their land nor the boundaries of their reserves.[22] Among the forty-one purchases made at this time was Castlepoint (275,000 acres), bought in June 1853. McLean reported that it had been difficult to get the tribes to sell and even more so to secure the land at the agreed price. He had told the rangatira that he thought the price too high and that the Governor might object, and that therefore they should offer an additional block of land. This they agreed to do, 'sooner than I should be subject to blame for giving too much'. Although he relished the regard in which he was held by the Maori, McLean did not hesitate to resort to such a tactic to reduce the price. The land had been secured at 'a wonderfully cheap rate' he told the Governor.[23] He believed that Maori had sold almost all the land they intended to sell. The Wairarapa purchases were distinctive in that 5 per cent of the subsequent return from the land sales to Europeans was to be paid back to the Maori vendors. Grey intended that this money should be used for schools, flour mills, hospitals and annuities to rangatira.[24] No payments were made until 1870.

In Wairarapa, McLean's negotiations differed from his 1851 transactions in Hawkes Bay. There he had brought together all those who had an interest in the land on offer and worked to get a consensus. Payment was made only on the signing of the deed of sale. In Wairarapa, however, McLean opened negotiations with one person who was eager to sell, and used this offer to pressure other legitimate owners to agree to sell. He made advances to rangatira before any agreement had been reached and then refused to call off the negotiations or to take back money that had been advanced.[25] McLean took advantage of the presence of Te Hapuku and other rangatira in Wellington to help him buy land in Wairarapa. That McLean made forty-one purchases in seven months suggests that negotiations were hasty and incomplete. Documentation for reserves was inadequate or absent.

Much of the 560,000 acres purchased by September 1853 had been indifferent land, McLean noted, but the real advantage was to have opened the country at a first cost to the Crown of less than 3d an acre. He told Dr Isaac Featherston, the first Superintendent of the new Wellington province, that he had secured large tracts of land, including the Forty Mile Bush, for £2000. To buy the unalienated parts of Wairarapa and Hawkes Bay would require, he estimated, a further £5000, 'but never again would there be such an opportunity'.[26]

In Wairarapa, Maori had sold three-quarters of their land, about 1,500,000 acres, between June 1853 and January 1854. Nevertheless, between November 1854 and February 1856 McLean kept up the pressure, acquiring one-third of the land remaining in Maori possession.[27] He made advance payments before any surveys had taken place, but final settlements were postponed until the actual size and detailed boundaries had been fixed – a departure from earlier purchases. The signatures on the deeds were few and some were signed in Wellington.[28]

In 1858, faced with growing opposition in Hawkes Bay, McLean resumed purchasing in Wairarapa. Searancke, the new District Commissioner, told McLean that he intended working down the Wairarapa Valley buying up all the small pieces of land as he went. The amount of land was not great, but it would help to prevent disputes over boundaries. Searancke had become exasperated with the Wairarapa tribes' continuing to dispute past purchases. Searancke complained that he had 'tried in a quiet way to do business with them' but had found them 'most atrocious schemers. They are all so much in debt and so completely out of credit that they are completely out of their wits' end for money.'[29] As in Hawkes Bay, rangatira were caught in the debt trap and would have to succumb to the pressure of the land-purchase officials. Searancke complained that 'a more unmitigated set of scoundrels than your Wairarapa pets it has never been my fortune or misfortune to meet'.

McLean's untidy and prolonged transactions, combined with an inability to get the land surveyed, frustrated the Wellington Provincial Government. It could not subdivide the blocks to make the land available for settlers and, meanwhile, was deprived of the money that would accrue from the sale of Crown land. William Fox, a member of the Provincial Council, complained 'these transactions have been of so very loose a character and so much is said to turn on the promises of Mr. McLean's that the terms of the Deed are no guarantee of the facts'. Dr Isaac Featherston, the Provincial Superintendent, remarked that difficulties arising from McLean's purchases were an 'almost daily occurrence'.[30] These situations arose from McLean's attempts to ward off disputing claimants where he had not gained consent to sell from all those with a customary interest in the land. This confusion was compounded by McLean's well-known habit of procrastination. Whether his failure to fulfil his promises arose from this trait or from a conscious attempt to mislead cannot be ascertained. He preferred a 'taihoa' policy in the hope that time might allow for the resolution of a difficult issue as he tried to wear down opposition. Yet the continuing failure to fulfil the promises given generated more discontent.

In Hawkes Bay by 1854 McLean had abandoned his earlier practice of open negotiations to buy land with the consent of all those who held a customary right. A factor in his thinking may have been his desire to obtain his own landholding in the district. Evidence for this is a letter from Alfred Domett, then Commissioner of Crown Lands at Ahuriri, in July 1854 saying that he would do all he could for him about a run but 'you must let me know your intentions respecting runs explicitly and rely on my forwarding your interests as much as I honestly can … I want you to concoct some plan for persuading these natives to sell their lands. The district will never do till that be done.'[31]

In April 1855 McLean visited Hawkes Bay and Poverty Bay. Staying at a settler's home north of Napier, he rejoiced at spending a Sunday in the company of 'intelligent and pious Scotchmen' with such a good knowledge of biblical and religious books. He spent the day reading Kitto's lectures on the Book of Job and finished the evening reading 'Family Prayers' and a 'Sermon on a Future State' by Dr Chalmers, the much-admired Free Church leader. His diary concluded: 'A day in thy sacred Courts O Lord is better than a thousand spent in idleness and sin however charming the allurements. What peace what holiness what contentment await the holy keeping of the blessed Sabbath Day.'[32]

The following day he made the final payments on the Mohaka block. At Waikare, when Maori complained at the small 'utu' they received for their land. McLean reminded them that they had agreed to the price. How to divide the money among themselves was their decision, he said, and if they thought the Mohaka people had too much they should talk to them and not complain to him. The land now belonged to the Europeans and, though they might think the payment small, they would have settlers coming among them to give their produce increased value. The rangatira Pikai Tohu lamented the loss of his land: 'mounted on his brown steed, he wheeled round, halted, his eyes flashing like fire and said, "McLean! Look at this large country! Look at its extent and look at the small payment for it! Only five hundred pounds for this large country! It is only a mouthful swallowed up by such a small compensation". With several other pertinent remarks the poor old chief seemed to feel as if his greatness was diminished to enrich the Pakeha.' McLean was pleased to have won him over as a friend, though he gave credit to a settler named Anderson and his nephew, 'whose acts of integrity and firmness towards the natives have a great effect in subduing their angry passions and making them good subjects of Her Majesty. Good settlers are unquestionably the best missionaries for the present transition state of the natives and may we have many who will perform the task with equal success as they are doing.'[33]

Once Alfred Domett, who had been Commissioner of Crown Lands in Hawkes Bay and had acquired property there, was elected to the General Assembly in 1856, McLean looked to him to advance the interests of the Ahuriri runholders by advocating a loan to buy more land in the district. McLean criticised frugal government policy, complaining that he had to take a heavy personal responsibility in purchasing lands. Having acquired nearly all the Maori land in the South Island, he said, those members objected to the Government spending money to buy land in the North Island.

The intervention of the King movement was also hampering McLean's land purchases. In November Cooper warned McLean that the Ngati Tuwharetoa rangatira Iwikau had been visiting Hawkes Bay and 'had done much mischief' by encouraging opposition to land sales. Iwikau had called a great meeting at Taupo to win support for halting land sales and encouraging squatters to lease land directly from Maori, and he believed several Hawkes Bay rangatira – Te Moananui, Tareha and Karaitiana – were to be present. He blamed the Anglican missionary T. S. Grace for stirring up trouble.[34]

In 1857 King movement delegates from the Waikato had attempted to prevent the sale of the Ngapaeruru block by taking money that the local tribe had received from McLean. The delegates offered to return the payment, but McLean declined. He did not recognise their right to interfere and would deal only with the real owners.

Increasing reluctance to sell more land by the Hawkes Bay rangatira drove McLean to the same kind of frantic and unfinished negotiations that he had shown in his dealings with South Island tribes. There was the further complicating factor that Searancke had observed. Ngati Kahungunu rangatira found themselves caught in a debt trap. Storekeepers had encouraged rangatira to take goods on credit. When the income from the sale of their agriculture produce was insufficient to pay their debts storekeepers acquired a mortgage over their land. When the rangatira could not meet the repayments they were forced to sell their land.

From 1854 McLean, with Te Hapuku's support, sometimes bought land in secret from those parties prepared to sell and excluded other rightful claimants who were then forced to sell to protect their interests. These deeds of sale show only a handful of signatures. Tautane (70,000 acres, thirty-two signatures, for £1000), Okawa (16,000 acres, four signatures, for £800), Kahuranaki (22,000 acres, four signatures, for £1100) and Te Umuopa (500 acres, five signatures, for £300) were sold by Te Hapuku, Hine-i-paketia, Hori Niania and other rangatira in 1854 while they were in Wellington helping McLean to buy land in Wairarapa.[35]

In 1855 McLean bought Waimarama (32,000 acres) and Ngaruroro (5000 acres, six signatures for £200) blocks in a secret deal while in Wellington, the Ngaruroro deed being signed by Te Hapuku and five other rangatira, including Hine and Hori Niania. (Cooper was unable to conclude the secret deal on Waimarama.) Later in the same year, the deeds of Otapahi and Te Totara were signed by Te Hapuku and four others while they were guests of McLean in Auckland. All these sales were later disputed as Maori opposition grew to Te Hapuku's initiating sales of land in which he had little or no customary right.[36]

McLean was prepared to wait for some years for possession, continuing to negotiate, sometimes making more than one payment for the same land. Three Hawkes Bay purchases – those of Porangahau, Tautane and Takapau or Omarutaiari blocks – illustrate McLean's tactics from 1853. With the Tautane purchase, McLean had neither visited the district nor consulted with the occupants of the block nor carried out any investigation there to determine who had claims to this block in which Te Hapuku appeared to have no customary right. McLean paid £1000 for 70,000 acres. References to a 5 per cent resale clause in the deed suggest that this was seen as a continuation of the Wairarapa purchases as the thirty-two signatures to the deed included some Wairarapa rangatira. In 1857 Cooper visited Porangahau and found the hapu objecting to the sale of Tautane and Hori's block (Te Umuopa). Cooper insisted that the money could not be returned but tacitly acknowledged the injustice of the sale, noting that the sellers were only secondary claimants and that none of the money had reached the principal claimants. Further payments had to be made on Tautane in 1858 and 1863 before all the rightful claimants were satisfied. In March 1858 when a further payment of £500 was made on Tautane, ninety signatures were obtained compared with thirty-two in 1854. This time the 5 per cent clause was excluded from the deed. In 1863 a final payment was made to Karaitiana for £150.

A mutually advantageous relationship had developed between McLean and J. D. Ormond, the Hawkes Bay pastoralist who was to remain his loyal lieutenant and close friend until McLean's death. Ormond had first come to McLean's notice when, aged eighteen, as private secretary to Lieutenant-Governor Eyre he was invited by McLean to join a land-purchasing expedition to Manawatu–Rangitikei in 1849.

Involved in illegal squatting on Maori land at Porangahau in Hawkes Bay since 1853, Ormond cultivated McLean's friendship in an attempt to protect his interests. In July 1857 he wrote privately to McLean to justify his illegal action. Having been private secretary to Eyre, he was aware that his action would not compromise McLean, he wrote, 'beyond an intimation that it would have been better not to have done so. Whilst on my part my very existence was at stake and there is no knowing what a man will do when he is fighting for his all. I am afraid my explanation is not so satisfactory as I could wish it. Still I trust the affair will make no difference in the friendly feelings you have so often evinced for me during the last few years.'[37]

Two days later Ormond expressed 'extreme pleasure that you are settling this long protracted purchase – good and welcome news it was to myself and the other *illegal* squatters settled here'. He suggested to McLean that the half of the bush area that the local hapu had agreed to sell should be that which was accessible for the settlers. Of the flat land, part was to be reserved for Maori, 'but the said flats are useless to the natives and are everything to me. I think a word from you wd. induce them to give them up. If you can do so you will render me a very great service'.[38] Ormond did not consider that if local Maori were to become part of the new pastoral economy, they too would require the use of these same flats.

The purchase of the Porangahau block was not completed until March 1858 when 145,000 acres were bought for £3000. This sale was criticised by Bishop William Williams. McLean responded that the Ngapaeruru block at Porangahau had been under offer to the Government for several years and, as it had been occupied by two pastoralists (one being Ormond), McLean thought it was desirable to buy the land. He said that he had been approached by two rangatira saying that their tribe wished to sell and asking for an advance payment. Uncertain whether they had the authority of their tribe, McLean had turned to Karaitiana, who advised him to pay part of the money and settle the question when he met the tribe. McLean had waited several days before giving £300 to the rangatira, Paora, to be taken to Porangahau and held until he arrived to apportion the money among the claimants, when he would pay a further £400. McLean denied that he tried to buy the land from two individuals or indeed that it had been bought at all. Although the parties had signed a deed ceding the sale, the transaction had still to be completed. McLean also condemned Bishop Williams for interfering in matters unconnected with his duties. If the Bishop had further criticisms of land purchases he would need to support them with 'something better than mere hearsay evidence derived from members of the Anti-land-selling Leagues and their sympathisers'.

McLean had to make three payments on the Takapau or Omarutaiari block of 11,700 acres, the first to Urupene in 1858 of £100. Two further payments were made while he was in Hawkes Bay in 1859, £50 in July and £400 in August. The signatories numbered two and four respectively. According to Samuel Williams, Renata Kawepo had complained that the owners had approached McLean telling him that this block, was not for sale as they had already sold most of their land and later they had found out that payment had been made secretly to two individuals with the remainder opposed the sale. Williams was with McLean when some Maori were leaving and heard McLean say that 'If people go away and are not present when I make the purchase their absence will give consent'. Williams was confident that McLean did not ask any of the opponents whether they had withdrawn their opposition before he paid money to the two sellers.

McLean denied Williams's version of the sale of the Takapau block, insisting that the block had been bought from the acknowledged owners after considerable discussion. Some had opposed the sale as members of the anti-land-selling league, although they admitted Hineipaketia's right to dispose of the land. McLean argued that he had to either admit the right of the anti-land-selling league from Waikato to forbid the sale or pay the rightful owners. He pointed out that this sale was later ratified by a large part of Ngai Tahu, a hapu of Ngati Kahungunu to whom the opponents of the sale belonged. The deed had been signed not by two but by four persons, said McLean, and had been witnessed by the principal rangatira of the district as well as the District Commissioner, Cooper, so the money could not have been paid secretly. McLean did not explain why there were only four signatures to the deed of sale compared with 200 or 300 signatures on the deeds of the earlier Hawkes Bay purchases.

Williams asserted that it had become evident to Maori that the Government was trying to provoke a quarrel with them so that it might have some pretext for depriving them of their lands and 'they declared that their heads and their land should go together'. They had fully made up their minds to resist any further survey of the last two purchases and had built a pa at Takapau with that intention 'so that we might have had the war here instead of at Taranaki'.

Cooper continued negotiations in 1856 and 1857. He proposed that the Maori sell all the land from Pariwahu to Waiamata and inland from Hori's block (this included Te Umuopa) and that money already paid out would remain as compensation for those who had signed the deeds. The hapu agreed, and demanded £5000. Cooper responded that McLean had set the price at £1400 but, as they had extended the boundaries making at least 100,000 acres available, and as the reserves they wanted were moderate, he thought McLean could ask the Governor to agree to £2000. At the end of a week of negotiation, the lowest price Maori would accept was £3500.[39]

McLean pressed Tareha to sell two blocks needed for the expansion of the township of Napier – land between the south side of Mataruahou and the Tutaekuri River. The township of Clive had been established when Te Moananui sold 200 acres at Waipureku, while the sale of Matau-a-Maui (29,000 acres) and Te Mata (16,000 acres) opened more land for pastoralists south of Napier.

McLean's actions in favouring Te Hapuku in buying land angered the other rangatira who felt their mana was diminished, especially as they too were ready to negotiate. Their frustration was compounded as Te Hapuku sold land in which they held the major customary rights. In March 1856 Cooper was struggling with Te Hapuku's offer to sell Tawhara's block when Te Moananui, Tareha and Karaitiana Takamoana were all opposed. Cooper advised McLean he felt that he could not make a payment as long as the three rangatira made it clear that they would view this as a *casus belli*. On the other hand, Te Hapuku insisted that unless payment was made, he would not accept money for the agreed sale of the Ruataniwha or Aorangi blocks and would prevent settlers from occupying these lands.

After difficult negotiations[40] Cooper reached agreement on payment for the Ruataniwha block and for the right bank of the Ngaruroro River. However, the next day, Cooper alleged, Te Hapuku tried to cheat by giving wrong names, which were those on the left bank. There was another dispute when Maori insisted that an amount of £2000 was to be paid for two blocks, South Ruataniwha and Aorangi, whereas Cooper had intended to divide the money over four blocks. The argument continued all day until he gave in and paid the money for the two blocks only. In 1856 two blocks only were purchased in Hawkes Bay, Aorangi (38,000 acres) and Maraekakaho (30,000 acres).

In 1857 Cooper had to deal with more disputes over payments in Hawkes Bay. As arranged with McLean, the sum of £1000 was to be paid for his Maraekakaho block but some Maori with a claim to the most valuable part of the block did not trust Te Hapuku and would accept the money only from Cooper. He believed that Te Moananui was deliberately refusing to take £1000 for the Matau-a-Maui block hoping to gain a pretext for taking back part of that block. Again Cooper saw the hand of Iwikau in this move. The inland part of the Ahuriri block was also disputed by a small but powerful hapu, Ngati Hineuru, who were backed by Iwikau, as McLean had excluded them from the 1851 negotiations. They pressed their claim, saying that they had received no payment.

In 1857 McLean had to deal with complaints from Te Hapuku and Te Moananui. Te Hapuku accused Cooper of siding with Te Moananui, complaining that 'Mr. Cooper is a bad man and a teasing man, the words of right he makes wrong and the wrong he makes right'. He asserted that Cooper and Te Moananui had taken his land – 'that land was my bald head'.[41] Te Moananui for his part alleged that Te Hapuku was taking payment for land that belonged to Te Moananui. He appealed to the Governor and McLean:

> you two must come that you see the good and evil of this place Heretaunga come you two and bring money a great quantity so that these places may soon be given into your hands so that evil may cease because all this evil arises from the lands which cause these people to live in an uneasy way so that those of your children may also live in peace and that our thoughts may rest.

The Native Minister, C. W. Richmond, minuted the letters asking McLean to go to investigate. Although it was unlikely that Cooper would side with Te Moananui, he thought the enmity between the two rangatira demanded McLean's speedy presence.

McLean and Cooper continued to negotiate with Te Hapuku for the purchase of the Heretaunga Plains, despite opposition from Te Moananui and Tareha whose hapu had their main interest in that area. The Revd Samuel Williams of Te Aute remarked that McLean had been known to say when buying land that he felt quite secure as long as he got 'Old Bunker' (Te Hapuku) to sign the deed and that Te Hapuku was knowing enough to see how far he was supported. Hawkes Bay Maori were complaining that the Commissioner was purchasing their land from Te Hapuku and they would not submit to it any longer but would 'risk their own heads in trying to put a stop to such proceedings'.[42]

Conflict between Te Hapuku and Ngati Kahungunu rangatira came to a head when Te Hapuku began to build a pa at Pakiaka Bush near Pakowhai, north of the Ngaruroro River. This site was outside his hapu's land, which lay to the south between the Ngaruroro and Tutaekuri rivers. Fighting broke out. There were casualties on both sides, with further skirmishes and consequent casualties in October and December. When McLean arrived at Napier on 27 December 1857, he found the dispute still unsettled, despite the efforts of Samuel Williams, Cooper and influential settlers. They had not succeeded in persuading Te Hapuku, who held that his honour was involved, to retire from the disputed territory. McLean remained at Napier for most of January and February, meeting separately with Te Hapuku on seven occasions over sixteen days and with Te Moananui and Tareha on another five days. Cooper and Grindell, another official, were also engaged. The extent of this mediation showed the care and patience with which McLean approached his dealings with the rangatira. Samuel Williams described how Renata Kawepo reproached McLean, saying that he had hoped to have done with firearms for ever and never thought he would have to take up arms to protect himself from the acts of the Government.

> 'Did you,' he said, 'consider that Hapuku, being a non-professor of religion, must be supported by you but that I being a professor of religion had my hands tied and was open game for you both to practice upon? Was religion sent to this country to open the way for imposition? It is useless,' he continued, 'for you to try and soften me down nothing but justice will satisfy me – Give my rights and I will have done with these things' at the same time throwing two cartridge boxes against the wall of his house.

Samuel Williams admired 'Mr. McLean's manliness in admitting that the error or the wrong was on the part of the Govt'.[43] This was unusual. McLean would rarely admit that he was wrong.

That McLean had acquired land for himself in this district gave an added incentive to his mediation. He feared that the region's development and his own prosperity would be hampered for years if fighting continued. He had a detachment of the 65th Regiment sent to Napier to reassure the settlers. His efforts succeeded. Te Hapuku agreed to evacuate the pa as soon as possible; Te Moananui promised not to intervene while the evacuation took place. Two months elapsed before Te Hapuku moved off the disputed land. Meanwhile, tribal deputations from Wairoa, Wairarapa and Manawatu arrived to mediate between the disputing parties. Not until March did Te Hapuku complete his evacuation by burning the pa and, accompanied by McLean and Cooper, moving south to Poukawa. As the rivers were too low to allow the passage of loaded canoes, McLean decided that the Government should assist Te Hapuku. He organised goods to be shipped from Auckland for the rangatira, hired drays from settlers and arranged for the side-cuttings on the road to Te Aute to be improved to allow the passage of carts as far as Poukawa. Until the move was completed McLean was obliged to remain in Hawkes Bay, as both parties saw his presence as the only guarantee that the agreement would be honoured.[44]

Gore Browne had some misgiving about departing from the principle of non-interference; yet, if Te Hapuku was killed, the Government would lose 'a firm and influential friend'. Te Hapuku was 'entitled to every protection that could be afforded without incurring a native war' he asserted. He proposed to his ministers that troops be sent and Te Hapuku advised to hold out until they arrived. Te Moananui should be told that 'though the British Government took no share in native feuds it would always afford shelter to the distressed'.[45] It is unlikely that this offer would have been made if Te Hapuku had been an opponent of land sales.

While McLean waited at Napier for Te Hapuku to move south, he overcame opposition to the formation of an overland mail route north through Taupo. Te Rangihiroa, the old rangatira of Ngati Hineuru living in that part of the Ahuriri block through which the road would pass, demanded payment from McLean for his interest in the block. McLean refused to renegotiate the settlement. When Te Moananui, who had received payment for the Ahuriri block (though admitting the justice of Te Rangihiroa's claim) protested that he had no money left to hand over, McLean advanced £50, on condition that the old rangatira renounce his claim. Te Rangihiroa's brother accepted, but would not uplift the money until Ngati Tuwharetoa and other tribes had been consulted. McLean noted in his journal that the 'natives have had several meetings which so far gratified their pride and weakens their opposition'.[46] The outcome was that work began on a road which McLean saw as of vital importance to the colony because it would link Hawkes Bay and Auckland.

After the 1857 conflict at Pakiaka, the Ngati Kahungunu rangatira, except for Te Hapuku, combined to prevent secret sales of land. Samuel Williams quoted them, 'Exert yourselves to build a whata [an elevated store] to keep the provisions out of reach of the Dogs (those natives who sold land by stealth) and appoint a keeper for the whata by whom alone the provisions may be served out'.[47] In September 1858 the rangatira decided that the 'system of selling land through the rangatira should be abandoned and that any one who should hereafter be guilty of selling another's property or of misappropriating any payment for land should be punished with death'.[48] At the same time, writing to the Governor, they made it clear that the blame for selling land without authority lay with Te Hapuku rather than with the Crown. The rangatira wished to retain control over management of their lands themselves rather than rely on the Government to intervene.[49] Such was the strength of McLean's mana that he escaped their censure.

In April 1859 a meeting of rangatira at Pa Whakairo at Waiohiki agreed to set up a runanga. They showed significant support for a Maori king without going so far as proclaiming allegiance. The runanga decided that it would not allow further land sales in Hawkes Bay. In 1859 the sale of Moeangiangi block was vetoed by the Hawkes Bay runanga and it took three separate deeds to satisfy claimants. At the same time the runanga demanded that settlers pay market rates for their illegal grazing on Maori land, while pastoralists who allowed their sheep to stray and graze on Maori land would be compelled to pay 'grass money' or have their stock impounded. McLean and his brother Alexander became subject to these fines.

Rangatira continued to protest. Bishop Williams reported that Renata Kawepo wrote to the Superintendent of Hawkes Bay province in 1860:

> Listen while I tell you of the last errors of Mr McLean after we had wiped his former ones [referring to Omarutaiari and Ngapaeruru]. You appear to suppose that by getting hold of a single individual you can gain an advantage over him. Hereafter whenever a majority shall consent to a sale it shall take place. Let us have no more blundering all our troubles have arisen from faulty working and on this account it was that the door of selling was shut. But when the system of buying is amended the door will be opened that the sales may be conducted on a regular plan. Whenever the Government shall have laid down some equitable system of land purchase and when calm is once restored, then the tribes who are for selling will sell their lands under a properly regulated system.[50]

Unlike in Taranaki and Waikato, Hawkes Bay rangatira were prepared to negotiate further sale of land if they were satisfied that negotiations were openly conducted and proper consent obtained.

If Hawkes Bay rangatira were alarmed at McLean's land-purchasing activities for the Crown, settlers were ready to condemn him for pandering to Maori. A letter to the *Hawke's Bay Herald* fulminated: 'We have allowed strong stockaded villages to spring up instead of uprooting them as foul obnoxious weeds ... We have fed this people with gold and satisfying their outcrying with silver ... but still they cry out with unappeased appetites – More, more, more, give us more!... the whole native policy is a mass of abominable rubbish ... [who] should be speedily carted away along with all the other purulent imbeciles who flourish upon that pestilential heap, the Native Department.' There must be a determined stand against the natives 'instead of one or two proclamations, followed by a series of cajoleries, flatteries, and general wallowing in the mire before these uncircumcised Philistines'.[51]

In 1859 McLean returned to Hawkes Bay to buy land, remaining there for more than four months despite appeals from the Governor and the Native Minister to return to Taranaki to complete negotiations over Te Teira's offer to sell land at Waitara. In reporting to the Governor, McLean made no reference to Taranaki, but implicitly justified his presence in Hawkes Bay by stating that his efforts would soon result in important land purchases in Hawkes Bay. He did not tell the Governor that, between June and August, he had also been buying several small blocks to add to his Maraekakaho run. He had bought 400 acres of the run, being the balance of the unpurchased 10s-per-acre land, the money coming from the sale of his wool clip. He was glad he had secured this land, he told his brother, even though he was now without a penny. Between 1857 and 1859 he freeholded over 2000 acres of his run.[52] McLean was sensitive to insinuations of jobbery in combining his private purchases with his duties as a Land Purchase Commissioner. He denied that his private business would 'ever delay him an hour' if he considered doing so was 'in any way detrimental to the public service'.[53] Domett took a more cynical view: 'I trust you are by degrees feathering your nest, a process which you Scotch Birds generally are said to understand very well.'[54]

In 1860 Bishop William Williams had made known his concern at the conduct of McLean and his district commissioners. In a detailed report, which also included quotations from a concerned letter to *The New Zealander* by his nephew, Revd Samuel Williams of Te Aute, Bishop Williams asked the Governor to forward his letter to the Secretary of State in London. He urged that land purchases should be made subject to regulations that would make it impossible for irregularities to occur. Under a regulated system, the Bishop was convinced that Maori would soon abandon the King movement and the anti-land-selling leagues. He analysed land purchases in Hawkes Bay since 1854, alleging that rangatira complained that purchases had been made in secret without full consultation or the consent of all who had an interest in the land. Whenever ownership was disputed, Maori alleged that the commissioners supported the selling party and would disregard the rangatira's authority if he disputed the sale. Samuel Williams made similar allegations, pointing out that the local tribes could have sought help from other parts of the island to hold onto their lands but that the response to these tribes had been 'mind your own business and leave us to arrange our differences with our Pakeha in a quiet manner'.[55] He believed the rangatira that had wanted to settle these land-purchase disputes themselves and to persuade McLean to allow them to exercise control over offers to sell. Instead, they feared they were being forced to retain their lands 'by force of arms'.[56] The moment force was used Maori confidence in the Government, already much shaken, appeared to break down and 'it was with much difficulty that many of them were prevented from giving way to feeling of despair'.[57]

McLean's response to the Williams's charges was self-righteous repudiation. Was his conscience troubling him? As a young man he had dedicated himself to the advancement and benefit of Maori and settler. Now that he was finding it difficult to reconcile their interests he was unwilling to admit that he had abandoned his pledge and had placed settler demand for land ahead of protection of Maori interests. McLean accused Bishop Williams of making charges on 'the unproven assertions of others rather than the facts coming under his own observations'. Williams was supporting Maori who opposed further land sales. Referring to the feud between Te Hapuku and Te Moananui, he claimed that

Williams had got his information from one of the parties only and that the land question was only one element in this feud, as the rivalry between these two rangatira went back years before any land had been bought by the Government. McLean argued that Williams had failed to show how the later purchases had been 'conducted on any different principle' from earlier negotiations. It was not the system that had changed but 'the views of the Natives'. That a great change had taken place could hardly have escaped 'the notice of an attentive observer'. The present Governor, he said, had laid down more stringent instructions for land purchases than any of his predecessors. Maori had not been, as Williams asserted, handed over 'to the tender mercies of the Land Purchase Department' as they had always had free access to the Governor. On the contrary, there were numerous instances where land-purchase officials had refused to negotiate for valuable land because this might lead to disputes and quarrels, resulting in ill-feeling towards the Government among those wishing to sell.

McLean was correct in saying that Maori attitudes had changed – they were no longer eager to sell. What he did not admit was that he too had changed tactics, no longer seeking the free consent of those entitled to sell. The evidence is clear. In 1848 McLean, in investigating rightful claimants, said that he allowed all who had claims 'to freely participate without distinction of rank or race' holding that a rangatira had no exclusive right and 'any paramount part he took in disposing of the land was entirely owing to the admission of superiority by his tribe of his right to take part in the disposal of it'.[58] By the late 1850s he was resorting to transactions with a handful of rangatira, sometimes in secret. The reduction in the number of signatures on the sale deeds confirmed the change. With the Waipukurau, Ahuriri and Mohaka blocks, the number of signatures was 376, 300 and 296 respectively. Later purchases in Hawkes Bay had few signatures: Tautane (Te Hapuku and thirty-one others); Okawa (Te Hapuku, Te Moananui and two others); and Kahuranaki (Te Hapuku and three others), for example.

In 1846, with a young man's idealism McLean had committed himself to the 'interests and social happiness and advancement of both races'. By 1859, over the twin issues of land and sovereignty, McLean struggled to reconcile the interests of the two peoples. His official policy statements on land purchases and the responsibilities of the Crown under the Treaty of Waitangi maintained his earlier views. What McLean said and what he did could differ. In practice, he had resorted to engineering consent to land purchases rather than securing the 'free and intelligent consent' of the tribes.

Chapter 11
The Waitara Purchase

The decision of Governor Gore Browne to press on with the disputed purchase of land at Waitara marked a turning-point in race relations in the young colony. Although the flashpoint of the subsequent war in Taranaki was the land-purchase methods followed by the Crown, it was also about the issue of sovereignty. The Governor was intent on enforcing the Queen's authority beyond the small European settlements. Maori rangatira feared that their tino rangatiratanga – their authority and independence guaranteed under the Treaty of Waitangi – was threatened. Ministers worked for the dominance of a settler Parliament in which Maori had no representation. For the British Government the implementation of responsible government in 1856 marked the surrender of its trust to protect Maori embodied in the Treaty of Waitangi; it had 'shuffled out of its moral obligations'.[1]

No government officer had a more comprehensive knowledge of the Taranaki region than McLean. He had been stationed at New Plymouth from 1844 until 1850 and he continued to be involved in Taranaki as Land Purchase Commissioner. In 1854 he was sent to mediate in the Puketapu conflict and he directed the work of Robert Parris as District Commissioner in Taranaki from 1857.

From the beginning of the New Plymouth settlement, the land at Waitara was seen by the settlers as vital to the economic progress of the region. The open, fertile plain to the north-east of New Plymouth was more attractive than the bush-covered interior land. The roadstead at New Plymouth gave no protection to shipping, whereas at Waitara the river was suited for development as a port. Soon after his appointment in 1844, McLean had offers of land at Waitara; these he declined, aware that any sale would be disputed. In 1848 Governor Grey had instructed McLean to arrange that Maori on the south-west bank of the Waitara River should abandon their claims and relocate to the north-east bank. Wiremu Kingi Te Rangitake refused. McLean had failed in his first important negotiation, and Grey later remarked that McLean had thereafter held a grudge against Wiremu Kingi.

Te Teira Manuka first offered to sell land at Waitara in November 1857. Parris refused the offer, as some rangatira, among them Wiremu Kingi, opposed the sale. Kingi was chief over several Waitara hapu and had been the leader of the migration south in the 1830s. Te Teira's offer may have had its origin in a quarrel with Wiremu Kingi over a kinswoman accused of adultery. Te Teira, aggrieved at what he thought to be inadequate payment of utu for this offence, sought to continue the quarrel by this offer to sell land in which Kingi had an interest. Three months later, Parris was writing to McLean to say that Te Teira was still eager to sell land at Waitara. In August 1858 McLean advised Parris not to push ahead with land purchases as a 'more general plan' was under consideration,[2] possibly a reference to C. W. Richmond's Native Title Bill. J. Flight, resident magistrate at New Plymouth, expressed the settler view when he told McLean that the Government should establish a policy that no man should forcibly interfere with another in the disposition of his land when he wanted to sell. Wiremu Kingi 'must be brought down to his proper level and not allowed any longer to mislead the people whom he had hitherto deceived'.[3] He said local Maori were expecting the Government to take some action in support of the land sellers.

The Governor, with McLean's support, decided on a new policy. Land could be bought from rangatira of hapu with a primary customary right who occupied that land. A leading rangatira of the iwi or larger tribal group should not have any right to block the sale of that land. This was consistent with McLean's intention of simplifying the complexity of land-purchase negotiations. That decision, however, did not concede that other hapu might also have some customary rights in that land or that the leading rangatira had a right to act on behalf of the iwi to which the particular hapu belonged.

In Taranaki intertribal fighting generated by quarrels over land sales went on intermittently from 1854 till 1859 when the warring groups agreed to a truce. In 1856 Ihaia Te Kirikumara had offered to sell land near Waitara. Te Waitere Katatore, usually an opponent of land sales, countered with an offer to sell a large area behind Bell block towards the mountain. Te Kirikumara, angered by interest shown in this offer to the neglect of his own, organised an ambush in which Katatore was killed. Gore Browne made no effort to enforce British law by arresting Te Kirikumara for Katatore's murder. When Katatore's supporters threatened Te Kirikumara's pa, however, he intervened to offer Te Kirikumara safe passage to the Chathams. Te Ati Awa concluded that British law was biased and was being applied only against those seen to be opposing land sales. In 1858 Te Kirikumara again offered land at Waitara, but the Governor would not proceed in the face of opposition from Wiremu Kingi, who, as the Governor acknowledged, had an interest in that land.[4]

The problem that confronted Gore Browne and McLean was how to reconcile the growing settler pressure for land to the increasing Maori reluctance to sell. McLean advised the Governor to resist settler pressure. Reporting on a memorial from the Taranaki Provincial Council in 1858 setting out its members' dissatisfaction at the Governor's inability to obtain sufficient land for colonists, McLean believed that local Maori occupied more land than they required. Every effort had been made to buy land at much higher prices than prevailed in other provinces. More aggressive action to buy land would result in fresh conflicts that might involve settlers and the Government. The Governor's requirement that the Land Purchase Department abstain from acquiring land if the consequences were in any way likely to cause conflict had been strictly observed by his officers, he claimed.[5]

In February 1859, Wiremu Kingi, alarmed at the prospect of settler expansion north-east of New Plymouth, wrote to the Governor and McLean that his runanga had banned the sale of land from the Waitaha Stream to Mokau in the north. Kingi reminded them that this decision was nothing new. Previous governors had heard it and now he told Gore Browne that he intended to hold on to his land. 'You O Mr McLean, are aware of that word of mine when you first came here and saw me, you heard the same word from me, I will not give the land to you.'[6] Browne and McLean were convinced that Kingi had placed himself at the head of an anti-land-selling league as these boundaries extended beyond Kingi's authority as an Ati Awa rangatira. Although Keith Sinclair has shown that a land league did not operate in Taranaki in 1859, it seems that tribes were exploring ways of making a common cause.

In 1859 Gore Browne set out on a round of visits to the provinces, arriving at New Plymouth on 7 March. Next day the Governor held an 'undress levee' that was not well attended. Were settlers showing their disapproval of his failure to buy land? That night McLean dined with the Governor. Gore Browne had written out the address that he was to deliver to the Maori the following morning and, no doubt, discussed the approach with his Native Secretary.

On 9 March, a large number of Maori gathered in the grounds of the Native Office's single-storeyed vertical weatherboard building to meet the Governor who was accompanied by McLean, Parris and C. W. Richmond in the latter's dual role of local member and Native Minister. McLean's diary noted only that it was 'a disagreeable close day' and no doubt the dress of the Governor's party – heavy woollen worsted trousers, long frock coats and waistcoats – contributed to the discomfort. Gore Browne addressed the Maori gathering, with McLean translating his speech.[7] The Governor was concerned that intertribal conflict in the midst of land occupied by settlers might lead to fighting between settlers and Maori. The Queen cared equally for all her subjects, he assured the gathering. Missionaries had given Maori the blessings of Christianity and translated the Bible for their use; indeed, 'it was not in the power of man to confer any other gift which will bear comparison with that of the Bible'. However, out of regard for them, he continued, he had caused an abstract of English law to be translated into Maori. He would not enforce English law except 'in districts where people were wise enough to use it'. He had two topics to talk about, criminal offences and land. Taranaki tribes had an advantage over other tribes as they were, to their profit, intermixed with the Pakeha. If they chose to live peacefully and cultivate their lands they would grow rich and multiply. Instead, they were constantly at war with each other, when their quarrels were 'about matters of little importance or about land which was not worth disputing for'. Gore Browne failed to see that these disputes over land had come about through his officials' pressure on Maori to sell more land. In future, the Governor warned, every man, whether Maori or Pakeha, who resorted to violence within certain districts would be arrested, tried and sentenced by a judge under English law. He would not allow settlers to be disturbed by evildoers. Those Maori who were not content to live in peace among the Pakeha should go elsewhere. In ending his address, he advised the gathering that they would be wise to sell the land that they could not use. He gave an assurance that he would never consent to buy land without an undisputed title. He would not permit anyone to interfere with the sale of land unless he owned part of it; on the other hand, he would buy no man's land without his consent.

After McLean had translated the Governor's speech, Te Teira came forward and, placing a parawai (superior cloak) at the Governor's feet, offered to sell land at Waitara. The Governor, having consulted with McLean and C. W. Richmond, agreed to accept the offer if Te Teira could prove his title. Gore Browne, taken by surprise at Te Teira's offer, believed that he had no option but to accept, having just stated his policy for buying land. Later, McLean was to state his reservations about the validity of Te Teira's title. In such a public forum, however, he would have found it difficult to express reservations that he might have been able to convey to Gore Browne in private.

In response to Te Teira's offer, Wiremu Kingi rose, telling the Governor that he objected to the sale of this land: 'Waitara is in my hand. I will never let it go, never, never, never.' Kingi, however, made no attempt to remove Te Teira's parawai, as was the custom when disputing a title.[8] What happened next is unclear, as eyewitness accounts of the day's events differ.[9] Gore Browne recorded that he was offended by Kingi's abrupt departure accompanied by his followers. McLean made no reference to Kingi's departure, merely recording that he then sat down. What probably happened was that Kingi walked away from the area where the speakers were gathered. The Governor should not have been surprised at Kingi's reaction as only one month before Kingi had written to him to convey the decision of 'our runanga' not to sell land between Waitaha and Mokau.

McLean had ceased to keep a regular personal diary after 1853 following the death of his wife; thereafter entries were spasmodic and limited to a few lines. For 10 March 1859, the day after the Governor's meeting, McLean noted, 'Long Taranaki meeting some truth elicited. J. Williams, Kopara and others.' The following day a settler deputation waited on the Governor asking that McLean return to Taranaki. McLean's diary shows that he found time on 12 March to ride over to talk to Ihaia Te Kirikumara, a government supporter and land seller. It does not record that, on the same day, there was another meeting of local Maori who, apart from Wiremu Kingi, offered no challenge to Te Teira's party's right to sell. McLean later commented that he was surprised that Kingi had not offered stronger opposition. It is significant that McLean found time to go and talk to Te Kirikumara, one of the rangatira most prominent in support of land sales, whereas he made no attempt to talk privately with Wiremu Kingi to explore the basis of his opposition or to persuade him to reconsider his decision. McLean did allow his personal reactions to influence his judgement. Men were either his friends or his foes. He cultivated those rangatira seen to favour land sales and ignored and avoided contact with rangatira like Wiremu Kingi whom he saw as leading the opposition to further land sales. 'Friendly' rangatira were more likely to be appointed as assessors and to receive pensions or gifts such as flour mills to develop the agricultural potential of their tribes.

The question then arises: how far was Te Teira's offer set up by Parris, Richmond and McLean? There is insufficient evidence to reach a firm conclusion. Was McLean party to a 'conspiracy of silence', as Sinclair maintained?[10] McLean hoarded his papers – inward letters, copies of his own correspondence, reports, draft memos and even his laundry lists – but for 1859 there is nothing in his own hand on Waitara and little from others, apart from a few letters from Parris. This dearth of material has been compounded by the loss of many of the Gore Browne Papers from National Archives. Keith Sinclair, while exonerating the Governor and C. W. Richmond, suggested that McLean's conduct over Waitara could be interpreted as 'dishonest and underhand', though whether it was of conscious intent, he thought it was not possible to decide. He concluded that McLean colluded with Parris to conceal their knowledge that Te Teira intended to offer to sell and that McLean was aware of his offer but chose not to warn the Governor when the two went over the content of his speech before the meeting.[11]

McLean and Richmond had known since 1857 of Te Teira's interest in selling land at Waitara and that discussions with Parris had been going on during 1858. They were aware that Te Teira could be a willing seller, but they may have told the truth when they denied any advance knowledge that Te Teira would make a definite offer during the Governor's visit. There had been discussions for over a year without any conclusion.

What can be established is that ministers and settlers had been eager to acquire land at Waitara, and that, during 1858, encouraged by Parris, Te Teira had been exploring the possibility of selling land, although he had not made a definite offer to sell. McLean knew of these meetings and would have been very conscious of growing pressure from ministers and Taranaki settlers to hasten the process. Likewise, Richmond, as Native Minister and as a Taranaki settler, would have known of Parris's activities and no doubt gave tacit approval. So when did McLean and Parris learn of Te Teira's decision to make a formal offer? Parris, speaking before a parliamentary select committee in 1860, after some equivocation, admitted that he knew beforehand of Te Teira's intention, but that McLean was unaware up to the morning of the meeting with the Governor. Did McLean meet with Parris before the morning of 9 March? His diary makes no mention. McLean himself, in giving evidence before the select committee, said that before the Governor's visit in March 1859, he was not aware that Te Teira or his party 'had determined upon making an offer'.[12] McLean believed in always telling the truth, but was he revealing only as much of the truth as he chose? He did not mention that he had been informed of the discussions during 1858 or whether he knew of the offer when he met with the Governor before the meeting on the morning of 9 March.

If McLean knew that Te Teira would offer to sell land, why did he not warn the Governor? It would not have been to embarrass or deceive Gore Browne, for McLean had a strong sense of public duty and a high personal regard for the Governor. When an offer to sell had been made, normal practice would have been that McLean as Chief Land Purchase Commissioner would refer this to the Governor for approval to proceed and to conduct negotiations for a price to be set by the Governor. McLean could have expected this procedure to follow Te Teira's offer, and would have been disconcerted when the Governor took charge. McLean was a man who had to work independently. He would not be hustled; he would carry out his duties in his own way and in his own time. He was reluctant to cooperate with other officials or to accept detailed supervision by his superiors. When Sir George Grey was governor, he made the decisions on the location, amount and price to be paid for land. Thereafter he never interfered in McLean's conduct of negotiations nor questioned his advice on whether to proceed or delay. Under Gore Browne, McLean had more freedom to decide on where and how land was to be bought. At Waitara, however, Gore Browne assumed detailed oversight of the negotiations over Te Teira's offer. McLean's subsequent inactivity might be attributed to a fit of pique at the Governor's unexpected intervention. It is noteworthy and surprising that McLean, the Governor's chief adviser on Maori affairs, had little personal contact with Gore Browne during 1859. He was with Gore Browne for a week in March while at New Plymouth; in May he accompanied the Governor on a visit to Wanganui and Hawkes Bay. For the rest of the year, a critical one for race relations, the Governor had no further meetings with his chief adviser.

The Governor directed McLean to send a formal notice to Wiremu Kingi to lodge any claim he might have within the block. McLean's letter to Kingi implied a partition of the 600-acre block; those who refused to sell could have their 'pieces' excluded. 'You are aware that with each individual lies the arrangement as regards his own piece; in like manner Teira has the arrangement of his piece.'[13] This reflected a change in government policy, signalled in the 1858 Native Titles Act. The reference to 'individual' claims appears to contradict McLean's explanation on communal land tenure before the Board of Inquiry into Native Affairs in 1856 and his evidence before the House in 1860. McLean, however, would have been addressing Kingi and Te Teira as rangatira of their respective hapu and not as individual owners.

McLean did not tell Kingi that, if he could show ownership, the Governor would not proceed with the purchase. He said only that the rangatira could keep any 'pieces' he owned and have them excluded from the sale. An undated map among McLean's papers does show that the 'pieces' occupied by Kingi and Te Teira were scattered throughout the block, so that it would have been difficult to exclude the lands of all those claimants who opposed the sale. This map shows the location of various pa. Some 200 of Kingi's followers occupied Te Kuikui and Werohia, while Te Teira's people lived at Hurirarapa, sited between the other two.

During March 1859, McLean, having made preliminary investigations into Te Teira's title, left the ongoing work to Parris who, rather than conducting an impartial investigation, concentrated on gathering evidence that might support Te Teira's claim. In April McLean moved on to Queen Charlotte Sound, where he succeeded in getting absentee claimants there and in other parts of Nelson province to agree to dispose of their absentee claims at Waitara. He wrote to Richmond that this would 'very much weaken the opposition of Wiremu Kingi and others', and that one of Kingi's rangatira supporters had become 'quite in favour of selling'. No price would be fixed until Parris had made further progress with the resident claimants.[14] The rangatira Ropoama Te One at Queen Charlotte Sound supported Te Teira's right to sell and, without their knowledge, attached signatures of some who did not agree.[15] When they protested, McLean appeared to ignore them. In 1860 when the House required that this letter be produced, he was alleged to have provided a translation that clouded the nature of the protest.[16]

McLean talked to a group of Te Ati Awa absentee claimants at Wellington but did not visit Otaki and Waikanae where there were other claimants. He justified this neglect by saying that it was unnecessary to go about the country 'raking up claims', though he had made a visit to the South Island where he knew the rangatira would support the sale. McLean did not return to Taranaki in 1859, despite urgings from both the Governor and the Native Minister and pleas from Parris, who had been left to continue negotiations alone. In April 1859, Parris told McLean that the local tribes were negotiating to bring an end to intertribal conflict; therefore he would await the outcome before proceeding, although Te Teira's party was getting 'anxious and restless'.

In September 1859, McLean was still dallying in Hawkes Bay although the situation in Taranaki was starting to escalate, while the King movement was beginning to threaten the Governor's control over the North Island. In response to Gore Browne's request for advice on ways to buy land to open up the country for settlers McLean set out his only comprehensive statement on land-purchase policy. Land purchases would be best secured, he argued, if the status quo was maintained by tribes selling only to the Crown and by continuing to recognise the absolute right of each tribe to retain and dispose of its own lands. Nothing, he stressed, would arouse a spirit of opposition and hostility more than a belief that the Government was resolved to take their land. 'Under such circumstances however the terms on which they might be invited to treat for the surrender of their rights, they would be offered in vain.' The Crown's pre-emptive right to buy land was seen by Maori as protection against settler pressure to sell. As long as they believed that the Government upheld their right to sell or to withhold their land, they felt secure from the consequences of the occupation of their country by a more powerful race. Relying on the repeated promises made by successive governors that the rights secured to them by the Treaty of Waitangi would always be respected and that their lands would never be taken otherwise than with their free consent, he claimed that they could contemplate without alarm the rapidly increasing settler numbers. It was essential that the Maori confidence in the 'paternal character' of the Government should not be disturbed. This was written when Gore Browne had been urging him to hasten to Taranaki to complete the purchase of land at Waitara without the consent of all those with customary rights – a purchase initiated on McLean's advice that Te Teira held a valid title – although Wiremu Kingi, the leading rangatira, had withheld his consent.

Any system for buying Maori land, McLean continued, had to 'be so presented as to avoid the appearance of seeking to force it upon their acceptance'. Maori should be allowed to believe that they were free to choose. The colonists generally held a very different view, said McLean. Few would admit that settlement depended on Maori consent. Maori land was regarded as the property of the colony merely encumbered with certain rights of occupancy of which it was the duty of the Government to clear them, as from time to time the land was required by the settlers. The Government was held to have failed in this duty where lands suitable for settlement remained in Maori hands. Colonists blamed the existing land-purchase system and urged the adoption of some new scheme.

The main object of the King movement, on the other hand, McLean noted, was a general assertion of the right of Maori to retain those parts of the North Island that they felt were necessary for the well-being of their race and to maintain their independence. 'To oppose the movement would be to strengthen it', McLean considered, whereas to counteract it, it was 'only necessary that the Government should be in position to show the tribes taking part in it, that such assertion of a right to hold back their lands is unnecessary, the right being recognised and respected by the Government in the case of each tribe in regard to its own lands though ignored as existing in any confederation in regard generally to lands belonging to tribes composing it'. (With Waitara, McLean identified Te Teira as representing the right of the tribe and Wiremu Kingi as being associated with an anti-selling confederation.)

McLean advised the Governor that the Government's land-purchase policy must be clearly established and the advantages of selling land made apparent to Maori. The Government should then wait until their appreciation of these advantages persuaded them to cede their land to the Crown. Both the Crown and the Maori should be protected from the pressures of settler demand. McLean also denied that he and his officers had continued to buy land despite opposition. Here McLean was misleading the Governor. As we have seen in earlier chapters, the activities of McLean and his commissioners after 1851 had generated opposition from rangatira in Hawkes Bay and Taranaki. McLean's claim that land had been sold with the free and intelligent consent of the Maori was no longer valid. Free consent had become an engineered consent. McLean's policy advice here is another example of where what he said differed from what he did. Perhaps he was taking the opportunity to convey his covert opposition to Gore Browne's determination to proceed with the purchase of Te Teira's block at Waitara.

He advised that 'a permanent and liberal system of dealing with the natives' should be entrusted to agents entirely independent of a colonial ministry subject to frequent change and therefore unable to provide the continuity that was 'necessary to secure the confidence of the natives and without which any system, however well devised, must fail'. No doubt he envisaged that continuity as identified with himself remaining in control. McLean argued for a permanent council appointed by and presided over by the Governor. The Governor's management of native affairs would rest on a more secure basis were he advised by a council composed of men who 'would watch over the interests of the aborigines and possess their confidence and who would be beyond the reach of political influences'. The Governor would need wide discretionary powers and sufficient resources to enable him to promote 'the civilisation of the native race' concurrently with 'the acquisition of their land for colonising purposes'. In other words the Governor and McLean would remain in charge.[17]

Letters from William Martin, former Chief Justice, and William Swainson, former Attorney General, said McLean, stated the arguments so conclusively that he deferred to them as an expression of his own views. Sewell's draft Native Council Bill met with McLean's approval as 'comprehensive and liberal with appropriate provisions'. (This provided for a council nominated by the Governor and allowed for a 'bi-racial systematic colonisation of specified districts'.) This council would buy land and return significant portions to Maori on an inalienable title, set aside land for religious and educational purposes and sell the rest. The Governor referred it to the British Parliament for enactment, but settler lobbying ensured its rejection.[18] McLean said it was important that the Crown had the right to set the terms for the cession of land. Native title should be extinguished over a whole district before any settlement took place. He recommended that negotiators deal with each tribe separately and 'in many cases treat for such portions as the proprietors may be willing to sell. Where ownership is divided among several tribes an attempt to insist on a general agreement requiring the consent of all parties concerned would almost inevitably fail.'

He disapproved of the provisions in the draft bill for the cession of Maori land in blocks of not less than 30,000 acres and for the authorisation of grants to Maori in return for the surrender of their territorial rights. This fell far short of what was required, nor were sufficient resources made available to carry out a scheme intended to provide a satisfactory solution to the land question. The powers vested in the Governor, he pointed out, were constrained by the control of a council in which Maori were not represented.

Sewell's provisions, he submitted, were not suited to the region north of Auckland where Crown and Maori lands were interspersed and settlement well advanced; but for the unsettled part of the island he saw no objection. Maori interests required that the Governor, when negotiating to buy land, should be empowered to make such arrangements as might secure to the Maori owners 'a proper possession for their wants, present and future'. He proposed that a portion of the land be reserves so that part could be reconveyed by a grant from the Crown to give a proper title that should be inalienable or sold only with the consent of the Governor. Reserves should also be set aside for endowments for religious, educational and charitable institutions for the benefit of Maori and a proportion of the land sales' proceeds should be appropriated at the direction of the council. It did not occur to the Governor or McLean that the Maori rangatira should be consulted about this proposal to set aside reserves. They would decide what was best for Maori. McLean proposed that reserves should be three-tenths of the area of land sold to the Crown with two-tenths allocated to individuals ranked in four classes (see Appendix 4). This should be sufficient for Maori needs and should include villages, cultivations, sacred places and occupied land. In the North Island, this would have amounted to nearly 500 acres to each individual. McLean thought this would be enough for Maori needs which he seemed to define in terms of their traditional subsistence way of life. McLean's proposal for reserves was not followed up.

The bill, by partitioning and defining boundaries of Maori land, would help Maori define their intertribal and other boundaries and so tend to 'promote their civilisation', McLean argued. He dismissed the colonists' argument that to disentangle the complications of Maori title would remove one motive for selling land to the Crown, affirming that there was a moral obligation on the Government to promote the improvement of the Maori race. Rather than making Maori title the subject of special legislation, McLean recommended that provision be made under the Native Districts Regulations Act 1858 to enable Maori to define boundaries and to individualise title.

McLean opposed a proposal by the Auckland politician, William Daldy, to remove the Crown's right of pre-emption and allow settlers to make direct purchases from Maori considering that 'confusion and conflict would soon follow its abandonment and the natives are fully aware of this'. The Waikato league, formed to stop all land sales, showed the strength of Maori feeling. The Land Purchase Department's difficulties had arisen not from arguments over the price of land but 'from the reluctance to part with land and that independence which attaches to the possession of the territory of the country and to give place to a superior race whom they have scarcely learnt to trust'. If Maori wished to sell land, they preferred to treat with the Governor to whom they could look to for protection from any unforeseen ill consequences. Whatever the system adopted, it had to be stable and permanent; changes merely for the sake of experiment would destroy existing Maori confidence in the British Government. He believed the interests of settlers and Maori were linked together. However, as McLean had earlier pointed out, the attitudes of settlers and Maori over land purchases were very much opposed. Indeed they were to prove irreconcilable.[19]

This statement on land-purchase policy was perhaps the only major presentation by McLean of his views. It also conveyed something of McLean's apprehension at the Governor's handling of the Waitara purchase. Existing policy, wrote McLean, recognised the absolute right of each tribe to retain or dispose of its own land. Nothing would hinder purchases and arouse opposition more than a belief that the Government was intent on appropriating Maori land. Was this a reminder that the Governor was creating just such an impression with Wiremu Kingi? It was typical of McLean that the paper dealt not with the principles underpinning the policy, but with the status quo and with pragmatic responses to current problems. This paper revealed McLean's covert opposition to Gore Browne's handling of the Waitara purchase when he warned that any system for buying land must be so handled as to avoid any appearance of seeking to force it on Maori acceptance.

McLean's apparent reluctance to become involved in negotiations over the Waitara purchase was highlighted by the Governor's subsequent actions. Gore Browne, eager to complete the purchase, was frustrated by McLean's inaction. He chose to write to Parris, outlining his own views on the situation and asking for Parris's opinion. Gore Browne, who felt a need to take his ministers with him, also consulted Richmond. They decided that they could rely on Parris to complete the Waitara purchase. Gore Browne told Parris that he had 'complete confidence in your knowledge and discretion in native affairs' and that he and Richmond wished Parris to make an advance to Te Teira for the sale of the land 'to any extent you like'. However, he instructed Parris 'not to allow any survey or act of ownership to be performed until Mr McLean arrives'.[20]

The Governor's confidence was misplaced, however. Parris did not fully understand the intricacies of Maori land tenure, nor was he a well-educated man. Although not unsympathetic to Maori – Richmond wanted him reprimanded for always 'hanging about Maori pa' – Parris, a Taranaki settler, and eager to succeed in his new role of District Land Commissioner, wanted to record his first success in buying land. Parris queried the Governor's instruction to make an advance payment, arguing that, as it was the planting season, it would be unwise to arouse excitement that might cause Te Teira and his party to lose the opportunity to plant their crops. Moreover, he thought the amount so small that there was no advantage in paying by instalments. The Governor's response was that Parris should go on with the payment 'if he had no positive objection'. Parris was clearly uncomfortable and feeling out of his depth at having sole responsibility. He wondered whether McLean was 'come-at-able' because there had been no replies to his many letters. He wanted to talk to McLean and, hoping for McLean's expected return, had taken no action on Te Teira's offer. Meanwhile, he found Wiremu Kingi as 'doggedly obstinate as ever'. He assured McLean that there could be no doubt about Te Teira's claims – one of the best proofs had recently been advanced by Te Teira: 'viz., that when they came from Waikanae in 1848 Wm. King asked leave of Teira and his father to build Pa's [*sic*] on the South-west bank of the river, explaining his reason for doing so, on account of the Waikato's [*sic*] considering the South side safer than the North-east in case of an invasion.'[21]

After returning to Wellington near the end of April, McLean accompanied the Governor first to Wanganui, to begin negotiations for land at Waitotara, and then to Ahuriri. McLean remained in Hawkes Bay from May until early September, completing land purchases and settling disputes. Both the Assistant Native Secretary, T. H. Smith, and J. Rogan, a District Commissioner, warned McLean that the Governor was irritated by his prolonged dallying in Hawkes Bay. McLean was there to continue land-purchase negotiations, in which he was successful. Although Gore Browne may have expressed frustration at McLean's remaining in Hawkes Bay, his letters did not betray this. In August he wrote: 'I wish you were here to advise me but I know you are well employed where you are; and unfortunately you cannot cut yourself in pieces.'[22] A month later he wrote that he was 'delighted in your success at Napier [in purchasing land] which is worthy of yourself … I write in great haste. Do, as you always do, what is best and having done it get on to Taranaki. I rejoice in your letters so write when you can.'[23] Referring to the situation in Taranaki, he had heard that Wiremu Kingi was 'determined to resist and if he does we must pitch into him'. Gore Browne did not seem to sense any danger over Waitara. If the Governor was firm, he thought that Kingi would then capitulate. He had received a 'very sensible letter' from Parris, 'who gives me entire satisfaction', and thought that, if Parris was satisfied that Te Teira and others who offered to sell had an undisputed title, an advance payment should be made at once. The sellers would have to understand that the purchase could not be completed until McLean visited Taranaki. The Taranaki settlers were, Gore Browne considered, 'impatient and very bumptious; and I am rather anxious to give them a rebuff. It is not to please them that I would hasten Teira's purchase but because it ought to be completed. Their impatience is the chief obstacle to the attainment of their wishes.'[24]

McLean's old New Plymouth friend, Dr Wilson, also condemned his fellow colonists. Writing to McLean at the end of October, he thought that the Governor should say to them, 'gentlemen, if you really be so eager to procure land go to Ahuriri – go to Canterbury – go to Otago and you shall have more than you or all of you can muster ready cash for – is NP [New Plymouth] your Natale Solum forsooth that all your early affections are concentrated on it or are you not so far strangers in a strange land, that good land is alone what you require. Well then take it where I have got to give it but do not coerce the aborigines to part with what is just as dear to them as it can be to you.'[25] Available Crown land in Taranaki had not been taken up by settlers because it was less attractive than the open, fertile land around Waitara.

In September McLean moved south from Hawkes Bay to Wairarapa, firmly rejecting efforts by local runanga to intervene in land purchases and resisting attempts by aggrieved Maori to reopen negotiations on earlier land sales. After visiting his run at Akitio, he journeyed south past Castlepoint to stay with the Moores at Waikaraka on the Wairarapa coast. Here, on 16 November, he was laid up with a severe bout of rheumatic fever. He described himself as being very ill and feverish and had 'literally experienced being doubled up [it] is like being bent almost in two'.[26] He was attended by Dr Sprott and by Dr Featherston, Superintendent of Wellington province, who had a run at Akitio next to McLean. It was a month before he could travel and he had to be carried in a litter to the beach at Castlepoint to board a waiting steamer for Wellington.

Gore Browne was delighted to get a letter in McLean's handwriting – a sign that he was recovering – but urged him not to overwork as 'your life is too valuable to your friends and to the public to be trifled with'. The Governor reiterated his trust: 'I need not say you are my right hand and as such must not be overworked or allowed to wear yourself out for want of any change that is good for you.' McLean asked for two years' leave to visit England and Scotland. He proposed Rogan as Chief Land Purchase Commissioner and Smith as Native Secretary in his absence. If McLean decided to take leave, Gore Browne asked that he fully brief Smith. It seems that McLean had indicated that he was prepared to give up the position of Chief Land Purchase Commissioner as Gore Browne said he wanted a decision as soon as possible if he still wished to be relieved of those duties. He thought Dillon Bell the only person who could replace McLean in that post and he wanted to engage him before he accepted some other position. It is significant that McLean not only wanted to surrender his land-purchase role but that Browne did not attempt to change McLean' mind. Their views seem to have diverged by this time.

When he learnt of McLean's illness, Parris wrote hoping that his health would soon be restored, 'for when the Head of a Department is disabled the whole gets faint and every branch seems disordered'. District commissioners looked to their patron with his superior mana as the man able to resolve stalemates over negotiations. He also briefed McLean on the situation in Taranaki. Te Teira was to be paid an instalment on his land the next day. Parris detected disagreement among Kingi and his followers, some wishing to raise the Maori King's flag. Kingi, who opposed putting his land under the Maori King's mana, threatened to return to Waikanae. Parris feared that this was too good to be realised. 'I assure you Mr McLean this matter gives me great anxiety lest we should have a repetition of Rawiri ma's massacre. The justice of Teira and other claims emboldens them to other propositions which I find it necessary to restrain lest evil should come of it.'[27] When the payment was made, Parris reported that Wiremu Kingi and his followers appeared to repudiate the sale but that, when asked to discuss the matter with Te Teira,

Wiremu Kingi had admitted the superiority of Te Teira's claims. When challenged, however, Kingi evaded the question of justifying his opposition and merely said, 'it is enough, their [meaning Te Teira and party] stomachs are full with the sight of the money which you have promised them for the land they have set afloat but I will not consent for it to be sent to sea but will take possession of it and cultivate it'.[28] Parris reported that Te Teira and his party were staying in New Plymouth, considering it not safe to return to Waitara after receiving the payment.

Parris remained anxious. Writing privately to McLean, he said that he was disappointed that his chief commissioner's return was still uncertain as there were many questions that he was eager to talk over rather than writing letters to head office in Auckland during McLean's absence. He reported that the Waitara question was quiet though Wiremu Kingi had been offended by the payment of the instalment on Te Teira's land. He was still optimistic that the purchase would proceed and that other rangatira were ready to offer to sell land at Waitara. Parris appealed to McLean to return and complete the deal. 'You may now Sir immortalise your name in New Plymouth ... I do most sincerely trust that your health will enable you soon to come for I verily believe that now is the time for turning the tables – a little show of determination with the present favourable changes will settle the whole question if some liberal provision of land is made for all.'[29] McLean did not respond to this invitation to achieve immortality, as he was about to take sick leave in Canterbury. Nevertheless, the Taranaki settlers chose to recognise McLean's contribution. When the town of Waitara was laid out, the main street was named after him, while the two governors, Browne and Grey, had to be content with lesser side streets.

In December 1859 McLean was convalescing at Christchurch. His diary recorded that he met with the Governor and discussed who should act as Native Secretary and as Chief Land Purchase Commissioner while he was on sick leave. This was the first occasion on which the two had met since May. The Governor would certainly have surveyed developments over the Waitara purchase and asked McLean's opinion, yet McLean chose to make no note in his diary. Confirmation that Gore Browne confided his forthcoming plans is found in a letter from H. Halse, Sergeant of Police at New Plymouth, in response to a communication from McLean dated 29 December. 'You will oblige me greatly by sending early intelligence of the Waitara expedition. Your apprehensions are significant.'[30] The Governor would have told McLean of his intention to proceed with the survey of Te Teira's land and to empower Colonel Gold to declare martial law, later confirmed at the January meeting of the Executive Council. That decision was a political one. McLean would have had no part in making it. Did he air his 'apprehensions' to the Governor or did he acquiesce, accepting that Gore Browne would not be moved?

That McLean had contemplated giving up his post as head of the Land Purchase Department suggests some crisis of the spirit arising in part from the debilitating effects of his illness. Although only thirty-nine, McLean felt the burden of his years. Writing to his elder brother Alexander, he regretted he had little money and urged him: 'Do for goodness sake save every penny shilling and pound you can, remember life is short, you and all of us have seen the best of it and where is the provision for sickness, old age and infirmity.'[31] Other signs had been his irritation with ministerial control, his procrastination over Waitara in 1859 and an increasing sensitivity to intemperate newspaper criticism. For example the *Wellington Independent* of 29 April 1859 condemned McLean for his failure to buy land for the province, only £45,000 of £500,000 being expended in the preceding three years. The province had been 'cruelly neglected' and a very great responsibility on the officers of the land-purchase department 'for their supineness (a supineness, which, if the statement by Mr McLean be correct, is most culpable) must the non-extinguishment of native title be solely attributable'. The *Taranaki Herald* of 6 March 1860 complained that the 'conflict of laws would have been cleared by this time had the responsible ministry been allowed to work freely for the benefit and civilisation of the native race instead of being hampered by the 'do nothing policy' and 'the jealousy of those who doing nothing ... are determined that no one shall succeed where they have failed'.

The Government was in a dilemma. Ministers detested McLean and longed to be rid of him. His blatant assertion of independence from their control, his supposed influence over the Governor and his petty obstruction of the lines of communication between Governor and ministers, all roused their enmity. At the same time ministers knew that McLean was indispensable. His influence among the rangatira was unrivalled. No one could so rally friendly Maori to the Government's side or mediate in tribal disputes.

In March 1860 the Governor paid a brief visit to New Plymouth, where he instructed Colonel Gold to ensure the survey of Te Teira's block and empowered him to declare martial law. When Kingi's followers obstructed the survey, Gold issued the declaration. On 17 March, after Kingi refused to evacuate a pa he had built on land he believed to be his own, Gold attacked the position without success. Subsequently Kingi abandoned the pa. Kingi's followers were soon reinforced from the south by Taranaki and Ngati Ruanui who plundered settlers' farms, killing six men and boys. The Taranaki War had begun.

That same week McLean, now recovered from his illness, had postponed taking leave and had gone to Taranaki on the Governor's instructions. He broke his silence over Waitara to warn Gore Browne that the military force was insufficient to protect the New Plymouth settlement. Taranaki and Ngati

Ruanui with 1200 warriors were preparing to attack the settlement, while Kingi and his 300 immediate followers would fight to the last at Waitara. There was an even greater threat as tribes had agreed to stop their intertribal feuding and to give their allegiance to the Maori King, Potatau. The possible intervention of several thousand Waikato warriors aided by the 'numerous and disaffected East Coast tribes' would be 'with a view of asserting their national independence and throwing over their nominal dependence to Her Majesty', McLean observed. He recommended the Governor obtain a force of not less than 5000 troops without delay to protect the scattered Taranaki settlements and vindicate Her Majesty's sovereignty.[32]

Auckland settlers were becoming alarmed, convinced that an attack by Waikato tribes was imminent, but Gore Browne refused to be swayed by their panic. He told McLean in April that rumours had the missionary, J. Morgan 'rushing into town; his horse white with foam and 500 natives at his tail!!! Everybody saw him; everybody knows it is true but I cannot learn that he has left Rangiwahia.'[33]

Gore Browne had not expected Wiremu Kingi to resist, nor did the fighting in Taranaki meet his expectations of a 'very short war'. As a military man himself, he was exasperated by the dilatory and cautious performance of Colonels Gold and Murray. Taranaki settlers were further outraged when on 28 March, at Waireka, Colonel Murray left the local militia to their fate from which they were rescued by sailors from HMS *Niger*. In New Plymouth this action was greeted as a victory, with a report of up to 150 Maori killed, though research suggests that the sailors did little more than capture an unfortified and undefended camp.[34]

Writing to his brother about the Waireka action, McLean remarked: 'the natives have got a sound thrashing 11 of their rangatira killed and some 30 others. We lost 2 on our side and 9 wounded. This will cure some of their boasting. They murdered in cold blood 5 of our unprotected men at least 3 men and 2 boys.'[35] McLean might wish to avoid war but, once engaged, he had no doubts that British imperial power must triumph. Gore Browne, however, told McLean that he was disappointed that reports of the number of rangatira killed were untrue and that several, including the principal rangatira of Ngati Ruanui, were still alive.

The Governor had a poor opinion of the fighting qualities of the local militia. Gore Browne thought the military could have been more active and energetic, though he acknowledged that the difficulties General Pratt, the new commander of the British troops, had to encounter were

> very great and among them may be reckoned the independence of the really gallant fellows who compose the militia and the volunteers but who

> like better to fight when they please and correspond with the newspapers than to mount guard or obey in silence. Still I must think that if the Prelates could wield the 'sword of Gideon' and the Commanders could mount the pulpit we should have more energy in the field and more charity and forbearance in the Church.[36]

The Governor empowered McLean to mediate between military and settlers and to liaise with Maori allies and British troops in an attempt to overcome the friction that existed among the various parties. McLean advised General Pratt on ways to use the friendly Maori allies to advantage, recommending that the general deploy them as advance skirmishers who would discover any ambush, no doubt thereby saving British lives! Moreover, he believed it was desirable to bring them into direct conflict with the enemy and compel them to be identified as the Queen's men – an example of divide and rule.[37]

Having failed to gain his quick victory the Governor, worried and eager to avoid intervention by Waikato supporters of the Maori King, suspended hostilities against Wiremu Kingi on 20 April but continued to attack the southern tribes in Taranaki. In April and May the Governor sent officials, including McLean, to meet with the Waikato tribes – only the third time McLean had visited the Waikato in the last ten years. At this meeting, called by the King movement in response to the Governor's approach, McLean reported that the rangatiras' speeches had centred on preserving their land from further encroachment by Europeans, erecting the King's flagstaff and expressing sympathy with Wiremu Kingi's stand at Taranaki. He identified three groups. First, there was the large majority, staunch supporters of the King movement. Second, the moderate supporters, whose objectives were to preserve a distinct nationality, retain their land and look to the adjustment of grievances while keeping the peace. Third, opponents of the King movement, who feared it would lead to war between Maori and European and that it would not result in any gain or, if it did, that it would favour one group at the expense of others.

The King's staunch supporters were prepared to fight to the last and looked for any opportunity to start a general war. McLean alleged that they had been spreading 'glaring untruths' about the Europeans to gain the sympathy of other tribes for the Taranaki War. This group had been using the fame of Potatau as a warrior and his mana as a rangatira in support of their plans to attack the settlers. Among the rangatira he listed Hoani Papika, Porokou Tihipa, Te Kehirini, Wiremu Tamihana and Te Heuheu.

The second group included Potatau's relatives, who supported the movement from family pride, but were reluctant to fight unless certain of success. They believed that it was only Potatau who was keeping the peace. Others, keeping their options open, gave the King movement 'quiet support' without openly committing themselves lest they might prejudice their relations with the Governor if the King's party collapsed. McLean thought that a considerable number of the Waikato including Tamati Ngapora, Huirama Tarahawaiki and Ihaka Takanini, belonged in this group.

The third group clearly supported the British Government 'so far as they can comprehend the nature of their obligation, without reference to any immediate advantage to be gained'. Among these rangatira were Wiremu Nera and Te Ao o te Rangi. McLean assessed that this group would increase in size as Maori became aware that Potatau's authority as King might restrict their independence and interfere with their property rights.

McLean told the Governor that he had spoken to the gathering on the history of the Waitara purchase from the time of the first sale to Te Teira's offer in March 1859. He had reminded the Waikato tribes that they had sold their right to land at Waitara, acquired by conquest, to Governor Hobson, therefore they could not in honour repudiate the act of their great rangatira, Potatau. Justifying the Governor's actions, he said that, at the tribes' request, the Governor had intervened to stop their feuding, and that he had not made war over 'a paltry piece of land' but to protect the rights of some Maori from being trampled by others. He added that land had not been offered by one individual – seventy claimants supported Te Teira – and had been presented at a meeting of all the rangatira. Nor had the Governor acted hastily, having considered his options for at least a year.

McLean did not continue his speech the following morning. He believed that he had been prevented from doing so because the King's party was alarmed by the effect it had had on the assembly. However, he also needed to depart before the King's flagstaff was raised. McLean considered that Potatau had hitherto proved himself loyal and had been conciliatory, in their conversation, assuring McLean that there was no intention of attacking Auckland. He considered Potatau 'a fine specimen of an intelligent New Zealand chief' and regretted that he had become 'subject to the evil council of his ambitious Maori adherents and their unprincipled European advisors'. McLean viewed the King movement not so much as a vehicle for regaining of national independence as a means of exacting a recognition of the chiefs' rights in their attempts to preserve their declining influence and power.[38] This was a change from McLean's assessment the year before when he had given priority to their wish for national independence.

Gore Browne told McLean that he had approached the Waikato rangatira Takerei for his views on a peace settlement, assuring him that he did not link Ngati Ruanui and Taranaki with Kingi. He asserted that he 'was not a stealer of land', but that the disputes between Kingi's people and the Europeans had become 'so acrimonious that we could not hope for peace while we occupied the same country'. He thought it reasonable that Kingi should cede his land on the south-west bank and cultivate the north-east bank of the Waitara River. As for the southern tribes, they must surrender the 'murderers' and agree to a boundary. He awaited their response. For Kingi, however, the Governor's plan presented real difficulties; it threatened his mana and left the utu balance between his people and Te Teira's unresolved.

On 29 April Gore Browne outlined his plans to Parris for making peace with Wiremu Kingi. He was adamant that there could be no permanent peace until Kingi and his followers removed themselves to the north-east bank of the Waitara. He believed that, if reinforcements arrived from the Waikato, Kingi would again fight and, he hoped, '(by God's assistance) he will be thrashed'. Kingi could then be prompted to make an 'acceptable proposal' that would have to include the sale of all property belonging to himself and his people on the south-west bank of the Waitara. In that event, compensation could be offered. The Governor ended, 'These are my wishes. I do not know if they can be carried into effect but ask your opinion and if you think them practicable, your co-operation'.[39] Sensing McLean's covert opposition the Governor seems to have decided to use Parris to continue negotiations over Waitara.

The following day, however, Gore Browne was writing to McLean expressing his support. 'You must use your own judgement, be guided by circumstances as they arise and act for the best, resting assured of my support always.'[40] Apart from the Waitara situation his trust in McLean appeared unimpaired. He thought that McLean's assessment of the Waikato tribes' intentions was not encouraging, 'but we are for it now and must fight out of it if necessary in the best way we can'. He agreed with McLean's advice to attack the Taranaki and Ngati Ruanui tribes, and would act upon it as far as he could. 'You desire that the murdering tribes should severely punished and so do I but the question is how to do it ... I told Gold to attack the murderers if he saw any way of getting at them and not to attack W. King unless he commenced hostilities.'[41] The Governor had been worried that an attack on Wiremu Kingi would bring the King movement tribes from Waikato to his aid.

In May the Governor had already drafted terms for peace in Taranaki. He told McLean that if he did not agree about the terms he should say what he thought should be done. 'Ministers are prepared to give pensions and act most liberally at Taranaki so that the chiefs will have the choice between good and evil, between cash with peace or war to the knife.'[42] If Wiremu Kingi rejected the offer, the Governor had instructed Colonel Gold to attack him. He advised McLean that, when he spoke of the terms 'on which I would make peace I think it desirable to lay stress on what we will not do rather than say positively what we will do'.

Any rumour that the Government was offering peace terms to Wiremu

Kingi, McLean replied, would be construed by Maori as a sign of weakness. He accepted that there was now a stand-off, so let Kingi be the first to propose terms. Until he did so, no terms dictated to him would be regarded as binding. The best way to make Kingi submit and avoid a general war would be to punish Taranaki and Ngati Ruanui, making it a lesson to deter other tribes from murdering unprotected settlers. Such an action would have the sympathy of most Maori. Unless this was done before Kingi was attacked, a general war might result. Any belief that the Government was making war to bring about a partition of land or to gain territory beyond Te Teira's block would threaten the settlers' safety throughout the island. Moreover, wrote McLean, it would confirm Maori suspicions that the Government was changing its policy and making war to obtain land.[43] He was offering prudent advice on the consequences of Gore Browne's actions over Waitara.

The Governor, perhaps frustrated by McLean's reluctance to return to Taranaki, no longer relied solely on him for advice on Waitara. By early 1860 Gore Browne was turning to Parris for advice, saying that he had read his reports to the Assistant Native Secretary and thought them very valuable. He asked Parris to report directly and confidentially to him adding that 'you might perhaps like to say to me what you would not wish recorded in the office'. This proposal to bypass McLean showed that Gore Browne had some unspoken doubt about McLean's commitment to implementing his policy

Increasingly confident that he understood the intricacies of Maori customary land rights, Gore Browne, believing in the righteousness of his policy, determined to subdue Wiremu Kingi. Writing to Gairdner at the Colonial Office, he complained that the 'virulence of party here is very lamentable. Some of the Bishop's friends declare that the war has been brought on by a breach of the tenth commandment while the public generally would be pleased to hear I was bent on exterminating the Maori race.' He outlined in detail what he saw as the erroneous claims advanced by Kingi and his missionary supporters; claims based on Kingi's rights as an owner and seigneurial rights as a rangatira. Anyway, the Crown had earlier bought the land first from Potatau, the Waikato rangatira, and again from those whom Sir George Grey had 'permitted to squat on it'. He relied on the judgement of his Native Secretary, McLean, 'whose integrity is beyond question and whose experience in the extinction of native title is greater than any other man in the Colony'. His responsible advisers, the ministers, had supported him 'spontaneously and in the most disinterested manner'.[44] This naive interpretation of his ministers' support conflicted with Gore Browne's earlier charge in 1859 that settlers were determined to get hold of Maori land, '*recte si possint si non quoque modo*' [rightly if possible, if not, by any means].[45]

Gore Browne was grateful for his ministers' support. In a later private letter to the Colonial Office, he pointed out that:

> You will see by the despatches that the high episcopal party are not very reasonable in their views and a glance at the newspapers will convince you the settlers are not more so. I cannot adopt the views of either party and do not therefore expect to give satisfaction but my conscience tells me I am right. It is however very satisfactory to know that in all matters there is no difference of opinion between my ministers and myself or between them and the Native Department. All unite in feeling that the purchase could not have been shirked without discredit; that having acquired the land equitably and shewn every possible forbearance and every wish to avoid collision it is necessary to enforce submission as soon as it is in our power effectually.[46]

Nevertheless, Gore Browne did have moments of doubt. In a confidential letter to McLean in July 1860 he wrote that some persons had been circulating questions about Te Teira's title. This had alarmed his ministers but, 'I have implicit faith in you and felt quite convinced that you would have told me if any thing was wrong and moreover that you would not have let me make the declarations I did in the printed statement I sent home from New Plymouth. I fear an attempt may yet be made to make political capital on this subject.'[47]

Gore Browne's correspondence gives evidence that, although relying on McLean for advice on Maori land tenure, it was the Governor who made the policy decisions. He was the driving force in a decision to impose the Queen's sovereignty on 'rebellious' rangatira. To convey what he might wish 'to say more distinctly' he submitted a private memo to the Duke of Newcastle, Secretary of State for the Colonies.

> I might rest the justice of my proceedings with WK upon the advice of Mr McLean the Native Secty. (whose experience in the extinction of native title is unequalled) and upon that of my Ex. Council confirmed and approved by a large majority of the chiefs assembled at the conference, of the Legislative Council and the H of R., but my Lord Duke I do not shrink from any responsibility which attaches to my office. The war was forced upon me by WK and could only have been avoided by humiliating concessions which might have delayed but could never have averted it.[48]

To assert that the war had been forced upon him, reinforces the view that Gore Browne believed that the real issue was the Queen's authority and that the Waitara dispute was the occasion to enforce this.

In June 1860 a contingent of Ngati Maniapoto came south to join Wiremu Kingi who had built a pa close to the soldiers' Waitara Camp. When British forces attacked on 27 June they suffered a substantial defeat at Puketakauere.

Both north and south of New Plymouth, the Maori tribes continued their attacks on settlers' property driving outlying settlers to seek refuge within the town. General Pratt, despite minor successes, had failed to achieve a significant victory.

The town of New Plymouth remained in a state of siege. Gore Browne, thwarted of his 'quick victory', sent McLean to New Plymouth to begin negotiations. Chiefs should be reminded, the Governor wrote, that

> we went into Taranaki when the natives were very few in number and that they returned to take advantage of the Queen's protection; that the two populations are consequently so mixed that we must have but one law viz. the Queen's law; that Wm King must submit to that law, lay down his arms and destroy fighting pahs; that a committee of chiefs should define the lands belonging to the different chiefs and that they should hold or sell as they please. Say nothing of King's going beyond the Waitara but say we will not have a peace on terms likely to be token, that we must have a permanent and consequently just peace.[49]

The Governor wanted to leave a door open so that local tribes could offer to sell the land needed to consolidate the settlement. The Taranaki tribes, however, encouraged by their recent success over British troops, were reluctant to enter negotiations. McLean made no progress.

At the end of August many Maori left off fighting to take advantage of the planting season. Puketakauere was abandoned. In September, a strong force under General Pratt was ambushed by a small Maori party and two weeks later Colonel Leslie's force suffered a similar defeat. In October the King movement fighters received reinforcements. Pratt adopted a new tactic constructing saps against the fortified pa but in March Pratt was still short of Te Arei fortifications when Maori agreed to a truce.

Chapter 12
The Aftermath Of Waitara

Following the beginning of the war in Taranaki, in July 1860 the Governor convened a meeting of North Island rangatira at Kohimarama. He asked McLean to consider what proposals should be put before the chiefs as, unless they had a constructive plan, the meeting would end in 'table talk'. Gore Browne wanted discussion on the following topics:

> Subordination of Native race to the authority of the Crown
>
> Relations between Native Race and Representative System of the English Colony
>
> Internal Government of the Native Race under the authority of the Crown
>
> Native Land Title as regards the actual occupation of Land by the Natives themselves
>
> Native Land Title as regards the alienation and transfer of land title from the Native Owners.

The Governor aimed to counter the growing influence of the King movement, to dispel rumours about his reasons for going to war in Taranaki and to sound out Maori opinion in general. Some 250 'friendly' rangatira were invited; most attended. The Waikato and Taranaki rangatira either were not invited or stayed away, suspicious of the Governor's motives. Any government today would be reluctant to mount such a major conference unless it was confident that the probable outcome would reinforce government policies. At Kohimarama, the Governor and McLean aimed to consolidate Maori support for their policies. McLean chaired the discussions and controlled the agenda.

In opening the conference, the Governor dwelt on the obligations of the Crown under the Treaty of Waitangi, reminding the rangatira that in return for substantial advantages they had ceded 'absolutely and without reservation all the rights and powers of sovereignty'. He seemed to be unaware of any contradiction between this statement and the assurance of tino rangatiratanga embodied in the Maori text of Article Two of the Treaty, nor did any of the rangatira raise this issue in their responses. Neither Maori nor Pakeha present seemed to look to the Maori text in the ongoing debate over Maori independence.

The Governor claimed that New Zealand was the only colony 'where the Aborigines have been treated with unvarying kindness. It is the only Colony where they have been invited to unite with the Colonists and to become one People under one law.' He told the gathering that their adoption by the Queen made it impossible for them to be unjustly dispossessed of their lands or property. Every Maori had the same rights under law as the English. Mindful of the threat of the King movement, he warned that it would be the 'height of folly' for the rangatira to violate their allegiance to the Queen and thus forfeit their rights and privileges as British subjects. If the chiefs had any grievances he urged them to make them known and, if they were real, he would try to address them. If they had suggestions for the better protection of property, punishment of offenders, settlement of disputes and the preservation of peace he would give them most favourable consideration. He ended by congratulating them on their vast progress in civilisation under the Queen's protection, saying that 'the old have learnt to be thankful that their sunset is brighter than their dawn, and the young may be grateful that their life did not begin until the darkness of the heathen night had been dispelled by that light which is the glory of all civilised Nations'.[1] Gore Browne remained firmly Anglocentric in his outlook. McLean, in translating the Governor's speech, skirted round the issue of sovereignty in Article One. The Maori text of the Treaty had translated 'all the rights and powers of sovereignty' as kawanatanga or governorship. This glossed over the real purpose of cession of sovereignty. McLean translated 'sovereignty' as nga tikanga me nga mana kawanatanga katoa, the authority and all the powers of governorship, a rendering that expanded on kawanatanga yet added little of the sense of 'sovereignty'.[2] He did, however, refer explicitly to the specific items in the English text of Article Two that had been absent in the Maori version – forests, fishing places and other possessions – taonga.

On subsequent days at Kohimarama McLean asked the rangatira to respond to the Governor's address, translating it to the gathering and commenting on some aspects. He reminded them of the Treaty provision for the Queen to protect them against foreign aggression, pointing out that she had kept her word, as no foreign power had disturbed the country. On the guarantee of the rights and privileges of British subjects, he said that some had complained that the laws for Maori were not the same as the laws for Pakeha. This was true, as 'children cannot have what belongs to persons of mature age; and a child does not grow to be a man in a day'. This may be seen as an example of McLean's patronising paternalism and also as a debating tactic in his efforts to counter the appeal of the King movement.

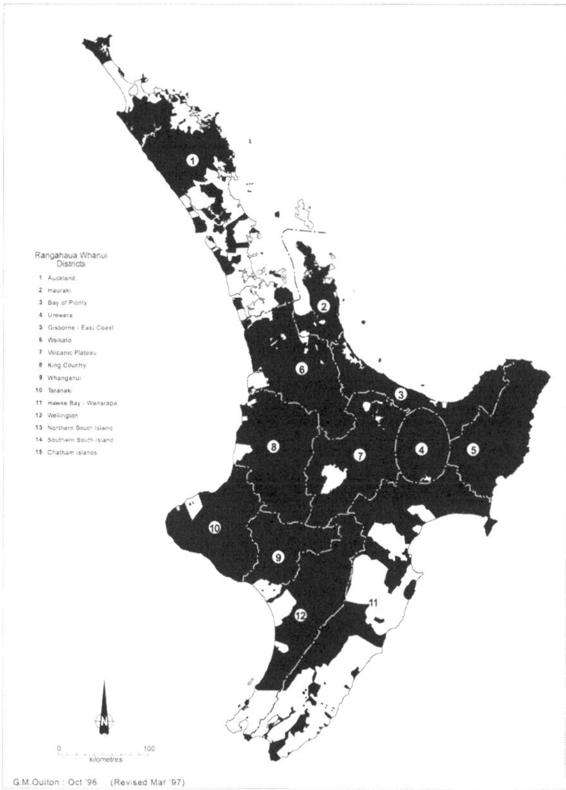

Map 3. North Island Maori Land at 1860 (shaded area)

Referring to the Treaty guarantee of the possession of their lands as long as they wished to retain them, he insisted that the Crown had strictly observed its obligations. In no single instance had Maori land been taken from them, except when they were willing to sell. 'Where is the man who has been deprived of any of his land?' McLean claimed that he bought land from those with the strongest title. Rangatira like Wiremu Kingi in Taranaki and Renata Kawepo in Hawkes Bay would have challenged this assertion had they been present. McLean continued that if the chiefs believed the Governor had violated any of the Treaty terms, he invited them to take the opportunity to tell him and, if anyone had a grievance, it should be made known at the conference. The Governor wanted them to know that this applied to the King movement which, although its original motive might have been good, involved setting up an independent nation. Such an act would 'prove a great hindrance to the establishment of peace ... The protection of England has been solicited and accepted by this country and it is therefore wrong to talk about any other sovereignty.'

McLean spoke of the Governor's concern about customary land rights, inviting the conference to come up with better ways of defining tribal boundaries and making provision for more secure tenure. No fixed law existed, only various customs that lacked permanence, and the endless complications of such customs were usually resolved by the 'Law of Might'. (McLean was exaggerating the extent to which Maori customary rights led to warfare over land.) He said the Governor looked to the co-operation of the chiefs in devising measures to simplify native tenure and to enable them to leave the land they had inherited in the undisturbed possession of their children. This approach reveals the ethnocentrism that motivated British policy in the nineteenth century. An indigenous people's customary rights were seen as inferior and better replaced by a European system of land tenure.

McLean, noting that the rangatira had been commenting on the Taranaki War, said it was important that they should understand the nature of the differences between the Governor and Wiremu Kingi. During 1860 McLean had been called on to justify the Governor's actions on several occasions, including before the House of Representatives. His explanation to the rangatira was probably his most important statement since he was aware that his audience, unlike the members of the House or the Colonial Office, had an intimate understanding of the intricacies of Maori customary land rights and of the status of rangatira and would challenge any doubtful interpretation or inaccurate definition.

He traversed the history of the land at Waitara from the time of Colonel Wakefield's purchase in 1839. He told the rangatira he believed that the main cause of the current situation was the existence of the King movement with its intention to prevent further land sales, thus moving the argument away from the relative merits of the claims of Te Teira and Wiremu Kingi. He did not concede increasing pressure of his district commissioners to acquire land may have caused the dispute. When Wiremu Kingi lived at Waikanae, said McLean, he had been well behaved but, when he returned to the land that previously belonged to his tribe, his attitude changed, he displayed 'both good and evil'. Taranaki Maori had been living at peace with one another but, after Kingi's arrival, feuding began and murders were committed. Some chiefs present might say that, if the Governor had asked them to intervene, peace could have been restored but they did not know the Taranaki Maori as he, McLean, did, who had long experience of their ways. Te Waka, who was present at the conference, Potatau and others all knew that the Taranaki tribes would not listen to reason. The Governor constantly urged them to end their feuds; that had been the purpose of his visit to Waitara in March 1859. This contradicted the opinion McLean had expressed some years earlier that, so long as the Governor had insufficient troops, it was preferable to have Maori fighting among themselves than uniting to confront the settlers.

At that Waitara meeting, McLean continued, the Governor had also spoken about the land, saying that each man should be at liberty to sell or retain his own place, as he thought proper, and that no one should be allowed to interfere. Te Teira's offer, said McLean, was on behalf of the hapu Ngati Hinga and Ngati Tuaho, and his intention was to sell a small part of this land to the Government, leaving the greater part untouched. McLean then gave his version of what followed. Te Teira had said to the gathering, 'Listen it is my own land that I shall give'. Three times he had asked the Governor if he would consent to buy. The Governor had turned to McLean saying, 'If it is right and he is really the owner, consent'. McLean said he gave that assent and Te Teira brought a parawai and placed it at the Governor's feet. Others also offered land, but their offers were not accepted as the title was not clear. Wiremu Kingi had then risen, and without questioning Te Teira's title or right to sell, merely 'spoke a few words' to the effect that Waitara should not be sold.

McLean told the conference that, before he left Taranaki, he had instructed Parris to investigate carefully the claims to this piece of land and not to proceed hastily. For more than a year Parris had been inquiring into the title. Wiremu Kingi had been present at those meetings and continued to withhold his consent to the sale while admitting that the land belonged to the sellers. McLean said he believed that Kingi's opposition arose from his connection with the land league. He had been encouraged by the King movement. Without this support, Kingi would never have ventured to forbid the sale of land to which he had never had any claim. He conceded that Kingi might have some justification if it had been land over which 'the Native title existed in its original state'. (He had earlier stated that Waikato had surrendered to Governor Hobson their claim to their conquered lands at Waitara.) He described how he had visited the section of Te Ati Awa living at Arapaoa in Queen Charlotte Sound, whose principal rangatira was Ropoama Te One. This hapu insisted that Kingi had no claim to the disputed land though he did have claims on the north bank. They insisted that they were the ones entitled to payment, but he, McLean, had refused them until the investigation was completed. From there he had gone to Heretaunga (Hawkes Bay) and when he returned he had been unable to give any further attention to the matter.

'You know very well that no man's land is taken unjustly from him', said McLean. 'The Ngati Tuaho and Ngati Hinga in times past claimed the *totaras* and the produce of the Waitara river. Other hapu Ngati Kura and Ngati Tuiti recognised their right and sometimes exchanged other produce with them for *totara* and lampreys.' He mentioned the rangatira of these hapu, including Harewa and Ropoama, noting that Patukakariki might also have a claim though he had not asserted it. McLean insisted that the Governor had never refused to listen to any just claim if properly brought forward. 'Do not pretend to say that Te Teira alone received payment for the land at Waitara. He was not even the largest claimant, but merely the spokesman for the seller.' McLean then read out the deed of sale, pointing out that the inland boundary had remained uncut because of disagreement.

Some chiefs had been complaining of hasty action, he went on, but this question had been under discussion for many years. The Governor had not acted hastily. He had invited Wiremu Kingi to come and meet him, but Kingi had refused. When the surveyors came Kingi had driven them away, and when the soldiers came to protect the surveyors, Kingi waited around hoping that one of his men might be killed, thus providing an excuse for an attack. He had built a pa on the disputed land and 'treated with contempt' a letter from the military commander. Thus, argued McLean, did Kingi 'wrongly provoke the war' and, according to the Governor, had 'assumed to himself the right of forbidding other chiefs to do what they pleased with their own'. McLean did not acknowledge that it was the British troops that had fired the first shots.

At the Kohimarama conference McLean sensed that many rangatira had a limited understanding of the Treaty of Waitangi, while others were questioning the supposed benefits. He arranged a session on it, reading the text and assuring them that the Treaty was their safeguard. If it were set aside they would suffer. Some had said that Ngapuhi, who were the first to sign, were foolish and ignorant and that Heke's rebellion had been the consequence. McLean maintained that no ill feeling remained, as these past quarrels were seen only as 'acts of rebellious children against their parent'. Tamati Waka Nene and other chiefs had shown themselves to be wise men in asking for the Queen's protection. It was folly, he said, to accuse the past chiefs of ignorance. Did they imagine that they were intellectually superior to the 1840 chiefs or more competent to decide what would benefit their people? 'Let not their children now talk of repudiating the wise acts of their fathers who knew in their day what they were about as well as or better than the present generation.' The Treaty, McLean told the rangatira, had been a great boon to Maori. He noted that many tribes were represented at the conference, including some, like Te Arawa, who had not signed the Treaty in 1840.

Before the conference closed, McLean told the Governor the nature of the recommendations he intended the rangatira to approve. They included a pledge of full recognition of the Queen's sovereignty; disapproval of the King movement; justification of the Governor's actions in Taranaki; and deprecation of the murder of settlers.

Sensing the mood of the conference, he picked up a reference to the Treaty as a covenant and skilfully steered the rangatira, suggesting that they endorse and ratify the Treaty as a covenant.[3]

The outcomes were limited. There was only half-hearted support for the Government's policy over Waitara or for any condemnation of the King movement. The rangatira were offered in place of Fenton's over-legalistic and complicated version of the 1858 laws affecting Maori a simpler codification of British law drafted by Sir William Martin. Contentious issues relating to land, sovereignty and power sharing remained unresolved, though the rangatira indicated they wanted the Queen as their sovereign, that they were willing to be involved in European society and wanted to have some influence within the institutions of government. The value of official recognition of the rangatira by the convening of the conference was reflected in their petition that such a gathering be a permanent institution. McLean could feel that he had at least averted a widening conflict between the two peoples.

While the rangatira who had signed the Treaty in 1840, and those who had not, affirmed their commitment to the Treaty and said they wished the Queen as their sovereign, at the same time, they made plain their dissatisfaction that the Crown had failed to involve them in the legislative and administrative processes of government. McLean interpreted the final resolutions as a unanimous endorsement of the Treaty of Waitangi as a covenant signifying a recognition of the Queen's sovereignty and of the union of the two races.

After the conference, McLean, conscious of the concern of the rangatira at the loss of their independence, submitted to the Governor 'a plan for the settlement of existing difficulties among the New Zealand tribes. A council of the principal chiefs would meet as determined by the Governor to 'consider all subjects affecting their interest as a people'. Meetings could be held alternately at Wellington and Auckland; £5000 was to be available for transport and accommodation. The Kohimarama conference had shown the advantages of a council that would give Maori a legitimate means of having their wrongs redressed in a constitutional manner and make them think that the Government was concerned for their welfare. Such a measure would involve them in participation 'in those institutions by which they must in the process of colonisation be governed'. McLean proposed that the best and wisest rangatira be selected to manage the affairs of their districts through runanga. The principal rangatira of each runanga would have the authority to decide disputes and to refer his decisions to the Governor for approval or rejection. New Zealand could be divided into 100 districts with rangatira paid annual salaries ranging from £20 to £100 according to the nature of their duties. Some older rangatira should receive life pensions to ensure their co-operation in keeping good order and peace. McLean, however, would have kept the Governor and himself very much in control.

McLean's proposal reflected a system of indirect rule practised by Britain and other imperial powers in the nineteenth century in which established structures were retained, though modified, and administered through existing rulers. Lord Lugard, a colonial African administrator, wrote: 'An arbitrary and despotic rule which takes no account of native customs, traditions and prejudices is not suited to the successful development of infant civilisations, nor in my view, in accordance with British colonial rule.'[4] In New Zealand there was a significant difference; New Zealand was a British settlement colony, whereas in Britain's African and Asian colonies British settlers were a tiny minority. For McLean, indirect rule was to be but a temporary phase until full assimilation took place. McLean's plan would favour sympathetic rangatira and had a further advantage: it would cost less to pay rangatira a small annual salary than to create a new structure with a large number of government officials. Moreover, it would be a means of rewarding sympathetic rangatira.

In August 1860, the Government, faced with opposition demands for a committee of inquiry over the Taranaki War, deflected these by agreeing on a rare procedure: to call Archdeacon Octavius Hadfield and McLean before the House, rather than set up a select committee, to give evidence relating to the origin of the 'Native Insurrection'. They were to be cross-examined by members seeking to find out what had happened. Opposition members led by Fox assumed the role of a peace party, denouncing the Government for its aggression.

Gore Browne insisted that McLean first submit his account to Whitaker, the Attorney General and to Richmond, the Native Minister. He thought it 'might be advisable to avoid saying anything about the terms on which we would make peace until the chiefs have expressed their opinion on the justice of the war ... I beg you clearly to understand that I do not think of interfering with your better judgement on these matters. Pray consider yourself quite unfettered in every way and use your own unbiased judgement in all things.'[5] Although the Governor assured McLean that he had complete trust in his advice on the validity of the Waitara purchase, he remained nervous of any criticism. He worried over news that Featherston was about to produce a map showing that Kingi had very large claims on the disputed block of land at Waitara. He asked McLean what answer he should give to such an assertion. Smith, the Assistant Native Secretary, suggested that it was a forgery intended to enhance Kingi's claim.

In his evidence to the House, Archdeacon Hadfield believed, from his contacts with Maori, that the war was not being fought to uphold the Queen's sovereignty but was 'a sheer act of spoliation' arising from an unjust land deal. Wiremu Kingi, as the leading rangatira of Te Ati Awa, was speaking on behalf of his tribe. Hadfield insisted that he himself was an unwilling witness who had no distinct proof but was relying on statements made to him by Maori involved in the dispute. Under cross-examination the 'political parson' sometimes challenged his questioner, saying that he found himself unable to understand the question or that the question was 'perfectly unintelligible and irrelevant'. Hadfield, never ready to suffer fools, was trying to point out to the House that his questioners did not know what they were talking about.

McLean began his evidence by traversing the history of the district from the time of the Waikato invasion in the 1830s and the New Zealand Company purchases to Wiremu Kingi's subsequent return.[6] When Te Teira made his offer before the Governor in 1859, no one denied his right except Wiremu Kingi. McLean told the House that the 'actual owners of the soil, the men known and recognised as such' had agreed to the sale and that 'great pains were taken both previously to and after the offer to inquire who the real claimants were and to settle with them'. The reference to prior investigations seemed to acknowledge that McLean and Parris had been trying to buy this land for some time. McLean insisted that the principle applied at Waitara was identical to that of previous purchases in Taranaki, namely 'of acquiring land from the different clans and subdivisions of those clans which came in from time to time to offer it'. McLean asserted that most of the difficulties and opposition over the purchase originated with an anti-land-selling league. This league had made a general claim that 'grasped at the *mana* of the whole extensive territory between Waitara and Mokau', although the same land had been ceded to Governor Hobson by the Waikato tribe. The existence of any such formal league at Taranaki at that time has since been discounted,[7] but there is no doubt that McLean and the Governor were convinced of its existence. Although there was in fact no formal structure, it seemed to them that the Taranaki tribes were making a common cause to oppose further land sales.

Under cross-examination, McLean insisted that the claim of Te Teira's party was strong because the offer to sell had been made in public – 'the first and best evidence you could get of title'. Opposition politicians confronted him with statements he had made in earlier years that appeared to conflict with his interpretation of the Waitara purchase. McLean was asked to confirm his evidence before the Board of Inquiry into Native Affairs in 1856 that an individual Maori did not have a strictly individual right to any particular portion of land independent of the tribal right relating to the transfer of that land. McLean denied that he had changed his opinion, nor had he, over Waitara, in any way recognised a right of an individual to 'alienate land held in common by his tribe or by subdivisions thereof'. Hadfield, he said, was wrong in inferring that the 600 acres at Waitara was offered by an individual. The offer came from a decision of two important hapu, Ngati Tuahou and Ngati Hinga, as well as a branch of the Puketapu.[8] McLean denied that there were eighty

Map 4. Pekapeka Block, Waitara, showing Wiremu Kingi Te Rangitake's holdings

claimants to the Pekapeka block at Waitara. If there had been, his invitation to the rangatira to put in claims would have brought them forward. Tribal right in different parts of the country varied so greatly that it was impossible to set down any rule; there were 'very wide exceptions'. He explained that hapu did 'most frequently' have a right to dispose of land but custom varied; in some tribes the hapu had to be consulted, in others, the rangatira. The rights of the parties had to be established by inquiring of the people of the district. This meant that there was no settled rule for land alienation. When asked what applied for Te Ati Awa, McLean replied that a family of three or four people was seen as being entitled to dispose of its common property. Although it suited McLean to tell the House that there were no straightforward rules covering land alienation, he was acknowledging the complexities of Maori customary land rights in having to accommodate the major and secondary interests of several claimant hapu. The evidence given before the House suggests that the interests of the hapu involved at Waitara were difficult to sort out and probably beyond Gore Browne's comprehension.

In his evidence McLean sometimes reworked his knowledge of events to suit his argument. His testimony departed from his recorded statements of earlier years. In 1848, when negotiating for the purchase of land at Waitara, McLean had accepted Wiremu Kingi as the leading rangatira, empowered to speak for his people. In 1860 he denied that same right, arguing that two hapu wished to sell. In 1847 McLean had reported that the claims of the land sellers were so intermingled with those opposing a sale that they were scarcely accessible. In 1859, at the Governor's instruction, he had written to Kingi inviting him to identify his 'pieces' within the block offered for sale. The course of the inquiry was predictable. Members were trying to find out what had been going on. Ministers set out to justify their actions to the House and would not concede that Wiremu Kingi had any right to intervene. Opposition members sought to embarrass the Government. McLean, as a government official, had to defend the decisions of his superior, the Governor, and to justify his own actions. His evidence traversed only those facts that supported the government case or would assist in damage control.

Gore Browne was disappointed that Hadfield had appeared so much better prepared than McLean when he appeared before the House. It seems that the Governor, certain that Wiremu Kingi had no case, was disconcerted by Hadfield's evidence. An examination of the transcript of the two men's evidence, however, suggests that, under cross-examination, Hadfield admitted that he had no first-hand knowledge of the circumstances at Waitara, but relied on what he had been told by his Maori informants, two of whom had left Waitara thirty years before. McLean conveyed the impression of being in possession of all the facts, though he commented only on those that supported his argument.

From an unexpected quarter came evidence that McLean had reservations about the validity of Te Teira's claim. In an October 1860 letter to a newspaper, Archdeacon Hadfield recalled a discussion with McLean on 10 March of that year when McLean told him 'very distinctly' that he was surprised that William King had not spoken more strongly at the meeting on 12 March 1859. (McLean made no mention of this meeting in his diary.) McLean said that he had by no means made up his mind that Te Teira's title was valid and that he had, 'in consequence of this doubt, urged the Governor and Mr. Parris to use very great caution if they proceeded with the negotiation'. According to Hadfield, McLean admitted that he later made inquiries at Queen Charlotte Sound and Wellington but investigated no further at Waitara. Referring to his conversation with McLean over the survey of the Pekapeka block, Hadfield wrote: 'I will not say that he expressed surprise that no reference had been made to him before the important step taken by the Governor was resolved upon; but his language undoubtedly implied as much when he attributed the absence of any such reference to him to the probable wish of the Governor to avoid giving him unnecessary trouble or anxiety during his illness.' Given the level of public hostility between the two men, it is surprising that McLean should have expressed a view so contrary to his public stance over Waitara. Hadfield said that Matene Te Whiwhi, an influential rangatira of high rank in Ngati Toa, Ngati Raukawa and Te Ati Awa, had accompanied McLean on a visit to Taranaki in March 1860. Te Whiwhi had reported that McLean regretted that the Governor should have taken 'such a hasty and premature step as the forcible ejection of William King from Waitara without investigation'.[9]

How strongly Gore Browne's feelings were aroused by opposition over Waitara he revealed in a letter to Sir William Martin, acknowledging the latter's pamphlet on The Taranaki Question. Gore Browne implied that Martin's account was based on incomplete and inaccurate information.

> I am however firm in my own convictions; at the same time I am not either so prejudiced or so unjust as not to admit that you have an equal right with myself to enjoy a perfect freedom of opinion ... views put forward so temperately and with such earnestness must command attention and respect from all and from no one more than myself and if I refrain from continuing my visits to Tauraua [Martin's residence] (which have often thrown a beam of sunshine across dark hours) it is because the conversation of two men, having one interest deeply at heart yet differing in their views of how it can be best promoted, must necessarily be constrained.[10]

The Governor reserved his bitterness for Archdeacon Hadfield, pointing out it was plain from statements in the pamphlet that, if Hadfield had complied with

Kingi's letters asking him to convey his views to the Governor, war might have been averted. 'Much blood lies at his door.'

Despite moments of anxiety, Gore Browne remained unyielding throughout the Taranaki Campaign. In reply to a letter from Featherston he wrote that 'I have got hold of that part of Waitara which belongs to the two hapu who sold it and I will keep my hold like a Bull dog. Any concession on this subject besides being disgraceful would leave the settlers at the mercy of an uncivilised race who would make war upon them whenever they had an object to gain.' He went on to challenge Featherston's opinion that to bring about the resignation of the Stafford Government would advance the prospect of peace: 'the real stumbling in the way of peace is the language used by those who consider themselves the friends of the Maoris. I do not dispute their right to say what they please in a free country but it is absurd to complain that peace is not made while they continue to give such moral support to the insurgents both in speaking and writing.'[11]

In December 1860, in setting out the terms on which he would make peace, the Governor told the Secretary of State for the Colonies that no one desired peace more than himself, but he would not consent to a peace that was 'likely to last only as long as the Maoris find it convenient'. The terms on which he would make peace included a commission to partition the district between Waitara and Tataraimaka, surrender of those who had killed civilians, and compensation to settlers for destruction of property.[12]

McLean never wavered in his public justification of the Waitara purchase. His first defence was always that the negotiations for the purchase of Te Teira's block had taken no different course from other negotiations, and charges that his department's policy had changed were unfounded. This smacked of sophistry; if the process was unchanged, then certainly the tactics had changed.

By the mid-1850s growing Maori reluctance to sell land led McLean to attempt to simplify the complexities of customary land rights and to secure agreement, sometimes in secret, from only a few rangatira rather than all claimants. McLean was cautious. He paid only a first instalment and did not proceed to undertake any survey or subsequent occupation. He was prepared to wait until opposition died down, hastening that process by actively trying to detach elements of the opposition and making further payments.

His next ground was that European opponents of the Waitara purchase based their case on erroneous assumptions that the various hapu of Te Ati Awa composed a community holding their lands in common and that Wiremu Kingi was their rangatira, and that the course adopted by the Government had not taken account of any special circumstance connected with Te Ati Awa. He argued that Te Ati Awa themselves in their land transactions had never taken the position that they were one community. In other sales, hapu had been the negotiators. The general consent of the whole tribe or of any rangatira not directly interested in the land under question had therefore not been thought necessary.

At Waitara the two hapu represented by Te Teira claimed both ownership and the right to dispose of the land. Wiremu Kingi admitted that they owned the land in question. Even the right of alienation could hardly have been questioned by Kingi as a matter of right. As a rangatira, McLean argued, Kingi's influence might sway the minds of his people, so that his word would be law if he spoke for the tribe, but over Waitara the four hapu were divided. No right as a rangatira would be conceded in respect of land not belonging to his own hapu. As to the argument that Wiremu Kingi was asserting a tribal right as distinct from a proprietary one, McLean pointed out that his right to intervene had been ignored by the interested parties 'independently of whom it could have no existence'. He insisted that Kingi had not asserted such a right, quoting his statement at the time of the payment of the first instalment that he would not allow the owners to sell. Kingi had not said that the tribe would not consent. McLean acknowledged that Wiremu Kingi was an influential rangatira, and that he owned part of the Waitara district. Kingi had made it clear that he did not want European settlement to expand to Waitara. So long as the majority of the owners in the four Waitara hapu wished to keep their land, said McLean, Kingi was able to say that no land should be sold. When two hapu changed their position over selling land Kingi tried to stop them knowing that he could rely on support from other tribes involved in what McLean believed to be an anti-land-selling league. Although Kingi's European supporters based their endorsement for his stand on the grounds of his right as a rangatira to uphold his tribal title, McLean argued that such a right had never been claimed by Kingi's Maori supporters. McLean's assessment differed when dealing with a rangatira willing to sell land. In Hawkes Bay, he looked to Te Hapuku, an influential rangatira, to promote offers to sell throughout the province.

Historians have difficulty in reaching firm conclusions or in apportioning responsibility over the Waitara purchase and the subsequent war in Taranaki. There are reasons for this uncertainty. By 1859, after two decades of British colonisation, those in authority were still struggling to cope with situations beyond their experience. With the possible exception of McLean, they lacked any real understanding of Maori society on which they might shape their policies. What they did achieve was ineffective. At the Colonial Office, Rogers concluded that 'a case in all respects unanswerable cannot be made on either side'.[13]

Waitara roused strong passions that divided colonial society. As we have seen, Governor Gore Browne felt compelled to tell his good friend, Sir William

Martin, that he could no longer visit his home because of their difference over Waitara. McLean denounced Hadfield as that 'proud and mischievous serpent, more demon than deacon'; Hadfield retaliated that McLean was an uneducated, ignorant man.

The key to understanding how the Waitara affair developed is in the relationship between Gore Browne and McLean – one that was changing by 1859. Gore Browne has been portrayed as weak and indecisive, an erroneous interpretation to which this author may have contributed.[14] A study of Gore Browne's private letters to the Colonial Office show a shrewd and perceptive analysis of men and events. He was capable of acting decisively. In the disastrous Afghan campaign of 1839–1842 he was the only commander who succeeded in extricating his regiment intact during the retreat. When he arrived in New Zealand he spent his first year seeking expert opinion from officials, missionaries and settlers who had been associated with Maori. For a nineteenth-century military man, he had an enlightened management style. Having established his policy, Gore Browne refrained from intervening in the way that McLean, his trusted adviser, went about its implementation. Gore Browne did what he believed to be right, undeterred by opposition. If Te Teira had the right to sell, then Wiremu Kingi's intervention was that of a bully and the head of an anti-land-selling league. For the Governor the issue was the enforcement of the Queen's authority. He insisted that he would never have gone to war for '600 paltry acres of land' at Waitara.

Politicians, resentful of McLean's exercise of his independent empire, believed that the Governor was his puppet. In accounting to the Duke of Newcastle for his actions, Gore Browne was emphatic that, although he had the support of his ministers and respected the advice of McLean as the expert on Maori matters, the responsibility and the decisions were his alone.

McLean's role was equivocal. If he had been left to negotiate there would not have been a war. As with numerous offers to sell, McLean, having established the rightful claimants, would have paid the first instalment to Te Teira representing the sellers and then waited for years if necessary to negotiate his way round the opposition. Gore Browne acted from principle. McLean, always pragmatic, would not have allowed principle to impede a compromise. Moreover, unlike the Governor, whose grasp of Maori land tenure was theoretical, he understood first-hand the complexities of Maori customary land rights, that different hapu might have a right to sell land and for different reasons. Somehow these had to be reconciled or bought off.

Gore Browne continued to justify his handling of the Waitara affair. In October, as he was about to leave New Zealand for Tasmania, Gore Browne sent a McLean a confidential note, believing McLean was about to go to England: 'if all I hear is true you would do well to inform yourself thoroughly and lose no time seeing the Secretary of State. I hear that W. is declared a Hero the King Movement a Godsend Hadfield a martyr and Fox the most farseeing disinterested of patriots … This may all be bosh but it condemns you and I and all who thought differently as we did' He ended with a postscript: 'I look anxiously for your letters for my heart and thoughts are in New Zealand. If you should ever be called on again don't let your case break down again for want of care and preparation. Remember how well Hadfield prepared anything for the committee of the MHR.'[15] Arriving in Sydney, Gore Browne resumed his advice: McLean should go to the Colonial Office and speak to Cox or Fortescue. He told McLean that his taking leave was for the best, as it was clear that Gore Browne's successor, George Grey, intended to hand over responsibility for native affairs to the ministers. 'You would not be able to serve under them. When they have tried their hands at managing Maoris for a few months they will find the want of the only man whom the natives really confide in and will clamour for your return.'[16]

After the renewal of fighting in Taranaki following the outbreak of war in the Waikato and Governor Grey's decision to abandon the purchase of the Pekapeka block at Waitara, McLean took the view that the war in Taranaki arose from the unresolved issue of sovereignty which had been at the heart of the 'native problem' ever since 1840. He told Featherston in 1863 that 'there is no blinking the fact that we have come to the face to face policy in earnest' but that with the arrival of a new military commander, General Cameron, they could expect a favourable outcome. If Cameron's attack at Tataraimaka on 4 June 1863 was followed up by a few more successful engagements, McLean hoped that, even if they did not 'completely reduce the natives to submission, it will teach them that British power is not to be trifled with. McLean was convinced that British imperial power must be imposed by force in the last resort.

Returning in his letter to Featherston to his theme of the underlying conflict between Maori and British power, he wrote of the growing 'spirit of disaffection' that had been present since 1840. In effect he saw a common thread of reluctance to submit to the Queen's sovereignty. He thought it had not required much at any stage in the life of the colony to 'kindle a blaze'. It was 'all twaddle' to claim that this was the consequence of any particular act, and 'shallow reasoning' to attribute the conflict to any one particular cause; this revealed only 'a superficial knowledge of human nature and of the Natives' character'. The Waikato were trying to unite the tribes in one general struggle, which he believed had been an aim for many years, going back to Hongi's time and the 1843 massacre at Wairau. The conflict was 'an inevitable consequence' of the 'continuation of circumstances acting upon the two races'. McLean seems here to acknowledge that the interests of settler and of Maori had become irreconcilable. Yet he had some responsibility, despite

Gore Browne's intervention, for allowing a relatively minor dispute (when measured by the acreage involved) to become the cause of a major war.

As for the war in Taranaki, he asserted, the 'symptoms of disaffection' had been plain for the previous fifteen years 'and yet you and others will positively avow that the paltry 600 acres of land at Waitara has caused all this spirit of insurrection'. He continued: 'Passing events and the relinquishment of that land go to prove how very little importance the natives attached to it. I am as ignorant as can be of any valid grounds for giving up that land; except that it has become fashionable in New Zealand for one party to reverse what another has done, merely proving to the natives the instability of our Acts.'[17]

Although he had ceased to play an active role in government, McLean continued to follow the outcome of the Waitara purchase. In 1863, when Governor Grey decided to abandon the purchase, McLean condemned his action. He wrote to the then Native Minister, Francis Dillon Bell, wanting to know what had happened to bring about this change of policy. Bell replied setting out the so-called 'new' facts: that Te Teira himself had said that Kingi had been placed on the south-west bank of the Waitara River at the invitation of the people as security against the threat of the Ngati Maniapoto, that there were a number of Kingi's followers living on this land at the time of the sale, and that Te Teira said he was promised a reserve of 200 acres at or about Huriapa.[18] None of this was new evidence; it would have been known to McLean in 1859.

Bell remarked that the 'new' facts had not altered the view Gore Browne and McLean took in 1860, 'that the war was not about title to a piece of land but an insurrection against the Crown's authority'. Bell, however, was surprised that men like Martin and Hadfield in their 'voluminous pamphlets' had not come across this evidence, remarking, 'They often shaved the truth pretty near but never hit it'. He believed that the Government had decided to abandon the Waitara purchase, not because it had been unjust, but because, although 'a great humiliation', it had placed the invasion of the Waikato 'on a ground which no one can possibly dispute', in that the fighting could not be seen to be linked with the Government's attempt to acquire land by force.

C. W. Richmond had no reservations: 'The inevitable hour of conflict must come. It was one of the necessities of civilisation.' McLean preferred to delay that hour in the hope that the Queen's sovereignty might prevail without a racial war.

In 1860 McLean was called to give evidence before another Committee of the House. On this occasion, it was an investigation into the effectiveness of Fenton's attempts as resident magistrate in 1857–58 to 'introduce institutions of Civil government among the Natives of the Waikato district'. Gore Browne saw this inquiry as part of the battle with his ministers over control of native affairs. He told the Duke of Newcastle that the committee was 'in reality a Court assembled for the purpose of trying the Native Department in general and Mr McLean, its able Chief, in particular. This gentleman possessed Sir George Grey's full confidence and from this fact as well as from being what is termed my irresponsible adviser in Native affairs he has incurred the animosity of those who consider the reservation made in reference to the management of native affairs an act of injustice, and who desire to include all who are in any way connected with it in one general condemnation.'[19] Aware of the animosity between McLean and Fenton, Gore Browne sent McLean a confidential note warning him to be on his guard the next day in giving his evidence and not to 'let any dislike or distrust of Fenton appear' because his opponents would try to make it appear that he disapproved of his scheme because he disliked the man. He also advised him to limit his responses and not give 'any account of the past or proposals for the future'.[20]

The personality clash between McLean and Fenton hampered the development of a constructive Maori policy. The pragmatic McLean saw little value in Fenton's legalistic and pedantic approach. He was jealous of Fenton's attempt to take on the role of adviser in Maori affairs, a sphere in which McLean was acknowledged as the unrivalled expert. Contemporary and more recent judgements rate Fenton's intellect highly. W. Gisborne, one of the earliest public service administrators, assessed him as 'a man of great ability, of acute original thought, holding strong views of his own, careless of departmental routine and not very amenable to official control'. Fenton's aim he described as 'a political and administrative system suited and acceptable to the natives, established on a wide and strong basis independent of mere personal influence. He felt an intense hatred of a policy of palliatives and procrastination – a policy which he attributed unfairly, as I think, to Sir Donald McLean.'[21] Keith Sinclair thought that Fenton had an intellectual grasp of the changes taking place in Maori society and that his writings 'would do credit to a modern anthropologist'. He considered Fenton to be 'a man to design policies; McLean a man to carry them out'.[22] Fenton's later conduct as Chief Judge of the Compensation Court and the Native Land Court, however, did not give evidence of any empathy with Maori aspirations.

In his evidence before the committee, McLean said that, when the Governor visited the Waikato in 1857, Maori had asked for a simple code of laws. The Governor agreed, making it clear that he did not wish to force such things on them. Fenton, when appointed resident magistrate in the Waikato, began to introduce a new system of laws. McLean was critical of Fenton for failing to consult with the leading rangatira, Potatau. McLean alleged that, up to that time, Potatau had been lukewarm towards the King movement, but, finding the Government acting independently, had switched to support the movement. Not only had Fenton ignored Potatau, he had organised a Queen's party in opposition to the King movement. The Queen's party, McLean sneered, had themselves 'abandoned cultivations and all other useful pursuits, and talked of nothing but building courthouses, being appointed assessors or wardens or jurymen; and under these various designations were all looking forward to some employment under the Government'. In McLean's view, a government official was actively encouraging ill feeling between the tribes in circumstances that were likely to strengthen the King movement. He had advised the Governor to withdraw Fenton from the Waikato.

In response to questioning, McLean made it clear that he thought Fenton had little or no knowledge of the Maori language (this was unlikely), something he considered an essential attribute for such an official. McLean also said that he had had no part in the decision to send Fenton to the Waikato; and that Fenton took his instructions from the Colonial Treasurer, although, as Waikato was classified as a native district, he should have come under the control of the Native Department. Because of Fenton's background, McLean considered his appointment was undesirable, but he had not expressed misgiving, as the Native Minister had made the appointment. When asked if his department did not come under the Native Minister, he equivocated, saying that he did not know. It formed part of the Government of which the minister was a member but was more directly under the control of the Governor.

At the committee's request, McLean presented a memorandum on Fenton's recommendations for a new system of civil institutions suited to Maori. His response was similar to his comments on the 1858 legislation. He supported the recommendations 'viewed as an experiment', apart from two objections. The proposal to elect runanga would impinge on the power of the older rangatira, upon whom the Government had to rely in carrying any measures of a political character or in maintaining peace. A provision for district meetings would encourage combinations among the tribes, which McLean saw as undesirable. In his opinion, if established under favourable conditions in a native district, the proposal would succeed.

McLean insisted that 'fundamental changes in the social organisation of any community to be effected safely must be introduced gradually'. The proposed system involved such a change and would produce 'mischievous results' unless introduced with caution and with due regard for the institutions it would replace. The existing power and authority of the rangatira would have to be recognised independently of any new powers they might receive. 'The latter should be grafted as it were on the old rather than made to supplant it.'[23]

In a letter to Judge Johnstone in November 1860 McLean repeated his support for the introduction of new institutions for Maori if they were part of a comprehensive scheme and not 'mere spasmodic efforts' that set out to destroy the influence of the old chiefs and to unsettle the existing social structure. He feared that Maori were being made the subjects of 'untried experiments subservient to the ends of party politics'. Any comprehensive measure would demand substantial expenditure – something the General Assembly had not been willing to support.

> The so-called friends of the Maoris of the present day would not grant 1000 pounds for Native purposes two years ago; although they contribute at least 25,000 pounds to the yearly customs revenue, independent of their selling us land at a cheap rate, which we retail at a handsome profit. When it suits a party or political purpose, the natives or the Native Office is found to be a very convenient stalking horse ...

However, he doubted that generous promises made in times of danger could be relied on afterwards. Yet he was heartened that members were at last trying to grapple with the Maori question as that 'must lead to a more full appreciation and just recognition of their social and political rights'.[24]

Henry Sewell, a moderate on native policy, tried to coax McLean to make public his views on the proposals for new institutions, as he appeared to be keeping them back from public criticism. He thought that McLean was reluctant to support experiments because he felt that insufficient funds would be available to make them effective. Although he did not agree with McLean, Sewell wanted him to present his case to the public in a way that would do him justice.[25]

After 1859, McLean began to distance himself from aspects of Governor Gore Browne's policies. By 1860, McLean, perhaps shaken by his recent illness and continuing ministerial hostility, was looking to retire from public life. Loyalty and regard for the Governor, however, kept him at his post. Gore Browne could not be deflected from acting according to his conscience. His actions since arriving in 1855 show that he shaped a policy and sought to implement it to the extent of his powers as Governor under a system of responsible government. Gore Browne trusted McLean and gave him freedom of action to implement policy, but McLean remained an official responsible to the Governor for his actions and for complying with government policies. Over Waitara, the ever-pragmatic McLean seemed to have reservations, but decided that he could not persuade the Governor to change his mind. He was, however, prepared to compromise and delay.

McLean's resistance, though covert, was impressive. Because of his regard for the Governor, he would not openly oppose or advocate a different course, although, as Native Secretary, he should have given impartial advice. In 1859 McLean remained in Hawkes Bay in defiance of instructions. His serious illness later in the year left the Governor to continue his policy alone. Throughout, McLean tendered no written advice on the Waitara purchase – at least there is no record of any. He did, however, at the Governor's request, present a major paper on land-purchase policy in which he warned his superior, if obliquely, that any actions that might convince Maori that the Government was determined to seize their land would bring land selling to an end.

Some observers believed that McLean, through loyalty, felt compelled to support Gore Browne against his own better judgement. Gisborne, a senior public servant and a shrewd judge of men, was 'convinced from a knowledge of his character that he would never have counselled Governor Gore Browne to complete that purchase and enforce it by armed measures'.[26] Featherston, who opposed the Waitara purchase, later wrote, 'Say what you will, McLean, you will never convince me that you believed in the validity of the purchase from Teira. You simply from a spirit of chivalry backed up Browne when he had gone too far to recede.'[27]

McLean wished to withdraw from public life, but felt that 'a sense of public duty and private regard for the Governor induces me to help the colony in its present unsettled state. Indeed I believe that my exertions since recovered from my late illness has done much to avert a general war.'[28]

Archdeacon Hadfield's behaviour over Waitara was ambivalent. He was sincere in his devotion to the cause of his Maori converts and believed that the Governor's actions had deprived Wiremu Kingi and his people of land that was rightfully theirs. Hadfield has been portrayed by his biographers as a saintly figure, but in his day he was known as the 'political parson', with a liking for a fight. His behaviour in 1859 in withholding Wiremu Kingi's letters to the Governor angered Gore Browne, who believed that these could have averted the war. It was Wiremu Kingi's misfortune to have Hadfield as his champion. Rather than seeking to mediate and avert conflict in Taranaki, Hadfield had become obsessed with bringing about Gore Browne's downfall. While he denied it, there was evidence that he instigated and encouraged Maori to petition London for the Governor's recall.

Wiremu Kingi was a man of integrity and, like Gore Browne, he decided that the time had come to draw the line. Earlier, Governor Grey had acknowledged him as the leading rangatira of the district. He had supported Grey when in 1846 the Governor sent troops against Te Rangihaeata. Kingi felt that the advance of settlement north-east of New Plymouth threatened the future of his people at Waitara, a land to which McLean acknowledged that they had an 'unalienable attachment'. The Governor might speak of '600 paltry acres' but for Kingi this was the land of his ancestors from which he would not be parted.

In 1860 there were those who believed that war between the races was inevitable and to be welcomed. By that time the range of choice for the Governor had diminished. Like the tale of the Sibylline books, what might have been viable in 1840 or 1850 was no longer possible. In 1850 McLean's proposal for a native council might have averted the establishment of the King movement. Yet war was not inevitable. If decisions over Waitara had been left to McLean, the pattern of his past conduct suggests that he would again have backed off when he encountered opposition.

Sir William Dennison, Governor of New South Wales, had visited Gore Browne in New Zealand in 1857 and in 1860. Gore Browne now sought his advice on how to deal with the Maori situation. Dennison was critical of the views of the Governor's ministers whose policy, he considered, would lead to the annihilation of the Maori and the occupation of their land. Dennison however, insisted that the Maori was 'entitled to have his rights respected, his feelings considered'. Dennison thought the King movement a step in the right direction and should not be ignored (as McLean had earlier advised). If the Maori King was assured of recognition of his position and rights he would be unlikely to plunge into war. The consequence would be the cessation of land sales. Gore Browne should accept and be in no hurry to buy. As Maori became more civilised, in a short time they would be willing to sell if they could get a better price. Dennison recommended that the Government pay the full market value for the land rather than buy at 6d an acre and sell at 10s an acre.[29] Dennison's advice was wise but, in the context of the time, unrealistic. The strength of settler feeling was such that any decision to halt land purchases would have brought the Governor into conflict with his ministers. The British Government, having conceded self-government to New Zealand, would have been reluctant to stand by the Governor. On the other hand, if Gore Browne had followed Dennison's advice and halted all land purchases while seeking an accommodation with the King movement, that might have given time to address Maori concerns about sovereignty. In any case, Gore Browne had failed to retain the confidence of his imperial masters and was appointed Governor of Tasmania in 1861 in circumstances similar to FitzRoy's 1845 recall.

Chapter 13
To Retire From Public Life

Under pressure from ministers to review his control of Maori affairs, in November 1860 Governor Gore Browne encouraged Henry Sewell to propose a bill to manage Maori affairs through a native council. Its members, Gore Browne hoped, would include men like the former Chief Justice Sir William Martin, Bishop Selwyn and McLean. The bill reflected McLean's advice to the Governor in September 1859. The council would take responsibility for land purchases and for encouraging Maori to sell. In every Crown purchase, an area would be set aside for the sellers and their descendants under an unalienable Crown title, and a further area allocated for religious and educational purposes. Part of the proceeds of the sale to settlers would be used for supplementing the General Assembly's grant for Maori purposes. Settlers, however, lobbied against the bill when it was introduced into the British Parliament and it was allowed to lapse.

Ministers then introduced their own Native Council Bill which transferred responsibility for Maori affairs from the Governor to the General Assembly and set up a native council with advisory powers only. At first the Governor reserved this bill for the Colonial Office to review, but in a private letter to Chichester Fortescue, Parliamentary Under-Secretary for the Colonies, Gore Browne admitted that he had reluctantly to agree to the Native Office being placed under the control of ministers.

Gore Browne agreed with Fortescue's view that the British Government, by signing the Treaty of Waitangi, had accepted the role of guardian of the Maori and could not hand over that duty to an assembly in which Maori were not represented. However, he pointed out that the New Zealand Constitution Act made insufficient provision for the Governor to exercise this guardianship. The bill was a compromise that, in the circumstances, was the best he could make. One major difficulty was the absence of men capable of managing a native district, and he regretted that in New Zealand there were no trained administrators as there were in India.[1] Gore Browne clearly did not intend to allow Maori to control native districts.

The Governor, unwilling to admit that he had lost the battle for control of

Maori affairs, clung to the belief that the bill was an adequate compromise. McLean disagreed. He had become more openly critical of government policy. He condemned the Governor's assent to ministers' proposals for the management of Maori affairs, describing this as a surrender. Any transfer to ministerial control should not take place without the 'free and intelligent consent of the natives themselves', who would be most affected by it. In his view, Maori, in ceding the sovereignty of the country to Britain, had relied upon assurances, since repeated by every Governor, that no change should take place in existing relations between them and Her Majesty, the Queen. McLean insisted that the Native Council Bill was not a substitute for the powers conceded as a council could not act except on ministerial advice. The contemplated changes would weaken Maori confidence in the British Government. It was unreasonable to call on the Crown to surrender its control of Maori affairs and at the same time to bear the expense of any wars that might arise 'under the management of persons irresponsible to the Crown'.

Further, McLean argued, 'Justice and good faith demand that such pledges or assurances should not be broken; and that the obligations assumed by the Imperial Government should not be transferred – at least without a sufficient guarantee that they will be faithfully discharged by those to whom the transfer is made'. A permanent appropriation of a proportion of the colonial revenue would be such a guarantee. The Crown should give careful consideration before surrendering control of land purchases with 19 million acres still in Maori hands.[2] McLean asked that his letter be forwarded as an enclosure to the Governor's dispatch to the Secretary of State.

Sir William Martin, Colonel Nugent and McLean all declined the Governor's invitation to join his native council. Gore Browne pleaded with McLean:

> Now don't throw me over! I would not ask you to do anything which I was not convinced was for your own credit, or what I believe to be for your own good. If you are determined to retire into private life, this is the best mode of doing it, viz:- to do it gracefully.
>
> Don't leave your old friend.[3]

Gore Browne admitted that the bill might be better than it was, but McLean's rejection removed all chance of success. Only his presence would assure the confidence of both settler and Maori. He suggested that it would be better for McLean to forward his protest to the Secretary of State, and to say that if the bill were still to be approved, he would be prepared to assist the Government, even though he disapproved of the plan. The Governor tried to frighten McLean by suggesting that, if he refused, ministers would have no alternative but to ask Fenton to join the council and he doubted if McLean would want to bring that about![4] McLean remained firm, saying the measure provided for nothing but a few salaried officers. If the bill had contained a single clause that could lead to hopes that something could then be done for Maori, nothing would have delighted him more than to join the council.[5]

Gore Browne excused McLean's refusal on the ground that he was 'wearied of hard work and abuse'. Earlier, in August 1860, he assured McLean that he understood his need to go to England and as soon as ever the war 'gives us a moment's rest you shall go with my wishes for your health and happiness'. The next month, however, he was urging McLean to return to Auckland as 'you know how entirely I depend on you and how ill I get on without you'.

Gore Browne maintained his gratitude for McLean's loyalty. Before his departure for Tasmania he wrote to McLean,

> In leaving New Zealand few things will grieve me so much as the cessation of our intercourse. You have been to me a kind friend and an able, conscientious and disinterested adviser.
>
> Wherever I go and whatever happens to me I shall remember you as such and I want you to remember me as a sincere friend.
>
> As a trifling token of regard and esteem I send you a watch (Scotch) which I trust you keep for the sake of
>
> Yours most sincerely T Gore-Browne

McLean responded, thanking him for the 'handsome letter you have sent me and the kind present accompanying it which I shall preserve as an heirloom and think of the days spent under your administration in New Zealand thro' good and evil report with the feeling that I have invariably had the good fortune of enjoying your confidence and sincere friendship'.[6]

McLean's personal regard for Gore Browne was reciprocated. After his departure from New Zealand, Gore Browne continued to express his gratitude for McLean's loyalty over the Waitara affair. Harriet Gore Browne shared her husband's regard. McLean had been a regular visitor at Government House and Gore Browne told him, 'My wife seldom saw you going away without saying, "There goes one of the most chivalrous men living!" and so you are'.[7] – an attribute, the Governor remarked, that his successor, Sir George Grey, did not comprehend or know how to practise.

In 1860 McLean had applied for two years' leave of absence to visit Britain but his request had been deferred. The Governor and his ministers believed that McLean's presence was essential to prevent the spread of the war in the North Island. In March 1861 McLean was still awaiting permission to take his leave. Meanwhile, he approved of the new Native Minister, Frederick Weld. He wrote to Dr Sinclair that 'I am getting on with my official duties very smoothly in fact I have my own way to a large extent'.[8] However, Weld soon found himself confronted with McLean's ongoing obsession for control. Weld complained to McLean that papers had been removed from his ministerial desk without his permission; at the same time he was aware that McLean was withholding in his own office papers intended for the minister, weeks after they had been minuted.[9]

The King movement had become involved in the Taranaki War in part because three Taranaki tribes had given their allegiance to the King, in part because of a commitment to stop the sale of further land and because it appeared that the Governor was intent on enforcing sovereignty over areas that had maintained a de facto independence in the first twenty years of the colony's existence. In March 1861 the Ngati Haua rangatira Wiremu Tamihana, the driving force in the establishment of the King movement, seeking to end the war in Taranaki sent proposals for a truce. The Governor intended to go to Taranaki with McLean and two of his ministers, but his ministers thought this premature. They recommended instead that the Native Secretary find out the real state of feeling and assess the prospect of the Governor going to make peace. Arriving at New Plymouth on 18 March, McLean sent a message to Tamihana asking for a meeting, but fighting continued throughout the day with further casualties. The following morning Tamihana replied, appointing a meeting place.

McLean described this meeting in a long report to the Governor.[10] Tamihana, accompanied by a hundred followers, gave McLean and his officials a 'cordial welcome'. He told McLean that, if such a conference had been held at the start of the dispute, it could have clarified the issues and, if 'some impartial and decided course' had been adopted by the Government he 'should not have sought out a remedy himself'. Maori neither understood nor were satisfied with the Government's actions.

McLean's response was measured and conciliatory and was met by an equally reasoned statement of Maori concerns from Wiremu Tamihana. McLean set a very different tone from Richmond's desire for a '*casus belli*' or Gore Browne's wish to 'pitch into' Wiremu Kingi. He began by saying that he was glad to hear that Tamihana desired peace as that was also the Governor's wish. He asked Tamihana if he still wished to pursue his previous suggestion to refer the dispute to the British Government and whether he and other rangatira would abide by the decision of the Secretary of State for the Colonies.

McLean set out the Government's view on the unity of the two races. Despite what might be said to the contrary by some Europeans, its aim was to preserve the Maori as a people and to promote their welfare. He told Tamihana that every question that might disturb the harmony between the two races should be examined and some remedy applied. The Government had not intended to ignore chiefs' rights but they themselves had 'trampled on the rights of the weaker parties'. The Government was committed to impartial justice to all. If Wiremu Kingi had a just claim at Waitara, he had been invited to substantiate it. His response had been to assert the 'right of might' over the land and to ignore the claims of other tribes.

Why had Ngati Haua and Waikato taken up arms against the Government? Tamihana should set out their grievances in writing for the Governor, 'with a view to devising some means of their removal'. McLean recorded that Tamihana replied that the occupation of Waitara was the sole reason for their taking up arms. He was not prepared to say what might bring about a future conflict, as 'he knew where the wind blew from today; but he could not say whence it would come tomorrow, that today it blew from Waitara, at another time evil might arise in another quarter, in which case he would feel bound to interfere'. He believed that the Government had got itself into a quarrel through one individual (Te Teira) without taking any steps to arrive at a proper conclusion, that no rules had been laid down to deal with such cases, and that the title to the land had not been sufficiently investigated. Tamihana said 'the Natives were a foolish and ignorant people, which made it necessary that the Governor and the Europeans, who were endowed with superior wisdom, should inquire into and adjust quarrels arising between the two races'. He observed that, if their land had been apportioned among individuals under the English mode of tenure, this quarrel would not have arisen, but the Maori system was different. McLean pointed out that Maori customary land rights had difficulties that could be overcome if, 'instead of trampling upon and quarrelling about each other's rights', they would agree to a fair subdivision of their property by which each tribe could enjoy its own lands. All that was required to meet this difficulty was that each tribe should unite with the Government to decide upon some mutually agreed plan. The Governor was equally eager that such a plan should be carried out.

McLean tried hard to get Tamihana to agree to a conference, either with the Secretary of State or the Governor, with both parties represented. He promised that he would go with him and answer for his safe conduct. Tamihana was amenable but was dissuaded by his followers from going by sea, mindful of Governor Grey's seizure of Te Rauparaha. They had no objection to meeting the Governor on land near Auckland. Other rangatira spoke, wanting the Waitara dispute to be kept separate from the issue of the King movement.

On saying goodbye to Tamihana, McLean recorded his wish for a further meeting with 'this intelligent chief'. He regretted that this did not eventuate but felt that Tamihana could not commit himself until he had conferred with the Waikato tribes, after which he would be better prepared to 'enter more fully into the questions which had been agitating the Native mind'. Tamihana, for his part, stated that he would allow the Governor a month or two to make peace and, if not, he would be prepared to take further action. Meantime he agreed to a truce.

Two days later McLean met Wiremu Kingi at Pakana. Finding that the Waikato tribes had empowered Kingi to make peace on his own terms, McLean said that he would return to Auckland to brief the Governor and that the Governor would come to Taranaki to arrange a final settlement. He told Kingi that hostilities should cease and that his people should have 'access to their cultivations, peach groves and graves and that the white flag of truce should fly from his fortified places'.[11] Kingi promised to observe the truce. McLean then advised the Governor that this was the opportunity to bring the Taranaki War to 'an honourable termination'. Any advance beyond the existing area occupied by the troops would mean high casualties and, with the onset of winter, military operations would have to be curtailed. Moreover, he warned, the tribes throughout the North Island were in a very uneasy state. 'Great care is also necessary to prevent the Natives from becoming exasperated, sulky and revengeful by a prolonged struggle at that point. If this unfortunately becomes a phase of the New Zealand war, life and property will be more endangered by the acts of a few marauding individuals than if the whole race were to rise in bodies against the settlement.' A large military force would be needed 'until all the questions at issue between the races are definitely settled',[12] – that is, until the Queen's sovereignty had prevailed.

McLean remained in Taranaki to negotiate the peace terms. Gore Browne had insisted that the Taranaki tribes pay full compensation for the destruction of settler property. Indeed a peace without compensation would be unacceptable. He instructed McLean to arrange to have the Union Jack hoisted on the blockhouses on Sundays and festivals, saying 'I am very anxious about this and consider it very important',[13] Negotiations ran on into May. McLean thought that fighting had ended because the tribes were weary but that a war element still existed and much remained before a permanent peace could be arranged.[14]

The meeting between Tamihana and McLean, two powerful men representing the more moderate attitudes of Maori and Pakeha, offered perhaps a last opportunity to avert escalating conflict. Each man was prepared to listen, to explore the issues and to seek a solution. The opportunity was lost, however. In April, when the Governor invited Tamihana to meet him in Auckland, Tamihana refused. He wrote to McLean saying that if the subject was Taranaki, the Governor should come to Taranaki, if the topic was to be Waikato, then

Waikato should be the venue. He would not come to Mangere.[15]

Gore Browne, however, was determined on capitulation, not negotiation. Although McLean had by this time resigned as Native Secretary, the Governor sent him back to the Waikato in July where the Revd J. A. Wilson had been trying to arrange a meeting with Wiremu Tamihana. Wilson told McLean that Tamihana's intention to meet with the Governor had alarmed the rangatira, who would try to stop him, one threatening to seize and kill him. They were complaining that Tamihana had begun the King movement and was then the first to 'swerve from it'.[16] McLean failed to meet Tamihana. Perhaps Tamihana was held back by the more militant elements within the King movement; or perhaps McLean thought another meeting pointless when the Governor was determined on an ultimatum.

Gore Browne had come to view the powerful Waikato tribes as a more serious threat to the Queen's sovereignty than Wiremu Kingi's defiance. They could field greater numbers of warriors and were well placed to make an attack on the capital, Auckland, with many more settlers than at Taranaki. Gore Browne relied on John Morgan, the Anglican missionary at Otawhao (Te Awamutu), for intelligence about the movements of the King movement tribes.[17] For their part, the Waikato tribes suspected the missionary of spying on them.

McLean warned the Governor that Maori intended to attack Auckland as they had built a strong pa in the forest inland from Drury. They had supplies of ammunition, including a large supply of powder obtained with the help of foreigners, and had collected and stored food crops. He believed that Waikato Maori were making great efforts to bring about a mass rising and that some of the powerful tribes were preparing for 'a general struggle to maintain their nationality and independence'. They had spies in Auckland who kept them advised of the number of troops there and would take advantage of any reduction to attack. He urged the Governor to maintain a sufficient garrison to repel any attack.

Ministers were determined to restrict McLean's powers. Correspondence between Weld, the Native Minister, and the Governor in 1861 proposed that McLean give up his duties either as Native Secretary or as Chief Land Purchase Commissioner, the option to be at the discretion of the Governor and McLean. No doubt ministers would have preferred to see McLean give up his post as Native Secretary, where he had become a barrier between ministers and Governor. With the outbreak of war in Taranaki, the Native Land Purchase Department, confronted with Maori opposition to further land sales, had become inactive.

Encouraged by his ministers, the Governor prepared a proclamation to be presented at a King movement meeting at Ngaruawahia. The terms required submission to the Queen's sovereignty, acceptance of British law, acceptance that roads and bridges would be built through the Waikato region, and a commitment to cease to uphold a land league. McLean as Native Secretary, together with the Assistant Native Secretary, Smith, submitted a memo[18] opposing the 'Governor's ultimatum', and predicting that it would be resisted throughout the North Island. McLean queried whether the time was appropriate to set out in detail the views of the Government on the questions at issue and recommended only 'a general manifesto' of the Governor's views. He argued that the Government had not prepared the settlers for the possible consequences of Maori rejecting the terms and uniting in defence of the King movement – an issue that would bring greater unity than had the Taranaki War. The most defenceless settlements would be the first to be attacked; other settlers scattered over the island would lose their lives and property before troops could arrive. Settlers should be made aware of the danger before the Government committed itself. Certain items of the proclamation should not be presented to the Ngaruawahia meeting: the claim to build roads and bridges; reference to their land remaining with Maori as long as they were able to keep it, as this would be seen as a threat from the Governor; and the demand that the King's flag be hauled down and replaced by the Queen's. McLean considered that the proclamation committed the Government to an unnecessary recognition of the Maori King. He recommended further negotiations after consultation with rangatira sympathetic to the Government.[19] McLean's conciliatory approach would not have ruled out some concessions to the King movement provided it was prepared to recognise the Queen's sovereignty.

The reaction of the Governor and his ministers, meeting as the Executive Council on 29 May 1861, was to censure McLean and Smith for exceeding their duty in expressing dissent 'from the course previously determined upon by His Excellency in Council'. The Native Secretary had erred in not stating his opinion earlier, when invited to do so before the proclamation was decided.[20] McLean was unrepentant, considering his censure unjustified. Did he believe that Gore Browne could not be deflected from his proposed course? McLean's failure to respond to the council's request for his views may be attributed in part to his tendency for procrastination and in part to his ill-concealed dislike of ministerial control. He saw himself as appointed by and responsible to the Governor alone, and resented ministers' influence on the Governor. Nevertheless, Gore Browne had been the driving force behind the Waikato proclamation even, it would seem, against the view of his trusted adviser, whose opposition to the trend of native policy had become more apparent since 1860.

The Executive Council resolved to issue the proclamation but to omit the requirement that 'the flag of the pretended Maori King at Ngaruawahia be hauled down', though it held that this was inherent in the general demand for submission to the Queen's sovereignty. Moreover, this demand would be made once the 'Insurgents' had agreed to the terms.[21] McLean's memo and subsequent censure must be viewed in the light of the ministers' demand that McLean surrender the post of either Native Secretary or Chief Land Purchase Commissioner. McLean resigned as Native Secretary, but continued to hold the post of Chief Land Purchase Commissioner. The passage of the 1862 Native Lands Act allowing for direct purchase and the removal of the Crown's right of pre-emption had made the Department redundant. McLean told his father-in law that, if the Native Council Act was passed, he would also resign as Chief Land Purchase Commissioner, but as the ministers did not appear to support his claim for a retiring allowance, he would not give up that post until he got some recognition for his past services.[22]

McLean's former officials regretted his departure from office. In Hawkes Bay, Cooper was pleading for McLean to visit and help resolve difficulties with Te Hapuku over reserves, 'as I must confess the old savage is beyond me to manage altogether. Confound these natives, they are getting harder to manage every day.'[23] From Taranaki, Parris, conscious of the loss of McLean's patronage, lamented his departure. 'What a world of changes we live in. Your own sudden disappearance from the Command of the Ship. Your subordinates all about to be sent before the Mast or dismissed to make way for a Crew of upstarts who in their conceit fancy they are going to remodel the Natives by Magic.'[24] He ended with a criticism of the new Premier, William Fox, known to be an enemy of McLean.

McLean still felt a responsibility for the office he had surrendered, assuring himself there could not be a better opportunity to retire when there was a man like Grey to manage native affairs.[25] With Grey's permission he again determined to take two years' leave of absence to go 'home' this time accompanied by his son, Douglas, who was to stay on to receive 'a good English education'. Once more his visit had to be postponed. As Chief Land Purchase Commissioner, McLean continued to negotiate unfinished business. In 1862 he was engaged in negotiations over the Coromandel goldfields where he overcame Maori unwillingness to sell. Fox authorised him to buy at a price not exceeding 3s 6d an acre and to arrange that, for every digger licensed to dig on a block, £1 per annum be paid to the local tribe that owned the land. McLean was happy to have shed some of his public duties and could now 'look on with much indifference to passing events than I used to do'.

In 1862 Fox was defeated in a debate over the responsibility for the cost of the war. He was succeeded by Alfred Domett who took a hard line, seeking large-scale land confiscation. McLean complained to his father-in-law of the treatment he received from Fox, saying that he would wait a little longer to settle his own affairs and take his leave to suit his own convenience. He told Strang that he approved of Domett as Premier, 'certainly an immense improvement on that captious fellow Fox who has done more mischief during his short reign than can be easily remedied for years'.[26] Later, he rejoiced that Sewell and Fox 'like birds of a feather have been condemned to the seclusion from which I hope they will never emerge'. His attitude may have been a reaction to Fox and Sewell's attacks on McLean at the time of the House inquiry into Waitara.

From time to time F. E. Maning, an early settler in Hokianga, corresponded with McLean freely offering advice. McLean's attitude to the Taranaki War made Maning confess that he

> felt rebuked at hearing your noble and merciful views on the subject of war with the natives, and your unwillingness to cause any more bloodshed or ill feeling than was absolutely necessary and forced on us. I did not say much at the time but have often thought of them; and I believe that both as a Christian and a politician you are right. I am a bad Christian myself, and am apt to be fond of any plausible excuse for a proper row; but reflection tells me you are right and I am wrong.[27]

By 1856 McLean had become the dominant official in native affairs within the government service. Nevertheless, in 1861 he had decided to retire from public life. At the end of 1859 McLean had been invalided by a serious bout of rheumatic fever. This physical illness was accompanied by a psychological collapse. The Governor had taken direct control of the negotiations over the Pekapeka block at Waitara despite McLean's covert opposition in 1859. His untidy and incomplete land purchases in Hawkes Bay and the northern South Island were unravelling, ministers had forced his resignation as Native Secretary while his duties as Chief Land Purchase Commissioner had become nominal after the outbreak of war in Taranaki and the Waikato. He had failed to reach an accommodation with the King movement. At age thirty-nine, he lamented to his brother that he saw no future but ill health, infirmity and old age.

The melancholy that seemed to possess McLean after his serious illness remained with him. Perhaps on sudden impulse, in 1861 he drafted his will while travelling on the Piako River. Since 1853 he had ceased to record his private thoughts in his diaries, but the preamble to the will showed that his religious faith had remained strong. He began with his customary invocation to the Almighty:

> How great and manifold O Lord are thy blessings which thou in thy mercy dost bestow on thy poor creatures. We have the light of heaven to guide upon [?]

> wisdom and mercy. Thou sendst affliction but for a season and send us the light of thy countenance to guide and preserve us. Being now under thy shade the great author of all I commit my all to thy gracious keeping and preservation.'

He ended: 'in the humble hope that God may preserve my soul I confide myself to his glorious keeping and mercy. My earthly goods I bestow to those whom nature and thy Providence has left in my keeping.'[28]

To his son, Robert Douglas Donald, he left £200 for his education, board and keep until he was twenty-one, 'care being taken to instruct him in the Protestant faith and to acquire a good sound education as becomes his position in society'. Douglas was to inherit all his father's landed estate when he attained an age mature enough 'to manage and direct its disposition'.

To his sisters, while married, he left half the net annual product of all wool from the Ahuriri station, and to his brothers, Archibald and Alexander, one-quarter each until they could otherwise provide for themselves, and he left £40 a year to his Glasgow aunts. He named his partner W. S. Grahame as executor, and to ensure 'all just debts being duly discharged and peoples' property confided in my charge being restored to them'.

There were some curious omissions. There was no specific provision for a guardian for Douglas then aged nine nor any financial bequest for his youngest sister, Annabella, or his younger brother, John, both of whom he looked on with more affection than his other siblings. In 1859 Donald had lent John £300 at 10 per cent and annual repayment, but in August 1861 when John tried to borrow £1000 to buy property, Donald had to refuse.

When he finally resigned as Land Purchase Commissioner, he admitted to his brother John that, if he had had no ties in New Zealand, he would have left to seek his fate at the Cape or some other colony. Having retired to his Hawkes Bay estate, within two years he recovered his confidence and re-entered public life as a provincial superintendent.

Chapter 14
The Patriarchal Runholder

On McLean's first visit to the Ahuriri district in 1851 he had been impressed by this splendid land 'unsurpassed in beauty' and wished he had the means to own 10,000 acres. In April 1851, when a local grazier, Captain Thomas, offered him 370 sheep for 14s 6d a head, McLean took his first step towards establishing himself as a pastoralist. McLean saw sheep as the 'most certain investment I can think of and I trust that providence will increase and multiply my little beginning'. He arranged with Alexander Alexander, a fellow Scot, and Donald Gollan to graze the sheep on their run at Mangatarata near Waipukurau and, in return, take half the annual wool clip and a third of the increase at the end of five years.

As McLean had insufficient capital, he looked for a partner. In 1852, together with James Kelham, a prosperous Wellington merchant, he bought sheep which they placed with Alexander Grant, a Wairarapa runholder. He also bought cattle, selling his Wanganui farm to find the money.[1] In October 1853, less than four months after he negotiated the purchase for the Crown, he secured the leasehold to a 10,000 acre run at Akitio, on the east coast of the northern Wairarapa, in partnership with Kelham, who paid for the homestead block. The following year they added a further 9800 acres of Crown land, leaving McLean in debt to Kelham for £769.[2]

In November 1853 he made his first move to get land in the Ahuriri district. Alexander Alexander, who had been grazing McLean's sheep, applied for two runs in McLean's name. M. Fitzgerald, a surveyor, told McLean that he could get a very good hilly run on the west bank of the Tukituki River, though he would need to secure the freehold of all the patches of flat land to prevent others from interfering.[3] Nothing came of this proposal.

In 1856 McLean began his career as a runholder, applying for a Crown lease of land at Maraekakaho about 2.5 kilometres west of today's Hastings. Meanwhile, he employed a Highland shepherd for £60 a year to look after his sheep that were grazing on Gollan's run. McLean instructed his brother Alexander not to put any sheep on the Maraekakaho run until the purchase was completed, 'as I should be sorry to do anything which would have even the most distant appearance of violating the law'.[4] He expected to spend £200 in the first year on a house, woolshed, sheep pens and so on.

From 1857, when he first acquired land at Maraekakaho, McLean's run had needed his attention and supervision. Like other pastoralists, McLean was faced with a shortage of capital. He had insufficient money to acquire an entire run or to buy livestock. G. S. Cooper advised McLean that Frederick Tiffen, Commissioner of Crown Lands in Hawkes Bay, was going to make suburban land out of McLean's intended run. That would be to McLean's advantage, as no one would want to pay town prices inland at Maraekakaho.[5] McLean's ambition to be a runholder had to wait for fulfilment until February 1857, when he took possession of the Maraekakaho run of 8500 acres on the basis of an occupation licence and a pre-emptive right to an eighty-acre homestead section. McLean was granted a fourteen-year pastoral licence. He had to pay a deposit, stock his run with at least one breeding ewe for every twenty acres and pay an annual rental licence fee.

Insecurity of tenure was the disadvantage; only the eighty-acre homestead block was exempt from purchase by outsiders. To gain freehold title, he had to compete on the open market when sections of the run would be sold at an upset price of 10s an acre. Crown land ordinances provided for the issue of pasture licences up to a maximum capacity of 25,000 sheep for a period of fourteen years at an annual fee of £5 and a further fee of £1 for every 1000 sheep above 5000.

Between June and August 1859, while in Hawkes Bay to buy land for the Governor, McLean made private purchases for his Maraekakaho run of small blocks of 40 to 400 acres – in all 1100 acres – of his remaining unpurchased 10s-per-acre land. McLean having bought all the 10s-per-acre land, anyone who wanted to acquire the other parts of the run had to give him three months' notice of their intention. He told Alexander that he was 'without a penny' but they could now feel easy that the run was secure.[6] By 1859, over 5000 sheep were on the Maraekakaho run.

In 1860, obviously thinking about his future, McLean asked Alexander to let him know when and how they could secure the remaining part of the Maraekakaho run. Should they approach the Provincial Council for a lease with a right to purchase at the end of fourteen years, or to put some of the land up for auction?[7] Alexander seemed to have opted for auction. Two months later McLean promised to send cash to buy 200 acres of 10s-per-acre land and two or three plots of forty acres. Alexander must not to employ more men than was necessary, and keep expenses down as much as possible as it would only be by 'careful saving that the place will ever pay. Take care of this my dear Sandy that we may have the means of helping our sisters.'[8]

McLean found his leased lands threatened by colonists seeking to buy cheap land. To counter this, pastoralists tried to buy land they held under Crown leases. Those who could not buy all their leasehold land bought portions of it so as to diminish the value of the remainder to any but themselves. 'Land sharks' also used this practice to extract money from runholders. McLean faced this threat. To gain a freehold title he was faced with the choice of bidding at auction for sections of his run or holding back in the hope that there would be no bidders and that consequently he would be able to buy the land at the upset price of 10s or 5s an acre. Runholders resorted to devices such as 'spotting' (buying up the most desirable parts, such as those that controlled access to water) and 'gridironing' (buying alternate strips of land) to keep their runs intact.

At this time McLean had to face a threat to his Akitio property. C. Pharazyn tried to oust him by arranging for his sons to 'spot' the run. McLean rebuffed the attempt of 'that scoundrel Pharazyn' through the intervention of Dr Isaac Featherston, Superintendent of Wellington province and an adjoining runholder at Akitio. McLean's position as Land Purchase Commissioner meant that he was courted by those wanting to establish themselves on the land. It seems that Featherston, who had been McLean's opponent, was by this time indebted to him and was willing to repay a favour. He assured McLean that he would see that his provincial officials obstructed and delayed the Pharazyns' claims at Akitio.[9] The boundary between public service and private interest was defined more flexibly in nineteenth-century New Zealand and politicians and officials saw nothing inappropriate in overt use of public office to advance their personal interests.

The development of the colony depended entirely on overseas investment by British capital. London and Scottish banks, through their subsidiaries in Australia, were the source. Banks were unwilling to provide runholders with short-term credit on the security of land and stock. They preferred to lend to merchants, leaving them to carry the risks. Merchants provided the range of services needed by runholders. They supplied goods, operated current-account facilities where there were no banks, acted as auctioneers of stock and property, agents for insurance and shipping companies, and advanced money on the security of the wool clip and arranged for its shipment overseas.[10] In Hawkes Bay, McLean dealt with J. G. Kinross, a fellow Scot, and with Bethune and Hunter in Wellington and later Rattrays in Dunedin. He also dealt with the Union Bank of Australia when a branch opened in Napier.

McLean was fortunate to have another source of finance. The younger brother of the Earl of Dysart, the Honourable Algernon Tollemache, had emigrated to New Zealand in the 1850s to protect his investments in the New Zealand Company. He accepted government scrip in exchange for his existing claims and, with further capital of his own, bought 5s- and 10s-an-acre land in

Wairarapa and Hawkes Bay. His investments in Hawkes Bay alone amounted to some £150,000. He put settlers on his land, holding the Crown grants as security for his mortgages over their properties. If a runholder defaulted on his mortgage payments, Tollemache foreclosed and resold to another settler. During the 1850s and 1860s McLean borrowed a total of £17,000 at 7 per cent from Tollemache[11] at a time when his official salary was £400 a year. A close relationship developed between the two men. Each had something to offer the other: Tollemache provided much needed finance; McLean brought inside knowledge as head of the Land Purchase Department and through his valuable Maori contacts.

The introduction of responsible government in 1856 had meant the retirement of McLean's first patron, Dr Andrew Sinclair, as Colonial Secretary. As Sinclair was about to visit Scotland, McLean took the opportunity to send a letter to his uncle Donald McColl by 'my kind and worthy friend our late Colonial Secretary', who was retiring with a 'pension of 500 pounds a year and large estates and other sources besides', something Donald felt would impress his uncle. He enclosed a photo of his little boy, Douglas, of whom he saw little, since he was in the care of his grandfather in Wellington. He intended to take Douglas with him to Scotland when he had made a little money, but he had not saved enough to allow him to resign and spend a year in Scotland. However, his expenses were reducing, while his sheep and cattle were increasing; in a few years he would be 'tolerably well off'. His brother Alexander, being a good hand among stock, could expect do well and become a rich man. His younger brother, John, a seafarer, he considered an active, enterprising young man even though he had no money.

On the other hand, a young relative, Archy McInnes, had failed in every job though he had excellent opportunities. McLean lamented that he had been 'a source of great anxiety and vexation from the first and all the splendid opportunities he has had have been thrown away. He could not be kept from going after young girls and getting in court and other scrapes in consequence that might be got over if he would avoid his wandering gossiping Highland propensities.' McLean went on to list his efforts to help; first with work in his office, where Archy proved 'careless and useless'; then, when apprenticed to a surveyor he was 'too idle and proud' to learn. Later his work as a hand on McLean's own run under Alexander's supervision had been unsatisfactory. He complained that all McInnes wanted to do was to lead an idle life and associate with low persons. McLean's Presbyterian values were offended. Archy had been 'entertaining foolish ideas of becoming a rich man without working for it'. He had sent Archy home at his own request, but thought it 'disgraceful to see a lad in the prime of life and health leave a colony where he could make a fortune to be a burden on his family'. He contrasted Archy's attitude with that of other Highlanders who had come to the colony and were all doing well. 'There is room for more of them if they choose to come,' McLean assured his uncle. 'The climate is good, land productive, fish abundant and employment certain. The steady industrious working man is sure to make a fortune.'[12]

McLean also took pleasure in telling his uncle of a dispatch from Downing Street in which the Duke of Newcastle had written 'acknowledging the important services rendered by Mr. McLean, the Native Secretary, on many occasions when difficulties have arisen with the natives and of expressing my sense of the zeal and ability with which he has performed his duties'.[13]

Although not the eldest among his brothers and sisters, as a young man Donald had a patriarchal vision of a day when they might join him in his new country – 'if I have undergone the various changes of life as a lonely adventurer far from my father's house it would be my greatest pride to see some of my household encircled around me pursuing their several vocations'.[14] Between 1856 and 1863, Donald's vision took shape as he gathered around him three brothers and two sisters. His older brother, Alexander, an experienced farmer, was given charge of setting up the Maraekakaho run with help from Archibald, who arrived in 1858. The two unmarried sisters, Catherine and Annabella, joined their brothers at Maraekakaho in 1863 and cared for their nephew, young Douglas. Donald's younger brother, John, no doubt through Donald's patronage, was given command of the government steamer *White Swan* when he arrived in 1858. Next year, with financial help from Donald he set up a business in Christchurch and later became owner of Buccleuch station in Canterbury. Of the three brothers, only John's industrious conduct and reliable character met with Donald's approval. Alexander and Archibald exasperated him. Archibald, a mariner with experience in the China and North Atlantic trade, arrived in New Zealand penniless. A 'venture in cigars' was said to have destroyed his promotion prospects. He never managed to hold down a position, whether first mate or captain, but was not prepared to admit that his own conduct may have lead to his misfortune; he always blamed the machinations of others. Donald arranged for Archibald to help Alexander on the Maraekakaho run. Young Douglas thought his uncle a 'droll fellow' and delighted to mimic him: 'I may be only an old seadog but ...'. Archy, who knew nothing about farming, took to his new role with enthusiasm, assuring Donald that he was the only person on the station who had his interests at heart and was fighting to protect them. He accused Alexander of ignoring him, but Donald was not impressed: 'I am quite satisfied that Alexander is doing his utmost for my interest and that he studies to do as much for me as lies in his power … Of his management I have never complained altho' I have been kept in straits from his drawing so heavily at times. However I am sure that he and I can settle without your interference beyond assisting him in making the accounts.'[15]

Donald's confidence in Alexander's ability to manage the run never stopped him from writing long letters filled with detailed suggestions on the day-to-day operations – now was the time to sow grass seed, cattle should be sold while prices were buoyant – and incessant calls for economy. Donald made it plain to his two elder brothers that they depended on his bounty and that he expected a satisfactory return. If Archibald failed in New Zealand as well, it would be his own fault. Donald warned that he could do no more for him. 'All I require is that those who live there [Maraekakaho] should study industry and economy as they are both essential virtues more especially in a new colony. I dislike empty and hollow display when persons have not the means to support them.'[16] He returned to his theme some months later: 'the great things to be observed in a new place like that are sobriety, truthfulness, avoiding foolish promises and being economical'.[17]

One reason for Archy's inability to hold down a job became clear after his arrival in New Zealand: he had a 'drinking problem'. Donald despaired of him, telling Alexander that he did not know 'what Archy is fit for. I distinctly oppose the taking of any spirits on my run.' (Donald's personal accounts, however, show that he was a substantial buyer of spirits as well as ales and wines.) Nevertheless, he was pleased that Archy liked Ahuriri and expected he would settle down there as he was industrious though 'coarse and vulgar in manners'. As he worried that Archy and Alex would quarrel he arranged for Archy's wife to come out to New Zealand to 'keep him in better order' as she had great influence over him.[18]

Donald remonstrated with Alexander for being foolish in lending money when he knew that his brother had to pay a very heavy interest on borrowed money. They were poor and should not try to appear otherwise. Alex did not like to refuse when asked for a favour, but better to refuse at once, boldly. He should realise that the very people who made a convenience of him would refuse him a loan. When Alex was in Melbourne before coming to New Zealand he had squandered his money on 'Highland vagabonds' to make himself appear a great man in their estimation yet he had never sent his sisters a single penny. Donald gave Alexander full credit for his work at Maraekakaho. However, the amount he had spent, Donald complained, was enough to ruin him. In future, unless Alexander gave advance notice of what he intended to spend the money on, he would not meet any of his bills.[19]

One year later, Alexander continued to exasperate Donald. When he learnt that Alexander was responsible for £200 on account of young Domett, one of the station hands, Donald could not sleep for two nights. He would advise the bank he would not pay the money!

> The Bank must be laughing at you for your liberality. Once and for all, I'm tired of you being so generous at my expense. To spend money that was not your own on idle flatterers was cruel. Especially when some of your own family were in want. Those same flatterers might call you a fine fellow. When they get their money, however, they will be laughing at you for a simpleton and a fool. Pay off your own debts before you go security for others. How can you be trusted after your broken promises? Yes, Alex, you have worked like a horse at Maraekakaho, but to what use if you squander on one hand what you make with the other ... believe me Alexander that to speak this plainly to you is more painful to me in doing so to a brother whom I greatly esteem than it can be to yourself but I find that you are so thoughtless that I cannot allow my credit at the banks to be destroyed through your good nature.[20]

Donald's irritation was justified. Not only did he depend on his wealthy partners for the capital to increase his landholdings, but he had invested all his spare money in these ventures. He confided to one of his sisters that 'McLeans generally have extravagant tendencies'. Alexander's generous nature concerned him; he 'would give anything to save others from difficulty even if he had not the means to pay his own liabilities, we know how many people have been ruined by such folly. I am resolved that this should not be'.[21] Donald lectured Alexander on the need to keep the station hands at work. He would be astonished at what early rising and perseverance could do. He should get rid of any who were unwilling to work. 'We have to work ourselves for all we get and should make others who are paid for it do the same.' Every man who was careful and industrious would soon be well off in a country like New Zealand.

Alexander, too, found the whisky bottle an attraction. When he was sent south in 1861 with a cargo of sheep for Donald's newly acquired Otago run, his brother thought it necessary to warn him, 'Do like a good fellow abstain from all drink at Otago and keep up the credit of the family'. Not that Donald was a teetotaller. In his travels he sometimes enjoyed the company of fellow Scots. On a journey to Ahuriri in 1850 with Robert Park, the surveyor, he spent a night at the Rangitikei home of one McDonnell, 'who kept real Highland whiskey which he, through his usual excess of hospitality, compelled me to drink rather too freely, no doubt to the annoyance of J. M. Laurie, a sensible, shrewd Scotsman and Mr. McDonald. We had a wee bit talk about the McLeans that rather rose my temper as the spirits we were drinking.' Two days later Park persuaded him to join in a pledge to abandon drinking spirits 'as the effects of last night's late ride and a few glasses of gin caused some excitement that annoyed him'. McLean agreed to give up all spirituous liquors except wine and beer, 'to be aided in this sudden resolution, may I be countenanced by the Almighty'. Park decided to give up all liquor![22]

While convalescing in Canterbury in 1860, Donald had to lend his brother John £200 out of the proceeds of his wool clip. He wondered how he would find the money for his trip home to Scotland. He was impressed by the Canterbury McLeans, from the neighbouring Isle of Coll in the Hebrides, who had acquired four runs each of 100,000 acres. He regretted that his brother Alexander had not married into that family. He consoled Alexander by telling him that, once he had Maraekakaho in good working order, he would not be too old to marry and get a run in the South Island, where prospects were better than in the north.

Donald had family matters to concern him. He continued to write to his kin in Scotland, but only to his youngest sister, Annabella, did he show warmth and affection. In the midst of land negotiations in Hawkes Bay in 1859, he wrote that his property had been increasing in value and in time he expected to be 'pretty comfortable'. Then, 'You my little pussy will share in my fortune and assist [me] in preparing a history of New Zealand as Lord McCauley's [*sic*] sister has done recently'. Despite extensive borrowing to finance Maraekakaho, Donald had been remitting money to enable Annabella to remain at boarding school to complete her education. He told her that he would like her to learn 'Scotch music', but above all things she had to attend to her religious devotions, study her Bible and 'ask the Almighty's aid and guidance in all your undertakings'. Arithmetic was the next essential, as he intended her to keep his books and, with this in mind, she should keep account of all her expenses and 'avoid extravagance of every kind'. In every other branch of learning 'you may follow your own tastes and inclinations'.[23] Annabella and her sister Catherine were not to come to New Zealand until he sent for them. With his 'very rambly life', he could not look after them until he became more settled.

Donald admonished his Annabella:

> Next to your religious duties, as they concern all eternity, I wish you to acquire a good practical economy which requires that you should be proficient in keeping accounts, dressmaking is of less consequence, drawing is a very good pastime, music particularly Scotch is requisite as an accomplishment and a nice unaffected manner in society is very desirable. Now Annabella if you attend to all this it will give me much pleasure, early rising and a careful economy of time is very essential. Good bye my little pussy always your affectionate Donald.[24]

Donald required his sisters to be proficient in grammar, history and French. 'Industry overcomes many obstacles,' he admonished Catherine, 'Above all let your minds be stored with a good sound religious knowledge. Music, drawing and dancing I approve of as innocent and harmless amusements.'[25] He also advised Catherine and Annabella to replenish their minds by reading good books such as might prepare them for eternity. 'This world its anxieties and pleasure soon vanish but before there is an endless eternity where in God's providence I trust we may all be united and happy.'

Donald monitored his sisters' lives as well as his brothers'. He inquired about his sister Catherine's matrimonial prospects. 'What about your admirer. Is it all up? or do you look for a more polished and accomplished man. I do not know Kate what to advise you. Above all let the man you choose be prudent, sober and religious.' As for himself, Donald assured his sister that the report that he was to marry a Miss Sinclair was unfounded. Indeed, he was unlikely to marry anyone in New Zealand though he might feel inclined to remarry if he visited Scotland.

Prudence, for Donald, was a prized virtue. He told Catherine that he was 'fond only of those relations I find economical and prudent'. Archy's most redeeming feature was 'his readiness to share his last sixpence' with his sisters. Alexander, on the other hand, he found 'extravagantly disposed' and 'a good natured Highlander' who thought more of others than his own relations, never having sent any money to his sisters. Having analysed his siblings' weaknesses, Donald confessed to Catherine that 'you would think very little of me if you saw me, a broad faced ugly plain looking gloomy reflective character'.[26]

Although a dilatory correspondent, Donald always found time to write to his son. From Napier in 1859, he wrote reminding him that the Kingdons, with whom he stayed in Auckland, had been very good and kind to him and that he must be fond of them and do what they told him. Donald wrote that he was 'much pleased with the nice letter you sent me asking when I was going back to Auckland. It may be a long time before I get back to see you and I trust to find you by that time a good boy able to read your lessons nicely and to read that nice story about Washington when he was a boy. How very good he was he would not tell an untruth for any person. I hope and trust my little boy Duggy will never tell what is not true, if he does I shall be very vexed.'[27] In urging his son to say his prayers every night and always to tell the truth Donald no doubt believed that he himself told the truth. He may have been careful never to tell an outright lie but he could certainly be economical with the truth, offering only as much as would suit his purpose.

Donald was intensely fond and proud of his only child but, like any Victorian father, he hid his affection. As his official duties demanded long absences from Auckland and constant travel around the country, he saw his son infrequently, yet he was a doting father. His letters to friends and relatives would always include news of the boy's progress. In turn, when writing to McLean, not only friends and relatives but ministers and officials did not fail to mention that they had seen young Douglas and that he was well. Maori rangatira, too, found it politic to enquire after Douglas. Once Donald's sisters were settled at Maraekakaho, young Douglas was entrusted to their care.

By September 1860 Donald still thought that 'matters are not very bright' but was eager to make a start on the Otago run he had just acquired before he went home to Scotland. He told Alexander that the Maraekakaho run was so small that he would restrict it to breeding purposes with no more than 5000 sheep. It would be unwise to overstock and risk getting his sheep mixed up with the neighbours'.[28]

As McLean's income was limited to his salary as government official and the sale of his wool clip, to gain an Otago run he had to find partners. W. S. Grahame arranged for wealthy Auckland landowner Henry Walton to join the partnership. McLean secured Run 339, over 80,000 acres near Lake Wakatipu bounded in the west by the Remarkables and on the east by the Earnscleugh River. To put up the money for his share McLean had to borrow from Grahame. McLean's Otago agent described the run as well watered with 25,000 acres 'as fine pasture as one can see' and fit for winter pasture though, in a severe winter, stock numbers would have to be reduced.[29]

McLean, having decided to keep 5000 sheep at Maraekakaho, arranged to ship the remainder to his Hawkesburn run in Central Otago. Bethune and Hunter were to arrange the shipment and Alexander would see to their transfer. McLean favoured fellow Highlanders. Scots were sought after by New Zealand pastoralists for their experience in stock management. To look after the Otago run, he engaged Thomas Condie, from Tiree, as manager at £100 a year and a sixteen year old, Stewart, who had arrived in New Zealand with his Highland sheep dog, became a shepherd at £30 a year. Young Stewart was the son of the minister with whom McLean had boarded at Craignish while attending the parish school as a child.

The transfer of sheep from Maraekakaho to Otago in July 1861 led Donald to rebuke Alexander for failing to write and account either for the safe arrival of the sheep in Otago or for his expenditure. He demanded to be told how many sheep had reached the run, how many men were employed, what they were doing and what wages they were paid. He wanted these matters cleared up immediately. Alex had 'better return to Ahuriri as I cannot, from the way you transact business, entrust you with any matter in the Middle Island where partners are concerned. I am exceedingly vexed with you.'[30]

Donald wrote to his brother John, asking him to find out how many sheep had been lost and how many sold. The charter had cost £1100, 2869 sheep had been shipped and yet only 1000 appeared to reach the run. Alex had drawn £580 since he left for Otago but had not said what he had done with the money. He told John not to advance any money to Alex. His partners should not suffer from Alex's negligence but he would have to answer for his brother's shortcomings.

Alexander's response did not satisfy Donald:

> I received a few lines from you giving no other information except that you are coming up here. I wish you would do so at once as I am treated by you as if I were an enemy or a stranger. I know nothing of what you are doing and I am ashamed to meet anyone who is concerned with me in sheep from not being able to furnish an account. I must have a full account of every kind brought up in order that I may settle with parties at once. You do not appear to know the harm you are doing me by not writing and telling me what you are doing. It would be bad enough if the property were all my own when I have only a share in it. What are my partners to think when called to meet your bills without knowing how you spend what was already in your hands. I will not sanction your selling another animal of the run until I am satisfied as to what you have done already ... You may be able to explain matters but when explanations are too late they are of no value ... One of my partners who is in England [W. S. Grahame] expects and I have promised him an account by every mail and he must think I am deceiving him as he has never had an account. Mr. Johnson the lawyer has drawn upon me for his wool and I am really in a fix as to what I am to do. I would rather lose the sheep altogether than losing my credit as I must do from your sad neglect.
>
> ... I hear you have been very liberal with my money in making presents to parties in Canterbury although you were aware of the losses attending that trip. For your own credit and mine too do come and put matters straight. It would be unpleasant to send a stranger to do it but I will not be kept much longer in suspense as to my state of affairs which I am sorry to find are not as prosperous as I expected judging from the information already in my possession... I intend to make different arrangements about the station in future.[31]

Finances were further stretched when McLean set out to acquire all the unpurchased 5s-an-acre land at Maraekakaho. In July 1861 he applied to have the 5s-an-acre land auctioned in three months' time. To find the money, he got an advance against next year's wool clip from Bethune and Hunter, and managed to borrow a further £200 from his friend the Governor.[32] This says something about the close relationship between McLean and Gore Browne as it was unusual for the Queen's representative to personally lend money to a government servant. By October McLean had completed his purchase of the original Maraekakaho run. This, he felt, removed a 'great anxiety' from his mind. Meanwhile, he had tried, without success, to buy Domett's Hawkes Bay run.

Donald had other worries. In 1861 his brother Alexander was summoned for stock trespass on Maori land. Donald advised his brother to defend the case, saying that although Maori had received one payment that had been refused for several years. No land had been leased from the Maori owners. The Government had been paid all dues and taxes and a deposit had been paid on the extension to the run. If these circumstances were laid before a court he doubted a fine would be imposed 'especially as there has not been nor is there any intention to lease as the sheep are being removed to Otago'.[33] He need not have worried. The justices of the peace, all runholders, acquitted Alexander.

His brothers' actions sometimes embarrassed Donald. From the Hawkes Bay newspapers he learnt that Alexander had been taking up Crown grants on his behalf, which he had no right to do. Archibald was in trouble again when he tried to lease some Maori land. 'You must know it is an illegal act and that I have already had complaints sent to the Government about the occupation of native land.'[34]

In 1861, Hawkes Bay pastoralists, believing the Government would soon legalise de facto possession of Maori land, scrambled to lease Maori land. Alexander McLean urged his brother to secure the fertile Ngatarawa Plain they had been grazing from time to time. Donald agreed, instructing his brother to have the boundaries accurately described and to get a long lease of twenty-one years with a right of purchase clause signed by all the claimants should the Maori dispose of their land within that period. The agreed lease was for sixteen years at £250 a year.

In 1862, McLean extended his run. C. Nairn, who had been leasing the Mangaroa and Raukawa blocks, was to be evicted by the Maori owners. He arranged with Alexander McLean to sell his 13,000 acres and his stock for £2000. The rangatira agreed to lease the land to McLean for £200 a year. McLean expected to pay much more as 'I find like most of these transactions that there are two parties of claimants'.[35] These leases were illegal. As a government official, McLean had been required to prosecute squatters for illegal leasing of Maori land, yet he was now prepared to break the law himself. He told his partner, W. S. Grahame, that he had just bought a European squatter's right to Maori land that adjoined his run, as, although leasing had not yet been legalised, a bill was before the Assembly. Moreover, Colonel Russell and other Hawkes Bay runholders had not hesitated to lease Maori land.[36] Writing to Gore Browne in Tasmania he justified his actions: 'If leasing land from the natives is to be the order of the day I shall have no compunction in doing so, also as I wish to extend the boundaries of one of my runs.'[37] When the Government legalised direct individual purchases of Maori land the pragmatic McLean told Gore Browne that, although in principle he opposed the bill knowing it would lead to 'endless complications,' he expected the bill would become law and therefore 'I must benefit myself to some extent by the change'.[38] This bill became the 1862 Native Lands Act.

At Maraekakaho, McLean's financial situation worried him. 'Times are getting as bad as they can be, no market, high wages, high rents and heavy expenses must cause ruin to many who expected to be well off'. Like other pastoralists, McLean had insufficient capital. He had to borrow but, when wool prices fell, he struggled to pay the interest on his loans. However, his friendship with Tollemache made substantial mortgages possible. His account books show entries for annual payments of £500 to £600 to Tollemache. By 1867 land prices had fallen 30 per cent. In April he exhorted Alexander to ensure the 'strictest economy' and not to commit himself to 'wild speculations'. A week later, McLean resumed his lament: 'Sheep and land are falling so rapidly in value that nothing but the strictest management will prevent ruin. I never knew money to be so scarce or the banks to be so very strict. I am actually afraid to draw a cheque for a small amount and wethers which used to bring in something cannot be sold at any price.'[39]

The pastoralists' dilemma was that a better price for wool depended on culling inferior rams and replacing them with a superior breed, fencing to keep the sheep apart, and improving the processing of wool for sale. All this meant spending more when they had no ready money. McLean was aware that his flocks were degenerating compared with those of Purvis Russell and J. D. Ormond whose wool had been increasing in value. Something had to be done to increase the value of the clip. McLean's solution was to buy quality rams and wash and sort the wool. The effect was marked. Sheep numbers grew from 25,000 to 30,000 while the average weight of a fleece doubled.

When McLean retired from public life in 1862 he went to live on his Maraekakaho estate. McLean's estate was valued at £24,000, a fourteen-fold increase since 1851. As well as his original Maraekakaho run and the adjoining Aorangi block, he had half shares in Akitio and in Gollan's run with the accompanying livestock, and a share in Hawkesburn in Central Otago. He owned suburban land and three town sections in Napier. In Auckland he owned a house and fifteen acres in Parnell and some Remuera sections. In addition, there was an island in the Hauraki Gulf, probably Pakatoa, a town section and county land at Waiuku.[40] In 1858 he had bought thirty-two town sections at Clive (Waipureku). Clive, named after 'the great founder of our Indian Empire', was to be the main town of Hawkes Bay with Napier, the subordinate settlement, as its port. That these sections no longer appeared on McLean's list of properties in 1862 suggests that he sold them when he saw that Napier was becoming the main town, though it was still referred to as the Port of Napier. McLean found it much more comfortable to have his own home in Auckland rather than boarding at old Mother Tidmarshes. If only he could get a 'good wife' he would be 'quite content'.

By the end of 1862, McLean had added 21,163 acres to his Maraekakaho run. He bought the adjacent runs of Warleigh and Doonside when Tollemache, who held the mortgages, foreclosed on the owners, James Oliver and Frederick Ormond. McLean paid £7500 for the runs; 8000 acres were freehold and the remaining 13,000 acres were 5s-an-acre land on a fourteen-year pastoral lease. He borrowed £5200 from Tollemache at 15 per cent, to be repaid by 1870.[41] This land was added to his original run along with the Aorangi block, mainly undulating country suitable for sheep, the fertile alluvial plain of Ngatarawa and the Raukawa and Mangaroa blocks, all Maori leasehold land. To realise the potential of his estate, now more than 50,000 acres, McLean would have to seek additional capital.[42]

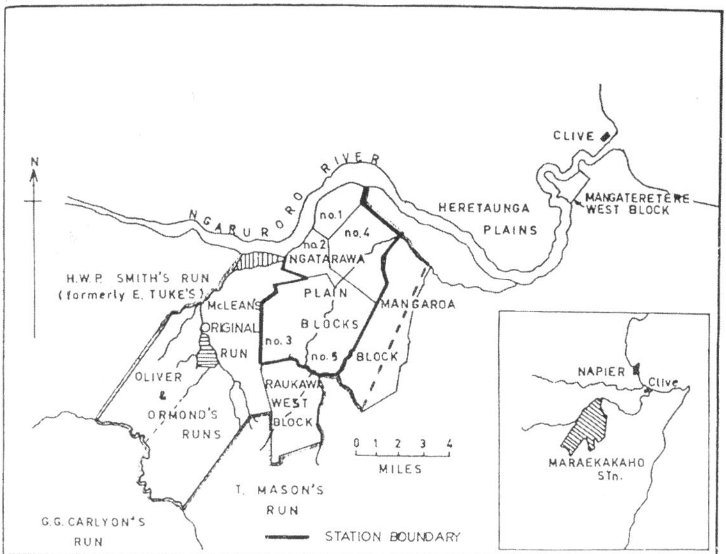

BLOCK.		ESTIMATED ACREAGE.	DATE OCCUPIED.
McLEAN'S RUN		8266 a.	1857
AORANGI SECTIONS			
NGATARAWA PLAIN:	BLOCK 1	1840 a.	1861
	BLOCK 2	1576 a.	"
	BLOCK 3	5000 a.	"
	BLOCK 4	5328 a.	"
	BLOCK 5	5375 a.	"
MANGAROA BLOCK (McLEAN'S SHARE)		2500 a.	1862
OLIVER & ORMOND'S RUNS		21163 a.	1863
GLENORCHY			
MANGATERETERE WEST BLOCK		900 a.	1867
RAUKAWA WEST BLOCK		4827 a.	1882
		56,775 a.	

SOURCE: A. KOCH'S MAP OF HAWKE'S BAY, April 1874, MAP COLLECTION, ALEXANDER TURNBULL LIBRARY

M.C.P.

Map 5. Maraekakaho Station 1857-1882

In April 1862 McLean told Alexander that he was being kept very busy in the 'present excited state of the Island'. Although retired from government service, he had been asked by the Governor to go to Waikato to calm the situation there. He lamented that property would fall greatly in value, not only in the troubled areas, but throughout the colony. By the end of 1862 McLean had finally retired. Writing to his father-in law, as well as giving news of young Douglas, he continued to comment on public business. He welcomed Governor Grey's return as he had always regarded him as a friend but, 'whether he will continue so I cannot foresee but will very soon know'. As for the departing Gore Browne, he believed he would 'like to fight out the New Zealand question but he may thank his lucky stars it does not devolve on him to do so'.[43]

Donald had encouraged Archy to send for his wife, Catherine, to join him, hoping she would keep him out of trouble. He thought her a 'solid sensible good woman' and he had 'every confidence that she would do her best to see things properly conducted about the station'. Donald told her that he hoped that Archy would get on better as he had been quite unhappy until she joined him.[44] Archy tried to persuade Donald to lend him money to buy a ship of his own, but Donald responded that Archy was not suited to the command of a steamer. Now that his wife was with him he should forget about the sea. He was too old to roam about as he used to do and should look to New Zealand as a good country in which to spend his days.

Donald approved of the changes Catherine introduced at Maraekakaho. Impressed by her business skills, he made her his confidant. Indeed, she became his Maraekakaho station detective, reporting on his brothers' activities. Although he valued Alexander's knowledge of farming practice, Donald was always troubled by his inefficient financial management. He asked Catherine to report on the station's expenses, the number of men employed, their pay and the work they were engaged on so that he could judge how Alexander was managing the run. He had hired J. Twigg, a former bank clerk, as assistant manager responsible for the accounts, but remained uneasy – especially as Alexander continued drinking. He sought Catherine's help to keep Alexander from visiting Napier. 'I hope you will employ his time in doing something at home, if he is not losing all respect for himself and all of us he will adhere to this.'[45] It seemed that the taverns at the Port were the attraction.

Donald's confidence in Catherine did not stop him from monitoring her activities. 'Do not feel annoyed at what I may have said in a previous letter. I know you will be able to explain all to my entire satisfaction when I see you. It was merely done by way of caution as I make you so much my confidant in all matters.' He told Catherine that he had not been able to sell his Auckland house as the road to it was so bad in winter, 'just such a road as suits a Highlander only'. He lived very quietly, seldom dining out. He was required to go to a ball, but was deterred as he would have to buy new boots and gloves, as his own were at Napier. His intention to travel to Scotland seemed to have lost its urgency. 'Being too late for the exhibition I am not now in such a hurry to go home in search of the heiress you talk of.'[46]

Donald decided to send Douglas to school in England. He thought this desirable, considering the unsettled state of the colony and the advantages of an English education. Donald settled for an English school as the climate would be less severe than Edinburgh. He thought Douglas was old enough to 'go home' as he had not had a day's illness for a long time. Meantime, he had been enjoying his school and his friends and had come to stay with his father every weekend. They went together to see a troupe of negro minstrels and to watch a review of the troops.[47]

Donald determined that Douglas would have 'a proper education' at an English public school as he was unhappy that 'such a mixture of all sorts of children' attended the colony's schools. Douglas had been attending one of the best, but Donald withdrew him as he was most unhappy with his being associated with the recently arrived sons of Grace, the missionary, 'not that we should visit the sins of the father upon the children yet there is significance in the old adage that as the old cock crows the young learn'.

In 1862 McLean had the Governor's approval to go home to Scotland on two years' leave, taking Douglas with him. He thought this was a good time to go, with a man like Sir George Grey as Governor to manage native affairs. The voyage home was again postponed. Within a year, McLean was to return to public office. The extension to his run also needed his supervision. Moreover, it seemed he was courting and had 'a hope that I cannot easily banish that Miss Lully might not be indifferent to my wishes'.

After McLean became Provincial Superintendent in 1863, the operation of Maraekakaho station continued to require his attention, although he had little time to visit the run as he spent most of the year in Napier – only some twenty miles away, but the roads were bad. When his sister Catherine was to visit Maraekakaho, Donald ordered the station trap to be sent to Havelock North two days before to give the horse a rest before the return journey.

Donald's youngest sister, Annabella, was his favourite among his siblings. She wrote to her brother that, although people were advising her to live in

Wellington, she was content to remain at Maraekakaho. It was quiet, she had few wants and no expenses and believed that her presence benefited Alexander – keeping him away from liquor? Nevertheless, she admitted being homesick: 'there is a void which costs me many a tear'.

Her nephew's exuberance disconcerted Annabella. She asked Donald to tell his son not to ride so much, as he was so enthusiastic that 'he must needs do everything over much'. Conversely, she could not endure him having too much time unoccupied. As he really liked his new subject, chemistry, she hoped this would take up his spare time. She reassured Donald that Douglas was 'a dear, good boy. When he attempts any frolic I have only to say would that be in accordance with your Father's wish. What ever it is he gives way at once.'[48] Donald delighted in his son's childish fantasies. Writing to the boy's grandfather he told of the eleven year old's ambition to become an admiral. 'He is to go to sea and when he is a lieutenant he will pay the station a visit. No one is to know him. You will be there and he is to say how do you do Mr Strang. Oh very well I think I have seen you before. Then he replies do you not know McLean. Then you exclaim oh dear oh dear it is you. He has any number of imaginary surprises of the most inventive description.'[49]

Young Douglas enjoyed his time with his uncles and aunts at Maraekakaho. He had been a sickly child but Donald was delighted that station life with its 'porridge and new milk together with healthy exercise and riding has done wonders for him'. He was delighted to hear he could ride well and even drive a carriage. He gave Douglas his own pony and encouraged him to take part in station life, helping his uncles burn fern and sow grass seed. Donald made his son aware of his priorities. 'I wish you always to be a good boy, to love God, say your prayers, to read nice stories to your aunts and always to tell the truth.'[50]

As Douglas grew older he would sometimes accompany his father on his travels. In 1861 he sailed with his father on the naval steamer *Fawn* from Napier to Wellington. Christmas Day on board had the sailors making merry and carrying Donald around the decks with Douglas on his knee. Their arrival in Wellington was delayed when the ship blew a boiler off Cape Palliser. Sea travel, though faster than an overland journey, could be unpleasant in a ship of a few hundred tons. In 1861 a naval ship carrying McLean took six days from Auckland to Napier. McLean's diary noted that it blew so hard that everything in his cabin was turned 'topsy-turvy'. With the 'wild waves flowing' the ship attempted to beat about in the dark. 'Bosun's shrill whistle often heard, men like crows running up rigging, Captain calling the officer of the watch, sentry repeating the call, bugle sounding men to quarters, the bluejackets and marines assemble.'[51] This scene led McLean to contrast the sailors' approach to their duties, 'delighting in a lark' and 'rejecting military drill and stiffness' with the soldier, 'fearful that he might be shot if he disobeyed orders'. He thought the military and naval services were 'wonderfully different each perfect in its way'. He saw them as different in practice as Puritanism and Episcopalianism in so far as these tended to influence English character. He thought each of these 'theological persuasions' had developed aspects of character that had moulded and sustained 'our present political fabric'.[52]

The forthcoming marriage of John's sister-in-law led Donald to deplore the expense to which John had been committed. He thought 'a quiet genteel private breakfast is all you should give. It is only a vulgarity nowadays to have barbarous displays and I well know you cannot afford it and men in business should be careful how they spend when they have not got it to spare. Believe me when I tell you people will not esteem you so much for doing so.' He was critical of John's mother-in-law for wanting 'to gratify her foolish pride' when she should have had 'more consideration for young people making their way in the world ... be kind but not indulgent let her know plainly you cannot afford such heavy expense'.

Douglas's departure for England was delayed until 1864. Donald arranged for Douglas to accompany the Tollemaches who were returning to England. He wrote to Douglas that he intended to see him before he left, urging him to continue to be 'a good, truthful and obedient boy'. He would miss him but he was happy that he was going to England and wished that his health would be improved by the sea voyage. At school he would

> become a clever scholar able to keep Papas books, copies of letters and to read history and conduct business in a methodical manner. I am sure you will obey Mrs Tollemache and feel also grateful for their kindness in taking you home.
>
> Goodbye my dear boy. May God bless you and expecting to see you soon
>
> I remain your affectionate Papa.
>
> Do not forget to say your prayers night and morning. Remember that you cannot prosper except God be with you'.[53]

Douglas spent two years at Temple Grove Preparatory School making up for the deficiencies of his New Zealand schooling. Tollemache secured a place for Douglas at Clifton, a public school in Bristol. He told McLean that he had been unable to get the boy into Eton, Harrow or Winchester because he was too old at age fourteen. While in England, Douglas spent his holidays with the Tollemaches at their home, Ham House in Surrey. McLean and Tollemache exchanged letters about the boy's progress and health.

Clifton, founded as recently as 1862, had a liberal and innovative headmaster in John Percival. He recruited talented staff including four Fellows of the Royal

Society. At a time when Classics dominated the public schools curriculum, Percival allowed boys to study English, French, German, mathematics, science and history as well as Latin and Greek. Percival had taught at Rugby where, even under the reforming headmaster Thomas Arnold, French and history could be studied for only one hour per week, while science was excluded as it might become too absorbing. Arnold wrote: 'Rather than have it the principal thing in my son's mind, I would gladly have him think that the sun went round the earth.'

At Clifton, the Victorian public school ideals of chivalry, loyalty and patriotism were inculcated. A boy was expected to write a letter of apology to his captain if he dropped a catch in cricket match. It was an old boy, Sir Henry Newbolt, who wrote the poem 'Vitae Lampada', an expression of the public school ethos that inspired those destined to carry 'the white man's burden' somewhere in the lands of the British Empire.

There's a breathless hush in the close tonight –
Ten to make and the match to win –
A bumping pitch and a blinding light,
An hour to play and the last man in.
And it's not for the sake of a ribboned coat,
Or the selfish hope of a season's fame,
But his Captain's hand on his shoulder smote –
'Play up! play up! and play the game!'

The sand of the desert is sodden red, –
Red with the wreck of a square that broke; –
The Gatling's jammed and the Colonel's dead,
And the regiment blind with dust and smoke,
The river of death has brimmed his banks,
And England's far and Honour a name,
But the voice of a schoolboy rallies the ranks;
'Play up! play up! and play the game!'

This is the word that year by year,
While in her place the school is set,
Every one of her sons must hear,
And none that hears it dare forget.
This they all with joyful mind
Bear through life like a torch
Bear like a torch in flame,
And falling fling to the host behind –
'Play up! play up! and play the game!'

Douglas enjoyed his time at Clifton. His father would have been pleased at the presence of practical subjects such as science and mathematics and reassured that Douglas was growing up among gentlemen. Douglas wrote conscientiously to his father with accounts of his school life and what he had seen of England. His father replied with family news and accounts of life at the station, how Douglas's ponies were in fine condition but he had had to take his dog Spring to town as he was too fond of chasing sheep. The Maori rangatira had been pleased to hear of his arrival in England. His father ended by urging his son always to read a chapter of the Bible every day and to remember the good advice Mrs Tollemache gave.[54]

It was fortunate that Douglas departed for a public-school education in England. His father would have found the erratic behaviour of an adolescent irritating and unacceptable. Douglas was a dutiful son, writing to his father by every mail. Donald could not write so frequently as he was caught up in the East Coast war. When he did write, he told Douglas how sad it was to see the Maori giving way to the 'evil of superstition' and ignoring Christianity. He exhorted Douglas to study hard as a great deal more would be expected of a boy who had been to England for his education. When Douglas wrote that he wanted to become a soldier, his father patiently replied that whether he was to be a soldier, lawyer, farmer, engineer or squatter, all of them required a good education. He should turn to the Tollemaches for advice but there was plenty of time. 'Get on with your lessons first and then a better judgement can be formed of what you are able to do.' Douglas continued to write long letters home. Tollemache told his father that his school marks and conduct were excellent.

Catherine, Donald's older sister, married Robert Hart, a Wellington lawyer, in 1867. Donald, who acted as master of ceremonies, told his favourite sister, Annabella, that he felt 'as stupid as an owl in performing'. He confided that he thought he must remarry as everyone else was getting married. Earlier, Donald told his uncle he accepted his advice about not remarrying until he returned to Scotland, 'that is provided I can select a nice lass of good family and some means that would be inclined to make New Zealand her adopted home'. Even in New Zealand he 'could marry one or more with several thousands of pounds'.[55] Although Donald talked of marriage it seemed he was reluctant. From time to time he discussed the marriage prospects of Annabella and himself. He told Annabella if she were in Auckland she might marry one of the naval captains of the visiting flying squadron. McLean had met the 'lovely Miss Todd' but her charms had not disturbed his rest though they might if she had been an heiress. The Governor, Sir George Bowen, had identified a rich Sydney widow for him but she was likely to marry another Scot. 'There I am done again. She is worth 3000 pounds a year.'[56]

Historians have described McLean as a dour Scot. It was fear of emotion rather than want of feeling that created that impression. Although he might appear cold, he was a man of strong emotions with the Gaelic temperament of a Highlander. Even as a young man he set out to charm those he encountered. As Sub-Protector of Aborigines, aged twenty-three, he won the confidence of men old enough to be his father or grandfather, whether Maori rangatira or British settler. As a Cabinet minister he displayed a politician's skill in convincing people that he had their interests at heart. Deputations would emerge smiling from their meetings with McLean certain that they had his support. Towards men whom he believed his enemies, in his diaries and private letters he allowed his vindictive feelings to surface. In his private life with his wife, Susan, he came to express his feelings openly and even to hint at the erotic pleasures of marriage. In his letters to his young son, like any Victorian father, he could not bring himself to openly express his love and pride; this was reserved for his accounts of his son's doings in letters to the boy's grandfather and his own family.

When Tollemache returned to New Zealand in 1870 to check on his investments, Douglas accompanied him. He had been at school in England since 1865 and was to complete his schooling in Auckland while staying with Dr Kidd. He used adolescent guile to thwart his father's instruction that he was not to join the cavalry. Douglas wrote that it was essential to have a horse as Dr Kidd was moving house 'a long way off' and he would need a horse to go back and forth to school in town. Douglas confessed to his father that he had already enrolled and been accepted in the cavalry as both he and Colonel Harrington had thought his father would have no possible objection. Indeed, Lady Bowen, the Governor's wife, had seen him in his uniform: 'I only mention this to show you it would not do for me to resign as it would look very bad.' He explained that the uniform was no dearer than that for the foot volunteers and that it would not do to join them as 'they are not as nice a set of fellows as the cavalry'. He hoped that his father would not be displeased as he had instructed Douglas to turn to Colonel Harrington for advice and this he had done, as he had had no letter from his father who, no doubt, had been too busy to write.[57]

Soon after his nineteenth birthday, Douglas, who had left school to study law, warily approached his father to confess that he had no wish to continue with his studies. His preference, he wrote, was to enter a merchant's office to acquire business habits, including bookkeeping, and especially a knowledge of the management of a sheep station like Maraekakaho. He was grateful for the opportunities provided for his education and acknowledged that he would have only himself to blame if he did not try to profit from them. He believed he had reached a time of life when he should make a decision on his future prospects.

> My disinclination for the law is on many accounts but I do not in the least take a dislike to it because I happen to know beforehand that it will entail much work on me. I do not wish to shirk from this in the least and do not see how I could get on in any sphere of life unless I work and trust that I shall henceforth as soon as arrangements are made to continue to work with perseverance at whatever I may have to do and feel that I have already lost much time and have myself to blame in a real measure for it and trust I shall in some measure be able to make up for it.[58]

Douglas had been nurtured by his father in the Protestant work ethic. He argued his case using words that identified the values approved by his father – 'grateful for opportunities', 'only himself to blame', 'entail much work', 'do not wish to shirk', and 'work with perseverance'. Donald, accustomed to having his own way, accepted Douglas's decision, perhaps gratified that his son had displayed such skill in outmanoeuvring his father. It seems that at one time Douglas considered entering the Anglican ministry. In 1877, however, after his father's death, Douglas went back to England to complete his law studies and in 1881 was admitted to the bar of the Inner Temple in London, though he never practised.

Douglas fitted readily into colonial life, became successful at rugby and cricket and once rode a penny-farthing bicycle from Napier to Wellington – an exhausting journey considering the state of the roads and the uncomfortable nature of the bicycle. He joined his father as a freemason. After giving up his legal studies, he gained first-hand experience of farming, at Akitio and then at Maraekakaho. Long and frequent letters to his father reporting in detail on station activities were evidence that, under Thomas Condie's guidance, he was acquiring a practical knowledge of managing a large sheep station. They also show an increasing maturity and confidence and suggest that he saw himself as a partner in his father's pastoral enterprise.

By 1869 the economic depression was alarming pastoralists. Having invested heavily in buying land and sheep, they were faced with falling incomes, insufficient to meet their loan repayments. Donald was worried. He told John, who had by then bought Buccleuch station in Canterbury, that he could not help him with finance. He asked about the situation in Canterbury, saying that he had heard that even Robert Rhodes, one of the largest landowners, was getting shaky. Donald hoped that John was not keeping an establishment beyond his means with two or three servants whereas he himself made do with one in an equally large house.

Having acquired 900 acres of the Mangateretere West block in 1867, McLean set out to complete the purchase in 1869. He was soon in trouble. Worgan, one of McLean's Native Department officials, acting for Sutton, a local merchant, secured mortgages over six shares which he converted into conveyances (the transfer of property from one owner to another). Sutton's intentions were outlined by F. E. Hamlin, a government interpreter. Mortgages, he said, in the past, had been entered into by merchants as security for outstanding debts. Later they came to use them as a way of getting hold of Maori land and depriving the owners of their yearly rents.[59] Sutton knew of McLean's interest in this block and intended to exploit his advantage. He offered to sell his share to McLean for £3000, much more than McLean had expected to pay the Maori owners. McLean refused and sought the opinion of the Attorney-General, but was told that there was no law to prevent Sutton's activities.

Meanwhile, as Alexander McLean and R. P. Williams had ceased to pay rent during the slump, Sutton, as owner of six-ninths of Mangateretere West, pressed for payment. Because the mortgage deed had been carelessly drafted it seemed that Donald McLean himself was liable for the unpaid rent. After consulting with McLean's brother-in-law, Robert Hart, the lawyer, Ormond told McLean that he was indeed liable for the rent, £1350. The best thing would be to assign the mortgage to Williams and Alexander McLean. Ormond, always ready to help McLean, told him that he would be a heavy loser but, as he saw nothing but more loss in the future, he advised him to get out altogether by selling his one share.[60]

By 1870 the slump was at its worst. McLean's Hawkes Bay agent J. G. Kinross, was becoming insolvent and could not carry any more of McLean's liabilities. The Union Bank refused to retire McLean's promissory notes unless he offered his sheep as security. As McLean had mortgaged all his properties, retrenchment was urgent. He sold his share in the Hawkesburn run in Central Otago to his partner, W. S. Grahame. It was the wrong time to sell and McLean found he had made little profit on his investment.[61]

W. K. McLean, an accountant in the Defence Department who had experience in pastoral finance, set out to restructure McLean's personal finances in 1871. Pointing out the need for a more economical approach given the large transactions involved, he estimated that 'the capital you have in use is costing you at least 20 per cent per annum … to add to this while you are occupied with your Public duties the Land Sharks of Napier are fleecing you in every way they can'.[62] He recommended that McLean conduct all his business through the New Zealand Loan and Mercantile Agency and to close his other accounts, including that with Kinross. McLean, however, was prepared to support a fellow Scot and kept Kinross as his agent.

Donald McLean reorganised the management of his Akitio and Maraekakaho stations. Thomas Condie had been moved from Hawkesburn to take charge at Maraekakaho. Condie had been unhappy at Hawkesburn but told McLean he would stay on until he found a replacement. It was not the salary but that he did not 'feel comfortable in this out of the way place'.[63] McLean improved productivity by importing stud merinos from Victoria and by fencing and sowing pasture; this meant that less culling was needed and sheep numbers increased from 25,000 to 30,000 in two years. McLean continued to insist that station expenses had to be reduced, and then wondered why Condie was 'so touchy as a manager but so thoroughly good, upright and honest'.

Although the colony was recovering from the depression by 1872, McLean was still heavily in debt and unable to pay off any of his mortgages. As the economy improved, investment in land became more profitable. McLean was forced to counter potential buyers by purchasing at auction Crown land he had been leasing at Maraekakaho and Akitio. His political opponent, H. R. Russell, sent an agent to the auction to run up the price so that McLean had to pay on average 13s 6d an acre for 5s and 10s land.

Station improvements at Maraekakaho were not confined to livestock. On one day McLean sent fourteen dozen trees to be planted at Maraekakaho. Varieties planted included natives as well as exotics: kahikatea and rimu along with quick growing pine (radiata, stone and maritime) and scotch firs and oak. Large vegetable gardens – potatoes, turnips, onions and cabbages – and orchards – plum, peach, cherry, pear and apple – provided for the household and the station hands. Some years earlier McLean and Ormond had commissioned Colonel Whitmore to bring back from England game birds, grouse and pheasants as well as blackbirds and thrushes. At another time McLean imported larks and sparrows. These imports reflected another aspect of nineteenth-century colonialism, the settlers' wish to feel at home in a strange land.

At Maraekakaho, under Condie's management, 29,219 sheep were shorn in the 1874–75 season, yielding fleeces weighing six pounds compared with two to three pounds in the early 1860s. In one season 3000 bushels of grass seed were sown to improve pastures. By 1875 W. K. McLean estimated that McLean's assets amounted to £117,625 (in today's values nearly NZ$15 million). Of this, Maraekakaho accounted for £77,975, Akitio £33,250, his Napier property £4000 and his Auckland house £1000. Liabilities totalled £35,930, the major debts being mortgages and advances owed to Tollemache (£23,000) and NZ Trust and Loan (£1500 on the Mangaroa block and £3000 on Akitio). In addition, the sum of £8430 was owing to short-term creditors. Within twelve years from 1863 the value of McLean's estate had doubled.

Chapter 15
From Provincial to Central Government

Since the establishment of Hawkes Bay province in 1859, deputations had been approaching McLean to stand for office as Provincial Superintendent. He had declined, saying that his public duty lay with his responsibilities as Native Secretary. In 1862, Ormond wrote to McLean to remind him that 'long ago I asked you to take what was then at your disposal. I shall be as glad to see you take it now as then' and assured him of his support.[1] McLean hesitated. He told his father-in-law that he cared nothing for the office and was not inclined to take it 'unless I may do so to keep any other out who might not study the general interests of the community'.[2] To Ormond he confided that he did 'not like to see the interests of the Province sacrificed to party ends for want of a person to undertake the duties who might not be inimical to the leading interests of the Province'.[3] No doubt he equated those interests with his own.

McLean accepted nomination and was elected Superintendent of Hawkes Bay province in 1863. At the age of forty-three McLean began a new career as a politician. He enjoyed the exercise of power; life on a sheep station could not satisfy him now he had recovered from his illness. The Superintendent did not have to be elected as a member of the Provincial Council, so he chose not to stand for a constituency, wishing to be seen as impartial. McLean wanted to retain his post as Chief Land Purchase Commissioner – Dillon Bell, the Native Minister, had told him that he could continue to hold his appointment as Chief Land Purchase Commissioner conjointly with that of Superintendent – but ministers insisted that the constitution did not allow this. McLean countered by surrendering his pay and other emoluments as commissioner but asked to keep the position on the grounds that there was much unfinished business over land negotiations. Unless he had that official status, he would be unable to negotiate. At the same time he lodged a claim for a pension in recognition of his nineteen years of service, asking for a lump-sum payment in lieu of an annual pension. Four years of haggling followed, with McLean doggedly insisting that the nature of his service over the years justified tangible recognition. Ministers blandly expressed sympathy for his claim but ungraciously sheltered behind their officials, who advised that McLean had no claim under existing legislation, either the 1858 or 1862 Superannuation Act. He could not comply with either fundamental condition: thirty years' service or retirement on grounds of ill health with a medical certificate. Ministers said they could do nothing more as it would be unconstitutional to make any recommendation to the General Assembly. They suggested that he might approach a private member to have his case raised in the House. The abolition of the Land Purchase Department, gazetted in 1865, meant the consequent disappearance of McLean's position. He finally wore the Government down. The Donald McLean Superannuating Act in 1867 granted him an annual pension of £273 10s calculated on the basis of twenty-one years' service to 1865 which included two years in which he had received no salary. Another clause provided that if within one year the annual pension was commuted to a lump sum, the amount paid was to be £1000.

In McLean's first provincial session he congratulated himself that he carried all the measures he wished without opposition. He welcomed Colenso's resignation as Provincial Treasurer: 'it is past time as hitherto he has been allowed to do as he pleased but I am not going to submit to this from him or any other Provincial servant and the subordinates are beginning to find this out'.[4] His officials, who had become 'very lax in their duties and exceedingly independent', were discovering that there was a firm hand in control. Government ministers who had been frustrated by McLean's intransigence as Native Secretary could have predicted that, whatever the position, he would use his powers to the utmost.

McLean described the Hawkes Bay Provincial Council's first session as 'a short practical hard working one' when he refrained from speaking unless really necessary. He did not allow standing orders to hamper him. Council minutes recorded frequent motions to set them aside. His Provincial Executive Council – J. D. Ormond, A. H. Russell and Smith – were 'all out and out supporters, all of them excellent men and more credible advisers than Colenso and Tiffen who are greatly chagrined at the change'.[5]

McLean had his way with the Provincial Council. He told his father-in-law that the council members gave him very little trouble, that he had 'only one speech-making opponent', Colenso, and that affairs were going to his satisfaction. As proof he enclosed newspaper clippings of his speeches. 'You see I am very mild and conciliatory but with a quiet determination of my own that no one can alter.'[6] Colenso, uncompromising, earnest and humourless, saw himself as the champion of the little man against the might of the establishment as represented by the pastoralists. His obsession, in the modern phrase, to keep the bastards honest, led him to oppose indiscriminately measures proposed by McLean and his supporters. Motions were savaged by Colenso in a stream of amendments. In 1864 he moved that, as the provincial government should be administered according to the law, the Superintendent be reminded to constitute his Executive Council in strict accordance with the Executive Act. A runholder, Buchanan, moved that there be tabled every order to supply the Natives with arms and ammunition and details of the funds used in treating the natives and conferring presents on them. At the opening session in 1865, Colenso tabled eleven motions, all challenging either the competence or the legality of the Superintendent's actions. He rarely mustered more than two or three supporters, so McLean allowed himself to be magnanimous. In proroguing the council in 1866, McLean affirmed that, as it was 'most essential under the free institutions we all enjoy that the acts of Government should form the subject of fair criticism, I take the opportunity of assuring those members who have differed from me in opinion that I fully appreciate the frank and courteous tone in which they have given expression to their sentiments'.[7] Despite their differences, Colenso kept in contact when McLean became Native Minister in 1869, offering unsolicited advice or seeking help in his personal affairs. McLean, for his part, commissioned Colenso to work on a Maori dictionary.

In his first address to the council, McLean outlined a proactive policy to advance the province's prosperity. Whatever the causes of Maori unrest in other parts of the North Island, he was confident that friendly relations would continue in Hawkes Bay. Local Maori were 'steadily progressing in individual pursuits and in the acquisition of property and wealth'. Even as McLean lauded the progress of the rangatira, he continued his efforts to buy the rest of the fertile plains on which their prosperity depended. Hawkes Bay, he boasted, possessed the finest climate and the best agricultural and pastoral land in the North Island. If the colonists were to turn these advantages to the best account, they must buy more Maori land as this was needed to attract labour and capital. The recent Native Lands Act of 1862, allowing direct sale to individuals, would put the province in competition with individual capitalists and speculators in whose hands land would be locked up to 'deny access to the industrious classes'. To guard against this possibility, he proposed to obtain a loan of £30,000 to buy Maori land for settlement and a further £30,000 for immigration, roads, harbour development and police. To secure permanent revenue from land occupied by run-holders, he proposed to grant leases with pre-emptive right of purchase, leases to be for fourteen years at 1d an acre for the first seven years and 2d an acre thereafter. To attract immigrants, the province would set aside land for special settlements on a system of deferred payments. Immigrants from the mother country should have priority, especially workers from the depressed north of England. German artisan immigrants, guaranteed by the Hamburg firm of Goddefroy, should be encouraged as they would produce many articles that the settlement otherwise had to import at high prices from foreign markets. McLean was advocating an expansionist policy of the kind that was to be implemented at national level after Julius Vogel became Colonial Treasurer in 1870. The policy measures were identical: borrowing to pay for the passage of assisted immigrants, construction of roads and railways, and purchase of Maori land for settlement.

McLean's Scottish respect for education led him to point out to his council that the money from the leasing of educational reserves was insufficient to meet the needs of a growing population. He urged the council to proceed with the building of an athenaeum in Napier; money had been raised for this purpose, but none had been spent. The building, opened in 1865, housed a library as well as the Mechanics' Institute, intended for the education of the 'industrious classes'. It was destroyed by fire in the 1931 earthquake.

As resources were limited, McLean proposed that the province concentrate on building main roads, leaving branch roads to be constructed by private enterprise with some grants-in-aid. The main route between Wellington and Auckland had to be taken along the eastern side of the main mountain range. Using Maori and other labour the province had already built part of the road from Napier towards Taupo and looked to Auckland province to complete its share. McLean also aimed to establish a better line of communication with the West Coast of Wellington province through the Manawatu Gorge. Although efforts to improve and dredge the harbour at Napier had been unsuccessful, other measures would improve the port, for example, establishing reserves to be held in trust and a local marine board. By his bold measures, McLean had committed some 2000 settlers to a substantial loan of £60,000 for land purchases, immigration and public works.

As a run-holder McLean was also aware of the financial drain of the effect of scab on sheep. He passed a Sheep and Scab Act to prevent the spread of the disease and to make individual pastoralists responsible for its control in their own flocks. The requirements included earmarking and branding sheep, the issuing of droving certificates before bringing sheep into Hawkes Bay, notice of intention to drive sheep through another pastoralist's land, and fines of up to 6d per sheep with scab.

The separation of Hawkes Bay from Wellington province in 1859 had required the allocation of a portion of the Wellington province debt to the new province. When Hawkes Bay disputed the amount, McLean set out to negotiate a settlement. Four years later, when there had been no solution, McLean proposed three commissioners – himself, Ormond and Whitmore – to negotiate with Wellington. They failed, and the General Assembly had to intervene and make a decision in 1868.

As Deputy Superintendent of the province, Ormond gave his support to McLean. Whereas McLean's procrastination and distaste for office work made him an indifferent administrator, Ormond was an excellent one, decisive in action and meticulous in attention to detail. It was Ormond who worked on the provincial estimates and negotiated contracts for roads and bridges. He did not hesitate to rebuke McLean when he found nothing done in the way of preparation for the council's meetings. 'What about the various acts you promised to prepare, pray look up the subject … Please attend this and have a speedy answer sent', and again, 'For goodness sake act decisively … I thought you had taken leave of your senses'.[8]

Both men were autocrats; both identified with the interests of the Hawkes Bay landed elite. Both saw peace between Maori and settler as crucial to the development of the province and to the prosperity of their pastoral enterprises. Ormond had a cold, austere personality, McLean, with his Gaelic background, was more outgoing in handling people. Despite this difference, their friendship was lifelong. When Ormond unveiled the stone cairn memorial at McLean Park in Napier in 1913, he claimed McLean as his closest friend and believed that McLean had held him in the same regard.

With the outbreak of war in the Waikato in 1863, McLean became alarmed that Ngati Maniapoto supporters of the King movement might threaten Hawkes Bay. Although he thought most Hawkes Bay Maori wanted peace, since they relied on an income from rents of lands they leased to pastoralists, there were others who had no revenue from that source and would be prepared to join the 'disaffected natives' in attacking settlers and destroying their property. He had reports that at Tarawera on the Napier–Taupo road Maori were being incited to kill the out-settlers at Pohue. In Poverty Bay the rangatira Raniera, McLean's source of intelligence, warned of the prospect of fighting: 'Listen, be attentive and on your guard. Do not be unprepared and let not my name be known.'[9]

McLean viewed Hawkes Bay as the most exposed and defenceless part of the island. Settlers had been petitioning for stockades to be built everywhere and to be garrisoned with troops. To grant all their demands would be 'preposterous', though he would do his best. As Superintendent, his response was to urge the Government to send 1000 military settlers to Hawkes Bay to be located on the north-east frontier and in the south at Seventy Mile Bush.[10] Six hundred men should be sent without delay. He assured the Government that the province would make land available – 3000 acres at Te Pohue and 14,000 acres at Puketitiri – for these military settlers, who would be used for road-making on the main trunk road from Napier to Auckland. A further 500 men should be recruited in England and sent direct to Napier with their wives and children. He expected to buy Maori land 'conveniently suitable for the location with advantage of settlers of the labouring classes'.[11] The Stafford Government did not respond.

Throughout 1864 McLean had been trying to acquire the remaining area of the fertile Ahuriri Plains that was still in Maori hands. The Provincial Council wanted not only to develop this land for agricultural settlement as it was close to the town of Napier, but to stop illegal leasing by a few individuals for grazing. As the majority of the council members were pastoralists, it seems that, having acquired land, whether freehold or Crown leasehold, they did not want competition from others, whose occupation of Maori land might give them an advantage once the land was bought by the Crown. The council was upset that the 1846 Land Purchase Ordinance had not been enforced against these illegal lessees.

In 1864 McLean himself was in trouble over leasing Maori land when a pastoralist, Chapman, laid a complaint with Whitmore, the Civil Commissioner for Hawkes Bay. McLean's response was to brand Chapman as troublesome and obstinate, suggesting that he was bribing some of the Maori claimants to support him. He told his brother, Alexander, to talk to the claimants and to bring all the relevant papers to the meeting where Whitmore would arbitrate. He feared Chapman had got one Maori party to side with him but was still confident of the outcome 'if the natives are true to their promises but they are so changeable and tricky that they require looking after'.[12] Around that time McLean had complaints from Chapman and Te Hapuku that his Maraekakaho shepherds were taking sheep from their runs. He asked Alex to caution his men as their action was most annoying. He complained about liquor on the station during drafting and shearing – 'if anyone does that and I hear of it, he must quit the station at once'.[13] As McLean was no teetotaller, his objection must have been to the effects of liquor on the men's work performance.

McLean sent an apology for his absence from the opening session of the Provincial Council in 1865 as he was engaged on the East Coast in 'securing the co-operation of influential tribes'. He told the council that the 'native question' under this 'new phase of superstitious belief' greatly increased the danger to the province because of 'the readiness with the native mind yields to the fascination of a new faith, accompanied as it is with the most determined hostility to the European race'.[14] On his return in June he told the council that the disturbed state of the North Island made it impossible to buy the rest of the Ahuriri Plains. He repeated his opinion that the rangatira were prepared only to lease land for settlement. Although the interests of the province made it preferable to buy rather than lease, the council must acquiesce in the only terms acceptable to the native proprietors.[15] In an earlier letter to Fox, McLean set out his perception of Ngati Kahungunu's objections to selling and his response. The chiefs, he wrote, feared a large increase in the settler population when their own growing sheep and cattle numbers would require large tracts for grazing. Their other concern, he identified, was that alienation of their land left them without authority or control. Leasing their land was preferable as it left them in control over the settler tenants. Taking these objections into consideration and bearing in mind the unsettled state of the country and Maori suspicions of the Government's eagerness to acquire land, McLean said he had abstained from 'using efforts which I might otherwise have done to acquire land by purchase'.[16] McLean's cryptic comment may have been a reference to his practice from the later 1850s in buying land from those willing to sell and waiting to wear down the opposition. This was an acknowledgement that his earlier tactics were no longer effective.

In the 1866 elections for the General Assembly, McLean had won the Napier seat with a substantial majority over Colenso, the sitting member.When approached to accept nomination, he told the worthy citizens that the flattering terms in which they desired to allow his name to go forward left him no option but to accept. Whether the approach was unsolicited or prompted by McLean or Ormond is uncertain. McLean believed his efforts to preserve peace and advance the interests of the province had, 'under Providence', been attended with such success that he was encouraged to persevere.[17] He had been contemptuous of parliamentary government with its quarrelsome factions. What brought about the change? Increasing unease at the Government's native policy. Since 1860, fighting in Taranaki, Waikato and the East Coast had disturbed the North Island and the Government seemed unable to secure a peace. His experiences as Government Agent on the East Coast had confirmed his dissatisfaction. A second reason was a need to promote the interests of Hawkes Bay runholders who sought someone more sympathetic to their interests than Colenso. As Superintendent, McLean had been proactive in advancing the interests of the province, interests that he equated with those of his fellow runholders.

With his election to the House of Representatives, McLean found himself with additional responsibilities. He remained Superintendent of Hawkes Bay province and was acting as Government Agent on the East Coast. The General Assembly and Provincial Council sessions were brief enough to allow him to continue to act as Superintendent. Was this the same man who, five years before, had determined to retire from public life? To his surprise he found that he enjoyed parliamentary life though he spoke little during his first session. McLean had acknowledged that he entered provincial politics to protect the interests of the Hawkes Bay landed elite. He came to recognise that these interests needed to be advanced in the General Assembly where he supported the provincialist faction. When offered the post of Government Agent on the East Coast he had welcomed the opportunity. Pastoralists' prosperity depended upon the pacification of the district. As Government Agent he would be in a position to extend the influence of the Hawkes Bay province north into the East Coast. Moreover, he would once more be in control.

In July 1867 Stafford had introduced an amendment bill to the Representation Act to provide members for Westland and the northern districts of Raglan and Franklin. He also urged support for Maori representation, saying that Maori should have equal rights with Europeans. South Island members, however, had the numbers to defeat this bill.

Later in 1867 McLean, at Stafford's request, introduced a Native Representation Bill to provide for four Maori members of the House of Representatives, three from the North Island and one from the South Island. Although J. E. FitzGerald had recently retired from the House, his cordial relationship with McLean continued. In responding to McLean's request to help to draft the bill, he advised him to show the draft to Richmond and Bell, 'who might be very mischievous if they opposed it' and to consult with the Auckland members, Carleton, Williamson and Graham. As early as 1856 McLean had proposed giving the franchise to Maori at a time when they outnumbered the European population. FitzGerald had dissuaded him then, arguing that he would place the Governor in an impossible position as the House would never agree and that could lead to a constitutional crisis.

FitzGerald acknowledged his own lack of success in achieving Maori representation as members had looked on him 'as a dreamer and theorist' whereas McLean's standing meant a real chance of success. He warned that most opposition would come from Otago members, as the bill would give more seats to the North Island. Conscious of South Island opposition, McLean had abandoned his earlier proposal to have eight Maori seats.[18]

It is difficult to determine from McLean's speeches on the bill how far his arguments were his own views or to what extent he tailored his advocacy to attract the support of members opposed to any significant measure of equality. Introducing the bill, McLean argued that as the courts of justice were open to Maori, so should the legislature be. Maori paid taxes and owned three-quarters of the North Island. The Government had recently been at war with the tribes. In seeking to establish peace they should offer representation which might allay any angry feelings that remained.[19]

Moving the second reading, McLean noted that various unsuccessful attempts had been made 'to govern the Natives to the satisfaction of the Colonists'. In a country inhabited by two such different races, 'it could not expect that complete harmony would prevail' during the process of colonisation. In the first years of the colony, settlers had placed themselves under the protection of the Maori as the 'ruling power' and Maori were entitled to great credit for the kindness they had shown the first settlers. Both inside and outside the House the view had been expressed that the Maori race should be under equal laws, with all the privileges and rights of Englishmen, but attempts to give effect to this had been unsuccessful. Although laws had been passed to apply to native districts, everyone knew they had been a dead letter. Apart from the Resident Magistrates Ordinance,[20] none met the needs of the native districts. The laws did not work, said McLean, because 'the native mind was not ripe to receive them'. The chiefs had seen them as interfering with their customs and diminishing their mana and as a government attempt to subvert their influence and authority, and they had determined to resist. The accumulation of what they believed to be serious grievances had led to a spirit of discontent that ended in war. A remedy had to be found to remove the causes of discontent, causes that affected 'every people who conceive that they have no voice in making the laws by which they are governed'. There was a special need to offer representation when there was

> a large proportion of them fixed to the soil and possessed of considerable intelligence such as we have seen displayed on various occasions – for it might be said that politics and war have been the history of their lives from infancy upwards – it would be a bare act of justice that this people should be admitted to the right of sending representatives to take part in making laws that might be enacted for the governing of the Colony.

The bill was a means of 'striking at the root of existing evils' and the time had arrived to concede the representation it sought: four members for 47,000 Maori. In the interest of the Maori, 'a highly interesting race of people who have fought us in politics and war for seven years', the House should give them a voice in the management of public affairs. McLean supported representation by Maori rather than Europeans, as some members wished, as Maori members would bring back information to their tribes and there would be a greater incentive to acquire a knowledge of English. Maori difficulties could not be got rid of until there was 'a greater desire to speak our language'. The bill passed with a substantial majority. Writing to Douglas in England, McLean confided that he thought it just, if Maori were expected 'to obey our laws, that they should have a voice in our councils'. They were such a 'fine intelligent race' that he hoped they might avoid the fate of other darker races when they came into contact with civilisation. He urged Douglas to include the study of race in his education as public men did not give this enough attention. They made mistakes when dealing with people when they did not understand the laws and instincts by which they were governed.[21]

McLean also supported Maori rights when the Stafford Government introduced the Princes Street Reserves Bill in 1867 requiring the House to determine the ownership of three acres of valuable land in the centre of Dunedin. The reserve had been intended as a canoe landing-place and a central market for local Maori, but to secure Otago support for his government Stafford had promised to hand it over to the Provincial Council. When a Maori petition asking the Supreme Court to determine the ownership of this land came before the Petitions Committee, Stafford had to admit that he had 'inadvertently' passed up to Governor Grey a Crown grant making over the land to the Otago Provincial Council and that Grey claimed to have 'inadvertently' signed this along with other grants in the bundle. McLean, who had presented this petition, spoke in support saying that the question should be decided in a court of law and not in a House composed of people with an interest in the outcome. He had been impressed by the evidence of those who were present at the time of the purchase. The House should not block any legal process but 'act justly towards a weak portion of the Native race, who perhaps had not sufficient strength in that House to represent them'.[22]

The impending visit of Prince Albert, the Duke of Edinburgh and second son of Queen Victoria, led McLean to urge the Premier to encourage some tribe to make its submission to the prince. He suggested Tuhoe, 'a wild tribe of inland mountaineers' who had hitherto resisted the progress of European settlement but were by this time ready to make peace. On the East Coast, former rebels had become 'our best friends' and would enthusiastically welcome the Queen's son. The Government should assure that good addresses were presented to the prince by the chiefs and, as far as possible, these should be 'spontaneous and genuine productions of their composition'.[23]

With the end of fighting on the East Coast in 1866 the region became attractive for settlement. Whitaker and McLean, the Auckland and Hawkes Bay Provincial Superintendents, engaged in a contest to incorporate the East Coast within their respective provincial boundaries. Competition was increased by the alleged discovery of oil springs within the region. Most East Coast settlers favoured inclusion in Hawkes Bay province, as did local Maori, who made three petitions to Parliament in 1865. Ormond and McLean had orchestrated these petitions, Ormond arranging for James Wyllie, a Poverty Bay settler, to travel the region to gain signatures. The means by which Wyllie secured these signatures led to allegations of corrupt practice. The Public Questions Committee of Parliament held an inquiry in 1866. Before the committee, McLean denied any involvement. As a politician he could be economical with the truth despite exhorting his son to be like George Washington and always to speak the truth. No doubt he convinced himself that he was not telling a lie, as Ormond made the arrangements and McLean had had no direct involvement.[24]

In September 1866 McLean introduced the Hawkes Bay and Auckland Boundaries Bill in the House which provided for the inclusion of East Coast region in Hawkes Bay province. This committed the province to contribute £50,000 to central government to go towards compensation and land purchases. Despite this attractive offer, the votes of fifteen Auckland members in the House ensured the defeat of the two Hawkes Bay representatives, McLean and Ormond. Stafford had decided that the East Coast should go to Auckland. McLean had been overconfident. He had already negotiated to buy two blocks, Nuhaka and Kopuawhara that were now located mainly within the Auckland provincial boundary![25] Stafford sided with Whitaker to ensure that the East Coast Land Titles Investigation Act placed the region within the Auckland provincial boundary.

When Ormond succeeded McLean as Provincial Superintendent, he reported that he was taking trouble to find the best line for the road from Napier to Taupo which was intended to form part of the main route to Auckland and to supply the Armed Constabulary garrisons manning the four redoubts between Napier and Taupo. Reports of gold in the Kaimanawa Ranges had encouraged Hawkes Bay settlers to set up a company to exploit this potential field, and Ormond believed that the Napier–Taupo road would become *the* road to the Kaimanawa. He deplored the attitude of Provincial Council members towards McLean now that he was no longer Superintendent; many of them had kept saying 'nasty things of any little irregularity without considering and referring to the many services you have done them'.[26]

Chapter 16
Government Agent 1865–1866

The war in the Waikato ended in 1864. General Cameron, commander of the British troops, having defeated the King movement forces and occupied the fertile Waikato valley, prudently decided against any pursuit into the hill country to the south held by Ngati Maniapoto. Later, new outbreaks of fighting occurred on the west and east coasts of the North Island. In 1864 supporters of Pai Marire, the religious arm of Maori nationalism, launched several attacks in the Taranaki–Wanganui area. By 1865 Pai Marire had become a focus for Maori resistance, the Maori King, Tawhiao, becoming a convert.[1] When the movement spread to the East Coast in 1865, local converts killed the Opotiki missionary, C. S. Volkner, believing him to be a government spy. The Government landed colonial troops and Maori kupapa to hunt down his killers.[2]

In March 1865 Frederick Weld, the Premier, appointed McLean to act as Government Agent on the East Coast, no doubt because of his ability to influence Maori and because he was located in Hawkes Bay close to the troubled region. He delegated authority to McLean to work with friendly Maori to preserve peace, to repel aggression and, if necessary, to forcibly detain or remove from the district seditious or actively disloyal persons. McLean's instructions empowered him to supply arms and ammunition to 'loyal natives' as well as Europeans and to offer substantial rewards to friendly Maori and pensions to widows. He had authority to call out the militia and to form a cavalry corps, but he was warned not to expect any support from British regular troops. Weld assured McLean that, in asking him to undertake this task, the Government placed 'full reliance on your discretion of judgement'.[3] In effect, McLean was authorised to act as a plenipotentiary with full power to act independently rather than as a subordinate official.

Weld told McLean to offer local Maori a handsome reward if there was any possibility of securing 'leading Pai Marire murderers or leading seditionists'. Doubting the competence of the military command, he advised McLean that, if he could find 'a dashing clever fellow, Native or European, make much of him, these are not times of routine'. If the military were obstructive, McLean should call his cavalry corps 'mounted police' and not allow the commander to have anything to do with them. The Government had earlier welcomed a proposal from McLean as Hawkes Bay Superintendent for a semi-mounted police force. Faced with serious Pai Marire threats of attack on both coasts, ministers gave priority to the West Coast with its larger settler population. Weld, however, assured McLean that he recognised the importance of the East Coast and told him to encourage the militia to hold out until the Government could help them with reinforcements.[4]

McLean's appointment was a sensible choice. He was the man on the spot and the one most capable of encouraging the 'friendly' Maori and of influencing the waverers against active support of the King movement. Nevertheless, having wide-reaching powers and not being directly accountable to Parliament, McLean used his plenipotentiary powers to act as a rival authority. For four years from 1865 he became the central figure in relations between the Government and East Coast Maori. His insistence on being in control, independent of the Government that appointed him, was to lead to conflict with ministers. They should not have been surprised at McLean's subsequent conduct, given his insistence on maintaining an independent empire when Native Secretary. McLean ignored ministerial policy over the conduct of the war. He made extensive use of Maori allies to fight 'rebel' Maori whereas ministers were alarmed that the Maori allies might at some future time use these arms against the settlers. Although at this time McLean supported confiscation of Maori land he opposed immediate confiscation as he wished first to protect and reward his kupapa allies on the East Coast.

Weld's self-reliant policy, dispensing with British troops and using colonial militia, was intended to avoid a system of divided control. The extent of McLean's authority, however, meant that problems persisted. When Stafford became Premier in October 1865 he tried unsuccessfully to limit McLean's practice of incurring unauthorised expenditure.

When McLean became Government Agent he had acted promptly. First, he set out to ensure the safety of Hawkes Bay settlers against possible attack from any King movement military advance from the Waikato. British troops from the 65th Regiment were to be stationed at Napier and another company would garrison the Waipawamate stockade in central Hawkes Bay. As McLean's trusted deputy in the provincial government, Ormond organised the commissariat for the East Coast campaign. In April 1865 he reported that he had arranged for all available colonial troops to reinforce the expedition to Waiapu near East Cape. He warned McLean that the Governor, Sir George Grey, was angry at an earlier report in the *Hawke's Bay Herald* giving the credit to McLean and Ormond for arranging for a regiment to be sent to Napier. Ormond said that Grey had been annoyed because General Cameron had accused him of surrendering to

McLean's influence. Grey felt that McLean's action had exposed him to attack by the general. Ormond told McLean that he had denied all knowledge and 'said the same for you. You had better make your peace with him.'[5]

In April 1865 McLean sent a number of rangatira, including Wi Tako, along with the Revd Samuel Williams, the Anglican missionary stationed at Te Aute, to the Bay of Plenty in an attempt to influence local Maori. Writing to his unofficial agent, the trader J. W. Harris at Turanga in Poverty Bay, McLean noted that Hawkes Bay province remained quiet except for Pai Marire converts in the Urewera, and at Wairoa and Petane on the coast near Napier 'upon whom, under the influence of this fanaticism, no reliance could be placed'. Formerly, he had been confident that he could anticipate the nature of Maori reaction 'but the new breed places all estimates and prediction beyond the bounds of calculation'.[6]

Sporadic fighting on the East Coast north of Gisborne began in June 1865 and lasted till the end of the year. While the Government made a clear distinction between 'loyal' and 'rebel' natives, McLean went further. He had grasped that the most effective way to maintain authority was to secure the active collaboration of a section of the indigenous people. He exerted his mana to secure active Maori allies to fight the war aided by local colonial militia. Maori took a different stance. Three groupings existed among the East Coast tribes: loyalists, neutrals, and the Pai Marire faithful and supporters of the Maori King. These groupings were fluid. Some tribes were lukewarm or prepared to change their allegiance to gain an advantage. The first phase of fighting on the East Coast from June to October 1865 amounted to a civil war among Ngati Porou, fostered by McLean. The opponents of Pai Marire led by Rapata Wahawaha triumphed with the aid of arms and ammunition supplied by McLean. The majority of Ngati Porou supported the Government but their support was qualified. Their primary allegiance was to their own tribe, but they saw support for the British Queen as the best means of preserving their land and their independence by keeping government control at a distance.[7]

Ngati Kahungunu, although sympathetic to the aims of the King movement, had not taken up arms against the Government during the Waikato War. They preferred to benefit from agricultural and pastoral development of their lands. However, Te Hapuku, McLean's trusted ally, and Tareha and Karaitiana Takamoana had been welcoming Pai Marire supporters. No doubt Maori hospitality required that they should welcome those who were not their enemies, but McLean called them together, expressed his disapproval and urged them to order 'such dangerous fanatics' out of the province. The rangatira signalled they were prepared to distance themselves, provided disputes between Te Hapuku and Tareha and Karaitiana and Renata could be settled. McLean proposed to refer these disputes to impartial chiefs from another district. He thought

Karaitiana and Renata were more willing to oppose Pai Marire, though their opposition might weaken Tareha's influence on the government side. If a war were to break out, this would lead to complications. 'However these questions must be met as they arise.' He told Weld that he had his hands full but believed his efforts had succeeded.[8]

Government decisions over the quarrel among Hawkes Bay Maori and the plan to deal with the Pai Marire on the East Coast followed McLean's advice. The Hawkes Bay Maori were warned that the Government would not let them fight among themselves when land disputes could be settled by arbitration. Karaitiana, however, had been decidedly averse, McLean told the Native Minister, to submitting disputed titles to arbitration, whether European or Maori, saying that the law may be good when applied to others but not if it interfered with his land claim.[9] Ministers were eager for a pre-emptive strike against the Pai Marire adherents but McLean advised the Government that the Pai Marire in Hawkes Bay should be left alone 'to dance harmlessly round their niu pole' unless they committed some overt act of aggression.

As an administrator McLean was prone to procrastination, but in a crisis he could act quickly and decisively. In July 1865 he was aboard a warship supervising the landing of rifles, ammunition kegs and cartridge boxes for his kupapa allies at Hicks Bay. In stormy weather the ship sprang a leak. McLean thought that to be shipwrecked on that coast would be a catastrophe: 'A lee shore, Pai Marire enemies, a leaking ship and Pai Marire prophesies vindicated by such an accident.' However, he had confidence in Captain Fremantle, the English naval officer, 'mild, gentlemanly, yet bold and courageous not knowing what fear is'.[10] The leaks were contained. The ship went on to Waiapu where McLean brought aboard a local Maori to point out the Pai Marire positions at which the ship's guns fired several rounds. Next day, McLean saw the Pai Marire Maori leaving their pa, frightened away, he believed, by the bombardment. Deighton and Fraser, local militia commanders, reported several skirmishes lasting three days with a total of twelve Pai Marire killed and that the militia and 'loyal' Maori were co-operating well. McLean went on to Hicks Bay where a party of loyalists left at daybreak to intercept a hostile party, although he did not approve of a large force going out on a Sunday!

The Minister of Defence, FitzGerald, panicked, fearful that the whole of the East Coast was 'in a blaze'. He made it plain that McLean as Government Agent was expected to produce military success. McLean reported to J. C. Richmond, Minister with Responsibility for Native Affairs, that it was 'war to the knife' from Hicks Bay to Tolaga Bay. He prophetically remarked that he expected to hear daily of some outrage at Poverty Bay. The Government had one great and decided advantage, he reminded Richmond, in that they had such faithful allies. The object should be 'a short and decisive war' making full use of their Maori allies and offering them every support. He asked for instructions about the fate of eighty Pai Marire prisoners as 'loyal' Maori said that they would not take prisoners if the Government was then going to set them free. McLean proposed that the kupapa be encouraged to adopt a humane code of warfare and to agree to take prisoners. Nevertheless, some understanding about the release of prisoners would have to be arrived at, taking account of the opinion of their Maori allies.[11]

McLean was uneasy, a nervousness he shared with Archdeacon Williams based in Turanga over the threat to Poverty Bay settlers.[12] He sent an officer and twenty-six military settlers there. He regretted that the force was so small but hoped it would influence the waverers to come onto the government side and show the Hauhau that government subjects would not be deserted. He provided additional arms, with orders that they were not to be distributed except in an emergency. McLean must have written to Weld detailing the extent of the victories of the Ngati Porou 'loyalists' against the Pai Marire as Weld responded that the greatest credit should go to McLean. Weld, who had resigned in October, said the East Coast campaign had been a great triumph for his ministry, especially as Sir George Grey would have done things differently if he had had his own way.[13]

Writing to Stafford, McLean complained of government delays in providing supplies, pointing out that, if arms had been sent when he asked, the war should have been ended. 'I have 260 men absolutely idle for want of arms which would with those now armed smash the "Hauhau". The friendlies now shedding their blood side by side with us cannot understand why they are not encouraged or their assistance availed of.' McLean's policy was to use his Maori kupapa allies to fight the war. The Stafford Government opposed their use, being wary of arming 'friendly natives' in case they might use their arms to attack the settlers.

In September 1865 local Pai Marire refugees from fighting on the East Coast moved south to Turanga, seeking sanctuary in a Pai Marire pa at Waerenga-a-Hika. On 1 November Stafford sent instructions to McLean to enforce peace in Poverty Bay by expelling all Pai Marire supporters; those not expelled were to be taken prisoner. Land should be taken to help pay for the cost of the war.[14]

McLean arrived at Poverty Bay on 9 November with a combined force of militia and 260 Ngati Porou. Despite the offer by Turanga Maori to meet with McLean, he refused. He issued an ultimatum based on Stafford's instructions. All Maori had to take the oath of allegiance, those who had fought against the Government were to be handed over, everyone who did not belong to the district was to be expelled and all arms surrendered. These terms were not negotiable and those who rejected them would have their land confiscated. When Maori were seen to have defied the Queen's authority or had been involved in killing civilians, or when his reputation depended on success, McLean was implacable. He made no attempt to sit down and talk.

When the ultimatum expired, government forces besieged the pa at Waerenga-a-Hika that surrendered six days later, the defenders having lost seventy-one killed. Many of the Turanga Maori had been reluctant allies and were suspected of passing information to the enemy within the pa and the day before, Major Fraser made prisoner one Maori fighting on the government side on suspicion of being a spy. This act was to have a disastrous sequel. The man arrested was Te Kooti Arikirangi Te Turuki, whose brother had been among the besieged within the pa. Te Kooti was released but Harris, a local trader, eager to acquire Maori land, complained to his friend McLean that Te Kooti and his brother were known thieves and that Te Kooti had been a spy. Te Kooti was again arrested when McLean and the Governor arrived at Turanga. McLean met with the Maori allies and got their approval that the prisoners should be shipped to the Chatham Islands. Their confinement would depend on their behaviour, though a term of one year was mentioned. Although Te Kooti protested his innocence he was not brought to trial on any of the charges made against him. He approached Lieutenant Wilson, his commanding officer at Waerenga-a-Hika, to intercede with McLean. Years later, Te Kooti recalled McLean's sudden appearance in Wilson's office and his angry refusal to listen to him.

Te Kooti was sent to Napier gaol where he wrote two letters to McLean. He asked to be told what he had done wrong and signed himself, 'Te Koti Queens Maori'. The second letter, also signed by his brother, accused two local traders, Read and Wyllie and some government Maori of selling guns and ammunition to the Pai Marire. (FitzGerald had made a similar charge against Read.)[15] Te Kooti and his brother were shipped to the Chathams on 5 June 1865, the day before the date given on their joint letter. Their inclusion in this batch of prisoners could be attributed to the presence in Napier of Captain Biggs, the militia commander at Poverty Bay. Biggs, an advocate of stern measures against Maori, along with the local traders, wanted Te Kooti out of the way, both as a potential troublemaker and as a rival who had been taking business away from European traders. Moreover, Biggs was occupying land that Te Kooti insisted he had not sold.[16]

Given the timing, it is unlikely that McLean considered Te Kooti's appeal before the ship sailed for the Chathams. It is possible that he did not even sight the letters as he was in Poverty Bay at that time.[17] The originals are located in the Native Affairs files in Wellington. There is no reference to his receiving or minuting Te Kooti's letter. If he did receive Te Kooti's appeal, it is probable he would have acted on the advice of Biggs as resident magistrate and militia commander for Poverty Bay. Te Kooti himself blamed Biggs who was in Napier at that time for his exile.[18]

After their defeat at Waerenga-a-Hika the East Coast Pai Marire had retreated to the mountains north of Lake Waikaremoana where McLean had sent them a letter advising them to come to terms.[19] This area later became a sanctuary for Te Kooti and his followers.

With the end of the war on the East Coast, Stafford, the new Premier, intended to confiscate Maori land to pay for the cost of the war and the establishment of military settlements to maintain the Queen's authority. Moreover, 'Maori who took the oath of allegiance and then broke it' would in future 'either be executed or transported or set to hard labour'.[20]

McLean in supporting Stafford said that he was confident the confiscated territory would more than cover expenses 'besides leaving a very handsome margin'.[21] Stafford was sceptical. He doubted there would be any money left from the sale of this land after making provision for compensation, reserves, military settlers and the like. The best that might be done would be to put on this land settlers who could be self-supporting and self-defending. He urged McLean to 'think this over seriously – it is the largest question we have to deal with both in its financial and political bearings'.[22]

McLean's priority remained the situation of the Maori allies. In 1866 he told Stafford that land confiscation was not possible until their lands were distinctly separated from those of the Pai Marire. McLean wrote that he rejoiced to hear news of the success on the West Coast and that Stafford was pleased with his efforts on the East Coast. He apologised for not writing sooner but, where kupapa allies were engaged, they needed vigilant attention. He was reluctant to be absent for any length of time.[23]

When McLean met Poverty Bay Maori in March 1866 he reminded them that he had warned them to refrain from fighting. As they had not taken his advice the Government would now take blocks of land on both sides of the fertile river flats of the Waipaoa River. The Maori protested that they would be left only with bush and scrub, but McLean insisted that the area was small. In desperation, the Maori made an offer of land that was rejected by McLean. He threatened them that, if they left it to the Native Land Court to decide, they would lose a large area. The court was not for their protection but for that of the Government; it was sent by the Government to take their land forcibly.[24] This frank admission of the Government's real purpose was unusual for McLean who tended to hide behind pious expressions of good intentions.

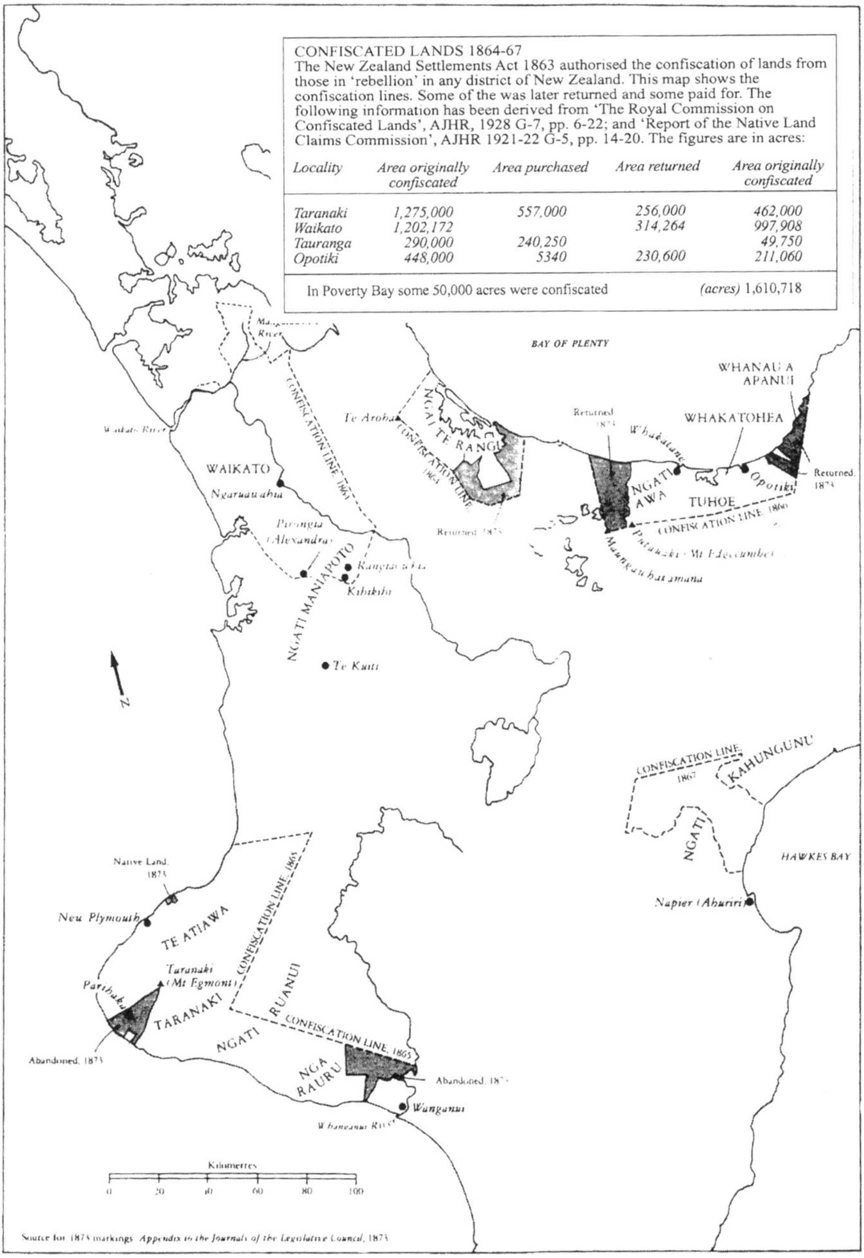

Map 6. Confiscated Lands 1864-1867

Stafford had first proposed to bring the land on the East Coast under the New Zealand Settlements Act of 1863 which entailed the confiscation of all land in districts where any section of a tribe had taken part in a rebellion since 1863. McLean initially agreed, advising that the next step would be to survey the land, set aside the confiscated territory and confirm the title of the 'friendlies' who had helped 'in suppressing rebellion'. As the kupapa had not been paid regularly, he recommended that they should be given part of the proceeds of the sale of confiscated land. At Poverty Bay, 'friendly' Maori should be compensated for the site of the town of Turanganui which should then be subdivided and sold by auction. Stafford, having doubts about the suitability of using the New Zealand Settlements Act after the British Government had made plain its displeasure by advising cession rather than confiscation, finally passed the East Coast Land Titles Investigation Act in October 1866 that provided for 'voluntary' cession rather than confiscation but really amounted to confiscation under another name. The act distinguished between Maori who had 'rebelled' and those who had not.

The Compensation Court had power to declare who were rebels and who were not. The Native Land Court could award land of those who had 'rebelled' to tribes who had not resisted. Where land was jointly owned by 'rebels' and non-rebels the court could partition out and award land to those who had not taken part in the fighting. This act gave a punitive role to the Native Land Court. Land belonging to 'rebels' became Crown land to be sold to meet the expenses of the fighting.

McLean indicated the cession of land would have the endorsement of the East Coast. In return, he proposed part of the land would be taken from the 'rebels' and given to 'loyal' Maori. At the same time the expenses of the war would be met out of the sale of the forfeited land.[25] Part of the land confiscated belonged to tribes who had not taken part in the fighting.

In November 1866 Stafford appointed Major Biggs as Crown Agent to the Native Land Court that would decide on the land to be ceded. McLean took offence, believing that having restored peace he was now to be excluded from participation in the peacemaking process. McLean believed that the Stafford Government was jealous of his influence over the Maori tribes and that this had been the reason for his being excluded from arrangements for the land settlement. Later, McLean would also blame Whitaker's intervention as Superintendent of Auckland province for his difficulties in bringing about a satisfactory settlement.

Although fighting had ended on the East Coast and Poverty Bay in August 1866, Pai Marire followers under their prophet Panapa were reported at

Titiokura and Te Haroto on the Napier–Taupo road in the territory of Ngati Hineuru. Settlers became alarmed at rumours of an attack on Napier, but McLean did not seem to consider that there was a threat. In September, Panapa and his followers had moved down to Petane in response to an invitation from McLean who sought to find out their intentions.[26] Te Rangihiroa, the rangatira of Ngati Hineuru, accepted along with Panapa, asking McLean to send soldiers to escort his party but that he not inform the local Maori. This suggests that their intentions were peaceful but that they did not want to surrender and take an oath of allegiance in front of other Maori. McLean, however, was in Wellington and the opportunity to achieve a peaceful settlement was lost. Panapa and his party remained at Petane for several weeks. Their presence there encouraged rumours of an attack on Napier. The party was running short of food and by the time McLean returned to Hawkes Bay on 4 October they had moved to the pa at Omarunui whose rangatira and his people moved to Tareha's Pa Whakairo. They were expecting to meet McLean there. Another Hineuru party led by Te Rangihiroa had set out from Te Pohue for Petane. Although Omarunui was close to Napier, McLean, instead of going to meet Panapa, sent three local rangatira to negotiate, inviting Panapa to go alone to Pa Whakairo to discuss a move to Napier, where the party was to renounce Pai Marire and take an oath of allegiance. Panapa's followers insisted that they all go – they 'were all Panapas'. McLean continued to send letters and Panapa to respond with confused and evasive replies. His last letter on 8 October concluded 'all talking is at an end'. McLean took this to mean that Panapa was prepared to fight, although an alternative interpretation would have been that this was merely a normal Maori way of concluding a letter. He ordered Major Fraser's force to move from Wairoa to Petane, and called out the Napier militia and invoked the help of his kupapa allies. McLean was under pressure. A hostile Ngati Hineuru was a potential threat to the important Napier–Taupo road. Colonel Whitmore was eager for a military solution and believed that Ngati Hineuru had been stealing sheep from his Rissington run. Moreover, Tareha and other local Ngati Kahungunu now wanted Panapa and his followers out of their district. They told McLean that if he did not remove them they would act themselves. Both McLean and Panapa appear to have changed their minds between September and October. McLean decided to issue an ultimatum rather than to talk and negotiate. Panapa perhaps swept up in the intensity of his religious fervour, was no longer prepared to submit, though not contemplating an attack.

By dawn on 12 October Colonel Whitmore's force and local Maori led by Tareha had surrounded the pa at Omarunui. McLean sent a letter to Panapa under a white flag saying that Panapa had not explained his reason for coming to Heretaunga and had refused to go back home. McLean required the party

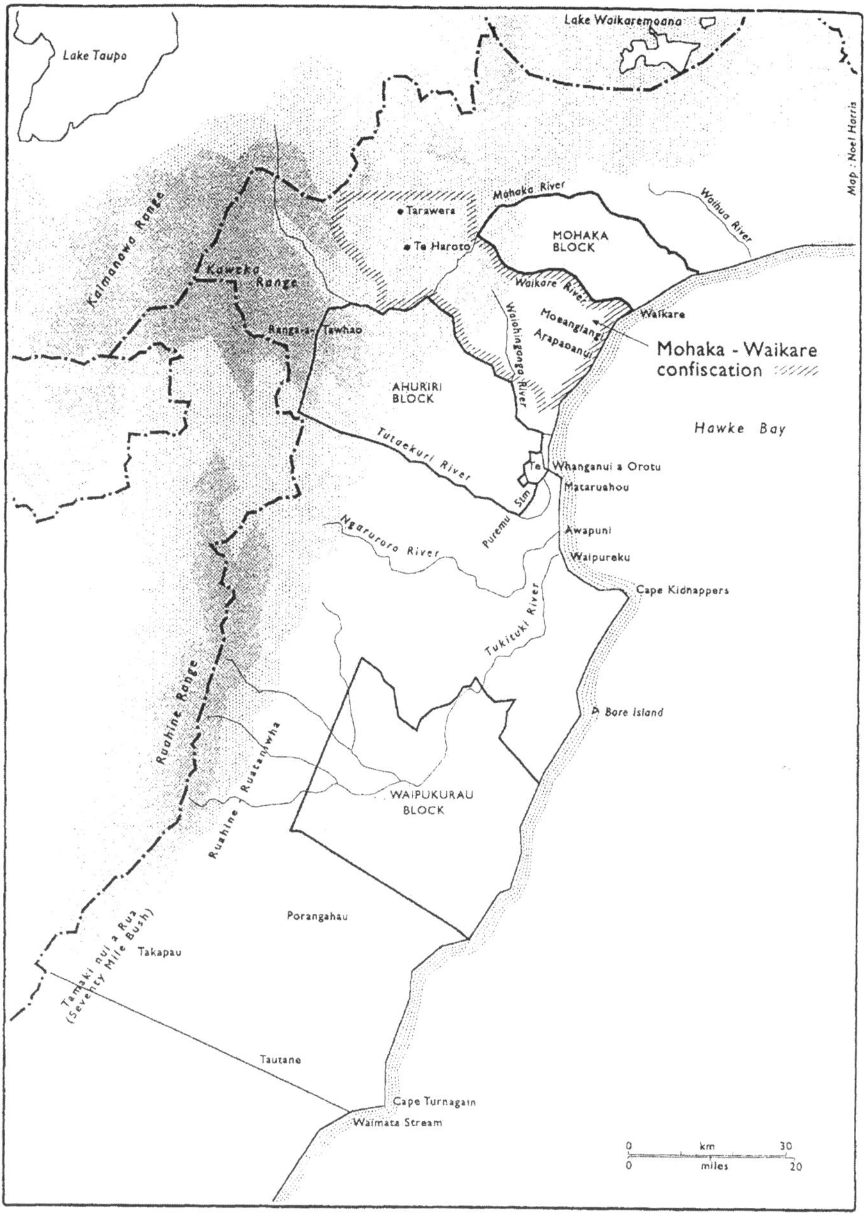

Map 7. Crown Purchase Issues 1858–1862

to give up their arms and surrender themselves within one hour of receiving the letter. This was the same tactic he had used at Waerenga-a-Hika in 1865 – assemble a strong force of militia and Maori allies, surround the pa, deliver an uncompromising ultimatum and then attack.

McLean and Whitmore were confident that Panapa's party would surrender. The militia and volunteers under Colonel Whitmore were accompanied by some 200 Ngati Kahungunu led by Tareha, outnumbering the Pai Marire by about three to one. When no reply was received, they waited a further hour before they hauled down the white flag and raised the Union Jack. The order to attack was given and the bugles sounded the advance. Although Panapa's party had occupied the pa for a week, they had made no attempt to fortify it. The Pai Marire force was overwhelmed, losing twenty-four dead, thirty wounded and fifty-eight taken prisoner. At Petane, Fraser ambushed Te Rangihiroa and his twenty-four warriors, killing twelve, including Rangihiroa. The captured men were imprisoned without trial and shipped to the Chatham Islands.

Napier citizens erected marble obelisks to commemorate the victories at Omarunui and Petane, while an unknown Napier bard proclaimed the exploits of their gallant settlers:

> Hark the warning bugles soundeth; peaceful townsmen
> rouse to arms;
> Fierce barbarians dare approach us; rise, and teach
> these raving bands,
> That though peaceful yet we scorn, all their boasted
> threats defy,
> When Aurora wakes the morn, we will conquer them,
> or die.
> We the sons of great Britannia, we will, like our
> sire of yore,
> For our homes and country, we will bleed
> at every pore.
> Forward, Onward, is the order; lay the vaunting
> rebels low ...

A description of the preparations for and of the battle itself follows and then the victors' magnanimous response:

> Ha! the white flag waving yonder; yield they now
> our work is done;
> See oh see the suffering wounded mercy show
> The battle's won

Gallant Napier, embrocity, thou hast done a noble
part;
Thou hast set a bright example, thou wilt prove
thy generous heart.
Thou wilt show the conquer'd savage, that, tho'
justice may demand,
Yet in mercy thou wilt spare the wretched remnant
of their band.[27]

Donald McLean, who had been a spectator at the engagement, sent a newspaper cutting describing it to a kinswoman, Mrs Skinner, widow of a British general. She replied that she was delighted to find that the martial ardour of the McLeans remained undimmed and that Donald had added to the honour of the clan. Stafford, the Premier, congratulated him on his success: 'You appear to have waited just the right time, laid your plans skilfully and struck forcibly.'[28]

The sequel to Omarunui was the confiscation of some 193,000 acres of land in the Mohaka–Waikare area, the last of the confiscations carried out under the New Zealand Settlements Act of 1863. In recommending to Stafford that 'rebel' land be confiscated, McLean noted that while the land was of very little value being hilly, rugged and unproductive, it was essential that natives who had 'so wantonly disturbed the peace' should be punished. In fact, half the land seized was from Maori who had taken no part in the fighting. Three factors appeared to lead McLean to recommend confiscation. First, there had been a long-running rivalry between the coastal Ngati Kahungunu – seen by McLean as 'friendly' – and the inland Ngati Hineuru. Ngati Kahungunu were to be rewarded with part of this confiscated land. Tareha was to receive a large block in his own name. Second, after his 1851 purchases McLean had little success in buying land between the Mohaka and Ahuriri blocks. Squatters who had taken up land there were now attempting to acquire land under the 1865 Native Lands Act. McLean seemed to have decided that confiscation was the solution rather than having to work through the Native Land Court in competition with the runholders. A third reason was the strategic importance of the Napier–Taupo road that ran through Ngati Hineuru territory. McLean wanted to use this road to cut off the King movement tribes of the interior from linking up with those of the centre of the island and of the Urewera. In Hawkes Bay, McLean had already built redoubts at Te Pohue and Tarawera to protect the road and telegraph line.

Chapter 17
McLean's Continuing Role on the East Coast 1867–1869

Biggs as Crown Agent to the Native Land Court had made no progress with the proposed cession of land, partly because of faulty drafting of the East Coast Land Titles Investigation Act. In November 1867 Stafford had to turn again to McLean who, resentful at his exclusion from the land settlement after suppressing the 'rebellion', did not respond. Ormond tried to persuade him to accept in order to help the colony, but advised him not to promise success, given the confused situation on the coast.[1] J. C. Richmond, the Native Minister, assured McLean that he had no desire 'to filch any title of your credit and honour in the matter for myself or the Government'. Ministers could not expect any 'brilliant settlement'. If McLean could make the arrangements, pay the expenses and secure 'some sort of position for rebels who return', he would have done as much as the Government could expect. Richmond warned that any payments of money must be made out of the net proceeds of the sale of the ceded land as the Government had no other funds available.[2]

McLean finally responded saying that endless complications had occurred and a complete settlement could not be expected. Although he could not promise to effect much, he would endeavour to do his best in the interests of the colony. He went on to demand an independent commission with almost unlimited powers and a budget of £56,000. Stafford would not agree. McLean must be accountable to the Government. He offered to give McLean a place on the Executive Council and to make him Resident Minister for the East Coast, stationed at Napier. McLean rejected the offer.

Although McLean had told Poverty Bay Maori in 1866 that the Government intended to keep the Pai Marire prisoners on the Chathams for only one year, he had advised Stafford to leave them there until the confiscation/cession of the East Coast lands had been completed. In July 1868, frustrated at the prospect of delayed return, Te Kooti seized a ship at the Chathams and sailed with 298 men, women and children, landing at Poverty Bay. Local Maori loyal to the Government believed that Te Kooti would cause no trouble if left in peace; it seems McLean conveyed this opinion to the Government. Te Kooti himself had told government messengers that he would fight only if pursued and attacked.[3] He aimed to settle on the shores of Lake Taupo; 'going into the wilderness' to set up the tabernacle of the ark of the covenant. Major Biggs and the local volunteers, however, set out to cut off Te Kooti's party, but were ambushed and put to flight. At the same time, the Government tried unsuccessfully to open peace negotiations with Te Kooti.[4]

Meanwhile, Titokowaru's victories on the West Coast of the North Island led the Government to transfer there some of the Armed Constabulary who had been pursuing Te Kooti. This transfer upset the East Coast settlers and angered McLean. During the 1868 parliamentary session in September, McLean, although Government Agent, joined the Opposition by moving two motions expressing alarm at the Government's handling of defence and native affairs. McLean charged the Government with failing to deal with those issues on which the peace and prosperity of the colony depended. Despite the impending crisis the Government had taken no steps to strengthen relations with friendly tribes from whom they had received full co-operation and whose services had been invaluable as veterans in the art of war. The Government should have made every effort to ensure their reliable support, he said.

McLean also attacked the handling of the wars. On the West Coast a war begun eight years before showed no sign of ending; the Government appeared to have no plan. At the same time there was war on the East Coast, while the tribes in the interior were in 'a state of sullen defiance'. The Government had to deal with a 'highly intelligent and, I must say, very chivalrous race, who are watching our every movement, who are skilled in the art of war, and who have the sagacity to ascertain and the ability to take advantage of our position'. The colony had to meet these threats with reduced resources and without the support of the British Government. McLean claimed that the conduct of military operations lacked any system. Military and civil authorities were in conflict and the Government had surrendered its power of directing policy to the military. As long as this power remained unco-ordinated among the districts, they could expect nothing but disaster. By following a cheese-paring policy the Government had allowed the escape of prisoners from the Chathams.

As for Hawkes Bay, McLean said that as Provincial Superintendent he had never asked the Government for assistance. The settlers themselves had checked the 'spread of fanaticism and war' (a reference to the fighting at Omarunui), but the Government must be prepared to meet such a threat if it reappeared: 'A bucketful of water will extinguish a flame when it appears but it will take a hogshead to quench if it is allowed to spread. You may bring hundreds of men and fail to put down a rebellion which twenty men would have been able to crush at its commencement.' McLean claimed that he had warned of danger yet Stafford had moved Major Fraser's force to the West Coast, depriving Hawkes Bay of the assistance asked for – an act of 'hardhearted cruelty' to the settlers, as this small band was the only force of trained men available in an emergency. He warned the House of a crisis that 'will yet cause this country much trouble, vexation and expense' and reminded members that in the past he had given public warnings that had turned out to be true, and thought that, so long as the present Government continued in office, there was no hope of seeing an end to the war.[5]

Stafford, in reply, said that for some time the Government had been unable to cooperate with McLean or accede to his demands. Ministers were not prepared to spend £56,000 on one district, though they were agreeable to make some money available if McLean were to become a minister responsible to the House and act as Resident Minister on the East Coast. Every step in the East Coast campaign, Stafford reminded the House, had been taken with McLean's agreement. If McLean had believed that the Hawkes Bay settlers were threatened, he had the power to call out the local militia, but he chose not to. The Government had been prepared to leave Te Kooti alone when he returned but it was the local militia commanders, Biggs and Charles Westrupp, who had taken precipitate action. Stafford accused McLean of moving the resolution because of his disappointment when the Government refused to give him money and unlimited power. The Government had not the power, said Stafford, to determine when the war should end. 'We do not believe we can at once absolutely change by a rapid convulsion the minds of semi-savages nor profess to ensure that respect for law and order shall at once reign in a people some of whom have only in the last few years given up eating their own relatives in order to murder and eat Europeans.'[6] That the Premier should speak in such a way shows a gulf in understanding that must have dismayed the Maori members of the House.

On McLean's second motion, the Government barely survived. Writing to his son at school in England, McLean remarked that he had nearly turned the Stafford ministry out. The division was 32–32; the Speaker's casting vote had saved the ministry. He said that he had no desire to take office, but had been dissatisfied with the ministers' handling of affairs and believed that the country would in future be better prepared to face up to 'our native difficulties'. He promised Douglas, aged sixteen, that he would send him some of the debates 'for your amusement'.[7]

When fighting was renewed on the East Coast in 1868 with Te Kooti's return, McLean, still nominally Government Agent, offered his services to the Premier. He made this offer, he said, 'apart from any political considerations, conceiving it to be the duty of every Colonist to assist at a time like the present, also from a desire to avert war if possible and to induce cooperation on the part of the friendly natives'. In return he asked for the support and cooperation of the Government for the authority to negotiate with Maori in the region and to control the activities of all officers, military or otherwise.[8] The Government accepted, aware that it depended on McLean to keep its Maori allies in the field against Te Kooti. In response to McLean's memorandum of 10 October insisting that he control the activities of all officers, civil and military, Richmond replied that the Government would 'hear with much attention all Mr. McLean's recommendations as to the location and movements of the Colonial forces within the district'.[9] Such an equivocal answer left the matter open to further disagreement when dealing with an autocratic McLean.

Richmond followed with a letter the next day conveying some reservations, not unreasonably in view of McLean's openly expressed opposition in the House. The only approval the Government aspired to, Richmond pointed out, was selecting the right man and achieving success. Since McLean had chosen to join the Government's opponents he made it impossible for the Government to 'altogether neglect the means of restoring that personal consideration for ourselves which your action has tended to damage'. Ministers were prepared to accept his offer of help and to give him his due share of the 'honour of success'. Richmond continued, 'Regard not for ourselves only but for the position of the Government generally requires that we should not let our hottest opponent stand altogether between us and any part of the native population'. McLean himself had chosen to make the native question 'the turning point of a parliamentary battle' and the Government could not ignore this challenge. Any payment of money to the East Coast Maori would be made directly by the Government or through some officer who was not likely to be an opponent. As McLean had raised the subject of money, Richmond thought it necessary to speak his mind, especially after the experience ministers had had of 'the mischief of silence'.[10]

Richmond authorised McLean to secure the support of the friendly tribes and to assure those that were hostile or neutral that no action would be taken against them so long as they remained quiet. McLean was to use the telegraph to communicate with the Government, but in an emergency the Government would support him in any measures he was required to take. Richmond made it plain that McLean must seek ministerial authority for any expenditure.[11] McLean's duties as Superintendent in Hawkes Bay were assumed by his deputy, Ormond, who would also efficiently organise the military commissariat for the East Coast campaign.

When Te Kooti landed in Poverty Bay in July 1868 he intended to retire towards the Urewera. The local militia under Biggs and Westrupp tried to cut off his retreat. Meanwhile the Government hastily organised three columns to pursue Te Kooti; one from Poverty Bay another from Wairoa and a third from Napier with Colonel Whitmore in overall command. Whitmore, with a force that included Maori allies recruited by McLean, took up the pursuit as Te Kooti made a fighting withdrawal towards the Urewera where he remained for two months after defeating Whitmore at Ruakituri.

On 9 November, Major Biggs was writing from Wairoa to assure McLean that 'we are all right here at present though of course there are often alarms about enemy being close to us'. He reported that Te Kooti's men were supposed to be cutting a road through the bush towards the settlement.[12] On the same day, McLean was writing to Biggs, worried over the absence of information about Te Kooti's movements.

On midnight 9–10 November Te Kooti made a successful surprise attack on the settlement of Matawhero, killing twenty-nine Europeans and part-Maori, including Major Biggs and then twenty-two Maori prisoners.[13] Te Kooti's success in attacking the settlers at Matawhero in Poverty Bay further discredited the Government's handling of the war. When he learnt of the killing of settlers, McLean wondered if this meant a new kind of warfare and what the consequences might be.

McLean reacted promptly to the attack on Matawhero, an attack which he insisted he had earlier warned Biggs. He rushed all available troops to Poverty Bay, including twenty-two Armed Constabulary, seventy Turanga allies under Westrupp and two hundred Ngati Kahungunu volunteers from Napier. McLean sent a steamer to Hicks Bay for Ngati Porou reinforcements and despatched arms and ammunition to settlers at Mohaka. Although he did not expect any immediate attack on Napier, as a precaution he organised Hawkes Bay settlers from Meanee to Te Pohue to report on any enemy movements. He recommended unsuccessfully that the Government station a company of British troops in Poverty Bay and Wairoa to support the friendly Maori in the field, as they could not be expected to carry on continuous warfare.

On 17 November Te Kooti began to retreat from Poverty Bay pursued by Ngati Kahungunu and Rongowhakaata kupapa forces. With superior numbers, Te Kooti held them off for a time. McLean was trying to attempt a pincer movement from Wairoa with more Ngati Kahungunu and Ngati Porou forces. McLean had no time for Major Lambert, the militia commander at Wairoa. He considered him incompetent and unwilling to cooperate with Maori allies; moreover Lambert was a staunch Stafford supporter. McLean sent his own man, F. E. Hamlin, to organise the expedition. Lambert sabotaged his efforts and five days were lost.[14] McLean wanted Lambert removed as too old for field service and unsuited to command Maori troops. Richmond refused, and

McLean temporarily acquiesced. When the Wairoa expedition finally reached Makaretu on 3 December, Te Kooti had withdrawn his women and children and most of his warriors to a new position inland of Ngatapa.

In December, when the Government responded to McLean's request for additional troops by sending Colonel Whitmore to command the combined forces on the East Coast, McLean protested. Maori allies disliked Whitmore so much, he said, they would not take the field under his command. McLean asked the Government to recall Whitmore; he even organised a petition. Writing to Archdeacon Williams at Turanga, McLean confided that he could think of nothing more offensive to the inhabitants of Poverty Bay than to have Whitmore among them so soon after their losses. The Government ignored McLean and sent Richmond to Poverty Bay as their representative.

When Richmond accompanied Whitmore and his combined force as they surrounded Te Kooti at Ngatapa, McLean concealed his displeasure. He told Richmond that, if Te Kooti tried to hold out at Ngatapa, this would prove to be his death blow. He was 'exceedingly glad' Whitmore was giving so much satisfaction and 'no one will be more rejoiced than I shall to see this unfortunate war ended'.[15]

Featherston told McLean he was angry that McLean's plans had been handicapped by ministerial interference actuated, he believed, by petty jealousy. As McLean appeared about to succeed, Richmond and Whitmore had hurried to Poverty Bay to reap all the credit for crushing Te Kooti. Featherston was scathing. 'The idea of Richmond conducting native operations or himself going to the front – a man who trembles in his office at every threatening Maori letter, is rich in the extreme.'[16] Ministers should not have been surprised that McLean resented what he saw as interference. Although Richmond made an effort to conciliate him, the Government had failed to clarify the precise extent of McLean's authority.

Whitmore found that he would need reinforcements if he was lay to siege to Ngatapa. McLean was uncooperative. He transferred 400 Ngati Kahungunu to Wairoa and Whitmore had to wait for Rapata and his Ngati Porou kupapa troops to return from their northern homes. On their return and with 200 Armed Constabulary Whitmore attacked the pa at Ngatapa. Te Kooti and his followers escaped but many were summarily executed by Rapata's men in the ensuing pursuit.

The campaign against Te Kooti was handicapped by enmity between McLean and Whitmore. Yet in earlier years the relationship between them had been positive. Whitmore had sought McLean's assistance in acquiring land to establish a run in Hawkes Bay. In 1866 Whitmore's handling of the Omarunui encounter had received McLean's unqualified approval as a 'brilliant success'. The McLean 'blarney' was lavishly applied, Whitmore being assured of McLean's 'highest commendation' for his 'wonderful tact' in managing such a mixed force, most of whom had never seen active service.[17] Whitmore, a former British regular soldier who had been military secretary to General Cameron, was by far the most capable of the colonial commanders. He was also 'cursed with the personal charm of a rattlesnake'.[18] He antagonised his own troops, the local militia and his Maori kupapa allies. When Poverty Bay volunteers refused to pursue Te Kooti outside the district boundary, for example, Whitmore made them dig their own graves and plead on their knees for their lives.

Given their autocratic personalities, it was probable that Whitmore and McLean should clash especially as they differed over the conduct and control of the campaign against Te Kooti, although they maintained a formal politeness and expressed co-operation in their correspondence. Still McLean insisted on complete control over the military; Whitmore, encouraged by ministers, intended to conduct his own campaign. McLean came to regard Whitmore as his enemy. The enmity between McLean and Whitmore was reflected in factional squabbles between McLean's followers and government supporters. Captain Charles Westrupp, a McLean man and the local militia commander at Poverty Bay, complained that he had been removed from his command by Whitmore: 'My opinion is not asked for on any subject in fact my presence is almost ignored.' He warned McLean that Whitmore was 'very bitter' against him.[19] Westrupp also warned McLean that the new Armed Constabulary had been sent to the East Coast without revolvers or side arms and that nearly half of them had never fired a shot in their lives. They were fit only for garrison duty, as no officer should have to depend on them in the field.[20]

In their letters, both official and private, Richmond and McLean preserved a courteous if wary relationship. To Stafford, however, Richmond revealed the depth of his animosity towards McLean. He saw McLean as being as great a threat to the colony as Te Kooti. Not only were there differences over policy – for example, in the use of Maori allies to do the fighting – but McLean's successes threatened the life of the ministry. If the Government succeeded in the campaign against Te Kooti, Richmond believed, the country would be relieved not only from anxiety and danger,

> but also from the serious evil of the personal ambition of a man at once incompetent and puffed up with silly flattery to the extreme of vanity. To destroy McLean's

Colonel Whitmore

Te Hapuku

Renata Kawepo

Tareha Te Moananui

The Cottage at Maraekakao, built between 1862 and 1869

Christopher William Richmond

J. D. Ormond

Archibald McLean

Donald McLean c. 1870

McLean residence at Napier, 1870s

McLean's grave, Napier Cemetery

> prestige among Natives and Europeans, at once is to save the land from great expenditure, misery and shame. We are bound steadily to disembarrass ourselves of all dependence on native levies and to discourage warlike skills among them as fast as we can … McLean will do the reverse he has done all along.
>
> If we succeed in holding the reins this session … we shall break down the mischievous influence of McLean on the Coast.

Richmond claimed that he had established good relations with the Ngati Kahungunu rangatira, Tareha and Karaitiana, and believed they could be persuaded to support the Government, 'if we can keep McLean and his friends out for a year or two'.[21]

McLean resisted government pressure to settle the Poverty Bay land question. Any attempt to do so before the fighting had ended and while the recent massacre at Matawhero was fresh in people's minds would have unfortunate consequences, he argued. Te Kooti must first be beaten. He would be sorry if the local tribes got the impression that the 'acquisition of land is more sought after than the punishment of Criminals who committed the late atrocities'. From his long experience, he told the Government the time was inopportune. Richmond wished to proceed with the cession of land. McLean advised him that such a move would offend the majority of East Coast Maori and thus offset any temporary advantage.[22] Turanga Maori had indicated they did not want to negotiate with Richmond and Biggs but would negotiate with McLean.

The conflict between McLean and the ministers over government policy on the East Coast was not merely a clash of personalities. It became a struggle for political power. The provincialist faction took the opportunity to attack Stafford. In September 1868, when McLean moved his motions condemning the Government's handling of the war and of native affairs, such was his mana as *the* expert on Maori matters that the survival of the Stafford ministry was threatened. J. C. Richmond, writing to Stafford, acknowledged that Biggs's inability to settle the land question on the East Coast and his subsequent death meant the ministry had 'suffered a great loss of influence' and their political enemies were saying that McLean would have succeeded. 'Even now the miserable curs are trying to claim the credit of settling for their chief.' Ministers needed to dispose of the land question without McLean's intervention, as their authority among East Coast Maori had 'become a shadow'. They must assert their authority 'even to the point of overruling McLean and his favourite natives'.[23]

McLean, for his part, claimed that the Government had broken faith over the agreed conditions of his appointment, and he listed the breaches. Colonel Lambert, who was in charge of the Wairoa militia, not allowing Mr Hamlin, a government official, to carry out McLean's wishes; ministers sending Colonel Whitmore to Poverty Bay against McLean's protests; attempting through Colonel Lambert to induce a Ngati Porou contingent to go to the West Coast without McLean's knowledge. The Government's memo of 12 October had stated that they would 'treat with much attention' all Mr McLean's recommendations about the colonial forces. Why had this not been done in Whitmore's case? Why were men not raised and sent to Hawkes Bay after repeated applications by McLean? McLean complained that ministers in Wellington thought that they knew more about the required troop movements than the resident agent.

The ongoing friction between McLean and ministers emerged again in McLean's request on 15 November that all instructions to military officers on the coast should go through him. A successful campaign, especially with mixed forces, he argued, would be impossible 'if even a semblance of divided authority is allowed to prevail'.[24] Militia officers were openly partisan; they were seen as McLean's men or government supporters. At Wairoa, Colonel Lambert, a Stafford supporter, assured McLean that he was doing all he could to restore confidence. He complained that Ngati Porou forces were unsettled while the Europeans were 'a set of Drunkards'. He would be able to hold his own but he was not surprised at the reverses they had sustained considering 'the material our forces are made of. I have closed the Public Houses and yet we have half the men drunk – this must be remedied before we can do anything with the Maoris.'[25] Deighton, a McLean man, was critical of Lambert for his handling of his kupapa allies: 'his old world military ideas upon all subjects are so totally at variance with their pre-conceived notions that there is a continual clash'. Deighton had warned Lambert that if he wished to keep the Ngati Porou he should interfere as little as possible.[26] McLean followed up, advising Lambert that the Ngati Porou should be handled very delicately and allowed to do things in their own way, as too much discipline would soon drive them off to their homes and it would not be easy to get them back again.

Richmond resisted McLean's efforts to be rid of Lambert. It was a time for mutual support, he said: everyone should 'throw away clique feelings as well as personal feelings'. He thought Lambert had some great qualities that were lacking in some of their dashing young men. Richmond went on to instruct McLean to have the East Coast Pai Marire disarmed immediately without waiting for any overt act of treachery. 'Do not be soft hesitating about this. I write this separately that it may be made a record when the need for privacy has gone by.'[27] This rebuke for being 'soft' was a response to McLean's policy of leaving the Pai Marire alone so long as they did not embark on overt attacks.

Friction over Lambert's competence continued. Richmond instructed McLean not to remove him. Denying Richmond's allegation that he had any personal feeling against Lambert, McLean maintained that, in the public interest, if he found Lambert unsuitable in a command he would transfer him. Yet he was prepared to, 'as you seem to think differently let him go on as he is for the present'.[28] Richmond responded by denying that the Government had fettered McLean with inflexible instructions and implying that, if McLean were to give proper instructions to Lambert making clear their intent, Lambert for his part would be found ready to take any risk to carry them out.

Again McLean tried to have Lambert removed from his command. He condemned 'that old fool Lambert' who had, without instructions, joined the Maori force McLean had directed to pursue and attack Te Kooti. He believed that Lambert had ordered this force to abandon the pursuit and return to Wairoa, and suspected Richmond's involvement. He demanded that Lambert be disciplined by the Government. He repeated his request that officers receive instructions direct from himself, 'otherwise divided authority must lead to disasters'.[29]

Relations between McLean and the Government deteriorated. Ministers were exasperated with McLean, who, although their representative on the East Coast, chose in the House to oppose their native policy and their conduct of the war. McLean, for his part, remained irritated by what he saw as ministerial interference in his handling of the East Coast campaign. Among Hawkes Bay militia officers, Major Carlyon, a McLean supporter, had been passed over for promotion. McLean suggested that the ministers had found him 'too able and independent' and 'true to their usual practice they resort to a mean and discreditable course to deprive me of your assistance and the district of the beneficial reforms that were taking place under your command. I have had as you know a great deal to put up with but I feel bound to sacrifice personal feelings and conduct for the common interest.'[30]

McLean's friends kept him informed of settler fears. From Poverty Bay Harris told McLean that it had been a mistake not to proclaim martial law after Ngatapa and to try all prisoners by a drumhead court martial. Karepa, who had guided Te Kooti, should be 'destroyed as you would any other rabid animal'. Settlers did not dare to return to homesteads or live inland; they had to keep together and be always armed.

Over in Taranaki, the killing of the missionary, John Whitely, at White Cliffs spread alarm. Helen Wilson told McLean that outlying settlers who had to come into New Plymouth were facing starvation. She doubted whether the Government would do anything. Rogan, by this time a Land Court judge, wrote to McLean about Whitely: 'You see these odd murders you so prophetically spoke of to me in our occasional evenings at St Georges Bay are cropping up in every corner of the land'.[31]

On 2 March 1869 McLean telegraphed Haultain, the Defence Minister, that Rewi Maniapoto with 700 men was about to join Te Kooti. There was talk of an attack on Titiokura on the Napier–Taupo route. While the Maori allies of the Government at Taupo were prepared to fight, they were too few. Another attack on Napier was threatened by way of inland Patea and the Ngaruroro Gorge in the Kaweka Range.[32]

Faced with war on two fronts, ministers decided that Titokowaru's force was a more serious threat to West Coast settlements than Te Kooti's guerrilla campaign against a smaller number of settlers on the East Coast. With insufficient troops to campaign on both coasts, it gave priority to dealing with Titokowaru and decided to move the Ngati Porou kupapa contingent by sea to the West Coast. When the steamer reached Napier, however, it seemed Rapata, the leader of the contingent, changed his mind. There was an exchange of telegrams between McLean and Haultain. McLean said that Rapata had asked him if he approved of Ngati Porou going to the West Coast; if not, he had no desire to go. McLean advised Haultain that it was unwise for Rapata to leave while the East Coast was threatened and suggested the Government reconsider its decision. Haultain insisted that the Government placed the greatest importance on reinforcing the West Coast. He asked McLean to use his influence on Rapata. McLean replied that Rapata did not want to continue, but that he would speak to him the next morning. After another telegram from Haultain, McLean responded that Rapata had 'no heart or inclination' to go to the West Coast leaving his own district threatened and his own people unprotected.

Haultain asked Ferris, the government agent who had travelled with Rapata's men, to set out the grounds of the agreement. Ferris said that each man had agreed to go to Patea in southern Taranaki and that Rapata, until he got to Napier, had been eager to proceed. Rapata had gone ashore at Napier and Ferris had found him in a 'half state of intoxication' and told him to hurry back on board as they were about to sail. Rapata did not return and the ship weighed anchor. It steamed slowly about until a boat came alongside with an order from McLean to remain until the following morning, when there was an order from Rapata for all his men to go ashore. Ferris complied and heard Rapata tell his men that none of them were to travel on in the steamer.[33]

On 10 March in another telegram, which the Government did not table in the House, McLean complained that there had been no reply to his previous telegram, that Rapata was pressing for a reply and seeking his advice. In the present state of the East Coast, reported McLean, aware of recent intelligence of planned attacks, he could not 'find it consistent with my view of my public duty to advise of his going to the West Coast and have told him so'.[34] McLean followed up two days later with a report to ministers on the East Coast situation. Various settlements were threatened with destruction, murders had been committed and 'life and property deemed quite insecure'. Deserters and Te Kooti's spies had infiltrated Poverty Bay, Opotiki was exposed to attack, with support expected to arrive from Waikato tribes. Maori allies had been bewildered by conflicting instructions and were at a loss to know what steps to take. McLean went on to complain that, although constantly appealing to the Government, he did not think that ministers had placed him in position to act with sufficient authority. He recommended that the East Coast tribes be encouraged to act immediately against Te Kooti and Te Waru Tamatea, his major supporter, to stop them strengthening their forces and before the Waikato tribes could intervene. Such an action would relieve government anxiety over the East Coast. If action were delayed, a much larger force would be needed to redress the disasters that would almost certainly ensue. Rapata and his men, if aided by a small European force could check the growing difficulties at Opotiki and the East Coast. If ministers approved, he was willing to offer every assistance.[35]

The Government's tolerance had expired. Stafford wrote to McLean that, in accepting his services, ministers were justified in expecting his loyal support. McLean's role in advising Rapata and his party to break their engagement to join Whitmore on the West Coast was 'so vicious an example in itself and exhibits such an irreconcilable difference between yourself and the Government as to the import of such terms as assistance and co-operation and as to the proper mode of dealing with the Maori population'. The Government therefore withdrew McLean's authority as its agent.[36] Vogel wrote to McLean to condemn 'Stafford's insulting notice about you' in the *Gazette*. 'Ill it must fare with the Colony when the head of its government can take such advantage of its position as to forget the services of a lifetime in the desire to gratify his feelings of petty spite.'[37] Stafford's 'insulting notice' was in fact the standard formal notification from the Colonial Secretary's Office.[38] McLean's conduct over Rapata's failure to go to the West Coast was the occasion for his dismissal rather than the cause.

In the 1870s political parties had not yet evolved in New Zealand. The formation of a government centred on factions and personalities. Although the ministers had accepted McLean's assurances of help in his role as agent, neither party really overcame its profound mistrust of the other. McLean felt that the Government, contrary to assurances, had intervened in military appointments and failed to support his authority. Ministers believed that they had made every effort to establish an effective working relationship with McLean, but found that he ignored instructions and persisted in acting independently.

As Government Agent McLean insisted he must have unfettered control. Having had previous experience of McLean's approach, the Government was therefore at fault in failing to set out precisely the conditions of his appointment in terms that could not be misinterpreted. Stafford and Richmond made an effort to accommodate McLean, but he remained intransigent. His dismissal followed. The conflict between them was to move to the floor of the House of Representatives.

Neither McLean nor the ministers really trusted one another. McLean resented what he saw as government interference in his mission and a reluctance to provide the support he required. Ministers believed they had tried to cooperate with McLean but had been rebuffed. For them McLean's role as a government representative and his leading role in the Opposition attacks in the House on their conduct of the war could no longer be tolerated.

In 1869 the Government's decision to remove McLean from his post as Government Agent brought an immediate reaction from Ormond: 'The miserable brutes have withdrawn the agency from you in the most spiteful way open to them but that of course was to be expected'. He advised McLean to have nothing to do with them beyond acknowledging Stafford's letter and denying any interference with Ngati Porou, as this was the issue on which he would be attacked. Ormond set out what could be done to 'retaliate on the wretches'. He had called a public meeting to petition the Governor to recall the General Assembly without delay. McLean should call a meeting in Napier and pass similar resolutions. If Hawkes Bay led, other parts of the colony would follow. Ormond sensed that there would be strong provincial support to overthrow the Stafford Government and urged McLean to write to leading people in Otago, Canterbury and Auckland asking them to take action. He suggested Rolleston in Canterbury and Vogel and Reynolds in Otago. Ormond was convinced that this simultaneous demand across the colony would 'shake this funk-stick of a Govr. and he wd. do what is wanted'.

McLean wrote to Dillon Bell on the need to convene the General Assembly:

> Each day the present men hold office is a black day for New Zealand and to us who reside in the scene of hostilities it is a matter of life and death that a change should take place that will restore the confidence of both Europeans and natives. The Stafford ministry is reduced to great extremities when it can only get such supporters as an ex-parson, a dismissed officer of the volunteers and a vain, silly man like Lord Henry Russell.

At a Hawkes Bay meeting of 500 people, only six had opposed resolutions condemning Stafford, he said.[39] Ormond's plan for the recall of the General Assembly failed; the Governor refused to act on the petitions.

Ormond reacted vehemently to the news that Stafford had appointed H. R. Russell as Government Agent in place of McLean. 'What a pass the country is coming to when a panic stricken ass as he is entrusted with the peace of the district.' Judge Johnstone regarded the Government's action 'with mixed indignation and contempt'. George Preece, serving with the colonial forces at Patea, warned McLean that Whitmore was leaving no stone unturned to do him an injury by spreading false reports and 'the dirty way he does it'. He accused Whitmore of attacking McLean in the *Hawke's Bay Times* under the title 'Our Own Correspondent'.[40]

When the Assembly convened in June, before a crowded gallery, William Fox moved a motion of no confidence in the Government. He condemned Stafford's arbitrary dismissal of McLean and deplored the loss of the one man whose mana had kept the Maori allies fighting in the field against Te Kooti. McLean seconded the motion *pro forma* but took no further part in the debate. Fox and McLean no doubt met together to plan their tactics and perhaps it was Ormond who decided that McLean should be silent while he spoke on his behalf.

Ormond charged ministers with encouraging Archdeacon Hadfield to accuse McLean of responsibility for the catastrophe at Poverty Bay thus showing he still 'cherished an old vindictive spite'. Ministers, Ormond alleged, had withheld information from McLean, including their order transferring Ngati Porou, McLean's most reliable allies, to the West Coast. Ormond had earlier warned McLean that he was vulnerable over Rapata's decision not to go to the West Coast with his Ngati Porou, but in the House he challenged the Government to offer one scrap of evidence to show that McLean had persuaded Rapata not to proceed. Ormond said that he had been present at most of the meetings between Rapata and McLean. Rapata had told them that government officers at Poverty Bay said that McLean wanted him to go to the West Coast, but, when he heard from McLean that Te Kooti was likely to attack Poverty Bay, he decided not to proceed and to leave his people unprotected. Ormond insisted that McLean had done nothing to prevent Rapata from going on but had refused to accede to the Government's demand that he use his influence to make Rapata proceed.[41] Ormond's defence was shaky. Not only had McLean's warning that Te Kooti was about to attack Poverty Bay been sufficient to discourage Rapata, but McLean himself had contradicted Ormond. Writing to the Defence Minister, he admitted that in the existing state of the East Coast he could not advise Rapata to proceed and had told him so.[42] Ormond concluded that if the opposition became the Government, they would replace 'the bad administration, weakness and incompetence of the present Native Minister with the vigour of Mr. McLean'. Stafford's reply centred on justifying the Government's treatment of McLean as Government Agent.

The Government was defeated 40–29 on the no confidence motion. The opposition that had united to overthrow Stafford soon fragmented. At first, Fox's only ministers were McLean and Vogel, later joined by Dillon Bell and Gisborne. McLean was Native Minister and Defence Minister. He had moved from being a provincial leader to a key role in central government.

Following his acceptance of a ministerial post McLean resigned as Provincial Superintendent in September 1869. Ormond, who was elected in his place, told the council he could not hope to achieve as much success as McLean: 'I do not possess that peculiar gift which Mr. McLean so pre-eminently does, of making friends on all sides and offending rarely, nor do I nor does anyone else in the Colony possess the same influence with the native race.'[43] Ormond's comment draws attention to another aspect of McLean's character. As a politician he was skilled at convincing people that he supported them while avoiding any specific commitment. He kept his own counsel.

Chapter 18
'To Glide Into a State Of Peace'

After helping Fox to defeat Stafford, McLean was rewarded with the portfolios of native affairs and defence. When he was a government official, McLean's role had been to implement policies determined by successive governors. For the first time in his career McLean was in a position to shape government policy. Settlers looked to McLean as the one man who could handle the Maori and persuade them to accept a settler-dominated peace. In Cabinet he had the acquiescence of his colleagues, along with the active support of the powerful Julius Vogel. Despite these advantages, McLean was to be frustrated by a settler Parliament that would reject his proposals to admit Maori to any effective form of power-sharing.

The Fox Government that took office in 1869 was committed to reducing military expenditure and restoring peace, but it had first to deal with the threat of Te Kooti who still eluded capture. The Government had other problems. By 1870 the economy was languishing. Prices for wool and wheat were low; goldfield production had declined. Vogel, the driving force in the Cabinet, had a plan to revive the economy and encourage growth through an extensive public-works programme, including road and rail construction, as well as a subsidised immigration scheme. This would require substantial overseas borrowing and an increase in the colony's debt. The sum of eight and a half million pounds was set aside for public works and land purchases and £500,000 for immigration. Immigrants would work on the roads and railways and then farm the land thus opened for settlement. McLean and Vogel became firm allies. They were the two outsiders in Cabinet in terms of education and ethnicity. Unlike their colleagues they had not attended English public schools or universities, and McLean was a Scot and Vogel a Jew. Vogel drew on McLean's experience in similar expansionist spending in Hawkes Bay in the 1860s. Vogel believed that his schemes would solve the Maori problem by peaceful means rather than by a war of extermination. His proposals would open up communications in the North Island thereby assisting pacification and giving employment to Maori on public works. The reconciliation policy pursued by McLean to bring peace to the North Island became not only desirable but essential. The colony could not maintain the existing level of military expenditure, nor could settlement expand so long as the threat of war remained. The Crown had to resume land purchasing to ensure that land was available for the roads and railways that were to open up areas for settlement by the new immigrants.

For the remainder of the first parliamentary session until 3 September, McLean behaved like a veteran minister. He replied to parliamentary questions with bland reassuring statements; he introduced a number of minor and uncontroversial amendments to legislation relating to his portfolios, including the Armed Constabulary Act, Native Lands Act, Native Reserves Act and the Poverty Bay Grant of Land Act. He even seconded an opposition bill to restrict the giving of credit to Maori, supporting it as a move in the right direction: 'There was such a desire to obtain money and when obtained an equal desire to get rid of it which would lead to very disastrous results if not speedily checked.'

The 1870 New Year led McLean to wish:

> May peace and goodwill prevail throughout the Island; and may New Zealand be extricated from its complications and difficulties; and a new and more kindly feeling grow between the races.
>
> A New Year should always cause us to aim at a new and better ordering of our affairs; and may the Great Power who governs the earth be our Guide in ruling for the good the destinies of New Zealand.[1]

When he took office in 1869 McLean hoped that he could resolve the problems of dealing with the Maori in two years and then be free to retire to his estate in Hawkes Bay. The major issues that confronted McLean were to:

- end the fighting in the North Island;
- bring about a reconciliation with Maori, especially with the King movement;
- abandon the policy of confiscation of Maori land;
- legislate to deal with problems arising from the operations of the Native Land Court;
- respond to issues involving Maori self governance and political representation and the welfare of Maori.

His responses show how he was ahead of his contemporaries in his thinking. Perhaps his greatest achievement was to persuade the disaffected tribes that there could be an honourable end to the wars of the sixties. No other politician had the mana among Maori to achieve this end. At the same time, like other politicians of that time, he was prepared to use public office to advance private interests. In his striving to consolidate and to expand his pastoral estate in Hawkes Bay, he remained a Scotsman on the make.

On becoming a minister, McLean bought a house in Wellington and required his youngest sister, Annabella, to move from Maraekakaho to act as his hostess, so 'necessary for the maintenance of his proper social position as a member of the ministry'. McLean confided to Annabella that he felt 'happy and jolly as possible with plenty of hard work early and late, no end of responsibility yet the work must be done'.[2]

Having been a destructive critic of the Maori policy of the Stafford Government, McLean had to develop an alternative that would bring an end to fighting that had lasted for nine years. In practice he followed the policies of his former mentor, Governor Grey: a show of justice towards Maori and a search for a kind of peace that was based on his personal influence. McLean once acknowledged that he was not 'a deep thinker'. Keith Sinclair thought that he lacked 'intellectual grasp' and was 'not capable of devoting deep thought to fundamental questions of policy'.[3] His administration was marked by pragmatic responses to specific situations. Principle was never allowed to impede a solution to a particular problem.

McLean had become a major public figure. As a Cabinet minister and as a leading pastoralist he was involved in a great variety of issues, having to make important decisions under pressure of time and often in a state of hectic confusion. In one week McLean might attend a Cabinet meeting to consider proposals for financing and building roads and railways, and authorising the Agent-General in London to speed up the despatch of emigrants. As Native Minister, he would be required to report on progress in buying additional land for the above purposes and on the state of negotiations for peace with the King movement. As Defence Minister, he would be called on to explain to his colleagues why once again his troops had failed to capture Te Kooti. He would try to win support for his new Militia Bill to reform the armed forces. Back at his office McLean might have a letter from a militia officer advancing his own claim for an award for bravery for his conduct on the battlefield, and lengthy reports on the state of the Maori from his district officers. Letters from Maori rangatira needed replies; to others he would write granting a pension or a gift of agricultural machinery to encourage loyalty to the Government – and to himself. (The only substantial collections of Maori letters among private papers are those in the Grey and McLean papers.)

Much of his time he was absent from Wellington. On leaving a Cabinet meeting, he might travel by sea to New Plymouth to meet first with settlers and then with former 'rebel' tribes, hearing their grievances when he would tell the Maori that they would have to learn to live with the settlers and that he intended to impose his kind of peace and would not concede their demands. Then he would go once more by sea and down the Waikato River to meet with Rewi Maniapoto and patiently to foster a reconciliation with the King movement. Before he sailed from Wellington he might learn of a further fall in wool prices. A letter from the manager of the Union Bank in Napier would advise that his account was in overdraft and that there was no money to pay off his loans that were due. Another letter from his sister-in-law at Maraekakaho station would tell him of the problems arising from his brother Alexander's worsening alcoholism.

When he was absent from Wellington, McLean would keep up a flow of telegrams to his Native Department officials with detailed instructions for action or demands for reports on the state of the Maori in their districts. There might be, for example, a telegram to Locke, the Civil Commissioner in Hawkes Bay, to tell Tareha that McLean was much opposed to his selling any land at Waiohiki; to the Coromandel to hasten the opening of the gold-field and to the Honourable Maurice O'Rorke in Auckland asking him to influence the newspapers from printing anything about the opening of the gold-field; to his old friend, J. D. Ormond, by this time Minister of Public Works, that he now saw his way clear to an adjustment of the land claims between Waitotara and Waingongoro; an instruction to the Public Works Department at Tauranga not to proceed with building a road until McLean had secured the agreement of the local tribe; and to Clarke at the head office of the Native Department about a pension for a loyal Whanganui. Somehow he would find the time to write his regular letter to his son, Douglas, and to send detailed instructions on sowing pasture, sheep-dipping and seeing that the Maraekakaho station hands were all kept busy. No wonder that, during the 1870s, McLean's working day extended to fourteen hours. His letters, both private and official, show the extent of his workload.

McLean had to wait until the end of the 1869 parliamentary session to deal with his most urgent objective, the final pursuit and intended capture of Te Kooti. In October 1869 Colonel Thomas McDonnell's troops with the substantial help of his Maori allies captured the pa at Te Porere near Lake Rotoaira south of Turangi but, once again, Te Kooti escaped. Not all the Cabinet had approved of McDonnell's appointment. Vogel told McLean that St John Branigan, head of the Armed Constabulary, did not think him fit for the post. McDonnell's near success at Te Porere, however, was acclaimed by McLean as justifying his choice.

When McLean had been Government Agent on the East Coast, it was Ormond who maintained the administrative support. Now Government Agent himself, Ormond kept McLean fully informed, writing frequent letters. His meticulous attention to detail was complemented by his capacity for prompt action. Moreover, he was ready to comply with the Government's intention to spend less on the campaign. Political opponents charged that, by his parsimony, Ormond had hampered the military in their pursuit of Te Kooti. Ormond himself told McLean that he thought the Taupo operation costly, although he had been feeding the force almost entirely on meat and potatoes as 'the former is not dear and the latter cost nothing'. Supplying the forces was 'fearful work', as there was no feed available for the horses which had to be relieved after two or three weeks. As Hawkes Bay Superintendent, Ormond said he would close the Provincial Council session as soon as he could, and, as Government Agent, 'go to the front to decide how arrangements could be improved'.[4]

The Cabinet accepted McLean's proposal that the next move against Te Kooti should be an expedition composed of an entirely kupapa Maori force to encircle the Urewera. The plan was that the Arawa would advance from their own district, the Whanganui tribe under Te Rangihiwinui and Topia would move from Poverty Bay along with Rapata and Ngati Porou, while Henare Tomoana would bring Ngati Kahungunu from Wairoa. McLean proposed that, if Te Kooti or Kereopa (the killer of Revd Carl Volkner) were captured or killed, all four groups should be rewarded by a payment of £5000 each. If they failed they would get no pay.[5] They failed.

Ministers were united in their determination to have Te Kooti captured or killed. In January 1870, when J. C. Firth, a Waikato merchant, accepted Te Kooti's invitation to meet to discuss the possibility of peace, ministers' reaction was one of disgust. Fox instructed McLean that Te Kooti must be attacked whenever and wherever possible and, if Firth had been the cause of his escape, he should be prosecuted. Ormond suggested that Firth should be shot. McLean himself, in the House, alleged that Firth had supplied Te Kooti with arms. Firth denied this charge asking that his reply be tabled in the House. He then complained that McLean had refused permission for this.[6]

In February 1870 a band of Te Arawa under command of Lieutenant Gilbert Mair caught up with Te Kooti near Rotorua. They forced him to retreat. Te Kooti again took refuge in the Urewera where the Maori allies hunted him until 1872 when he retired to the King Country under the protection of the Maori King.

★

Among those exiled with Te Kooti to the Chathams had been a 'half-caste' Maori of powerful physique, Eru Peka Makarini, also known as Peka Te Makarini or Edward Baker. He was to become Te Kooti's lieutenant in the subsequent East Coast campaign. He was bilingual, said to have received a good education and been employed in an Auckland lawyer's office until dismissed for theft, when he fled back to his mother's people on the East Coast. In the encounter near Rotorua in 1870 Gilbert Mair shot and killed Te Kooti's lieutenant. Peka Makarini was rumoured to be Donald McLean's illegitimate son. James Cowan described him as 'a herculean young savage, so fair skinned that he seemed almost a pakeha', who had tattooed across his broad chest in blue letters his name Peka Te Makarini. Cowan discreetly referred to him as 'the reputed son of a notable pakeha colonist' who 'out did even the full blooded Maori in pitiless ferocity'.

After Makarini was killed, Te Arawa kupapa tied his body to a cabbage tree. Later the remains were taken by the tribe living at Mohaka, thirty of whose people had been killed by Makarini. They made his bones into fish-hooks and flutes. The story went that McLean was dining at a regimental mess one night when he saw one of these bone flutes and proceeded to play a waiata on it. Another story had it that, as Minister of Defence, he ordered that Peka Makarini was to be shot on sight.

These rumours appeared to originate with Colonel Hamilton-Browne, a man of doubtful veracity, described by Judith Binney as the 'fraudulent George Hamilton-Browne'.[7] Contemporary New Zealand historians made no mention of any allegations. Given McLean's prominence in nineteenth-century New Zealand public life, his political opponents might have been expected to embarrass him either in public or private gossip. The only other sources are Cowan, writing in the twentieth century and advancing no verification and referring only to the son of a 'high government official', and W. Hugh Ross, who in a biography of Te Kooti relied on the contemporary account of Colonel Hamilton-Browne.

As McLean did not visit Poverty Bay until 1851 the child of any liaison would have been only sixteen when he returned as Te Kooti's lieutenant in 1868. However, as Maori women did travel by ship from Poverty Bay to Auckland there was the possibility of an earlier encounter. That Edward Baker took the name of Makarini, a transliteration of McLean, does not prove any blood link with Donald McLean. At that time it was a practice for Maori to take well-known Pakeha names. The Harold Williams Memorial Library at Gisborne that holds the whakapapa of East Coast Maori last century has no record of Baker or Makarini yet of course Maori always acknowledged 'half-castes' in their whakapapa.

The McLean Papers contain no references and McLean hoarded paper, even his laundry lists. There is nothing among McLean's personal accounts that suggests any regular payment for schooling nor any correspondence with a Baker in relation to Peka Makarini. McLean's will first drafted in 1860 make no mention of Peka Makarini, who could have been still at school. In the absence of firm evidence, it seems improbable that Peka Makarini was McLean's illegitimate son.

As Minister of Defence, McLean initiated a reform of the armed forces. The last British troops were withdrawn in February 1870. The colonial forces that took over included military settlers recruited from Australia to protect the confiscated land of the Waikato and Taranaki, and local militia and volunteers. After 1867 this military force became the nucleus of the Armed Constabulary. McLean had papers prepared on the armed forces of Switzerland, Norway, Sweden and the Netherlands and another on Cardwell's reform of the British Army. At the same time Colonel Whitmore's proposal for a colonial rural police force was considered, along with Colonel Rookes's plan for a reorganisation of the New Zealand Cavalry.

The outcome was McLean's Militia Act passed in 1870. Settler militia were disbanded, being replaced by reliance on an Armed Constabulary that was to be halved in number to 1000. McLean preferred to use his Maori kupapa allies as the main force in pursuit of Te Kooti. Acting as a paramilitary force, more a police force than an army, the Armed Constabulary was to garrison redoubts and blockhouses. Initially they had been called on for road making but McLean preferred to contract local Maori labour with a view to bringing Maori into contact with Europeans.

McLean extended his responsibilities as Native Minister to the supervision of land purchases and public works. He would not allow roads to be built through Maori territory until the consent of the owners had been received. The land-purchase officers, located in the Public Works Department, included many who had worked under McLean in the 1850s and still looked to him as their patron. By 1873 McLean had had them transferred to his own Native Department. In the same year the sum of £200,000 was set aside for land purchases; 771,849 acres were bought for £86,319 with a further 556,569 acres under negotiation. McLean estimated that by 1874 the Government would have nearly 7 million acres being prepared for settlement.[8] A return to peace had not brought an end to the acquisition of Maori land; rather, it speeded up the process.

★

Although Fox deferred to McLean on native affairs, McLean's independent attitude irritated the Premier.[9] When McLean failed to attend Cabinet meetings before a forthcoming session of the House, Fox reminded him that there were 'many most important matters' affecting native policy that could not be conducted by telegraph. Cabinet did not wish to hurry him, if either public or private affairs required his presence in Hawkes Bay, but he should not be surprised if Cabinet made decisions in his absence.

McLean followed a policy of conciliation in Taranaki. He kept Robert Parris as Civil Commissioner despite Fox's efforts to dismiss him for being pro-Maori. The compromise was to establish a Taranaki Native Board, comprising five rangatira and five settlers, selected by McLean because they would work with Parris.[10] This was typical of the way McLean operated, acting without reference to his Cabinet colleagues and establishing a network of his own supporters who owed their position to his patronage. Fox reluctantly accepted this board, but insisted that it should be only a 'board of advice'.[11] Fox told McLean that Parris must not be allowed to interfere with the 'good work' being done by Major Noakes, the officer commanding the militia in the Patea district. To get the settlers back onto their land, he insisted, it was essential that all Maori be kept out of the block from Waihi to the Waingongoro River. 'If we allow any of the ex-rebels to return they will not be long there. The settlers have made up their mind to it and mean it.'[12]

When Noakes began to check the movements of Maori within his district in 1871, the Taranaki Native Board complained that his restrictions were hindering road building and the erection of telegraph lines. McLean ordered Noakes to take no action that was likely to irritate either friendly Maori or those who had been in arms against the Government but now wished to live in peace. Nevertheless, he should be vigilant and report at once any action that aroused his suspicion. McLean pointed out that every effort had been made to conciliate hostile Maori such as Titokowaru, who now moved freely throughout the district without causing trouble. At Patea, however, Noakes was treating even friendly Maori with suspicion and such a practice, McLean warned, would inevitably lead to renewed fighting. He ordered Noakes not to make his instructions public, presumably expecting angry protests from settlers.

When Fox became aware that the Taranaki Native Board had allowed so-called 'rebels', including Titokowaru, to return their old haunts, he decided to confront his Native Minister. Fox ordered Noakes to suspend any instructions from McLean and to refuse permission for any Maori to return south of the Waingongoro. The Premier told the Cabinet in April 1871 that McLean had acted without due consideration in changing a policy, when Fox had earlier assured the House that 'rebel' Maori would not be allowed to return to the country between the Waingongoro and Wanganui. Fox warned that, if Titokowaru and his armed followers were to appear south of the Waingongoro, 'there is not a settler who has a gun who would not take it and go to seek them. A collision would be inevitable.' He regretted this difference of opinion between himself and a minister who had otherwise zealously carried out government policy. As McLean's approval of the Taranaki Board's actions was in opposition to government policy, Fox referred the matter to Cabinet for a decision.[13] The Premier did not gain his colleagues' support and McLean remained Native Minister. Fox may have been Premier, but he was unable to control a powerful minister like McLean. Gisborne, also a member of the Cabinet, was critical of Fox, noting that, as Premier, he 'followed where he should have led, was unable to control his colleagues and was out of touch with his party'.[14]

Whatever the Cabinet decided, Fox seems to have persuaded himself that he was in charge. Eight months later, he was writing to McLean that Noakes, 'under instructions he holds hitherto' was doing all he could to keep Maori out of the district south of the Waingongoro and prohibit them from settling there. Fox was alarmed that Titokowaru's followers were settling on the north side of the river in defiance of the Government. He asked McLean to go immediately to Wanganui where he 'would be better able to judge and interfere with effect if necessary'.[15] In response, McLean insisted on his right as Minister of Defence to control his own officers, and removed Noakes from his post. Vogel and Gisborne had to mediate between Fox and McLean. Vogel advised McLean that he had gained all he required with Noakes' removal. Fox might be angry but Vogel had persuaded him not to persist and to accept that another post should be found for Noakes. Vogel warned McLean that his colleagues did not want the ministry broken up over such a matter.[16]

In pursuing his policy of reconciliation, McLean first sought to reach an accommodation with the King movement in the Waikato. McLean was the only minister with the mana to negotiate with the Waikato tribes. To advance his policy, McLean visited the Waikato on 9 November 1869 to make contact with the King movement and to explore on what terms they might accept peace. In his journal he noted that the Maori King, Tawhiao now seemed 'well disposed' and had checked 'the actions of the wilder spirits' who had wanted to join Te Kooti. He recognised Tawhiao's problem in maintaining control when each hapu, if not consulted on every subject, became defiant and obstructive. From information that he had received, McLean believed Rewi Maniapoto could become a valuable ally and optimistically surmised that, if Te Kooti escaped to the King Country, Rewi would surrender him. McLean's party included Louis Hetet, a man of considerable influence through his marriage to the daughter of a leading Ngati Maniapoto. McLean remarked that 'the few natives we met appeared to have a scowl on their countenances. The events of this day will I trust with God's providence be pregnant with the best results for the colony.'

The lengthy entry in his journal showed the importance McLean attached to his mission. Although much of the Waikato land had been confiscated, the Maori King had retired to the hill country to the north where Ngati Maniapoto remained a rallying point for disaffected tribes. The party was greeted by some of the leading rangatira of Waikato and Maniapoto. Tawhiao had wished to be present but was prevented by an accident. McLean, who had waited according to custom for the tangata whenua to speak first, was himself invited to speak. Expressing surprise at this departure from Maori protocol, McLean said that he did not care whether he was there by invitation or of his own accord. He was not going to talk about peace only, as he believed they would have both war and peace. There was no point in trying to ignore this and talking about a peace that did not exist. However, he believed that they could work together to 'put down evil'. McLean's tactic was to force the tangata whenua to speak their mind. Turning to Tamati Manuhiri, McLean reminded him they were not strangers; in the past they had spoken together freely. It was the host's place to have spoken first. Why was he silent now? Even if they were enemies, they should be talking so each knew what the other meant. 'If it is to be evil let it be understood now. If peace, let it be understood. The world is made up of good and evil, let us cast aside one and choose the good. It is now for you to speak.'[17] McLean had limited room to manoeuvre. He had to keep faith with the previous Government's decisions and at the same time try to calm things down. A 'taihoa' policy was appropriate in order to avoid any suggestion that he was trying to force the pace.

It was Rewi Maniapoto who responded, acknowledging McLean as the man who was able to settle hard and difficult questions. 'This is my word. Kati-Kati-Kati me mutu. Cease-Cease-Cease [fighting], let it end; and here is another word; let my land at Taupo be restored; you have got the men, but leave the land with me.' Te Heuheu Horonuku had been foolish in taking up arms in support of Te Kooti at Te Porere but McLean should be merciful and set him free. Likewise, Te Hura had been sufficiently punished and he should be handed over to Rewi. (Te Hura, a Pai Marire supporter had been sentenced to life imprisonment.)[18] In reply, McLean assured Rewi that if he and all the tribes under his influence put an end to the fighting and killing he would do his part. 'Then in reality will peace be established, a peace which shall not afterwards be broken.' As for Te Hura, he was prepared to release him if Rewi would answer for him. No land would be confiscated, and Te Heuheu would be released.

Rewi rejected McLean's demand that he surrender Te Kooti if the latter were to take shelter in the King Country. As long as Te Kooti lived in peace Rewi would not molest him, but should he prove troublesome he would hand him over. For his part, McLean assured him that he would not pursue Te Kooti's followers as long as they remained quiet. The only man he wanted was Te Kooti, as he was the 'cause of the evils'. McLean ended by asking the gathering to select a chief whom they could trust to help the Government to put a stop to misunderstandings that had arisen. They should take time and carefully consider this proposal before replying.[19] McLean congratulated himself that his remarks had satisfied the rangatira and that countenances that had been gloomy were now cheerful. McLean was encouraged by the prominent part taken by Rewi, who said, 'Let the sun shine and the rain fall upon what has been said. It is enough. There are times and days in the future ... Enough! There are days in store, a marama [moon] of light is now opened. It will spread. Is it a small thing to have seen you and met you, to me it is a great thing.'

After his visit to the Waikato, McLean sought FitzGerald's advice on how to deal with the King movement.[20] On 20 November 1869 McLean commented in his diary, 'What a dreadful calamity war is to both races'.[21] No doubt to clarify his thoughts in preparing his advice to Cabinet, he set out his terms for peace: English law was to be the law for both races. In territory occupied by the Maori King constitutional power was to be given to him to exercise all local municipal purposes with a superintendent and council to advise him. A leading chief should be appointed to cooperate with the Government in adjusting differences and bringing about a peaceful settlement. Land not sold to Europeans should be given to the Waikato, and Tawhiao should be recognised as head man of the Waikato and Ngati Maniapoto. The Government would not go to war over those who had committed murder but would let the law take its course. Those who had 'fought openly should not be considered enemies but brave men who had fought for a cause as our own troops had done ... that all that should be in the past and forgiven'.[22] McLean rejected Searancke's suggestion for a further meeting with the Waikato tribes as he thought this would show 'great anxiety to push matters forward'. He believed Maori did not like to be hurried in anything they undertook to do. He would not hurry them beyond their inclinations.[23]

Land confiscation after the wars of the 1860s had fanned Maori resentment and continued to trouble the Government. When he took office McLean set out reconcile the disaffected tribes. He assured the rangatira that there would be no further confiscations and that they would be left alone provided they were prepared to keep the peace. In November 1869 McLean told a gathering of Ngai Te Rangi at Tauranga that the confiscation of their land had been the act of previous governments in which he had not been involved. It was not in his power to return any of the land. The Government had warned the tribes of the consequences if they took up arms, and as minister he would uphold what previous governments had done. Anyone who promised to return these lands – a reference to Karaitiana Takamoana – was deluding them. He dismissed Karaitiana as 'a land schemer from Napier' and one who was looked on with distrust by his own tribe. Raniera Te Hiahia of Tauranga called on McLean to return half his land. He accepted that confiscated land would not be returned. But he himself had not taken up arms against the Government, yet his land had been taken as if he had done so.[24] The rangatira's situation was not uncommon. In Taranaki, as in other parts of the North Island, confiscation had extended to land of tribes who had taken no part in the wars or had been loyal to the Government. The Government was swayed by settler pressure to acquire good farming land. McLean did set aside some 50,000 acres as reserves and later made payment to tribes who had refused to recognise the confiscation of their lands so that their land could be available for settlers.[25]

After fighting had ended, Maori retained their independence in three areas: the King Country; the Urewera, because of its isolation; and that part of Taranaki centred on Parihaka through the influence of Te Whiti, even though surrounded by settler land. In Taranaki, settlers were eager to acquire all the confiscated lands. McLean resisted this pressure. He made payments as compensation for land confiscated and promised that reserves would be set aside. Convinced of Te Whiti's peaceful intentions he would not allow surveys to be made or roads to be built through land at Parihaka. He was prepared to wait for years, if necessary, to negotiate his way around opposition. John Sheehan and John Bryce, his successors as Native Minister, did not share his subtlety, his patience and his understanding of the Maori mind. In 1881 when Te Whiti's followers, carrying out his policy of non-violent resistance, obstructed government surveyors, Bryce sent troops to Parihaka, evicted the inhabitants and burnt the dwellings.

In February 1870 Sir William Martin, the former Chief Justice and a strong advocate for Maori interests, sent McLean two lengthy papers on relations between the Government and Maori and the constitutional issues arising, believing that McLean was prepared to welcome his suggestions 'made honestly and after due consideration'. The constitutional issue of Maori participation in the administrative and legislative processes of government had long been Martin's concern. His first paper dealt with the relations to be established between the Government and those who had opposed it, the second with Maori who recognised the Queen's authority.[26] Martin advanced three proposals: establish native districts where the tribes would make their own rules and administer as they thought fit and where provincial laws had no force; blocks of land within the confiscated territory should be made available to any dispossessed hapu; and no Pakeha should be allowed to reside within a native district except with the tribes' consent and a licence from the Governor. Martin also argued that, if the material well-being of those who accepted government rule proved to be in advance of those who rejected it, the King movement's supporters would diminish.

When McLean circulated Martin's proposals to other ministers, the Premier was not impressed. Fox annotated the memoranda at length and recommended that the Government not commit itself to any approval. He believed Martin's proposals would promote the isolation of the Maori race at the very moment when they were giving evidence that they were about to quit their seclusion. As for returning a portion of the confiscated lands, he believed that large areas should be handed over to the Government's 'native allies' to replace the original owners.[27]

Martin's papers had been couched in general terms. The Government's immediate concern was with the King movement, and in September 1870, McLean prepared a Cabinet paper on future dealings. He reminded ministers that for the past ten years the North Island had been caught up in a war that had been fatal to its progress and prosperity. Now that fighting had ended and there was comparative peace the transition from war would require 'careful but firm treatment' and any new system should be introduced gradually as previous efforts had tried to do too much at once. Full recognition of the influence and power of the King was essential. He was preparing ministers for the policy to which he had already given Rewi a commitment.

One solution proposed by men who had devoted a great deal of thought to the subject (a reference to Martin and himself) McLean said, was to define districts within which Maori would carry out their own laws and usages. The Maori King's adherents would favour this policy because they were already exercising an independent jurisdiction. They were 'not subject to the restraints and annoyances of progressive colonisation which we might see as advantageous to them but they recognise as the extinction of their nationality and independence'. Peace, however, would gradually overcome their strong anti-progressive tendencies, but to rudely interfere with those prejudices would be most unwise. If the King movement wished to maintain a friendly neutrality, the Government should respond. Yet if Europeans were violently attacked by Maori, the supremacy of British law must be enforced. The example of the United States after two centuries of warfare, McLean noted, showed that President Grant had arrived at a similar conclusion; that any system looking at the extinction of the Indian race was too horrible to contemplate. The President planned to set up large reserves and allow the Indians to set up territorial governments for themselves. What McLean did not recognise was that the United States policy had already resulted in the near extermination of the indigenous people. Therefore the remnant could be safely confined to reserves where they could be permitted to govern themselves.

As Maori were designated British subjects, it had been argued that no separate system of laws could be allowed. McLean dismissed this view as 'mere theory'. It would encourage the colonists to expect the Queen's writ to be enforced throughout the country, and would exasperate the large section of Maori who, he believed, denied the right of any foreign power to exercise jurisdiction over them. The Government should decide that English law would prevail only within certain regions that had a large European majority and that it was not prepared to offer protection to any who chose to reside beyond the frontier of territory acquired from the Maori.

Although he could not predict all the terms to which the King movement might agree, McLean thought it essential that they included the surrender to British law of offenders guilty of murder and the maintenance of order within the districts. Even though European settlement would be excluded for a time, the Government should regard such an agreement as a great step in the right direction. The punishment of past criminal offences presented a problem. On February 1869 a small party of Ngati Maniapoto warriors had attacked the redoubt at White Cliffs and killed several settlers and the missionary, J. Whitely. Ngati Maniapoto were holding aloof until they knew the fate of the White Cliffs murderers. Titokowaru was in a similar situation, said McLean, but 'To prolong the war for the sake of capturing them is beyond the means of the colony, to forgive them may appear humiliating and yet I do not see any other course open beyond proclaiming them outlaws'. No mercy, however, should be extended to Kereopa and Te Kooti as notorious murderers. Hostile tribes who had fought against the Government should never be placed in a better position than those who were friends or allies of the Government.

McLean reminded his colleagues that he had always stressed the importance of meetings with the chiefs and of instituting a Council of Chiefs elected by their people to represent the feelings and wants of their respective tribes. He advocated local self-government in districts where Maori desired it, but thought it should be open alike to European and Maori residing in the district. The Government should tell the tribes that it did not intend to revert to a policy of confiscation though it would punish 'the perpetrators of crime and outrage'.[28] At the time of the Taranaki and Waikato wars, McLean had supported the government policy of confiscating 'rebel' land. By 1869 he had become convinced that it was 'no longer politic or judicious' to confiscate further land. He believed his Cabinet colleagues had accepted that the confiscation policy had been an 'expensive mistake'. McLean's change of policy was based on a pragmatic recognition that losses associated with confiscation were greater than any gains. Voluntary cession of land, where and as required, would not necessitate a standing army to maintain possession. Moreover, the British Government, from which ministers were seeking assistance in the form of troops, was strongly opposed to confiscation.[29]

McLean's paper was accepted by his colleagues and became government policy. The objective – that it was possible 'by judicious management to glide into a state of peace without specific terms' – reflected McLean's distinctive approach, a patient pragmatism. It also revealed his understanding of the Maori mind. In making a contract, Maori looked not to the terms but to the intention of the person making them. McLean was able to convince them of his sincerity. He recalled past meetings and associations to reinforce that trust.

During his term as Native Minister McLean attempted to introduce measures to give Maori some control over their own affairs. After the wars of the 1860s, unofficial local runanga continued to operate alongside the resident magistrates' courts fostered by McLean. Maori had been pressing for their runanga to be given official status with the power to make laws along the lines of the scheme earlier proposed by Governor Grey. In 1870 Sir William Martin had approached McLean with proposals that led him to introduce a Native Councils Bill late in the 1872 parliamentary session. In approach, his legislation resembled Grey's proposed 'new institutions' of the 1860s which were intended to establish local and district councils under the supervision of resident magistrates and civil commissioners.

The bill provided for local runanga to make and enforce by-laws dealing with 'the familiar problems of puremu (adultery), sanitation, drunkenness, noxious weeds, dogs and trespassing stock'.[30] The runanga would also have the power to investigate and determine disputed land boundaries, their decisions to be ratified by the Native Land Court. Introducing the bill, McLean reminded the House of numerous Maori petitions to be allowed to manage their local affairs subject to the advice and direction of the resident magistrate. McLean could have pointed out that, under his supervision, resident magistrates had already had some successes in areas where the King movement was not influential.[31] The bill's provisions would apply only to native districts and, in cases of land disputes, would have the additional advantage of allowing a preliminary inquiry to enable differences to be settled before any application to the Native Land Court.

The attempt to establish runanga in 1856 (Grey's new institutions) had not succeeded, McLean said, as Maori felt that the colonists were trying to thrust British law upon them. Now, he asserted, Maori were unanimous in support of such a bill. Indeed, no measure of this kind would succeed without Maori cooperation. It was the duty of the General Assembly 'to lead the Native mind in any direction that would harmonise with our institutions and the present bill was a step in that direction'. McLean seems to have seen his bill as fostering assimilation as well as providing for Maori participation in administration of their own districts. The Government wished to apply the bill in only a few districts and then to report to the House next session on the results.[32]

Despite McLean's advocacy and the bill's tentative limitation to two or three districts, most members were strongly opposed; only the four Maori members and two others spoke in support. The Maori members went further, wanting to abolish the Native Lands Act and the Native Land Court. The settler majority found justifications for their opposition. The bill was rejected as an attack on the authority of Parliament; it had been introduced far too late in the session; it was a backward step to have different laws for Maori and Europeans; Europeans would have no vote yet the native councils had the power to make laws binding on Europeans. William Rolleston, a former Under-Secretary of the Native Department, denounced the bill as one of the most dreadful pieces of legislation he had ever seen and predicted that it would be productive of evil. Local bodies were opposed on the ground that there should be one law for all. For their part, Maori leaders wanted the response to their concerns to be at government, not local, level. In the 1870s, the Repudiation, Kotahitanga and King movements were all seeking greater control of local issues by Maori.

McLean was not able to reconcile Maori and settler aspirations. He withdrew the bill and in the 1873 session introduced an amended version that attempted to meet objections. This bill restricted its application to Maori customary land and allowed settlers to opt to come under its provisions and to elect members to the councils. Opposition to allowing Maori any say on land titles or to make laws suited to their circumstances made even the amended bill unpalatable to the House. The pragmatic McLean acknowledged his defeat, withdrew the bill and made no further attempt to respond to Maori demands for a measure of self-government.

McLean had found himself engaged in another struggle to maintain his control over native affairs after Sir George Bowen succeeded Grey as Governor in 1868. Bowen had had a distinguished career at Oxford with a first in Classics and being twice elected President of the Union. Before coming to New Zealand he had been Chief Secretary to the Ionian Islands and then Governor of Queensland. Bowen favoured a conciliatory policy towards the King movement and supported McLean in his efforts to bring peace. A pompous, self-important man, he travelled throughout New Zealand making regular visits to Maori communities, convincing himself that he was gaining their goodwill. His ministers were less enthusiastic. In response to an enquiry from Vogel about Bowen's object in visiting Waiuku, McLean replied that he had no idea, 'unless he wanted food for a despatch to the Secretary of State'.[33]

By 1872 Bowen, confident that his intervention would overcome all difficulties, was eager to take a leading role in the reconciliation of the Waikato Maori. Born in County Donegal in Ireland, a member of the Anglo–Irish ruling class, he believed he understood the ways of keeping the natives in submission. His despatches to London took the example of the pacification of the Highlands after the Jacobite rebellion and stressed the value of building roads towards the King Country, roads that before long 'would render future wars and rebellions impossible'. Although Bowen in his despatches gave full support to McLean's policy of reconciliation, McLean was alarmed at the Governor's inclination to interfere. Ormond was brutally frank. He told McLean that the Governor seemed to think that, no longer subject to ministerial control, if he went to the Waikato, the native difficulty would be at an end. 'He told among other things – that you had a fair knowledge of what was going on along the Coast but hadn't anything like his (the Governor's) knowledge of the state of the interior. What an ass the man must be. However, he can do little harm except by his stupid talk ... By all means keep him at the Pheasants – that is more in his line.'[34]

McLean assured the Governor that he had tried to uphold his authority.

> Nothing consistent with the respect due to you has been omitted to bring about a meeting with the Waikatos and if they choose to shift their ground as the Hauhau section of them are proverbial for doing it is not from any neglect on my part ... I regret very much that your patience has been taxed so much but I can assure you it is only trifling in degree compared to what former Governors and officials have had to experience in dealing with native matters.

He pointed out that, if the Waikato Maori agreed to terms, he had planned for a body of influential chiefs to accompany the Governor. 'As however, you desire to visit Hamilton and Cambridge I waive my plans and opinions.'[35] Despite the deferential tone, he could not conceal his irritation that Bowen had not acquiesced in his arrangements.

In reporting to Cabinet on the Governor's visit to Taupo, McLean's exasperation at Bowen's continued meddling in 'delicate negotiations' was evident. He had made it plain to the Governor that his interference would imperil the prospects of a settlement. He complained that Bowen, while apparently acquiescing, would revert to the need to meet the King movement – presumably, alleged McLean, to impress the British Government. He found it very embarrassing in negotiations to be interfered with by persons with no direct responsibility. He had impressed on the Governor, he said, the need to abstain from interfering until negotiations had been settled. Then, as Her Majesty's representative, he could meet King movement representatives to ratify the arrangements entered into between his responsible advisers and Maori. McLean complained that the Governor failed 'to realise the old adage, so frequently true in native affairs, that the more haste the less speed'.[36] When differences arose within the King movement, McLean avoided any hasty step. He briefed his colleagues 'to guard against any attempts which may be made to refer prejudicially to the course of action which in the interests of both races I considered my duty to follow'.

The Governor's persistent intervention in matters relating to McLean's native affairs portfolio led the latter to confront him on a constitutional issue. To prevent any misunderstanding, he first set out his reasons (sixteen pages of them) for failing to arrange the requested interview between the Governor and the Waikato, which 'I believe has been looked upon by you as a misfortune'. Waikato Maori would view a visit by the Governor with suspicion and apprehension, McLean stated. Without an invitation from the Maori King, the journey to the King Country would have placed the Governor in the awkward position of being subject to demands with which he could not comply. Instead of reconciliation it might have led to a rupture in relations 'with disastrous consequences to the colony'. McLean reminded the Governor that, under responsible government, since 1863 ministers had responsibility for native affairs. Any change would require the sanction of the British Government as well as the colonial legislature, as the party assuming responsibility would incur a heavy financial liability. Whether the British Government would be prepared to resume this responsibility, he left as a matter for the Governor's consideration, though he thought it proper to point out the consequence. McLean was aware that the Governor could expect no support from Britain. Twisting the knife further, he ended, 'Should Your Excellency continue to hold the views I have alluded to, it would be advisable they should be laid before the Secretary of State for the Colonies and in that case I request that this memo accompany your views'.[37] Although McLean briefed his colleagues on the advice he tendered the Governor, it is surprising that it was McLean, rather than Fox as Premier, who assumed responsibility for raising a constitutional issue – particularly as Fox had been a champion of responsible government in the 1850s. Now it was McLean who had to remind the Governor of his constitutional limitations.

In February 1873 the new Premier, George Marsden Waterhouse, had to deal with a further attempt by Bowen to intervene in native affairs. He told McLean that he could not reconcile the Governor's actions to constitutional usage and feared he might precipitate a crisis at any moment by pressing for an amnesty for Maori 'rebels'. Waterhouse declined to bring the matter before the Executive Council until formally approached by McLean as Native Minister.[38] Bowen, however, did not persist, aware of the limitations of his constitutional role, and careful to avoid outright conflict with his ministers.

In August 1872 Stafford carried a vote of no confidence in the Fox ministry, attacking maladministration and waste in its public-works policy and its handling of Maori affairs. Fox resigned and Stafford took office in September. It was rumoured that McLean was to join the new ministry but this was denied by Stafford and McLean. McLean had rejected an approach by some Auckland members saying he had always been united with Fox 'on all matters of importance'. He told the Governor that 'no good could result from allying myself with those I whom could not cordially work'. Within a month Stafford was forced to resign when three members voted against the Government and the Governor refused Stafford a dissolution. George Marsden Waterhouse became nominal Premier but Vogel was in control and became Premier early in 1873 on Waterhouse's resignation. McLean meantime had resumed his two portfolios.

After the failure of his 1873 bill to give some measure of self-government to Maori McLean did, however, persevere in developing racially integrated administration at a local level. He continued to appoint Maori assessors and police, and encouraged Maori participation on school committees which supervised native schools under the guidance of a resident magistrate. The number of native schools grew from thirteen in 1870 to thirty-three by 1873. McLean also tackled the liquor question. Maori resented the 1847 Sale of Spirits Ordinance because its prohibition applied only to Maori. McLean gave districts an option to approve the sale of liquor and, in districts with at least two-thirds Maori population, applicants for liquor licences had to have the written consent of the district assessor. Legislation establishing licensing courts in 1873 provided for a Maori assessor to sit on the bench with a power of veto over new licences and renewal of existing ones.[39]

Such legislation was a response to Maori aspirations. Resentful of being placed under any legal disability, even of a protective kind, Maori wished instead to share the opportunities and institutions of the settlers, provided those were modified to take account of special Maori needs and values and involved Maori leaders in responsible roles. In the 1870s McLean's administration went some distance towards accommodating these aspirations.[40] Despite his efforts, however, McLean failed to resolve the two essential areas of conflict between Maori and colonist: the unrelenting settler pressure to acquire Maori land, and the Maori wish to retain their independence and to share in the administrative and legislative processes of government.

During the 1870s McLean had to grapple with ongoing Maori grievances arising from the legislation of a settler Parliament, particularly the consequences of the Native Lands Acts that allowed private individuals to buy land from Maori. Among Maori complaints were the restriction of ten grantees to a title, that grantees had been induced to sign deeds of sale, and mortgages the contents and purpose of which had not been fully explained, and that storekeepers allowed Maori unlimited credit and then foreclosed on mortgages when Maori could not pay. McLean's response was to try to remedy the more flagrant injustices in the operation of the Native Lands Acts and, as discussed, to introduce a Native Councils Bill to establish native districts that would give Maori responsibility and involvement in their administration.

The Native Lands Acts of 1862 and 1865 had replaced the Crown right of pre-emption with the opportunity for direct purchase by individuals. The Native Land Court established under these acts was to determine who owned customary Maori land and to replace this customary title with one derived from the Crown. The 1862 act had given Maori some input by providing for district courts to act as a commission of inquiry, with panels of chiefs under the chairmanship of a resident magistrate. Under F. D. Fenton as Chief Judge, however, the court became centralised and operated like a supreme court, with disastrous consequences for Maori. Often, only those who could travel long distances had their claims considered. Major Biggs of Poverty Bay spoke the truth when he described it to Maori as the 'land taking court'. Although this was a reference to the Poverty Bay Commission, the Native Land Court was intended to separate Maori from their 'unwanted lands'.

In an attempt to protect Maori against the unscrupulous practices of purchasers taking advantage of Native Land Court proceedings, Henry Sewell, as Minister of Justice in the Fox Government, introduced a Native Land Frauds Prevention Bill in the Legislative Council in 1870 providing for the appointment of trust commissioners, who were to be officers of the Native Department authorised to examine transactions in Maori land and to disallow any that appeared to be a breach of equity or if liquor or arms formed part of the sale. McLean's opponent, Henry Russell, a member of the Legislative Council, carried an amendment to make the legislation retrospective with the intention of bringing McLean's private purchases under scrutiny. McLean, however, declared the amendment objectionable and had this provision deleted by the House of Representatives. He acknowledged, however, that the object of Sewell's bill was 'a very good one which has much pressed on the attention of the government'.[41] The bill was passed.

Despite McLean's attempts to remedy some of the worst injustices in the 1865 and 1867 Native Lands Acts and the introduction of the Native Lands Frauds Prevention Act in 1871, the system still gave inadequate protection of Maori interests. In 1873, McLean as Native Minister asked the former Chief Justice, Sir William Martin, and former Native Secretary, Edward Shortland, to draft recommendations for a new bill. Apart from a provision for sale by public auction, McLean incorporated their recommendations in his 1873 Native Lands Bill. These included the Native Land Court meeting on the land in question instead of only in the main centres, having its own surveyors, excluding lawyers and agents, making inalienable reserves and supervising the distribution of payments. In place of the ten-grantee system, which had resulted in land sales occurring without the wider consent of their people, the hapu could be the focus, with all owners to be listed on the title. The main effect was to allow individuals to sell their individual interests to the Crown or to private buyers. This had the effect of retarding the alienation of land by making it more difficult to complete a purchase, as the consent of all the owners had to be secured first. Nevertheless, the act came to further undermine customary Maori land rights by giving title to many individuals, who in turn would pass on their shares to their successors until hundreds came to have an interest in a very small piece of land. Although politicians insisted that the Maori system of communal land-holding was invalid under British law, they ignored situations where corporate title was a normal practice – for example, land held by the Anglican Church.[42] District officers were to inquire into the good faith of a claimant, to arrange for inalienable reserves of fifty acres for every man, woman and child. (In 1859 McLean had proposed reserves of three-tenths of the land sold.) These officers were to draw up maps of tribal boundaries and compile tribal genealogies. McLean's intentions for the 1873 bill were made more explicit by his law draftsman, John Curnin, when he gave evidence before the Rees–Carroll Commission in 1891. He said that McLean had envisaged that dealings could be with hapu and not individuals. However, other evidence presented to the 1891 Commission pointed to unabated individualisation since 1873. The work of the district officer in compiling genealogies and maps of tribal boundaries had been viewed by McLean as potentially the equivalent of a Domesday Book so that there could no longer be any disputes in the courts over ownership of Maori lands.[43] The district officer scheme however, had been under-resourced and therefore ineffective.

McLean, in moving the second reading of the bill, said that the intention was to identify the owners of the land by less costly means than under the existing acts. There was a need to ascertain and more accurately define title to tribal land by mapping and recording boundaries. He regretted that some judges (a reference to his old enemy Chief Judge Fenton) had followed 'a most vicious principle' in recognising only the evidence of people who had been able to appear before the court, so that sometimes the wrong people had been given title. Maori had come to believe that a Crown title was a device on the part of the Europeans to get hold of their land.

One of the Government's objectives was to settle sufficient land as a permanent home in which Maori might feel safe and secure against any change in the law or administration. McLean did not define what he meant by 'sufficient', but he seems to have seen it as being adequate for traditional subsistence farming. This did not take into account increasing Maori participation in the pastoral economy, which required extensive areas for grazing sheep. Hapu should retain land to hold as an 'ancestral patrimony' that could not be disposed of, he said, where they could settle down and live peaceably side by side with Europeans while preserving their traditional way of living in villages. McLean believed that Maori should feel that 'in their own country, under the Treaty of Waitangi, they had that treaty observed to the fullest extent'. It was clear, however, that he saw the Government, rather than Maori, deciding what was 'sufficient'.[44]

The bill, said McLean, had been explained to the Maori members of the House, who agreed with the general principles while suggesting valuable improvements. The Maori members, however, expressed differing views. Parata, member for Western Maori, supported the bill, affirming that, without the Native Land Court, the island would not have been so prosperous. He argued that if Maori did not want the court they could leave it alone. When Maori came to grief, it was not through the actions of the court but through themselves. The other three Maori members disagreed. Karaitiana Takamoana, opposed the bill, saying that he could vote for it only if it allowed retrospective action for lands that had been improperly dealt with. He could not support the policy of the Native Minister; he had been in attendance with the minister in his dealings with Maori and did not approve of what he had done. He charged McLean with saying one thing in the House about particular cases but, when they came before the courts, 'quite a different thing was done'.[45] Takamoana underestimated the influence of Chief Judge Fenton on Native Land Court proceedings.

Nevertheless, Maori could not always trust McLean. What he said and what he did were sometimes at odds. Evidence before the Legislative Council in 1871 and the Hawkes Bay Lands Alienation Commission in 1873 showed that McLean made promises that were not followed up. In Parliament, he might state government policy and show a politician's skill in convincing people that he had their interests at heart, but in practice he would respond pragmatically to a particular situation in a way that sometimes overturned policy.

McLean ignored Karaitiana Takamoana's criticism perhaps because of his association with the Hawkes Bay repudiation movement. Replying to matters raised during the second reading, he explained that he had not consulted with the judges of the Native Land Court because he was not satisfied that people who had to administer the act were always capable of giving the best opinion or of taking an impartial view. Maori had complained that, when land was dealt with by the Native Land Court, 'it slipped out of their hands, they could not tell how'.[46]

The personal conflict between McLean and Fenton as government officials in the 1850s had ended with McLean's resignation in 1862 and Fenton assuming the role of adviser to the Government on native affairs. Their conflict was resumed when McLean became Native Minister in 1869, Fenton having been appointed Chief Judge of the Native Land Court in 1865. Chief Judge Fenton denounced the 1873 bill, declaring it would destroy the judicial authority of his court. He produced his own draft, sneering that McLean's bill was framed 'to do celestial justice which I always believe to be impossible in this wicked world'. Fenton found support. Both Colonel Haultain, who had been appointed by McLean to conduct an inquiry in 1871, and C. W. Richmond, as chairman of the 1873 Hawkes Bay Lands Alienation Commission, recommended against major change and supported retaining the court as a judicial authority. Fenton's opposition, together with the views of Haultain and Richmond, influenced the House. Many of McLean's safeguards were removed from the bill, though some reforms, including the provisions for inalienable reserves, survived into law. Fenton considered that the new act was unworkable; he and his fellow judges decided not to implement the requirement for inalienable reserves. With that decision went any chance to protect traditional Maori society as an enclave within the settler economy.

In 1874, partly in response to objections from the Native Land Court judges, McLean introduced a further Native Lands Bill.[47] However, he claimed that their objections were impractical and that Maori were generally satisfied. He ignored Karaitiana Takamoana's claim that all Maori petitions to the House had opposed the bill and his demand that the Native Land Court be abolished. McLean insisted that criticisms of the 1873 act were unjustified as its provisions had yet to be implemented. In the past, difficulties had arisen because title had not been investigated. The present bill insisted on prior investigation and that land should not be acquired until title had been established. All legislation relating to Maori, he reminded the House, would have to be altered with the changing circumstances of the country, and he was prepared to make changes to the present legislation the following year.

As settler demand for land was undiminished and most of the North Island was still in Maori hands, McLean's task was to press on to acquire more land. The 1873 and 1874 acts had made it more difficult and expensive in theory to buy Maori land. Every individual owner had to be found and the block resurveyed to separate sellers from non-sellers. Individual buyers found costs so excessive that the Crown became the main buyer.[48] As a result, some politicians accused McLean of trying to regain control over land purchases and to bring back his old Land Purchase Department.

In September 1876, when McLean made what was to be his last speech in the House, it was appropriately on a bill to increase Maori representation. It was necessary, he said, for Maori to be represented in the House, because not only were they taxpayers, but the laws affecting them were passed by that legislature. He still believed that a separate Maori Council of Chiefs would have been more successful than limited representation in the House, as the council would have enabled Maori grievances to be brought before the House and would have provided a better representation of Maori opinion. He also affirmed that the removal of the Crown right of pre-emption over the sale of Maori land had been a mistake that had disadvantaged Maori. What he did not say was that, if Crown right of pre-emption and the Council of Chiefs had been in place, then he as Native Minister would have remained very much in control.

The only way to achieve fair representation, McLean argued, was to promote the English language among Maori children to place them on a common footing with the European population. As a Highland Scot, raised bilingual in Gaelic and English, McLean was conscious that the success of the Highland Scots around the world in the nineteenth century had depended on their mastery of English. Maori could not have equal laws with the Europeans so long as their circumstances were not equal. 'When they considered how different in ideas and language the two races were, it would be seen that in one generation it was not possible that they could remove the prejudice existing among them.' Education was the way to overcome this difficulty. Already up to 1800 young Maori were learning English and 'rapidly conforming to European habits and civilisation'. Once, education had been available in boarding schools only. Now, government policy was for Maori children to be taught in their own villages. His aim, he concluded, was to see Maori and European placed on a common footing. Assimilation was still his goal.[49]

Chapter 19
McLean Under Attack

At the same time as McLean was attempting to alleviate the adverse effects of legislation on Maori he found himself under attack for his conduct as a government minister and as a private landowner. The parliamentary opposition, led by Sir George Grey, attacked the Government's intention to abolish the provincial system of government and questioned the propriety of McLean's dealings as Native Minister while Hawkes Bay settlers and Maori accused him of impropriety in his private land dealings. McLean's close friend J. D. Ormond was associated with McLean in these allegations as a minister and as one of the Hawkes Bay landed elite. There is no doubt that Ormond supported and encouraged McLean in his dubious private land dealings with local Maori.

Under McLean, the Native Department took a proactive role, with officials intervening in disputes between Maori and settler. By merging the head office staff of the Native and Defence departments McLean congratulated himself that he had made a saving of £645 a year. Nevertheless, the Native Department staff expanded. McLean increased the number of resident magistrates to sixteen together with two district civil commissioners, located mainly in regions of dense Maori population – Northland, Waikato, Bay of Plenty, the East Coast and the West Coast from Taranaki south. With the aid of their Maori assessors, resident magistrates were effective in quickly resolving disputes between Maori or between Maori and settler in many North Island areas, apart from the King Country, the Urewera and Te Whiti's territory in Taranaki. Medical officers were increased from five to twenty-four; and Maori assessors to 150 and Maori police to 180.

In the 1870s Native Department staff at head office totalled twelve, with another sixteen in rural districts; there were also ancillary staff, interpreters and clerks, as well as medical officers and native school teachers. Salaries for the Native Department amounted to £16,000, while its total vote increased from £27,000 in 1869 to £34,000 by 1872. A significant part of the vote was set aside for contingency expenditure, to the fury and frustration of the members of the House in their attempts to control the minister. Contingency expenditure was accounted for by gifts to Maori of food in return for hospitality, of seed, stud stock, farm machinery and loans to buy coastal vessels. Other payments were for services rendered or to mollify grievances over land. Native Department expenditure in this category continued to rise. As McLean was also Defence Minister, he did not hesitate to shuffle funds from one department to the other.

McLean had appointed G. S. Cooper as Under-Secretary of the Native Department. However, by 1873 he had accepted Cooper's inability to work effectively with Maori and had him moved to head the Colonial Secretary's department. H. T. Clarke, who had been an effective Civil Commissioner in Auckland, Waikato and Bay of Plenty, took his place. McLean used him to cope with the administrative work while he personally conducted negotiations and controlled his field staff.

As Native Minister, McLean often bypassed his officials and conducted his own negotiations. He wrote to Maori explaining his policy, he visited the disaffected areas, both King movement and Pai Marire, and, by his use of contingency expenditure through gifts of stock, seeds and agricultural machinery, encouraged these groups to return to farming their land. He supported the education of Maori children, providing places in boarding schools for chiefs' sons, and awarded pensions or other gifts to Maori for services rendered. Above all, he made plain to the tribes that the Government would leave them alone. There would be no more confiscation of their lands. Departmental officers were expected to encourage and support the 'friendly' tribes and to persuade the Pai Marire and King movement followers to abandon the thought of war. McLean used Rapata Wahawaha and Te Keepa Te Rangihiwinui to negotiate with the 'rebels' and to supervise them when they returned to the reserves he had made available to them.

McLean was very much a hands-on minister. Whenever absent from Wellington, he kept in regular contact with his Native Department officials and with Maori, sometimes by personal visits, often by letter or the recently introduced telegraph which allowed him to remain in control when absent from his office. In one month, February 1873, McLean despatched 258 telegrams. The majority, 117, dealt with Maori affairs, land purchases or Cabinet business, 17 related to defence and 24 to private business – his own land transactions in Hawkes Bay. In the same month he received 72 telegrams: 48 on Maori affairs, land purchases and Cabinet business, 14 on defence and 10 from Ormond relating to McLean's private land purchases in Hawkes Bay.

McLean required his district officers to be intelligence agents, reporting on the social, economic and political state of their tribes. He also expected them to conform to his own Protestant work ethic. On 27 December 1872 he telegraphed H. T. Kemp: 'Any fresh news. Many happy returns of the season.' The next day another telegram demanded: 'Were the Christmas festivities so urgent that you have not been able to reply to my telegrams of the last day or two.'[1] McLean complained to Ormond: 'Confound these holidays. Telegraph offices are to be closed.'[2] He would not tolerate any procrastination in his subordinates yet this trait was a distinctive feature of his own character. Prominent in his personal affairs when he was a young man, procrastination also hampered his work as an administrator and as a negotiator. Unfulfilled promises in land-purchase negotiations generated Maori mistrust. As an administrator, McLean was better at handling men than dealing with paper. Perhaps his greatest weakness was his inability to delegate, though given the inadequate calibre of many of his subordinates this was understandable. When combined with his innate procrastination this resulted in a crisis-management approach.

As public servants depended on their patron for their continued employment, McLean's officers set out to present themselves in the most favourable light, writing frequent private letters as well as their official reports. They were not averse to denigrating the work of their colleagues. Brissenden, a Native Department official, wrote to McLean that it was better not to communicate with him by telegram as he believed that James Mackay, Civil Commissioner for the Waikato, had access to all government telegrams. This inhibited him from keeping McLean posted on developments in native affairs. He told McLean that the principal King movement Maori sent their communications direct to Te Wheoro – a Waikato rangatira and, later, a member of the House, who acted as an intermediary between the Maori King and the Government – rather than to Mackay, 'whose manner of doing business with them they dislike'. Te Wheoro said Mackay told him not to write to the Government direct but only through him and that that was at McLean's wish. Brissenden thought that Te Wheoro doubted Mackay's honesty and had no confidence in him.[3] McLean, however, had himself selected Mackay as commissioner for the Waikato to deal with the difficult negotiations there, and other accounts suggest that he was skilful and enterprising.

The conduct of McLean's departmental officers came under scrutiny in 1871. There had been complaints about George Worgan's activities in Hawkes Bay and the East Coast. When stationed in Hawkes Bay, Worgan had acted for McLean and other pastoralists and merchants in negotiating their private land purchases. W. K. McLean, who had represented McLean at the Hawkes Bay Alienation Commission hearings in 1871, had warned him that the commission had made 'very severe remarks' about Worgan's dealings with Sutton, a Napier merchant. He thought Worgan was on very dangerous ground.[4] In June 1872 W. K. McLean wrote again to warn McLean that Sutton and Worgan had been 'engaged in some sort of nefarious practice' and that Sutton possessed evidence that placed Worgan in his power, and that Worgan knew more than he pretended.[5]

In 1872 the West Coast activities of George Worgan had led to an investigation on behalf of the Premier by Colonel A. H. Russell, former Native Minister and a Hawkes Bay runholder. Following Russell's adverse report, the Premier was advised that the Government would not be justified in retaining Worgan's services. However, as he was an important officer in McLean's department, nothing could be done until the Native Minister returned to Wellington.[6] Another report on Worgan followed, stating that the management of native affairs on the West Coast was in 'a most unsatisfactory position' and required the Government's immediate attention. The report concluded that there existed 'a general conspiracy to defraud both the Government and the owners of the land and the whole case goes very far to prove the origin and cause of our native troubles'.[7] Worgan asserted his innocence, saying that he had given the Government 'the fullest and clearest information'. He told McLean that he had refrained from writing as much that he had to say 'was better said than written'. He complained that he had been 'grossly ill used' and only his wish to see McLean had given him the patience to endure it.[8]

McLean defended Worgan. He acknowledged that his subordinate had departed from the spirit of his instructions by assisting private individuals to acquire Maori land while employed by the Government to perform the same duty. McLean excused Worgan's conduct, however, saying that he had been placed in a position of 'peculiar difficulty' as the Government had been eager to get the matter settled and numerous private individuals had already entered into negotiations with the Maori owners, while the provincial government also wanted to lease or buy some of the land and had applied for Worgan's services. Although this competition for the land had drawn 'much odium' on Worgan, he did not appear to have lost sight of the Government's interest, even though 'acting most imprudently in dealing with private individuals'.[9] McLean's disingenuous interpretation of Worgan's behaviour highlighted the absence of any clear protocol of conduct for officers of his Native Department.

On this occasion Fox stood up to McLean. There would have to be an inquiry into Worgan's 'pocketing government money and defrauding natives and others of it'. Fox had accepted McLean's assurance that he had not been personally involved, though he reminded McLean that Worgan had been boasting that he had the minister in his power and that McLean would not dare dismiss him. A subsequent commission of inquiry found Worgan guilty of forgery and he was imprisoned.

Worgan, as a government officer, did not hesitate to assist his patron, McLean, in advancing his private interests. McLean reciprocated by defending him and continuing to employ him as an official. McLean was loyal to his officials even when faced with evidence of dereliction of duty, as with Worgan's corruption or, in another case, with James Grindell's alcoholism. In the latter, he offered to find Grindell another government post provided he promised to abstain from alcoholic liquor. This was yet another instance where Fox seemed overawed by McLean. In complaining to McLean about Grindell's behaviour as a Native Department official in insulting a prominent settler, the Premier said that twice he had had Grindell dismissed from the public service, only to find him taken on again 'to repeat his offence on some new victim'.[10]

Gisborne, the first head of the public service, thought that McLean showed

> a want of discrimination in the choice of his officers. He occasionally chose persons who had knowledge and experience of natives, but who were devoid of the moral qualities which were essential to success. Sometimes he preferred to those who were moderately clever but good, men who were very clever but not good at all. The natural consequence was that his confidence was abused and that he met with worse than common failure which redounded to the discredit of himself.[11]

Gisborne's interpretation was generous. McLean was aware of Worgan's illegal activities but chose to overlook them as he himself had benefited from Worgan's help in acquiring land to expand his Maraekakaho estate.

In May 1875, Ormond provided evidence of a smoking gun when he told McLean that Worgan had been playing a 'dishonest game', taking bribes from private individuals. It was difficult to prove, but 'still we know that Worgan is not nice to a shade and of course proof of such proceedings would-be very damaging to us ... I agree with you that he is capable if only he wd. be honest'. In June, Ormond warned that Henry Russell was to lay a charge of forgery against Worgan for forging the signatures of grantees in the Coleman block in Hawkes Bay. If Russell succeeded, Ormond feared that all other cases in which Worgan was the interpreter 'would be next to worthless'.[12] As early as 1870 Kinross had advised McLean that he doubted that Worgan was 'quite trustworthy'. Ormond's comments indicate that McLean was aware of Worgan's dishonest and illegal transactions but chose to take no action against one of his own officers as he himself had benefited from such activities.

Competition to acquire Maori land in Hawkes Bay resulted in vitriolic rivalry between two factions of runholders: McLean and Ormond against Henry and Purvis Russell in association with Frederick Sutton, a Napier merchant. The Russell brothers, who were Stafford supporters, used the *Daily Telegraph*, owned by Sutton, to attack and discredit McLean politically. The *Hawke's Bay*

Herald became the organ of the McLean faction, led by Ormond, Kinross and Colonel A. H. Russell. Each faction, righteously indignant, denounced the other for the same practices they themselves were applying: devious or possibly illegal tactics to separate Maori from their land through the operations of the Native Land Court. The enmity between the Russell and McLean factions had a sequel when Ormond and other pastoralists narrowly failed in an attempt to force Russell to resign from the Hawkes Bay Club for 'ungentlemanly conduct' over his support for the Hawkes Bay Maori in their Repudiation movement. This movement attempted to overturn land purchases of Maori land under the Native Land Court since 1865. Ormond refused ever to enter the club again.

The origin of this feud is obscure. On first meeting Henry Russell in 1859, McLean approved of him as 'an excellent, enterprising settler'.[13] McLean and Russell were on friendly terms in the 1860s. Russell trusted in McLean's 'friendly aid' in one of his land transactions, hoping that Locke was 'making it all safe for me with the Reserve'. He could jest about the expansion of McLean's estate: 'What a land cormorant you are after all!! Your territory will by and bye be as wide as many an English Lords of the first magnitude.'[14] Three years later Russell told McLean that his wife had sent him an invitation to her ball 'and she quite sets her heart on opening the affair with you. Now don't plead business but put that aside for a day or two. The change will do you good.'[15]

A perceived Pai Marire threat to settlers in 1865 led to a disagreement between Russell and McLean. Russell, who founded the town of Waipukurau, demanded that the militia be called out and troops stationed there to protect the settlers. McLean thought Russell was panicking and refused. Later, of course, Russell was appointed Government Agent on the East Coast to replace McLean. This is another example when McLean's friend became an enemy once McLean believed he was thwarting McLean's plans. Russell's subsequent dismissal when McLean became Native Minister after the fall of the Stafford Government in October 1869 contributed to the feud. After 1870 Russell ceased to correspond with McLean until 1872, when he wrote about a Supreme Court hearing involving Te Hapuku's debts. The forms of address he used were no longer 'My dear McLean' and 'Yours always' but a formal 'The Hon. D McLean' and 'I am, dear sir Yours truly'. McLean responded in the same style.

Though he himself had been under investigation for his land dealings, Ormond believed that the Russell faction's real target was McLean, as they were Stafford supporters and wanted to destroy McLean politically. In May 1872 Ormond told McLean he had decided to give up his public works portfolio in the Fox Government but to retain his position as Provincial Superintendent in order to keep control of Hawkes Bay affairs that involved their private interests.

'Since you left it has become more apparent that it wd. be suicidal on our part for me to give up the key to command here. Those wretches the Russells are more active than ever.' He listed all the land transactions, including his own and McLean's, that Russell was trying to bring before the Supreme Court and complained that he meant 'real mischief' and that 'counteracting the schemes of these scoundrels' was taking up a great deal of his time. The Russells were spending hundreds of pounds in their encouragement of the Repudiation movement that had roused Maori in a ferment. Ormond deplored the power of mischief that one or two unscrupulous men had with the Maori. He also assured McLean that he did not think the 'enemy' had uncovered anything new about his private transactions. Nevertheless, the Russells hoped to upset the Locke and Lyndon Deed, arranged on McLean's behalf, with their own deed and then as trustees they would get control of the land that McLean had bought from Te Hapuku.[16] In 1871 telegrams went between McLean and Ormond, Locke and Kinross as they struggled to rescue Te Hapuku from a probable bankruptcy that would deliver the purchase into Russell's hands. Both McLean and the Russells had tried to get Te Hapuku to sign a deed to sell land at Ngatarawa. Both factions accused the other of plying him with liquor to secure his consent. Te Hapuku himself acknowledged his problem as he got further into debt and was taken to court. In 1871 he confessed to McLean, 'I am in trouble; it is not caused by any person, it is through my own fault – the craving of my heart for the food of the European. I am now suffering from my excesses; the cause of my trouble is rum.' Te Hapuku was an example of how a Maori became entrapped between the operation of an alien system of British law through the Native Land Court and his own indebtedness.

H. R. Russell continued to encourage the Repudiation movement to harass McLean over his titles to Mangaroa and Ngatarawa blocks. However, McLean travelled to Napier in November 1874 and, exerting his superior mana, secured a twenty-one-year lease on Ngatarawa No. 2 for £100 a year and completed the purchase of No. 3 block for £3300. Russell did not give up. He persuaded one of the parties to the sale to lodge a caveat against the title, though this was later withdrawn. In 1875, Sheehan, legal counsel to the Repudiation movement and a Russell supporter, arranged for Te Hapuku's share in Ngatarawa No. 4 and No. 5 blocks to be assigned to Sir George Grey, even though a deed of conveyance had been executed on McLean's behalf in 1871. When Te Hapuku found out that Grey's power of attorney would give him ownership of his share, he refused to sign, as his aim was to regain his land.

The nature of McLean's personal relationship with the Hawkes Bay rangatira was highlighted by the actions of Tareha and Te Hapuku. Both, while despondent at having to part with their land, were emphatic that, if they must sell, they would sell only to McLean. They seem still to have looked to him for support even while they denounced the iniquities caused by the operation of the Native Land Court. To sell to McLean would enhance their mana, such was McLean's status. In their eyes he ranked next to the Governor. The rangatira would look to McLean for some form of reciprocity following an agreement to sell.

McLean's ministerial responsibilities left him little time to monitor activities on his own estate. To ease his workload, Ormond volunteered to oversee McLean's private interests. 'In any matter of your own do not hesitate to ask me to do anything you want seen to. I don't mind trouble as you know and will do my best for you in anything. Your run question is getting in a mess I fear.'[17] The Maori owners of the Ngatarawa land leased by McLean at Maraekakaho were now willing to sell and McLean had to find the money to take up this offer or risk other buyers acquiring parts of his run. Ormond arranged for a mortgage of £1200 on McLean's Maori lease and instructed Locke as Civil Commissioner to follow it up. By July 1870 Kinross, acting as McLean's agent and working through George Worgan had secured an agreement to sell from four of the seven grantees of Ngatarawa block No. 4 and seven out of ten of Ngatarawa block No. 5. The risk of outside interference remained. D. Lindsay, a merchant, registered a caveat against one grantee's share and McLean had to pay Lindsay £120 to remove his caveat. Worgan advised that the 10,000 acres of this fertile land could be bought for 4s an acre,[18] leaving 375 acres for a Maori reserve. McLean was eager to buy before the land fell into 'the hands of numerous sharpers who were looking after native land'. The Maori owners were prepared to accept £3000 for the two blocks, £1000 more than McLean intended to offer. To head off possible competition, he agreed. The Maori owners' mortgages owing and their debts for stock and goods from Maraekakaho station amounted to £2355,[19] leaving them with only £645 as a result of their sale.

McLean had been negotiating with Tareha to buy his and Karauria's one-ninth share, 1253 acres, in Big Bush, part of Mangateretere West block. Tareha had refused to sell but said if he ever did sell, he would sell to McLean for £300. In March 1870, Tareha approached Ormond wanting payment of £300 owed by McLean on this alleged purchase. Ormond had the money lodged to his credit in his own bank and he asked McLean whether he should pay.

This transaction came under scrutiny. The *Hawke's Bay Times* remarked that McLean as Native Minister had referred to the Native Lands Acts as imposing restrictions for the protection of Maori property rights, but had himself taken advantage of the pressure on Maori to sell. 'If there is one man in the colony who should not have concluded this good bargain with this improvident chief for the purchase of land belonging to him and the heirs of a brother slain in battle that man is the Native Minister.'[20] Ormond warned McLean that the authors, Henry Russell and his lawyer, Wilson, were arranging to reprint the article in other newspapers. He thought the article in the *Hawke's Bay Times* 'very vindictive and spiteful' and complained that there really was 'a malignity in their hatred to you that far exceeds any feeling they have against me'.[21] It seems that payment for Mangateretere West was not finally made until 23 May 1872.[22]

In 1871 McLean came under attack in the House over the Government's handling of the sale of land confiscated after the wars of the 1860s under the New Zealand Settlements Act of 1863. An opposition motion sought a return listing the sale of all confiscated lands with the names of the purchasers, the amount and price of the land and the date of the authority under which the sale occurred. The members' intention was to implicate the Native Minister over improper conduct over the sale of the Piako swamp (86,000 acres at 2s 6d an acre) to a syndicate led by Thomas Russell, an Auckland lawyer and leading businessman. Members alleged that the Government had acted contrary to the law and that the land had been 'given away for a mere song' and spoke of bargains made with 'capitalists in back parlours', hinting at 'gigantic jobbery' and 'wanton waste of the public estate'.

McLean assured the House that the return for confiscated lands would be prepared and tabled at the earliest possible date and the Government had already indicated that the sale of confiscated lands would be brought under ordinary land laws. He defended the Piako sale as sound public policy. When Thomas Russell had applied to buy the land, the price offered had been rejected as being too low. McLean had insisted on the upset price of 5s an acre, a price at which land could not be sold in the Waikato. The Government wanted to connect Piako with the Waikato region. As it would be costly to build a road through the swamp, it agreed to sell to Russell on condition that his company build the road. McLean believed the Government could not have got better terms if it had put the land up for auction. He admitted that the transaction was incomplete and that the Government had no authority to proceed. However, he justified the sale on the ground of expediency and pointed out that the Government had the power under the New Zealand Settlements Act to pass regulations, though these had not yet been issued.[23]

There were further accusations of impropriety in 1872. Again, McLean was the target. In 1871 the House had called for a return listing all persons holding land under Maori tenure. The Registrar-General of Land objected that this would give undue publicity to private affairs, so the Government did nothing. A year later, E. J. Wakefield moved a similar motion. He attacked the Government, and McLean and Ormond in particular, saying that the Government had tried to conceal the large private interests of its own members, and suggesting that the two ministers, the only Hawkes Bay members in the House, would refuse to provide information that might be useful. Reynolds, member for Dunedin City, supported Wakefield quoting from a letter from 'A North Island Settler' in the *Otago Daily Times* (written by McLean's opponent, Henry Russell of Hawkes Bay). The writer claimed that in the absence of regulation on the sale of Maori land, valuable areas had been bought for a very small consideration and that Maori had been supplied with liquor illegally by 'rapacious and unscrupulous parties'. The writer then warned South Island people that Maori, having disposed of all their land, would 'become a race of sturdy beggars who will prove a heavy burden on the colony'. Buckland, an Auckland member, said that there was no reason to fear that 'natives would become beggars' while they owned four-fifths of the North Island though this was nearly all neglected and uncultivated, and the 'sooner they got rid of the land the better it would for the Europeans and the Natives themselves'.

Replying for the Government, McLean referred to letters from the Registrar-General of Land and the Attorney-General and said that, on their advice, the Government did not deem it advisable to lay the information before the House. The Government was justified in protecting people from having their private affairs exposed, especially as no good whatever would be attained by such a course. As for the Hawkes Bay members, however, they would be only too glad if the fullest inquiry were made into land transactions in that province. The Premier, William Fox, submitted that any questionable transaction could be brought before the Lands Alienation Commission and indeed that had happened in Hawkes Bay. The government majority ensured the defeat of the motion.[24]

In land matters Hawkes Bay Maori, like other tribes, had many complaints. These included the restriction to ten grantees on a title; that grantees had been induced to sign deeds of sale and mortgages, the contents and purpose of which had not been fully explained; and that Maori had been allowed unlimited credit by storekeepers only to find their creditors foreclosing on their mortgages. Numerous Maori petitions to Parliament had sought redress, but none had succeeded.

By 1872 a young Ngati Kahungunu rangatira, Henare Matua, had founded the Repudiation movement with the aim of having investigated all deeds of sale, leases and mortgages that had passed through the Native Land Court since its first sitting in 1866. The movement sought to have the Native Land

Court abolished, land sales in Hawkes Bay since the passage of the 1865 Native Lands Act revoked and the land returned, or at least to have unfair land dealings remedied by ascertaining the loss Maori had sustained and these amounts recovered. Samuel Locke, the Civil Commissioner for Hawkes Bay, told McLean that he estimated the area to be investigated as 700,000 acres, much of which had been subdivided and resold. The Repudiation movement had the support of H. R. Russell, but his motives were suspect as he relished any opportunity to embarrass his political enemies, McLean and Ormond. Nevertheless, Russell seems to have had a genuine concern for the plight of local Maori, and supported the Repudiation movement to an extent that endangered his own financial position. Ormond was baffled by Russell's action in supporting a movement that must harm the economic power of the landed elite: 'The men are mad and will hesitate at nothing. The spirit of revenge is at the bottom of all they do and has no limit.'[25]

Samuel Locke warned McLean that any movement to remedy land grievances, whether real or supposed, would be sure to gather followers. He admitted that some injustice had occurred: there were cases in which local Maori 'with truth' considered themselves injured and deceived and that such grievances required careful examination.[26] Ormond, who could be relied on to blurt out the truth, also acknowledged injustices, telling McLean: 'Of course as we know, many of the natives have been cheated out of their land and all are ready to get it back if they can and seemingly they really think they will get it back and are proportionately elated.'[27]

As the Repudiation movement gathered support from the rank and file, some Ngati Kahungunu became uneasy at the challenge to their traditional leadership. Karaitiana Takamoana aimed to placate the movement by seeking a public inquiry. As member for Eastern Maori, in 1872 he introduced the Hawkes Bay Native Lands Alienation Bill to establish a commission to inquire into alleged illegal land deals. McLean gave his ostensible support, saying that there was a great necessity for an inquiry, not only in Hawkes Bay but in Poverty Bay, Wairoa and possibly Wairarapa. There were also three or four unsettled government purchases that he intended to bring before the commission.[28] McLean sometimes used this tactic in the House when confronted with a hostile motion, though finally exercising the government majority to defeat it. McLean appeared confident that his own private land dealings were beyond reproach. He remarked to his brother that 'sometimes I wish all the native runs were in the sea but I am satisfied that if there has been any fault it has been too great a liberality towards the natives and the dealings with them have always been fair and above board'.[29]

The 1873 Hawkes Bay Native Lands Alienation Commission appointed by the Government to inquire into Maori grievances in Hawkes Bay consisted of two Pakeha judges who were unsympathetic towards Maori – the chairman, the former Native Minister, C. W. Richmond, by that time a Supreme Court judge, and F. E. Maning, a Native Land Court judge – and two Maori, Wiremu Te Wheoro and Wi Hikairo, a native assessor. McLean thought that the members would have the confidence of both races, but the cynical Ormond had no doubt about the commission's intention. He told McLean that it was a political tool in the hands of Richmond and Russell: 'having got all they can on my a/c [Heretaunga] they are going to give the enemy the opportunity of throwing all the filth they can at you'.[30] Ormond did not mention that Maning, as a good friend of McLean, might provide a counterweight to Richmond. Indeed, McLean was rumoured to have had a private meeting with him before the commission convened.

Maori lodged over 200 complaints. Nine were against McLean, associated in several of these with Kinross and a pastoralist, Hugh Campbell. With the Mangaroa block, the complainants were Karaitiana Takamoana and Henare Matua, who disputed the validity of the alleged sale. With Mangateretere, Waka Kawatini and Paora Torotoro disputed all the alienations. The Ngatarawa blocks drew five complainants, including Karaitiana Takamoana, Henare Matua and even Te Hapuku, who had been McLean's ally in the 1850s. Te Hapuku alleged that no settlement of rent had ever been made; he had never mortgaged this block to anyone; that he had been induced to sign a deed agreeing to sell to McLean by being told that all the other grantees had sold, which he found out afterwards was not true; no price had been fixed before the signing of the deed; that he had rejected £3000 and wanted £7000 or the land returned to him. Ormond worked to keep Te Hapuku as an ally, but complained that the Russells had 'plied him with liquor' and kept him 'fearfully weak and foolish'.

McLean chose to visit the West Coast of the North Island as Native Minister, leaving his financial adviser, W. K. McLean, to represent his interests before the commission. W. K. McLean told him that, although Te Hapuku had lodged complaints, he insisted that, whether or not McLean had to pay £7000, no one but McLean should have Ngatarawa. He thought it plain that the old chief had been put up to do what he had done by the Russell faction.[31] A month later, W. K. McLean reported that he had been occupied in 'keeping the natives in the right frame of mind' and in gathering to counter the 'vile insinuations' of the opposition. Some had behaved honourably, insisting that they had no complaints against McLean. Ihaka, under oath, had said that the Maori Repudiation Committee had induced him to lodge complaints against McLean, but he wished to have them withdrawn.[32]

Complaints over the purchase of the Heretaunga block originally illegally leased by Thomas Tanner in 1864, concerned unfair pressure, inadequate price, failure to carry out the conditions of sale, supplying of liquor and threats of extreme measures. This block had been divided into twelve shares held by seven pastoralists, known as 'The Twelve Apostles'. How far was McLean involved in the Heretaunga purchase? He did not hold any share, though his closest friend, Ormond, was one of the purchasers. However, in evidence before the commission, Ormond admitted he had 'probably' asked McLean to approach one of the owners, Tareha, as McLean had considerable influence over him, to facilitate the sale and that it was 'excessively likely' that McLean had spoken to Tareha.

John Sheehan, the lawyer assisting H. R. Russell, in cross-examining Ormond before the commission, asked whether it was not his duty as Government Agent 'to protect the Natives from being unfairly dealt with by the Europeans'. Ormond responded: 'Certainly not. I should not have consented to act had I understood it to be my duty to interfere in their transactions with Europeans.' His attitude that Maori had to look after themselves and learn how to compete in a European economy reflected the nineteenth-century laissez-faire economic philosophy.

The commission cleared Tanner and his fellow apostles of illegalities. It found that the prices paid for the land were adequate and that the ten grantees did represent all the interested owners. No case of fraud had been found that would invalidate the purchase. Keith Sinclair found this 'a conclusion it is impossible to believe and which probably no one believed then'.[33] The commission did criticise provisions of the Native Lands Acts, including the restriction of title to ten grantees. Richmond and Maning also condemned the Maori grantees for their improvidence and extravagance in amassing large debts. What did emerge from the evidence, according to Richmond, was that 'the leading chiefs of Heretaunga seemed to have an alarming lack of understanding about money, finance, credit and debt'.[34] They had exchanged their land for perishable goods, food and alcohol, rather than money. Allegations that Ormond and McLean had used the influence of their official positions to put unfair pressure on the complainants to force them to sell their land were rejected by Richmond as 'so vague and entirely unfounded on any tangible fact' that 'to make any further remark would be to lend to them an importance they do not deserve'. Hikairo strongly disagreed with Richmond, arguing that there were hapu and individuals whose interests had been overlooked. The ten grantees should be seen as trustees for all who had an interest in the land; therefore they were not entitled to sell as individuals. He felt that the prices paid were inadequate and did not think 'this was a proper way of making a sale of land'.[35] The Maori claimants were disappointed when they discovered that the commission had no power to redress grievances, only to report to Parliament on the effect of the land laws.

The commission, having heard only a quarter of all the complaints, and those mainly about the Heretaunga block, reported to the House without inquiring into other allegations, including those against McLean. According to Turton, the complaints against McLean had been placed low on the list because they had been purposely held back by interested parties who intended to prefer them in person before the commissioners and to argue that Maori had no confidence in government officers. Turton told McLean that he had tried unsuccessfully to have McLean's Ngatarawa purchase considered. It would seem from the manner in which the commission treated Tanner and the other purchasers of the Heretaunga block that McLean too would have been exonerated, particularly as he had not been involved in enticing Maori into ever-increasing debt, as had merchants like Sutton and Maney. There was one transaction, however, where Maori debts of some £400 to Maraekakaho station were included as part-payment.

Karaitiana Takamoana went to Auckland in a last-minute appeal to ask the Government to buy the Heretaunga block and advance £3000 to pay Henare Tomoana's debts. Karaitiana said that McLean 'agreed to it but it was not agreeing. I asked him twice and he answered the same each time.' Here again was McLean the politician, trying to pacify a petitioner without making any firm commitment. However, when Ormond went to see Takamoana on his return to Heretaunga and was told that McLean had agreed, he replied that that was not correct, as the Government had no money.[36]

Settlers were relieved that the commission did not uphold the complaints. Judge Maning later agreed with McLean that even 'a very small encouragement' from the commission would have caused trouble that would have spread like an epidemic across the North Island. He was relieved that the evidence did not support any finding favourable to the claimants.[37] Fenton thought the alienation commission 'very dangerous', no doubt because it threatened his authority as Chief Judge of the Native Land Court. He assured McLean that he was prepared to do or say anything in opposition to such inquiries.[38]

Although Maori continued to petition Parliament and to appeal to the Supreme Court over unjust land transactions, it should be noted that by the end of the century, some four million acres of Maori land in Hawkes Bay had been bought by fewer than fifty Europeans, a landed elite that included McLean and Ormond.[39]

In 1873 McLean went to Taranaki rather than appear before the Hawkes Bay Lands Alienation Commission. His intention was to meet the tribes and deal with issues arising from lands confiscated after the 1860s wars. Writing to Harry Atkinson, member for Egmont, he said that he agreed on the necessity of grappling with the return of some confiscated lands.[40] He would deal with it in a fair and impartial spirit and trusted that the settlers would not throw obstacles in the way. The return of Maori to their lands to which they had an undoubted legal right could not much longer be postponed. He was confident that Atkinson would use his influence to reconcile the settlers to this necessity.

McLean made a plea for Maori to live in unity with the settlers. At New Plymouth, one Ngati Maru rangatira told him, 'I have seen distress and now I have turned my attention to searching for what will benefit me. You are the first member of the Government I have seen .... Salutations to you the parent of the people and of the land. My former parents I discovered to be without knowledge and I want you to be my parent.' McLean responded by stating a view that he had advanced since he first became a land-purchase commissioner. What was the use of Maori letting the land be idle, he asked?

> When you get up in the morning you see nothing but the same trees the same gullies and the same streams that you saw the previous day. What benefit can you derive from leaving your land in that state? Land was made by God for the use and benefit of men and not to lie idle. It is for you to act in such a manner as will lead to our mutual benefit. It is a good thing to dispose of unoccupied land upon which to locate your friends the Europeans so that they may see you and you may see them. It will then be easy for you whenever you desire to come out to the Coast to do so.

Wi Parata, member for Western Maori, urged the tribe to give their allegiance to the Government irrespective of any offer to sell land. If they did sell, they must make sure they did not 'trench upon what belongs to another'. McLean endorsed his statement.

At the next meeting, Te Pakakohi and Nga Rauru wanted to discuss a return to their confiscated lands between the Waitotara and Tangahoe rivers. The rangatira Taurua said that when he and his people returned from Otago (where they had been sent as prisoners), they had promised that they would not return onto their land without McLean's sanction. McLean had kept his word but he doubted whether there was sufficient land for all his people. Another rangatira, Pehimana Te Tahua, said that he wanted to return to the land of his ancestors, but all the land on that side of the Waitotara River had been given to Pakeha. McLean responded that Nga Rauru had the same advantages as other tribes when the Compensation Court, which had been set up under the New Zealand Settlements Act 1863 to apportion confiscated lands, made its awards.

McLean reminded the tribes that the 20,000 acres inside the confiscated block would provide for those who had no tribal claim on that side of the Waitotara. The Whanganui rangatira Mete Kingi argued that the reserve should concentrate the tribes in one particular area. He criticised the allocation of several small blocks scattered among European settlements since this would lead to trouble as Maori did not understand the need to fence all their land. Mete Kingi's suggestion was impractical, replied McLean, as the land had already been disposed of for schools, railways, reserves and special grants, though he was prepared to consider minor alterations. The Government's Maori supporters had the last word. Wi Parata told the gathering that they should be well pleased with the Government's allocation. Te Keepa (Te Rangihiwinui) insisted that the tribe had been restored to their liberty and to their land.

On meeting Ngati Ruanui, McLean pointed out that some of their confiscated land had been handed to settlers and could not be touched, but part of what remained in government hands could be returned. He claimed, however, that if their land was returned, they could not use it all. The actual area should be further discussed, as 'a state of peace is the best under which to seek refuge, a state of quiet and steady work is a boon much to be desired'

Puketapu Maori were the next to hear from McLean. He said that he came to settle the troubles that had disturbed them, promising that he would reconsider the 1866 court decision that had ignored the claims of some members of the tribe.

When McLean met Waitara Maori, Te Teira, in a reference to his 1859 offer to sell land announcing himself as 'the man who broke the canoe', asked whether McLean was going to return the confiscated land. Another, Pita Hongihongi, welcomed McLean as 'the man who set the minds of the people at rest' and appealed to him to 'now set the land right'. He asked that he be given back his land. McLean's reply was cryptic. He told them that he had nothing much to say, but nothing was more important than peace. As for the land, some had been dealt with, some was still vacant. Hongihongi brought McLean back to the issue, charging that McLean's 'old words' had been that he would not take the land of Ngati Rahiri as they had remained loyal. What wrong had they done? He wanted his land restored. McLean agreed that he had been loyal, but said that some of that hapu had been 'foolish enough to go away to do wrong' and only the loyal were entitled to protection. However, he would meet with those who had turned against him to talk the matter over and warned them not to hide those faults that had lost them their land.

Of the land confiscated, 15,000 to 20,000 acres had been returned, McLean reminded the gathering.[41] He admitted that Ngati Rahiri had been loyal, but their land taken had been very small (300 acres). It had been taken under a former administration and he was not able to restore it. However, the present government was willing to compensate them in addition to what Mr Parris had already been authorised to do. The rangatira continued to insist that they had been treated unjustly, as they had been deprived of their land, even though they had done no wrong. Money was no compensation, they wanted their land returned as the remaining land was insufficient for them and their children. McLean was unyielding: the bulk of their land had not been touched, but they were now asking for more.

At another meeting of Ngati Ruanui, Te Ati Awa, Puketapu and Taranaki, McLean was equally uncompromising. He refused to return land between Okurakura and Kai Iwi, saying:

> You were often advised how fruitless must be any attempt to resist the increasing power of the Europeans and how inevitably those tribes must suffer who opposed their progress and settlement ... you must make up your mind to the influx of a large European population and be careful how you act towards the dominant race. You can no more prevent the Europeans coming to this country than you can arrest the flowing of the tide. You must be moderate in your requests and expectations. Let the law be supreme ... Your best course is to turn your attention to the cultivation of the soil.

McLean spoke with the assurance of a man who believed in his imperial mission to bring peace, order and good government to 'lesser breeds without the law'. At the same time, he had to reconcile settler pressure for more land to Maori demands to return to their lands. Maori had to accept their subordinate role and acknowledge the superiority of their colonial masters.

McLean was equally blunt in rejecting settler protests at the Government's allowing 'rebel' Maori to return to their Taranaki lands. At a Hawera meeting, settlers insisted that Fox, when Premier, had promised that no Maori fires should again be lit south of the Waingongoro. McLean replied that that promise had applied only when danger was imminent and was no longer valid in the present time of peace and tranquillity. He reminded the settlers that, a year before, he had told them that Maori had a clear title to their reserves. The Government had now decided that it was time for the native owners to occupy them. They must accept that they would be more secure if Maori were residing among them rather living in the inland forest. McLean made it plain to both settler and Maori that there was to be peace, but it was to be his kind of peace on his terms. Throughout his time as Native Minister in the 1870s, McLean was resolute in withstanding settler pressure.

Governor Grey had offended McLean when he reversed the decision over the Waitara purchase in 1863 and they had no further contact until 1868 when

McLean, now a member of the House of Representatives visited Grey in his retirement on Kawau Island. Grey's charm and hospitality so dazzled McLean that he declared that the former Governor could do more for New Zealand as a private settler than any other man. Indeed, in 'old Roman Catholic times he would be regarded as a saint of much higher qualities than many that had been canonised'. Perhaps it was the tranquil atmosphere of the island that affected McLean. However, when Grey was elected as member for Auckland West in 1875 he became a bitter political opponent of the Vogel ministry. Vogel and McLean had originally been staunch provincialists but by 1874, now in control on the national scene, Vogel and McLean saw the provinces' demands as the barrier to their plans for the economic development of the colony. Grey unsuccessfully led the opposition to the abolition of the provincial-government system that he had established in his first term as governor. Thereafter he singled out McLean as the target for his attacks on the Government's native policy. Grey and McLean became political enemies and in time Grey's attacks became personal. McLean retaliated with some reluctance.

On 8 October 1875 Grey led an opposition attack on McLean when he condemned the purchasing of native lands by government officers or agents for their own or for other people's advantage when it was their duty to buy land for the public interest. Such officers had no lawful right to buy these lands for themselves or for other private individuals. Grey moved two motions in the House. The first affirmed that 'the purchase or leasing of Native lands, directly or indirectly, for their own interest or advantage, or for other persons, by Government officers or agents, whose duty it was to purchase Native lands for the public is contrary to the public interest'. His second motion sought to have all lands so purchased since the 1870 Immigration and Public Works Act to be taken as part of the public estate and compensation made to the purchasers to the extent of the actual sum expended. Grey argued that, by English law, an agent employed to purchase cannot purchase for himself. McLean as Native Minister was responsible for buying Maori land for the public. The House had voted £700,000 to acquire a large public estate in the North Island. This large sum of money had been entrusted to the Native Minister with absolute power over its expenditure, yet no part of this money had been accounted for. Grey alleged that large tracts of land had been bought by the Native Minister and his agents for themselves or third parties. He called for justice to be done for the people of New Zealand.[42]

McLean in reply, said that the Government intended on a course of action on the lines of Grey's first motion. This was another example of McLean's tactic of deflecting criticism by appearing to concede merit in the opposition's case. At present the law allowed any person to acquire land wherever possible. Competition had made it difficult for the Government to acquire the public estate required by the House. Nevertheless, the Government had acquired a public estate of some 6 million acres in the North Island. He agreed with Grey that government officials should not be allowed to purchase land for private individuals and this would be enforced. The second motion, however, amounted to confiscation. The law allowed people to buy land after it had passed through the Native Land Court. What possible objection could there be to acquiring land in a legitimate manner, as he himself had done? He thought it unnecessary to reply to the personal allusions made by Grey. Further, he pointed out that the money entrusted to the Native Department had been audited, though of the £700,000, half was unexpended. Once more a government majority defeated Grey's two motions.

In nineteenth-century New Zealand it was accepted that men would use their public office to advance their private interests. In 1884 Vogel and Robert Stout would take office to protect their interests in the Waimea Plains Railway Company. In 1861 McLean had told Governor Gore Browne that he was illegally buying Maori land, knowing that legislation would be passed to make this legal. As other runholders in Hawkes Bay had already done so, he did not intend to be disadvantaged. McLean did not appear to accept that as Native Minister he had a responsibility to safeguard Maori interests and should avoid any possibility of involvement in illegal transactions. Pragmatism again took precedence over principle.

In October 1875 McLean's private land purchases again came under attack in Parliament. Sheehan, who had earlier acted as legal counsel for the Hawkes Bay Repudiation movement, moved that 'This House regrets to hear of the scandalous and dishonest dealings of certain Europeans in the acquisition of Native lands in the Province of Hawkes Bay, and of the fact that high officers have been either connected therewith or were cognizant thereof and considers that such transactions are a stain on the good name of the colony'. Sheehan charged McLean and Ormond, the two members representing Hawkes Bay, with abusing their high office in provincial and central government to advance their private land purchases. Under the old system, Sheehan explained, native land had been protected from seizure for debt and land could not be sold without the consent of all the people. As a consequence of the passing of the 1865 Native Lands Act, native title in Hawkes Bay had been almost extinguished, with a mere twenty-five or thirty settlers acquiring this land. Runholders, having gained a lease from Maori grantees, believed that they had a moral right to the freehold. In many cases they delayed or withheld the rent. This forced Maori owners to have recourse to hotelkeepers and storekeepers, who supplied liquor and goods on credit protected by mortgages, until the land 'slipped through the hands of the Natives', who 'were given up to one continuous drunk'.

Sheehan went on to attack the actions of McLean's Native Department interpreters in carrying on private land-purchase businesses on behalf of settlers while in government employment. He named F. Hamlin and his brother, and Grindell and Worgan. These men had been rewarded by the Native Minister with promotion within the government service, said Sheehan, claiming that McLean had refused to intervene because he himself had profited from similar transactions. Through these men McLean had acquired 20,000 acres (the five Ngatarawa blocks) at very much below their real value – land as valuable as 200,000 acres in any other part of the country. Most of these transactions had been handled by Worgan, who had later been dismissed from government service for fraud. When the Land Alienation Commission came to Hawkes Bay in 1873, Sheehan alleged that agents of the Native Minister took claimants into public houses, gave them a few pounds and got them to withdraw their cases.[43] McLean interrupted Sheehan to deny this charge.

In reply, McLean declared that almost all assertions could be proved to be unfounded. He condemned Sheehan for encouraging Maori to repudiate all fair and reasonable transactions they had entered into. Indeed, Hawkes Bay Maori had been better treated than those in any other part of New Zealand. McLean avoided any response to specific charges, resorting to the reports of Richmond and Maning of the Hawkes Bay Lands Alienation Commission, which had cleared the runholders of any misdeeds. McLean omitted to mention that the commission had made its report before it got around to hearing any of the complaints lodged against him. McLean justified his private purchases, saying that he was as entitled as any other citizen to purchase Maori land after it had passed through the Native Land Court. He ended by condemning Sheehan for 'exciting a spirit of antagonism' between the two races.

The government majority ensured that Sheehan's motion was defeated. Nevertheless, some members expressed unease at the impropriety and possible illegality of McLean's private purchases. They were probably correct, but the exact details of these transactions are hard to ascertain. McLean distanced himself from direct involvement in these purchases, saying that he left the negotiations to others. For example, with the Ngatarawa purchases he delegated Kinross, the merchant with whom he dealt, to handle the negotiations. Kinross in turn used Worgan to conduct the negotiations with the Maori. On another occasion, when buying land from Tareha, McLean delegated the transaction to Samuel Locke, the Civil Commissioner for Hawkes Bay. Given his detailed oversight of his officials, it is hard to believe that McLean did not keep himself informed about the nature of these transactions. His defence of Worgan when confronted by evidence of corruption, although due in part to loyalty to his official, suggests that Worgan's role in some of McLean's Hawkes Bay purchases would not bear close scrutiny.

Government land purchases were Grey's next target. He used McLean's failure to table the report of the native land purchase commissioners in Poverty Bay to imply impropriety and to attack McLean's handling of native land purchases. McLean explained that the Government had held back the report as it reflected on the character of a Native Land Court judge and other officials, who should first have an opportunity to reply to the allegations. Grey retorted that the minister was protecting persons accused by his own departmental officers. He again demanded to know what had become of £700,000 placed at the sole disposal of the Native Minister, implying that it 'had been squandered in a manner in which public moneys had never been squandered before'.

McLean was often absent from the House, sometimes through ill health, but this did not stop Grey from attacking his actions both as minister and as a private individual. Grey's persistent censure finally drew an indignant response from McLean, who said that Grey had singled him out 'for the mask of his displeasure'. This had not surprised him for, from the very first, Grey, rather than work harmoniously, had contrived to quarrel with the leading men of the colony. It was 'always a misfortune to possess so ill balanced a mind as always to surmise evil where none exists'. He deplored Grey's treatment of Lieutenant-Governor Eyre, his vilification of the pioneer missionaries and his perpetual strife with the early settlers. He condemned Grey's clashes with the imperial commanders during the Waikato War, when the interests of both races demanded unity of action.

McLean blamed Grey for failing to foresee the rise of the King movement after the influx of new colonists, or seeing that relations with Maori would change as the missionary influence declined. He thought it

> lamentable to see a gentleman whose talents are so rare and whose career has been so distinguished, descend to small purposes and petty devices. To break down the barriers that divide communities, to inspire a scattered population with common sympathies, to foster a common pride of country and mould them into a united people, an infant nationality. This would have been a work to gild the evening of a political life, to command admiration and enforce respect.

At the end of a long and remarkable official career, he said, Grey remained utterly without friends. 'If I were exempt from the effect of this chronic irritability I should consider myself either too insignificant for the Hon gentleman's notice or of a too compliant a morality, neither of which positions I am desirous to occupy.'[44] Friendship with McLean could not survive if that friend were ever to thwart McLean's plans. This was the case with Henry Russell once he supported the Hawkes Bay Maori in their Repudiation movement; with Colonel Whitmore when he threatened McLean's control of the East Coast campaign; and with Sir George Grey when he attacked McLean's handling and expenditure of native affairs and his private land purchases in Hawkes Bay. There were contradictory elements in McLean's character. His determination always to succeed was in contrast to his essential pragmatism when he settled for what was immediately achievable.

Grey's attacks on McLean in the House became more personal. He charged that McLean had bought native reserve land in Hawkes Bay for his own use and had admitted this. Grey told the House that he himself had bought land for the Crown in Hawkes Bay and advanced money for that purpose, with McLean as his assistant. McLean had heard him tell the natives that the real value he paid them for their land was not the small sum they got but the valuable estates he reserved for them. Grey alleged that McLean had acquired these lands and made himself 'enormously rich at his expense and that of the natives'.[45]

Wearied by ill health, McLean was unable to attend the House himself and counter Grey's charges. He wrote to the Premier, Harry Atkinson, asking him to say that, of all the land bought in Hawkes Bay before Governor Grey left New Zealand in 1853, he had not acquired a single acre. (His first private purchase was in 1857.) Therefore, how could he have become rich at either Grey's or Maori expense? The greater part of the land he acquired in Hawkes Bay he had bought from the Crown, land that was subject to competition at public auction. He had leased land from Maori only after it had passed through the Native Land Court after 1867. These leases he later had purchased on 'fair and acceptable terms'.[46]

Chapter 20
'I Remain Your Sincere Friend'

In November 1873 McLean had felt very much the death of his older brother, Alexander. Such a matter was beyond man's control, he wrote to his sister, Annabella, but he admitted that he was Roman Catholic enough to pray for his soul after death. Nevertheless, he told her that it was 'needless to mourn over the acts of the great power that rules the universe'.[1] At the end of the 1876 parliamentary session, McLean formally submitted his resignation as minister, having advised the Premier some months earlier of his intention.[2] For the previous two years his health had been poor and he had been advised to rest, but he resisted. His sense of public duty had driven him on, for he had unfinished business; to reconcile the Maori tribes to the settlers, and to consolidate the peace.

Moreover, finance had been an ongoing problem for McLean, as his estate carried a high level of debt. Despite boom times with high wool prices, most of his income went towards improving his land or buying more land. He tried to sell an area of rough hill country in Hawkes Bay but failed to find a buyer. In 1876 an Australian, James Armstrong, seeking a pastoral run in New Zealand, bought Akitio in Wairarapa for £35,000. McLean was thus able to reduce his short-term debt and, over the following years, to repay the mortgages on Maraekakaho held by Tollemache and the N.Z. Trust and Loan Company. At last he was free from the burden of debt.[3]

In 1874, after the earlier award of a CMG, McLean had been knighted, an honour for which he believed he was indebted to Sir Thomas Gore Browne. Apart from the recognition accorded two Speakers of the House, David Munro and Francis Dillon Bell, McLean was the first New Zealand politician to receive a knighthood. McLean found time to make his first voyage overseas since arriving in New Zealand in 1840. As Sir Donald McLean KCMG he visited the colonies of New South Wales and Victoria as the representative of the New Zealand Government. McLean had a secret mission. The Premier, Julius Vogel, had sent him to Sydney to raise a loan, but he was unsuccessful. His visit was more rewarding for his private pastoral interests. At the Sydney Exhibition he bought six draught mares and investigated Thomas Mort's pioneering experiments in preserving meat. In Victoria he visited 'splendid farms' and at Learmouth, famous for its stud merinos, he bought fifteen ewes and five rams. These, along with previous purchases, helped to make Maraekakaho merinos among the best in Australasia.[4]

McLean's farewell letter to Maori rangatira before his departure from public office expressed his thanks to those who had supported him in preserving peace and order, but the platitudinous ministerial prose did not really convey the nature of his relationship with the Maori people. It was through their efforts, wrote McLean, that peace and goodwill had prevailed and he earnestly hoped that the friendly relations that existed between the two peoples would never again be disturbed. The present Government's policy, he assured the rangatira, would not differ from that pursued in previous years and he hoped the rangatira would continue to cooperate with the Government in devising and carrying out measures for the benefit of both races. The letter ended:

> I shall watch with interest the progress of the Natives in industrial pursuits and of their children in acquiring a knowledge of the English language that they may be able to avoid such misunderstanding as have often arisen from ignorance of each other's language.
>
> Hoping you will be guided by moderation in the settlement of differences that may arise either with Europeans or other tribes and with best wishes for your welfare
>
> I remain
> Your sincere friend
> Donald McLean

When McLean returned to Hawkes Bay in December 1876 he was an ill man. His intention was to retire to his home on the Napier hill, but in fact he had come home there to die. Ormond and his family had been living in McLean's house at Napier awaiting the completion of their new home at Karamu on the Heretaunga block. Ormond, at his wife's insistence, told McLean in November that they would depart in time for him to return to his own home. Ormond failed to grasp the seriousness of his illness. He thought a rest and the more benign climate of Hawkes Bay would promote a quick recovery. Ormond told McLean that his plan of working with Tawhiao, the Maori King, would have to be deferred until he recovered his strength, 'Then if you see your work to the end yours should be the credit of doing it'. He urged McLean to defer his retirement until they had talked it over. Delay in completing the Karamu house meant that it would be the second week in December before the family could move and Ormond suggested that McLean would not mind waiting a short time. Meanwhile he could stay with Donald Gollan, another Hawkes Bay pastoralist and longtime acquaintance, as 'it would be quite quiet there'.[5]

Early in January 1877 McLean caught a cold. Although he rallied and appeared to recover, he took a turn for the worse at 6 a.m. on 5 January. Now and then he uttered a few words in his native Gaelic. He was attended by a few intimate friends, including the Reverend Samuel Williams who 'administered spiritual consolation'. He was mainly unconscious until he died at 4.10 that afternoon at his home on the Napier hill. The immediate cause of his death was announced in the *Hawke's Bay Herald* as 'a dropsical effusion on the heart and chest'.[6] That Williams, an Anglican missionary, should attend on McLean in his dying hours, rather than the Reverend Dr Sidey, Minister of St Paul's Presbyterian Church, of which McLean was a member, may have aroused comment in Napier. McLean, however, had never had any time for sectarian differences. He had had a long association with Williams from the time of his first purchases in Hawkes Bay, whereas Sidey had only recently been called to St Paul's. Moreover, though he was a foundation member of St Paul's congregation, McLean's ministerial duties kept him from Hawkes Bay and, when he was there, much of his time was spent at Maraekakaho.

On Sunday, 7 January between 2000 and 3000 people, including a considerable number of Maori led by their rangatira Te Hapuku, Tareha and Renata Kawepo, gathered for the funeral at Napier cemetery near McLean's home on the hill. A special train ran from Waipukurau for the country settlers; many more made their way by road. As McLean had been a District Grand Master of the North Island Masonic Lodge, the funeral ceremonies centred on Masonic rites. The arrangements were settled only after bickering among the local Masonic orders. The compromise was for the two local lodges to gather at the Scinde Lodge rooms for the first part of the service, and the funeral procession to be led by members of Victoria Lodge, whose chaplain would conduct the Masonic service at the graveside. The Oddfellows, Foresters, Good Templars and Hibernians marched in the procession but, on reaching the cemetery entrance, found that they were to take no further active part. The Artillery Volunteers and the band prepared to be part of the cortege but were told that they were not wanted, as the McLean family did not wish to have a military funeral. Rangatira who had known McLean since 1851 were refused permission to speak over his grave, being told that this would be contrary to European custom.

At the Napier cemetery, the Reverend Dr Sidey of St Paul's Presbyterian Church conducted the funeral service. The Masonic chaplain told his brethren that 'while we drop a sympathetic tear over the grave of our deceased brother, let us cast around his shortcomings, whatever they may have been, the broad mantle of Masonic charity and not withhold from his memory the commendation which his virtues demand at our hands ... our deceased brother has left behind him a name for amiability, kindliness and love which can never be forgotten in this country'.

The *Hawke's Bay Herald* told its readers that 'we have had many more skillful parliamentarians and many better departmental administrators but we have had no other statesman with anything like the same broad sagacity or the same calm wisdom in emergencies often of a most formidable character which enabled him to guide the infant colony safely through overwhelming seas of trouble and at the same time to subject, without exterminating, the aboriginal inhabitants of the island'.

Ten days after the funeral, some 800 Maori gathered in Clive Square and marched to McLean's Napier hill residence. A 170 strong firing party, led by Reihana, went through their drill and fired five volleys in honour of McLean. Ormond welcomed the rangatira who included Tareha, Renata Kawepo and Te Hapuku, and invited them to speak. The rangatira had two themes: lament for the loss of their greatest friend and protector, and anxiety for a future without McLean and for laws that lay increasingly heavy on Maori. Their eulogies made plain just how much McLean's effectiveness as government official and politician had depended on his personal influence. Tareha paid tribute to McLean,

> Go upon the path that thou hast chosen; go to eternal life ... We tried to devise means when the Europeans first came here whereby we might live amicably with them and make the same law serve us, that we might not go upon separate roads but work together. When McLean came here then I learned this word – we the Maori and European – should live united in peace. Then we tried to carry those plans with the aid of the friend who has departed. We both acted together for the benefit of the people.

Renata Kawepo exclaimed: 'Those Pakeha who are left behind we know not as we knew him.' He recalled that McLean had 'guided the canoe safely through the sea of strife' in the time of war and expressed their fear: 'Shall we hereafter move into a world of darkness? Will you, Ormond, will you, Locke, take Sir Donald's place now he is dead?' Paora Kaiwhata, expressing a sentiment held by other speakers, pleaded that the law be made clear now that McLean was no more: 'Those laws that bear heavily on us, it is for the Europeans to have them repealed. Let us the Maori have also a voice in the framing of the laws.'

The rangatira could speak of McLean as their friend despite his actions that led to the loss of their lands. Their mana was enhanced by their association with this powerful man. Although he adopted a paternal attitude towards Maori as a people, to any individual rangatira he accorded a fundamental respect for his human dignity. He spoke to him as an equal whose company he enjoyed.

When the rangatira had expressed their feelings, Ormond, Douglas McLean and Locke responded. Ormond said that, speaking as one who knew McLean better than any of his European friends, the great object of McLean's life had been to secure peace between the races. Douglas McLean followed, saying that if his father had retired from the Government two years before he might still be alive, but he had decided he had so much still to do for the benefit of the Maori. Therefore, it was the duty of the rangatira to honour his father's name by adhering to the laws they had had a voice in confirming, to send their children to school, to improve their land and to co-operate with the Government in carrying out measures for the benefit of Maori and European so that they might share alike in the wealth and prosperity of the country. 'By doing so you will indeed cherish his memory and raise an imperishable monument to it.'[7]

For McLean's memorial service in St Paul's Presbyterian Church, Napier, the Reverend Dr Sidey took for his text, Ezekiel 19:28 'Her strong rods were withered and broken'. He compared the strong rods that bear rule to the administrators of a country who 'conduct its affairs with wisdom, rectitude and benevolence … Government is an ordinance of God for the good of man.' He identified the qualities of the administrator as 'an intellect of keen insight, a heart of deep emotional sympathy running in the channel of divine and human interests and possessed under consecration of high moral obligation to God and man and specially adapted to engage themselves with matters of an administrative character'. Donald McLean had shown all these attributes he said, and that a very large part of the peace and prosperity of the colony was due to the 'sagacity, the humanity and steadfast dedication to duty of the late Sir Donald McLean … He was indeed a strong rod to bear rule.' There were some who had condemned McLean's native policy and advocated a war of extermination against the native race. It was to McLean's 'eternal honour' that he always opposed this attitude. 'Exterminate man', exclaimed the preacher, 'whence comes any right for one order of man to cherish such a sentiment against another? It embodies the spirit of the demon but not of the man.'

On McLean's Christian faith, Sidey doubted whether McLean was familiar with or cared about theological argument, but he was convinced that his mind ran in the 'common channel of an evangelical faith after the peculiar temperament of the Gaelic race'. Sidey ended by reminding his congregation that two duties devolved on the community: thanksgiving to God in raising such an administrator as Donald McLean and the need to see that fit men succeeded him. A nation reaped as it sowed. If its rulers were strong, the nation would prosper. 'Let us accept our duty and privilege, and act up to our opportunity in securing fit and honourable persons for these positions, and we shall have abundant reason to magnify our God and rejoice in His gifts. May God so help us.'[8] These were sentiments that Donald McLean would have endorsed.

Appendices

APPENDIX 1

Chief Protector of Aborigines: Instructions to Sub-Protector McLean

First.[1] You will consider the varied exercise of your official duties as connected with and based upon the primary intention of H.M. Government in the function of the Department with which you are connected, viz. to watch over the interest, to protect the persons and property, and advance the social and moral improvement of Her Majesty's Aboriginal Subjects.

2ndly.That in order to the more efficient accomplishment of these duties His Excellency has been pleased to divide the Colony into Districts. The Western will be your sphere of action, every inhabited portion of which you will consider it your duty to visit (except in cases where local circumstances may render it impossible) at least once a year.

3rdly. In all native cases, i.e. in disputes and quarrels amongst themselves endeavour in conjunction with the chiefs as far as possible to settle them in accordance with their own customs by compensation. Their more serious disagreements may be settled in accordance with the Native Exemption Ordinance in a Superior Court. There are not likely to be many cases in which reference thereto may be necessary.

4thly. In cases of continued and determined obstinacy, compulsory measures must be gradually but carefully introduced in accordance with the Ordinance. The assistance of the Chiefs must at all times be resorted to.

5thly. To prevent sudden ebullitions of feeling so apt to lead the natives to the Commission of Deeds which their better judgement would disavow, impress upon their minds the necessity of referring all their grievances to you and encourage them at all times to send for you, and as their own customs have from time immemorial taken cognisance of offences (and considered them grave which our Courts scarcely notice) and as these customs help to preserve Society in a healthy state, they will therefore deserve to be treated as gravely by you.

6thly. Impress on their minds the benefits arising from the establishment of a well organised Government amongst them. Let them see the practical results of it.

7thly. By your elevated character elevate theirs. Never descend to their standard but raise them to yours.

8thly. Let them distinctly understand that wars and the practice of Cannibalism must cease, that if persisted in, such conduct will eventually be visited with severe punishment.

9thly. Assure them that protection will invariably be afforded to their property and relieve their minds from any apprehensions that may arise on an increase of a European population by reiterating the assurances of the late Governor Capt. Hobson that in no case should they be deprived of estates and cultivations and that no lands may be taken possession of but those they have or may be willing to alienate.

10thly. Make yourself acquainted with every passing event in the district, note and inform the Head of Department and encourage the natives to write on all subjects.

11thly. Be careful in the reception of native reports of each other where interest or animosity activating them, neither credit all they say nor discredit everything.

12thly. Make great allowances for both Europeans and Natives in their little disputes owing to their ignorance of each others' language but always bear in mind that it characteristic for Europeans to tyrannise and assume a superiority especially when theirs is a difference in the shade of skin, and that he has an advantage in always being able to represent the case in his own language. An honourable union between Natives and European should be encouraged.

13thly. Transmit to me as Head of Department your half yearly report embodying in it statistical accounts of the Natives and Country more especially pointing out the increases or diminution of the Aboriginal population, its causes and whether local or general and its antidote. In addition to such reports you will keep up a regular correspondence with the Department informing me of every important event in reference to both the Natives and the Europeans as far as the Government and the former are likely to be interested by them for which you will be supplied with stationery and books in which you will be particularly careful to preserve a register of all documents you may receive together with an accurate copy of all letters you may transmit. I will embrace the earliest opportunity on the return of His Excellency the Governor of giving you special instructions relative to the choice of Native Reserves in Town and Country sections in and about New Plymouth.

I have the honour to be Sir
Your Obt. Servant
George Clarke
Chief Protector of Aborigines.

APPENDIX 2
Deed Of Sale: Wanganui Block

26 May 1848

Listen all people who see or know of this paper giving up or parting with land. Now we the people of Wanganui of Wangaehu of Kai Iwi consent on behalf of ourselves, our relations, children, and all who may who be descended of us or succeed us to entirely give up all our lands within the boundaries herein after written, the likeness of which is shown on this paper giving up or parting with land to Mr McLean for and on behalf of the Governor of this Island of New Zealand and for all other Governors that may be appointed by the Queen of England to come after him, that is, this land is to be a sure and certain land for ever for the Governor or for such Europeans as he the Governor agrees to give the said land to.

Receipt for 1000 pounds, compensation granted by Commissioner Spain in 1844

And for as much as we have consented to altogether give up our land within the boundaries which shall be presently written; the places made sacred or reserved for ourselves being always excepted; Mr McLean consents on the authority given him by the governor to pay us One Thousand Pounds (1,000) in money, which we have received from the hands of Mr McLean.

Boundaries

Now this is the last or concluding payment which was decided upon by Mr Spain in the Year One thousand eight hundred and forty four (1844) when he held a meeting with the people of Wanganui respecting the land which he then declared should be for the Directors or principal persons of the New Zealand Company and which sum he Mr Spain decided should be given in addition to what was given by Colonel Wakefield the Chief or Principal Agent of the said Company now residing in Port Nicholson and which was paid over by Mr Jerningham Wakefield to some of the Chiefs of Wanganui in the year One thousand eight hundred and forty (1840).

Now these are the boundaries of the land which we give up for ever to Mr McLean for the Governor and which have been shown and pointed out to us by Mr. Wills and Mr. White the Land Surveyors who accompanied Mr. McLean, that:, to Te Munu to Hapameriko and some other people of Kai Iwi to Patarapo to Hoani to Hekenaia to Henari to Taiaroa and also to Takarangi of Tunuhaere to Abraham to te Munu and to some other people of Wangaehu which have been marked by stakes holes and other marks and have been seen by those persons who walked the boundaries. The boundary commences at the mouth of the Mowhanau river and from thence to the stake which was driven by Mr. Wills on the south side of the Mowhanau and crossing that river it goes in direct inland to Wataroa to Matakitaki and crosses the river at Pungawakatere and goes from thence to Otareu and crosses over at Katiaka and goes from thence to Otahakino proceeding thence in a straight line till it crosses the Kai Iwi and from thence until it joins the end of the line at Otawa which was cut by Mr. White and Richard Deighton together with Takarangi and some other natives of Tunuhaere commencing at Otawa it proceeds along Mr.White's line through the woods which are named Tutirara and Tautawai till it reaches the Kahikatea tree named Kiwi and goes thence in a straight line to the river of Wanganui a little distance below the Pa of Tunuhaere and crosses from thence to the first or upper stake of the Native Reserve marked out by Mr.White at Kaiwaiki from thence it proceeds straight to the top of the highest wooded range of hills and continues along the top of that range to Waikupa to the Southern Boundary line cut by Mr. Wills surveyor in the presence of Mr.McLean Abraham and Munu and the Wangaehu Natives who accompanied them and continues along that line by Wakaokao Pukepapa Pukepoto Pirihira till it joins the sea.

Now all the land contained within these boundaries excepting the places mentioned in this paper as reserved for ourselves we have wept over and sighed over bidden farewell to and delivered up for ever to the Europeans; together with the rivers streams trees and all and everything connected with the said land.

Reserve no. 1

1. This is the first reservation for us. All our Eel and Inanga cuts at Wiritoa at Paure at Kaitoke at Okui at Oakura and other streams for fishing Eels within the boundaries which have now been given up to the Europeans.

Reserve No. 2

2. Second. The small wood called "Omanaia" close to the Eastern boundary line which was surveyed by Mr. Wills and shewn by him to Te Munu of Wangaehu and marked on the accompanying plan.

3. Third. A piece of the wood called "Te Marangai" containing nearly eleven acres the boundaries of which have been cut and shewn to the Natives by Mr. Wills surveyor in the presence of Mr. McLean Abraham and Munu of Wangaehu in One thousand eight hundred and forty six (1846) and of Munu and Mr. John Cameron in One thousand eight hundred and forty eight (1840) [*sic*].

4. Fourth. Inland from the Matarawa from the stake "Maungarau-tawiri in the direction of the line staked by Mr. Wills in One thousand eight hundred and forty six (1846) and shewn by him to Abraham Munu and John Williams in the presence of Mr. McLean. We are to be allowed to cultivate and use the timber on the wooded hills towards Waikupa from which the settlers are also to be allowed to cut and take

whatever firewood they may require.

5. Fifth. One section containing one hundred acres of land on the sea side of the lake Paure as marked out by Mr. Wills and shewn to Governor Paipai in the presence of Mr. John Cameron.

6. Sixth. A large block of land in the neighbourhood of Putiki Waranui. These are the boundaries – Commencing at Te Papa on the South bank of the Wanganui river the boundary there is a Mahoe tree shewn by Mr. Wills to George King and other natives of Putiki thence straight along the large survey line which was formerly cut from Te Papa by Colonel Wakefield's surveyor to a high Titoki stake known by the name of George King and driven by Mr.Wills in One thousand eight hundred and forty six (1846) and by him shewn to Maewae and other natives thence along the line cut by Mr. Wills in the direction pointed out by Mawae together with the natives Kemp and ford through the woods (in which numerous trees are marked) and Fern land to a pole known by the name of "Mawae" and driven in by that chief near another large Survey line formerly cut by Colonel Wakefield's surveyors and from that pole straight along the said survey line through the wood named "Te Oa" and through the swamp behind Putiki Waranui straight to the Wanganui River. This land is shewn in the plan given to us by Mr. McLean, however, from this block is excepted a piece of land shewn in the accompanying map and on the map given to us by Mr. McLean and containing about twenty nine (29) acres the properly of Messrs. Taylor and Watt the boundaries of which as marked on the ground by George King, Mawae and other natives have been surveyed by Mr. Wills. Our block exclusive of Taylor and Watt's piece contains One thousand three hundred and two (1302 acres).

7. Seventh. A block adjoining the last mentioned block and containing about six hundred (600) acres commencing at Awarua the mouth of the Waitahanui the boundary goes straight across to the Kaitoke stream thence round by the West side of the Kaitoke lake till it joins the line in the wood on its bank cut by Mr. Wills in one thousand eight hundred and forty six together the native (Kemp) sent by Mawae (in the direction pointed by Kawana Paipai) along that line it goes straight to a Kahikatea tree also pointed by them and continuing straight to a pole driven by Paipai in a hill above the Putiki Swamp thence straight to a pole close to Bell's Bridge on the Waitahanui. This land is shewn on the map given to us by Mr.McLean.

8. Eighth. A piece of land on the Sea side of the Purua stream the boundaries of which as marked by the Tahana and others of the Patutokotoko have been surveyed by Mr. Wills.

9. Ninth. The burial ground fenced in on the sea side of the Mataongaonga creek.

10. Tenth. A block of land about six hundred and fifty (650) acres on the south bank of the Wanganui river commencing at the mouth of the Kutuka stream the boundary goes up that stream to its junction with the Waipukura stream thence it goes up that stream to the end of the line cut in One thousand eight and forty six (1846) by Mr. White on the Makirikiri stream and shown by him to Tamihana and others of the

Patutokotoko Tribe then down the Makirikiri to its junction with Upokongaro and down the Upokongaro to its mouth. This land is shown on the map given to us by Mr. McLean. Also the small patch where the Church and other Native houses are erected the boundaries of which were marked by Tamihana and the Tahana of the Patutokotoko tribe and which patch has been surveyed by Mr. Wills.

11. Eleventh. About one hundred (100) acres of the land at Kaiwaiki which was shown to the Natives of Tunuhaere by Mr. White Surveyor in the year One thousand eight hundred and forty six (1846). This land is also shown on the Map given to us by Mr. McLean.

12. Twelfth. The cultivations on the north side of the Wanganui river from below Tunuhaere to the Kaipua stream the cultivation of Waipuna behind Tunuhaere Also the cultivations at Motuhou and Matakitaki and we will not extend or enlarge these cultivations but shall confine them to their present shape or extent at the date of writing this paper.

13. Thirteenth. We are allowed to cultivate those portions of the wood known as Ngaturi near Tunuhaere which have not been surveyed by the Surveyors for the use of Europeans, it will however rest with the Governor when Europeans settle near this neighbourhood that we the people of Tunuhaere should abandon the last named cultivations lest the Europeans be disturbed by our cultivations because we are provided with a large extent of land beyond the European boundary.

14. Fourteenth. A block of land at Aramoa containing about two hundred and forty 240 acres on the North side of the Wanganui river which has been surveyed and the boundaries pointed out to the Natives by Mr. White Surveyor in the One thousand eight hundred and forty six 1846 but this land is more clearly shown and described on the map given to us by Mr. McLean.

15. Fifteenth. A small patch at Tutaieka namely the burial ground which was marked in the presence of Mr. McLean by Wiremu Eruera and Hoani Rawenata of the Putiki Pa and which was surveyed by Mr. Wills.

Now this assuredly is the last of the lands which shall be reserved or made sacred for us within the boundaries of the Europeans and Mr. McLean consents on the part of the Governor of this Island that these reserves shall be surely and certainly for us for our children and for all our descendants and successors for ever.

And we further agree that we shall not dispose of the said Reserves to the Europeans until the Governor of this Island has consented to our doing so. And we also agree to leave entirely with the Governor of this Island and ourselves the understanding about any future arrangement that is made respecting the large roads which the Governor may hereafter decide on being used as public roads for ourselves and the Europeans within the boundaries of the reserves that are made sacred to us for ever. And forasmuch as we have chosen with Mr. Symond's sanction and consent the Reserves which are written in this paper giving up land in such places as we desired to have reserved we consent to give back to Mr. McLean for the Governor the places which were made sacred for us by Colonel Wakefield and Mr. Spain.

And having fully consented to all the conditions and particulars contained in this paper giving up land which has been publicly read and explained by Mr. McLean we subscribe our names and marks.

And Mr. McLean having also consented on behalf of the Governor to all conditions and particulars contained in this paper his name (Mr. McLean's) is also hereunto subscribed.

Here follow 207 signatures –
On Friday the 26th May 1848 ... 83
On Saturday the 27th May 1848 ... 114
And on Monday the 29th May 1848 ... 18–
the day on which the payment was given and the deed finally executed.

A True Translation.
DONALD MCLEAN, Inspector of Police.

No. 126. Received for Registration at 12 o'clock, noon, 17th November, 1848.
ROBERT R. STRANG,
Registrar of Deeds.

A True Copy of Original Deed, Translation, and Endorsement.
Wellington, August 6th 1875
H. HANSON TURTON

APPENDIX 3
AHURIRI BLOCK DEED OF SALE
17 November 1851

Translation

THIS DEED written on this seventeenth 17 day of November in the year of our Lord one thousand eight hundred and fifty one 1851, is a paper of the full consent of us the chiefs and the people of Ngatikahungunu at this meeting assembled whose names are hereunto subscribed on behalf or ourselves our relations and all our descendants who shall be born after us entirely to give up our land the plan of which is hereunto attached unto Victoria the Queen of England and to the Kings and Queens her successors for ever, and the Queen of England on her part agrees to pay us for the said land the sum of one thousand five hundred pounds 1500 of which monies one thousand pounds 1000 has been paid into your hands on this day by Donald McLean Esquire. The five hundred pounds 500 will be paid to us in the days of November in the year of our Lord one thousand eight and fifty two 1852 as a last instalment for that land for ever.

The Boundaries of the Land

The boundaries of the land as agreed upon by ourselves at our first meetings for negotiations with Mr McLean are these: Commencing at the place where the Tutaekuri and Puremu Rivers discharge themselves into the sea, the boundary runs in the Puremu to Tamihinu on reaching which place it runs in the Tutaekuri to Okahau when it leaves the Tutaekuri and proceeds along the survey line to Tarehas Post at Umukiwi and along the survey line of Mr Park the surveyor and ourselves to Kohurau on reaching which place it proceeds to the confluence of the Waiharakeke and Ngaruroro rivers thence the boundary runs along the ridge of Te Kaweka to the confluence of the Mangatutu and Mohaka Rivers and on in the course of the Mohaka to Mangowhata and on in the Mangowhata Stream to the Taupo road and along the said road to Titiokura and along the said road to Kaiwhaka and in the course of the Kaiwhaka to Opotamanui and thence to Waiohinganga to Whanganui-o-roto thence to our reserve at Te Niho thence to Rere-o-tawaki where our reserve ends, the boundary continues thence to Te Puka and on to the Puremu River. And we will not permit any Native to molest the Europeans within these boundaries.

At former meetings for negotiations between ourselves and Messrs. McLean and Park at Te Awapuni we agreed to entirely give up all the stony spit from Ruahoru to Ahuriri, we also agreed to entirely give up Mataruahou, Pukemokimoki being the only portion of Mataruahou reserved for ourselves, together with a small piece of land where the children and family of Tareha are buried during such time as it remains unoccupied by the Europeans.

Now we have in our assemblies sighed over wept over and bidden farewell to and solemnly consented entirely to give up these lands descended to us from our ancestors with seas rivers waters timbers and all appertaining to the said land to Victoria the Queen of England forever.

Now these are the portions reserved for ourselves:–

1st. The first. The island in the Whanganui-o-rotu lake named Te Roro-o-kuri.

2nd. The second. The portion surveyed by Mr. Park the surveyor named Wharerangi as a lasting possession for ourselves. The boundaries of the said piece of land commence at Te Niho thence along the survey line to Whakamarumaru turning thence to Ahititi on reaching which place it runs along the survey line to Rere-o-tawaki and on to Te Niho.

3rd. The third. Five hundred 500 acres at the place called Puketitiri with a right to snare birds throughout the whole of the forest of Puketitiri.

We also agree that the Queen's line of road may be laid off and constructed through our reserves at such times as the Governor of New Zealand shall see fit to commence such roads.

It is agreed that we shall have an equal right with the Europeans to the fish cockles muscles and other productions of the sea and that our canoes shall be permitted to land at such portions of the town as shall be set apart by the Governor of New Zealand as a landing place for our canoes.

And in testimony of our true assent in the presence of this assembly to all the conditions of this Deed which has this day been read over to us by Donald McLean Esquire we hereunto sign our names and marks.

And in testimony of the consent of the Queen of England to all the conditions of this Deed the name of Donald McLean the Government Land Commissioner is hereunto affixed.

(Signed) DONALD McLEAN
Land Commissioner
(Signed) TAREHA x his mark.
PAORA TOROTORO
KARANAMA TE NAHU x
and 297 other signatures.

Witnesses to these payments and to these signatures –
(Sd.) Robert Park, Government Surveyor.
Alex. Alexander, Settler.
Edward Spence Curling, Settler.

Frederick Sedgwick Abbott, Settler.
Wiremu Tako, Wellington Chief.
James Buchanan McKain.
C.L.H. Pelichet, Assistant Surveyor.
James Williamson, Clerk.
J.Thomas, J.P.

True Translation
(Sd.) Wm. B. BAKER
for the Chief Commissioner.

A True Copy of Original Deed and Translation.
H. HANSON TURTON.

Wellington, 17 February, 1876

APPENDIX 4
Land Purchase Reserves

The reserved portions should bear in each case a definite proportion to the extent ceded.[2] Three tenths of the whole would probably sufficient for the wants of the original proprietors. This should include the villages, cultivations, sacred places and land in actual occupation.

Prior to the cession of any block the name of any individual having a direct claim might be registered with a view to granted in [...]lty wherever considered expedient to do so. The parties or persons appointed on their behalf should make selections out of town and country land under regulations made on their behalf.

In fixing the quantity to be granted to each individual regard should be had to the rank of the grantee. I would suggest four classes:

First class to comprise principal chiefs
Second class, the younger chiefs
Third class, Wives of chiefs
Children of chiefs
Freemen
Fourth class, Wives of freemen
Children of freemen

Assuming that two out of three-tenths of the land reserved for native purposes would be available for grant to individuals, the following apportionment among the four classes above mentioned might be adopted.

To 1st. class Chiefs	one fifth
2nd. class chiefs	one fifth
3rd. class	two fifths
4th class	one fifth

The native population of this island is estimated at between 50,000 and 60,000 and its area about 26,000,000 acres This gives in round numbers nearly 500 acres to each individual. In the Auckland province however, the native population is greater in proportion to the extent of land and this would be scarcely 400 acres each, or 125 souls to every 50,000 acres Classified the numbers in each class would probably stand thus

1st. Class Principal chiefs	3
2nd. Class Young chiefs	7

3rd. Class	Wives of chiefs	9	
	Children	9	55
	Freemen	37	
4th. Class	Wives of Freemen	30	50
	Children of Freemen	30	
		125	

If allotments were made to each of these individuals according to the scale suggested above the grants to each out of a block of 50,000 acres would be as follows:
Two tenths of 50,000 acres – 10,000 acres

For each individual of class		666 acres
———	of 2nd. class	266
———	of 3rd. class	73
———	of 4th. class	33

I do not propose that any undeviating rule should be laid down. The utmost latitude and fullest discretionary power should be given to those who may be charged with carrying out of any system of dealing with native lands. The foregoing figures may, however, serve to show the proportions existing between the numbers of the native population, the territory they hold and the portion of it which should be secured to them.

With respect to native lands in the northern and settled portion of this province the mode of dealing with them proposed by Your Excellency appears to me to fully to meet the necessities of the case. As a general principle I think the commutation of native title objectionable. At the same time I think the Governor should have the power of reconveying by grant from the Crown land ceded for the purpose ...

APPENDIX 5

McLean's Wairarapa Land Purchases 1853–1854[3]

1853

	Block	*Acre*	*Price (pounds)*
June	Castlepoint	275,000	2,500
Aug	Homestead blocks		
Sep	Western Lake	200,000	1,200
	Eastern Lake	120,000	1,100
	Tuhitatara	40,000	1,000
	Tauherenikau	430,000	2,000
Oct	Whawhanui	40,000	1,000
	Pahawa	250,000	700
Nov	Waihora	12,000	300
Dec	Whareama (4 blocks)	188,000	1,000
	'Manawatu'	100,000	800
	Kuratawhiti (Greytown)	4,000	220
	Owhanga (Featherston)	18,000	1,000
	Kaiwhata	10,000	270

1854

Jan	Te Awaite	100,000	1,500
	Wharekaka	40,000	2,000
	Ahiaruhe	5,000	500
	Smith's	6,000	500
	Kuhangawariwari	150,000	1,500
	Awhea/Whawhanui	15,000	400

APPENDIX 6

Major Hawkes Bay Land Purchases 1851–1861[4]

Block	*Acreage*	*Date*	*Signatures*	*Price (pounds)*	*Reserves*
Waipukurau	279,000	4/11/51	276	4,800	4,378
Ahuriri	265,000	17/11/51	300	1,500	2,415
Mohaka	85,700	5/12/51	240	800	100
Tautane 1st		3/1/54	32	1,000	1,050
2nd	70,000	11/3/58	90	500	
3rd		26/1/63	Karaitiana	150	
Okawa	16,000	17/1/54	4	800	
		7/6/59	2	50	
Kahuranaki	22,000	9/1/54	4	1,100	
Matau a Maui	29,000	28/3/55	33	2,000	300
		24/2/57	11	1,000	
Te Mata	16,000	13/4/55	12	500	5,120
		13/11/56	10	500	
Ruahine					
Ruataniwha N.	130,000	1855–59		10,500	3,100
Te Totara	26,000	28/8/55	3	1,300	
Ruataniwha S.	31,000	1855	3		
		22/3/56	90	1,200	
Aorangi	38,000	22/3/56	88	2,000	803
Maraekakaho	30,000	20/11/56	18		
		4/7/57	16	1,000	
Ruahine bush	100,000	13/7/57	128	3,000	
Otaranga	50,000	15/3/57	27	1,000	
Porangahau	145,000	10/3/58	83	3,000	276
Omarutaiari	11,700	1858	1	100	
(Takapau)		16/7/59	2	50	
		12/8/59	4	400	1,000
Middle-south	16,000	18/7/59	2	400	1,300
Porangahau					
Kaweka	50,000	1859–75		430	
Moeangiangi	12,000	7/7/59	15	310	200

Glossary

aukati	a line across which the movement of people is ritually restricted
hapu	sub-tribe
iwi	tribe
kupapa	government supporters, neutral
mana	prestige, authority
pa	fortified village
Pakeha	European
puremu	adultery
rangatira	chief
runanga	council
taihoa	wait
tino rangatiratanga	chieftainship
utu	reciprocity, recompense, revenge
whenua	land

Notes

Chapter 1

1 L. Colley, *Britons: Forging the Nation 1707–1837* (London, 1996), 111.
2 Ibid., 139.
3 James Belich, *Making Peoples: A History of the New Zealanders from Polynesian Settlement to the End of the Nineteenth Century* (Auckland, 1996), 191.
4 Ibid., 186.
5 T. C. Smout, *A History of the Scottish People 1560–1830* (London, 1986), 186.
6 M. N. D. Campbell, 'The Evolution of The Hawkes Bay Landed Society 1850–1914', (PhD thesis, Victoria University of Wellington, 1973).
7 Smout, *A History of the Scottish People*, 209–11.
8 Ibid., 336.
9 The birth record of his daughter in 1824 no longer identifies him as a tacksman as with his older children.
10 Annabella McLean to Donald McLean, 13 Sep 1849, McLean Papers, MS 32/427.
11 Jan 1877, McLean Papers, MS 32/732.
12 McLean to Provost Lumsden, 18 Aug 1846, McLean Papers, MS 1308.
13 McLean, Diary, 18 Dec 1858, McLean Papers.
14 D. McColl to Mr McLean, 22 Jun 1840, McLean Papers, MS 32/405.
15 McLean, Account Book, 1842, McLean Papers, MS 1192.
16 J. H. Townsend to D. McLean, 14 Feb 1846, McLean Papers, MS 32/606.
17 Ibid.
18 Ibid., 1854.
19 William Colenso, Diary, 13 Mar 1846, quoted in A. G. Bagnall, *Wairarapa: An Historical Excursion* (Masterton, 1976), 196.
20 McLean to Charles Morison, 8 Jan 1846, McLean Papers, MS 32/761.
21 John McLean to Donald McLean, 5 Dec 1844, McLean Papers, MS 1306.
22 Morison to McLean, 1847, McLean Papers, MS 32/461.
23 Abercrombie to McLean, 29 Aug 1847, McLean Papers, MS 32/141.
24 Ibid., 19 May 1858.

Chapter 2

1 McLean to Sinclair, McLean Papers, MS 32/574.
2 McLean to Revd D. McColl, 31 Oct 1854, McLean Papers, MS 32/405.
3 Normanby to Hobson, 14 Aug 1839. *Speeches and Documents on New Zealand History*. ed. W. J. McIntyre and W. J. Gardner (Oxford, 1971).
4 Ibid.

5 Ibid.
6 Ibid.
7 Ibid.
8 Ibid.
9 Ibid.
10 McLean to Clarke, Report, 11 May 1844, Official Papers, Protector of Aborigines, McLean Papers, MS 32/1.
11 Clarke to McLean, 8 July 1844, McLean Papers, MS 32/1.
12 Clarke to McLean, 2 Aug 1844, Protector's Office, McLean Papers, MS 32/1.
13 McLean, Diary, 11 May 1846, McLean Papers, MS 1284.
14 Clarke to McLean, 3 Aug 1844, McLean Papers, MS 32/215.
15 Ibid., 13 Sep 1845.
16 Ibid., 11 Mar 1845.
17 Ibid., 13 Sep 1845.
18 Sinclair to McLean, 16 Sep 1844, McLean Papers, MS 32/574.
19 Clarke to McLean, 26 Oct 1844, McLean Papers, MS 1306.
20 Sinclair to McLean, 13 Sep 1845, McLean Papers, MS 32/574.
21 McLean, Diary, 26 Aug 1844, McLean Papers, MS 1284.
22 McLean to FitzRoy, Report, 8 Nov 1844, McLean Papers, MS 32/6.
23 McLean, Diary, 9 Sep 1844, McLean Papers, MS 1284.
24 Ibid., 27 Sep 1844.
25 Ibid., 16 Sep 1844.
26 Ibid., 13 Nov 1844.
27 McLean, Diary, 7 Jan 1845, McLean Papers, MS 1284.
28 Ian Wards, *The Shadow of the Land* (Wellington, 1968), 314.
29 Revd R. Taylor, Journal, 5 Jan 1845, vol. 4, Taylor Papers, MS 245. A copy of this section of Taylor's Journal has been included in the McLean Papers. This has caused some confusion, especially in the typescript copy, as the views expressed appear to be those of McLean, rather than those of the missionary.
30 McLean, Diary, 26 May 1846, McLean Papers, MS 1284.
31 Ibid., 7 Oct 1844.
32 W. J. W. Hamilton, Diary, 24 Nov 1844, MS 2302, ATL.
33 McLean, Diary, 29 Apr 1845, McLean Papers, MS 1284.
34 Ibid., 27 Apr 1845.
35 McLean to Clarke, 5 May 1845, McLean Papers, MS 32/2.
36 McLean, Diary, 19 Nov 1845, McLean Papers, MS 1284.
37 Ibid., 12 Nov 1845.
38 Ibid., 22 May 1845.
39 Ibid., 26 Nov 1845.
40 McLean, Diary, 22 May 1845, McLean Papers, MS 32/741.
41 Ibid., 22 Dec 1845.
42 Ibid., 25–26 May 1845.
43 McLean, Diary, 26 Nov 1845, McLean Papers, MS 1284.
44 Alan Ward, *A Show of Justice: Racial 'Amalgamation' in Nineteenth Century New Zealand* (Auckland, 1973), 73.
45 Clarke to McLean, 7 Feb 1846, McLean Papers, MS 1308.
46 Ward, *A Show of Justice*, 73.
47 McLean, Diary, 17 Feb 1846, McLean Papers, MS 1284.
48 New Plymouth settlers to Gov. Grey, 9 Apr 1846, McLean Papers.

49 McLean, Diary, 7 Jan 1847, McLean Papers.
50 McLean, Diary, 7 Feb 1846, McLean Papers, MS 1200.
51 McLean, Diary, 21 Mar 1846, McLean Papers.

Chapter 3

1 McLean to Clarke, 22 Aug 1846, McLean Papers, MS 1308.
2 McLean, Diary, 27 Apr 1846, McLean Papers, MS 1284.
3 James Belich, 'The Governors and the Maori', in Keith Sinclair ed., *The Oxford Illustrated History of New Zealand*, Auckland, 1990, 86.
4 W. K. Hancock, *Argument Of Empire* (London 1943), chapter 7.
5 Ward, *A Show of Justice*, 20–21.
6 M. P. K. Sorrenson, *Maori Origins and Migrations* (Auckland, 1979), 85.
7 J. Rutherford, *Sir George Grey K. C. B. 1812–1898: A Study in Colonial Government* (London 1961), chapters 15 and 16.
8 Richard S. Hill, *Policing the Colonial Frontier: The Theory and Practice of Coercive Social and Racial Control in New Zealand 1767–1867* (Wellington, 1986), 251.
9 McLean, Diary, 8 Jun 1846, McLean Papers, MS 1284.
10 McLean, Diary, 26 May 1846, McLean Papers, MS 1284.
11 Ibid., 26 May 1846.
12 McLean to Halse, 19 Dec 1846, McLean Papers, MS 1308.
13 McLean, Journal, 4 Mar 1847, McLean Papers, MS 1285.
14 Hill, *Policing the Colonial Frontier*, 269.
15 McLean, Journal, 8 Jan 1847, McLean Papers, MS 1285.
16 G. S. Cooper to Colonial Secretary, Report, 29 Apr 1854, McLean Papers, MS 32/124.
17 H. Halse to McLean, 31 Mar 1851, McLean Papers, MS 1314.
18 H. Halse to McLean, 17 Sep 1850, McLean Papers, MS 1312.
19 Hill, *Policing the Colonial Frontier*, 261.
20 Helen Wilson to McLean, 19 May 1846, McLean Papers, MS 32/644.
21 Ward, *A Show Of Justice*, 57.
22 H. Halse to McLean, 26 Oct 1850, McLean Papers, MS 1313.
23 Grey to Gladstone, 24 Jun 1846, *GBPP*.
24 McLean, Diary, 21 Mar 1846, McLean Papers, MS 1284.
25 Ibid., 2 May 1846.
26 Ibid., 4 May 1846.
27 Ibid., 12 May 1846.
28 Ibid., 5 Jun 1846.
29 Ibid.
30 McLean to Revd Taylor, 24 Apr 1847, McLean Papers, MS 1309.
31 McLean, Diary, 10 Jun 1847, Mclean Papers.
32 Jno. Cameron to McLean, 13 Jun 1847, McLean Papers, MS 1309.
33 This was a slip on McLean's part. Te Mamaku's principal people were Ngati Haua.
34 McLean to Lt. Gov. Eyre, 24 Apr 1848, McLean Papers, MS 1310.
35 Wards, *Shadow of the Land*, 349.
36 McLean, Diary, 11 Mar 1848, MS 1285.
37 David Young, *Woven By Water* (Wellington, 1998), 41.
38 Report of McLean on Wanganui Purchase 1848, *AJHR* 1861, C1.

39 Ibid.
40 Sinclair to McLean, 3 Jul 1848, McLean Papers, MS 1310.
41 Report of McLean on Wanganui Purchase 1848, *AJHR* 1861, C1.
42 McLean, Diary, 20 Jul 1848, McLean Papers.
43 McLean to McColl, 7 Oct 1848. McLean Papers MS 32/124.
44 John Jackson to Lieut-Gov Eyre, 14 Oct 1850, McLean Papers MS 32/124.
45 Draft reply by McLean, 24 Dec 1850, McLean Papers MS 32/124.
46 McLean, Diary, 28 Nov 1845, McLean Papers MS 1284.
47 Ibid., 26 Dec 1846.
48 McLean, Diary, 11 Jan 1849, McLean Papers, MS 32/741.
49 Annabella McLean to Donald McLean, 1847, McLean Papers, MS 32/427.
50 McLean, Diary, 8 Jan 1849 MS 1285.

Chapter 4

1 Though aware of the distinction between iwi and hapu, McLean often used the term to apply to either.
2 Alan Ward, *Rangahaua Whanui National Overview Report*, vol. 2 (Wellington, 1997), 8.
3 McLean, Diary, 2 Nov 1847, McLean Papers, MS 1286.
4 Ibid.
5 McLean, Diary, 4 May 1848, McLean Papers, MS 1285.
6 George Clarke, Notes on Early Life in New Zealand, quoted in E. W. Wilson, *Land Problems of the New Zealand Settlers in the Forties*, 119.
7 McLean to Lieut-Gov. Eyre, Report, 25 Oct 1849, McLean Papers, MS 32/12.
8 McLean, Diary, 21 Mar 1846, McLean Papers, MS 1284.
9 McLean, Undated draft, McLean Papers, MS 32/12.
10 Gladstone, 2 Jul 1846, cit. J. Rutherford, *Sir George Grey*, 176.
11 McLean to Colonial Secretary, 1 Feb 1847, Letter Books, Police and Native Land Purchase Department, McLean Papers, qMS 1206.
12 Ibid., 9 Dec 1846.
13 Ihaia to McLean, 24 Jan 1847.
14 Ibid., 5 Jan 1847.
15 McLean, Journal, 4 Mar 1847. McLean Papers, MS 1285.
16 McLean, Journal, 5–6 Mar 1847, McLean Papers, MS 1285.
17 Memo from Gov. Grey, 5 Mar 1847, McLean Papers, MS 32/16.
18 McLean to Thatcher, 30 Mar 1847, McLean Papers, MS 1309.
19 McLean, Diary, 17 Apr 1847, McLean Papers, MS 1285.
20 Ibid., 19 Apr 1847.
21 Ibid.
22 McLean to Gov. Grey, 12 Dec 1848, G13/1/39, NA.
23 Ibid.
24 Ibid., 13 Dec 1848.
25 McLean, Diary, 8 Jan 1848, McLean Papers, MS 1285.
26 McLean to Colonial Secretary, 10 Nov 1847, Letter Books, Police and Native Land Purchase Departments, McLean Papers, qMS 1211.
27 McLean to Grey, 4 Dec 1847, McLean Papers, MS 1310.
28 McLean, Diary, 8 Jan 1848, McLean Papers, MS 1285.

29 Ibid., 15 Mar 1848.
30 McLean to Eyre, 5 Apr 1848, McLean Papers, MS 32/12.
31 Ibid., 6 Apr 1848.
32 Keith Sinclair, *The Origins of the Maori Wars* (Auckland 1952), 197.
33 J. E. Gorst, *The Maori King*, 134. Copy with Gore Browne's annotation, ATL MS 0860.
34 McLean to Lieut-Gov. Eyre, 10 May 1848, McLean Papers, MS 32/124.
35 McLean, Journal, 14 Mar 1848. McLean Papers MS 1285.
36 Te Heuheu Iwikau to McLean, Pukawa, 5 Dec 1848, McLean Papers.
37 McLean, Diary, Jan 1849, McLean Papers, MS 1285.
38 McLean, Journal, 22 Feb 1849, McLean Papers, MS 1285.
39 Quoted in J. C. Wilson, *Early Rangitikei* (Christchurch 1976) Ch. 6 passim.
40 McLean to Grey, 23 May 1849, Letter Book, 1846–1852, McLean Papers, qMS 1209.
41 McLean to Colonial Secretary, Report, 21 May 1849, McLean Papers, MS 32/3.
42 McLean to Colonial Secretary, 12 Aug 1850, McLean Papers, MS 32/4.
43 Ibid.
44 McLean was mistaken. Te Oti Pohe was of the Ngati Rangi, Ngati Tama and Ngati Whiti peoples of Murimotu, the central North Island region south of Mt Ruapehu.
45 McLean, Diary, 12 Jun 1849, McLean Papers, MS 1285.
46 Ibid., 14 Jun 1849.
47 Ibid., 25 Oct 1849.
48 McLean, Diary, 17 May 1851, McLean Papers, MS 1286.
49 Ibid., 1 Jan 1850.
50 Ibid., 31 Mar 1850.
51 Ibid., 1 Apr 1850.
52 Ibid., 30 Apr 1850.
53 Ibid., 4 May 1850.
54 Ibid., 19 Apr 1850.
55 Ibid., 5 Oct 1850.
56 Ibid., 21 June 1851.
57 McLean to Grey, Report, 9 Nov 1850, McLean Papers, MS 32/127.
58 Thos. King to McLean, 14 Nov 1850, McLean Papers, MS 1313.

Chapter 5

1 A. J. Harrop, *England and the Maori Wars*, 56.
2 Tareha and others to Grey, 26 Apr 1849. S. McHugh, quoted in evidence before Waitangi Tribunal, Wai-119-201.
3 Colenso, Journal, 22 Dec 1848, vol. 1, 137, ATL.
4 McLean to Domett, 24 Aug 1850, G7/12 75 NA. S. McHugh, quoted in evidence before Waitangi Tribunal, Wai-119-201.
5 McLean, Diary, 5 Dec 1850, McLean Papers.
6 Ibid., 11 Dec 1850.
7 Ibid., 25 Dec 1850.
8 Ibid., 14 Dec 1850.
9 Ibid., 16 Dec 1850.
10 Ibid., 8 Jan 1851.
11 Ibid., 18 Dec 1850.

12 Ibid., 20 Dec 1850.
13 Ibid., 25 Dec 1850.
14 Ibid., 24 Dec 1850.
15 Ibid., 23 Dec 1850.
16 Ibid., 8 Apr 1851.
17 Ibid., 22 Dec 1850.
18 Ibid., 25 Dec 1850.
19 Ibid., 31 Dec 1850.
20 Ibid., 10 Jan 1851.
21 Ibid., 17 Mar 1851.
22 Ibid., 9 Jan 1851.
23 P. J. Goldsmith, 'Aspects of the Life of William Colenso' (MA thesis University of Auckland 1995), chapter 2.
24 McLean, Diary, 7 Jan 1851, McLean Papers, MS 1286.
25 Dean Cowie, *Rangahaua Whanui District 11B: Hawkes Bay* (Wellington, 1996), 28.
26 McLean, Diary, 29 and 31 Jan 1851, McLean Papers, MS 1286.
27 Ibid., 1 Feb 1851.
28 Ibid., 8 Jan 1851.
29 Ibid., 19 Mar 1851.
30 Ibid., 16 Jan 1851.
31 Ibid., 4 May 1851.
32 Ibid., 26 Mar 1851.
33 Cowie, *Hawkes Bay*, 28.
34 McLean, Diary, 28 Mar 1851, McLean Papers, MS 1286.
35 Ibid., 8 Apr 1851.
36 Ibid., 16 Apr 1851.
37 Angela Ballara, *Iwi: The Dynamics of Maori Tribal Organisation from c.1769 to c.1945* (Wellington 1998), 82.
38 McLean, Diary, 17 Apr 1851, McLean Papers, MS 1286.
39 Ibid.
40 Ibid., 5 Apr 1851.
41 Ibid., 2 May 1851.
42 Ibid., Oct 1851.
43 Ibid., 8 Oct 1851.
44 Ibid., 29 Oct 1851.
45 Ibid., 5 Nov 1851.
46 Ibid., 6 Nov 1851.
47 Ibid., 7 Nov 1851.
48 Ibid., 11 Nov 1851.
49 Ibid., 14 Nov 1851.
50 Cowie, *Hawkes Bay*, 51.
51 McLean, Diary, 17 Nov 1851, McLean Papers, MS 1287.
52 Ibid.
53 Ibid., 23 Nov 1851.
54 Waitangi Tribunal, *Te Whanganui-a-Orotu Report*, (Wellington, 1995), 45.
55 McLean's draft notes for his report, 27 Dec 1851, McLean Papers, MS 1287.
56 Vincent O'Malley, 'The Ahuriri Purchase', 162–67.
57 *NZPD*, 1875.
58 Cooper to McLean, 20 Jun 1861, ATL.

59 Cooper to McLean, 19 Mar 1860, McLean Papers, MS 1322.
60 McLean, Dairy, 20 Nov 1851, McLean Papers, MS 1287.
61 Ibid., 8 Dec 1851.

Chapter 6

1 McLean, Diary, 11 Jan 1849, McLean Papers, MS 32/741.
2 McLean to Susan Strang, 25 Jul 1849, McLean Papers, MS 32/826.
3 Ibid., 2 Jul 1850.
4 Ibid., 17 Sep 1850.
5 B. C. Parr, 'The McLean Estates: a study of pastoral finance and estate management in New Zealand 1853–1891' (MA thesis: University of Auckland 1970), 8.
6 McLean and his party halted for the first night at Buck's Hotel at Taita.
7 McLean to Susan, 30 Sep 1851, McLean Papers, MS 32/826.
8 McLean, Diary, 30 Sept 1851, McLean Papers, MS 1286.
9 McLean to Susan, 6 Oct 1851, McLean Papers MS 32/826.
10 Ibid.
11 Ibid., 15 Nov 1851.
12 Ibid., 16 Nov 1851.
13 McLean, Diary, 15 Dec 1851, McLean Papers MS 1287.
14 Ibid.
15 Ibid., 2 Nov 1851.
16 McLean, Diary, 23 Nov 1851, McLean Papers MS 1286.
17 See Raewyn Dalziel, 'Making us one': courtship and marriage in colonial New Zealand, in *The Turnbull Library Record*, vol. 19 no.1, May 1986.
18 McLean to Susan, 14 Jan 1852, McLean Papers, MS 32/826.
19 Ibid., 16 Jan 1852.
20 Ibid., 24 May 1852.
21 Ibid., 30 Jul 1852, McLean Papers, MS 32/827.
22 Susan to McLean, 24 Aug 1852, McLean Papers, MS 32/828.
23 McLean to Susan, 7 Aug 1852, McLean Papers, MS 32/827.
24 Ibid., 13 Aug 1852.
25 McLean to Susan, 14 Apr 1851, McLean Papers MS 32/827.
26 Susan to McLean, 28 [24?] Aug 1852, McLean Papers, MS 32/828.
27 McLean, Diary, 7 Nov 1852.
28 McLean, Diary, 24 Nov 1853.
29 McLean to Revd Donald McColl, 4 Aug 1853, McLean Papers, MS 32/405.
30 Rosemary Rolleston and Ormond Wilson, *The Master: J. D. Ormond of Wallingford* (Wellington 1980), 61.

Chapter 7

1 Belich, *Making Peoples*, 216–17.
2 McLean to Colonial Secretary, 5 Aug 1852, McLean Papers, MS 1315.
3 McLean to Cooper, 16 Aug 1852, McLean Papers, MS 1315.

4 Te Puni to McLean, 18 Oct 1852, McLean Papers, MS 1315.
5 McLean to Grey, 24 Aug 1852, McLean Papers, MS 1315.
6 Parata Te Huia to Cooper, 24 Jun 1852, McLean Papers, MS 1315.
7 Cooper to Parata, 26 Jun 1852, McLean Papers, MS 1315.
8 Cooper to McLean, 28 Oct 1852, McLean Papers, MS 1315.
9 Hill, *Policing the Colonial Frontier*, 274.
10 McLean to Cooper, 27 Mar 1854, McLean Papers, MS 1316.
11 Wilson to McLean, 6 Aug 1854, McLean Papers, MS 1317.
12 W. Halse to McLean, 7 Aug 1854, McLean Papers, MS 1317.
13 Turton to McLean, 8 Aug 1854, McLean Papers, MS 1317.
14 Cooper to McLean, 24 Aug 1854, McLean Papers, MS 1317.
15 McLean to Colonial Secretary, 11 Apr 1853, McLean Papers, MS 1316.
16 Cooper to McLean, 26 Aug 1853, McLean Papers, MS 1316.
17 Halse to McLean, 17 Oct 1853, McLean Papers, MS 1316.
18 Te Hapuku to McLean, 20 Mar 1852, McLean Papers, MS 1315.
19 Russell to McLean, 1 Aug 1853, McLean Papers, MS 1316.
20 McLean to Grey, 17 Sep 1853, McLean Papers, MS 32/4.
21 Rutherford, *Sir George Grey*, 284.
22 McLean to Grey, 17 Sep 1853, McLean Papers, MS 32/4.
23 Ibid.
24 McLean, Diary, Porangahau, 24 Nov 1853, McLean Papers, MS 1287.

Chapter 8

1 McLean to Revd Donald McColl, 8 Jul 1856, McLean Papers, MS 32/405
2 Votes and Proceedings of the House of Representatives 1854 Session 2 p.3
3 H. Turton, An Epitome of Official Documents Relative to Native Affairs and Land Purchases in the North Island of New Zealand, No. 50, 15 Jun 1854.
4 Ward, *A Show of Justice*, 97.
5 McLean to Colonial Secretary, 29 July 1854, in Turton, Epitome, No. 41.
6 B. Rigby and J. Konig, Muriwhenua Land Claim: A Preliminary Report on Historical Evidence, 128–9.
7 McLean to Kemp, 17 Nov 1855, *AJHR* 1861 C1 No. 6.
8 McLean to Donald McColl, 31 Oct 1854, McLean Papers, MS 32/405.
9 Gore Browne to Gairdner, 22 Mar 1855, Gore Browne Letter Book, MS 284, ATL.
10 McLean to Colonial Secretary, 30 Aug 1855, in Turton, Epitome.
11 McLean, Draft memo to Governor, undated, McLean Papers, MS 1299.
12 Henry Sewell, *Journal of Henry Sewell* vol. 2, ed. W. D. McIntyre, 263.
13 McLean to Smith, 9 Sep 1856, McLean Papers, qms 1839.
14 Sewell, 26 Aug 1856, *Journal of Henry Sewell* vol. 2, ed. W. D. McIntyre, 263.
15 McLean, Memo, 13 Dec 1856, McLean Papers, MS 32/9.
16 T. H. Smith to McLean, 15 Feb 1858, McLean Papers, MS 1320.
17 Gore Browne, Annotations to J. E. Gorst's *The Maori King* 112–13, MS 0860, ATL.
18 Gore Browne to Merivale, 2 Jun 1856, Gore Browne Letter Books, MS 284.
19 *GBPP*, vol. 47.
20 Native Department Chief Commissioner to Governor, 14 Apr 1856, McLean Papers, MS 32/9.

21 Gore Browne to Merivale, 15 Oct 1856, Gore Browne Letter Books, MS 284.
22 McLean to Governor, Memo, 4 Sep 1856, McLean Papers, MS 32/9.
23 J. E. FitzGerald to McLean, 16 Aug 1856, McLean Papers, MS 1301.
24 McLean to J. E. F. [FitzGerald], 16 Aug 1856, McLean Papers, MS 1318.
25 J. E. FitzGerald to McLean, 16 Aug 1856, McLean Papers, MS 1301.
26 C. O. Davis to McLean, 23 Feb 1856, McLean Papers, MS 1318.
27 R. Taylor to McLean, 17 Oct 1856, McLean Papers, MS 32/600.
28 R. Taylor to McLean, 21 May 1857, McLean Papers, MS 1319.
29 Ibid., 21 May 1857.
30 McLean to Governor, Memo, 17 Dec 1856, McLean Papers, MS 1318.
31 McLean to Governor, 21 Apr 1856, in Turton, Epitome, No. 53.
32 McLean to Governor, 20 Mar 1857, in Turton, Epitome, No. 51.
33 McLean to Kemp, *AJHR* 1861 C1, quoted in Rigby and Konig, 127.
34 McLean to Governor, 21 Apr 1856, in Turton, Epitome, No. 53.

Chapter 9

1 F. Dillon Bell to C. W. Richmond, 21 Mar 1858, Msy 2773, Richmond Papers, ATL.
2 Ibid.
3 Gore Browne to Gairdner, Gore Browne Letter Book, MS 284.
4 McLean to C. W. Richmond, 11 Apr 1857, McLean Papers, MS 32/5.
5 Ibid.
6 Gore Browne to Ball, Colonial Office, 26 Aug 1857, Gore Browne Letter Books, MS 284.
7 T. H. Smith to Governor, 21 Nov 1859, McLean Papers, MS 32/9.
8 Gore Browne to Gairdner, 26 Oct 1858, Gore Browne Letter Books, MS 284.
9 Memo from McLean in response to Ministers' memo, 29 Sep 1858, McLean Papers, MS 32/9.
10 Ibid.
11 Draft memo, undated, McLean Papers.
12 McLean Diary, 6 Apr 1853, McLean Papers.
13 McLean, Diary, 16 Jan 1851, McLean Papers, MS 1286.
14 Undated memo, McLean Papers.
15 McLean, Diary, 15 Apr 1855.
16 McLean to Mr Lewis, 6 Sep 1866, McLean Papers, MS 1300.

Chapter 10

1 Revd S. Williams, *The New Zealander*, 11 May 1861.
2 H. G. Miller, in I. L. G. Sutherland ed., *The Maori People Today* (Christchurch, 1940) 88–89.
3 *AJHR* 1860, E4, 11.
4 McLean to Sinclair, Colonial Secretary, 6 Dec 1854, Sinclair Papers, ATL.
5 Searancke to McLean, 9 Jul 1858, McLean Papers, MS 32/565.
6 McLean to Cooper, 15 Sep 1855, *AJHR* 1861.

7 Cooper paid the final instalments on the West Lake (£500) and East Lake blocks (£400) and on Kawawhawhanui (£400) and Kuhangawariwari (£100). The signatures to these deeds were few: eleven, seventeen, four and two respectively.
8 McLean to Cooper, 15 Mar 1856, McLean Papers, MS 1318.
9 Cooper to McLean, 19 Apr 1856, McLean Papers MS 32/227.
10 H. Evison, *Te Wai Pounamu*, 354.
11 G. A. Phillipson, *Rangahaua Whanui District 13: The Northern South Island* (Wellington, 1996) 127–84.
12 McLean, 30 Jan 1856, McLean Papers, MS 1318.
13 McLean 9 Feb 1856, McLean Papers, MS 1318.
14 Ibid.
15 *Dictionary of New Zealand Biography* vol. 1, 252.
16 *GBPP*, vol. 47.
17 McLean to Grey, 1852, *AJHR* 1862 C1, No. 11.
18 Bagnall, *Wairarapa*, 97.
19 Paul Goldsmith, *Rangahaua Whanui District 11A: Wairarapa* (Wellington, 1996), 23.
20 Ibid., 22–23.
21 Ibid.
22 Barry Rigby, *Report to Waitangi Tribunal on Wairarapa Crown Purchases 1853–1854.*
23 McLean to Civil Secretary, 23 Sep 1853, *AJHR* 1861, 252.
24 Bagnall, *Wairarapa*, 101.
25 Goldsmith, *Wairarapa*, 44.
26 McLean to Sinclair, 11 Apr 1853, McLean Papers, MS 1316.
27 Goldsmith, *Wairarapa*, 55.
28 Ibid., 56–58.
29 Searancke to McLean, 9 Jul 1858, McLean Papers, MS 32/565.
30 A. G. Bagnall, *Wairarapa*, 133, quoted in Goldsmith, *Wairarapa*, 62.
31 Domett to McLean, 15 Jul 1854, McLean Papers, MS 1317.
32 McLean, Diary, 8 Apr 1855, McLean Papers MS 1287.
33 Ibid.
34 Cooper to McLean, 16 Nov 1856, McLean Papers, MS 1318.
35 Cowie, *Hawkes Bay*, 36
36 Ibid.
37 J. D. Ormond to McLean, 10 Jul 1857, McLean Papers, MS 32/481.
38 Ibid., 12 Jul 1857.
39 Cooper to McLean, 19 Apr 1856, in Turton, Epitome.
40 Cooper to McLean, 17 Mar 1856, McLean Papers, MS 1318.
41 Te Hapuku to Governor, 28 Mar 1857, McLean Papers, MS 32/5.
42 Samuel Williams, Remarks upon Land Purchases in the Hawkes Bay Province, McLean Papers, MS 32/9.
43 Ibid.
44 Report of Chief Commissioner of visit to Ahuriri, Dec 1857, McLean Papers, MS 32/5.
45 Gore Browne to Ministers, Memo, 22 Jan 1858, Stafford Papers, ATL.
46 McLean, Journal, 6 Feb 1858, McLean Papers, MS 32/741.
47 Samuel Williams, Remarks on Land Purchases in Hawkes Bay, 1860, McLean Papers, MS 32/11.
48 Cooper to McLean, 30 Sep 1858, *AJHR* 1862 C1 No. 47.
49 Cowie, *Hawkes Bay*, 46–47.
50 Bishop William Williams to Governor, 5 Jun 1861, McLean Papers, MS 32/9.

51 Nemo, Letter to the Editor, 5 Nov 1859, *Hawke's Bay Herald*.
52 Donald to Alexander, 15 Mar 1860, McLean Papers, MS 32/947.
53 McLean to T. H. Smith, 20 July 1859, qms 1839, ATL.
54 Domett to McLean, 5 Jan 1859, McLean Papers, MS 32/245.
55 Remarks upon Land Purchases in the Hawkes Province, McLean Papers, MS 32/3A.
56 Ibid.
57 Ibid.
58 McLean, Diary, 4 May 1848, McLean Papers, MS 1285.

Chapter 11

1 W. K. Hancock, *Survey of British Commonwealth Affairs* vol. 2 part 1 (London 1940), 63.
2 Sinclair, *Maori Wars*, 151.
3 J. Flight to McLean, 10 May 1858, McLean Papers, MS 1320.
4 Sinclair, *Maori Wars*, 142.
5 *AJHR* 1861 C1.
6 Wiremu Kingi to Governor, 12 Feb 1859, *AJHR* 1860 E4.
7 Draft report of Governor's address, undated, McLean Papers, MS 32/728
8 B. J. Dalton, *War and Politics in New Zealand 1855–1870* (Sydney, 1967), 94.
9 Sinclair, *Maori Wars*, 136–37. There is a discrepancy between McLean's diary entries recording the date of the arrival of the Governor and his subsequent meeting with the local tribes and Sinclair's. The latter has the Governor noting his arrival in his journal on 5 March while the large Maori meeting took place on 8 March, quoting the *Taranaki News* of 10 March as his source. C. W. Richmond in 1860, responding to Gore Browne's request for his views on the state of Maori affairs, like McLean, gave the meeting date as 9 March.
10 Ibid., 149.
11 Sinclair, *Maori Wars*, chapter 11.
12 *AJHR* 1861, F3, 19.
13 *AJHR* 1861, E1, 36.
14 McLean to C. W. Richmond, 10 Apr 1859, Richmond Inward Letters, Msy 2773, ATL.
15 Sinclair, *Maori Wars*, 158–59.
16 Ibid., 159.
17 McLean to Governor, 23 Sep 1859, McLean Papers, MS 32/9.
18 C. Orange, *The Treaty of Waitangi* (Wellington 1987), 150–51.
19 McLean to Governor, 23 Sep 1859, McLean Papers, MS 32/9.
20 Gore Browne to Parris, 25 Oct 1859, McLean Papers, MS 32/184.
21 Parris to McLean, 7 Nov 1859, Private, McLean Papers, MS 1298.
22 Gore Browne to McLean, 13 Aug 1859, MS 1298, McLean Papers.
23 Ibid., 12 Sep 1859.
24 Ibid., 27 Sep 1859.
25 Dr. Wilson to McLean, 31 Oct 1859, McLean Papers, MS 1322.
26 McLean, Diary, 17 Nov 1859, McLean Papers, MS 1287.
27 Parris to McLean, 28 Nov 1859, McLean Papers, MS 1298.
28 Ibid., 5 Dec 1859, McLean Papers, MS 1298.
29 Parris to McLean, 12 Dec 1859, Private, McLean Papers, MS 32/9.

30 W. Halse to McLean, 2 Jan 1860, McLean Papers, MS 32/316.
31 Donald to Alexander McLean, 22 Nov 1859, McLean Papers, MS32/947.
32 McLean to Governor, 17 Mar 1860, McLean Papers, MS 1322.
33 Gore Browne to McLean, 4 Apr 1860, McLean Papers, MS 1322.
34 James Belich, *The New Zealand Wars and the Victorian Interpretation of Racial Conflict* (Auckland 1986), 87.
35 McLean to Alexander McLean, 31 Mar 1860, McLean Papers, MS 32/947.
36 Gore Browne to Fortescue, 3 Nov 1860, Gore Browne Letter Book, MS 284.
37 Gore Browne to General Pratt, undated [1860], Gore Browne Letter Books, MS 284.
38 McLean to Governor, 31 May 1860, McLean Papers, MS 32/12.
39 Gore Browne to Parris, 29 April 1860, Gore Browne Letter Book, MS 284.
40 Gore Browne to McLean, 30 Apr 1860, McLean Papers, MS 32/183.
41 Ibid., 1 May 1860.
42 Governor to McLean, 16 May 1860, McLean Papers, MS 1322.
43 McLean to Governor, 21 May 1860, McLean Papers, MS 1299.
44 Gore Browne to Gairdner, 28 May 1860, Gore Browne Letter Book, MS 284.
45 Keith Sinclair, *Penguin History of New Zealand* (Auckland 1980) 123.
46 Gore Browne to Gairdner, 27 Jun 1860, Letter Book, MS 284.
47 Gore Browne to McLean, 24 Jul 1860, McLean Papers, qMS 0616, ATL.
48 Gore Browne to Newcastle, 9 Sep 1860, Gore Browne Letter Book, MS 284.
49 Gore Browne to McLean, 12 Jul 1860, McLean Papers, MS 32/183.

Chapter 12

1 Report of Proceedings, *AJHR* 1860, E9. The following discussion draws on this report.
2 Claudia Orange, 'The Covenant of Kohimarama', *NZ Journal of History*, April 1980.
3 Claudia Orange, *The Treaty of Waitangi*, 148.
4 F. D. Lugard, *The Rise of Our African Empire* (Edinburgh 1893) vol. 2, 651.
5 Gore Browne to McLean, 13 Jul 1860, McLean Papers, MS 32/183.
6 *AJHR* 1860, E4, 15–24.
7 Sinclair, *Maori Wars*, 71.
8 Chief Land Purchase Commissioner to Governor, 1 Dec 1860, *AJHR* 1861, E1.
9 Hadfield in a letter to *New Zealand Spectator*, 10 Oct 1860.
10 Gore Browne to Martin, 7 Dec 1860, Gore Browne Letter Book, MS 284.
11 Gore Browne to Featherston, 2 Jan 1861, Gore Browne Letter Book, MS 284.
12 Ibid., 4 Dec 1860.
13 Dalton, *War and Politics*, 118.
14 R. W. S. Fargher, 'Donald McLean, Chief Native Land Agent 1846–1861 and Native Secretary 1856–1861' (MA thesis: University of Auckland, 1947), 52, 102. Also Sinclair, *Maori Wars*, 89, 202–3. Sinclair drew on material from my thesis when writing *The Origins of the Maori Wars*. Writing to me in 1948, he said he agreed with my opinion of Gore Browne though he did not think I had satisfactorily shown his indecisive quality. When I wrote my thesis in 1947 I was a self-confident young man. Having seen overseas service during the war, like other New Zealanders, I had acquired a healthy scepticism for the infallibility of those in authority over us, particularly of the British officer class. My prejudice led me to view Gore Browne as thick-headed and pigheaded and at the same time weak and indecisive. Maturity and further research changed my opinion.

15 Gore Browne to McLean, Oct 1861, McLean Papers, MS 1299.
16 Ibid., 15 Nov 1861.
17 McLean to Featherston, 17 Jun 1863, McLean Papers, MS 1326.
18 Dillon Bell to McLean, 20 Jul 1863, McLean Papers, MS 32/158.
19 Gore Browne to Newcastle, 4 Dec 1860, Gore Browne Letter Book, MS 284.
20 Gore Browne to McLean, confidential, 1 Oct 1859, McLean Papers, MS 1298.
21 W. Gisborne, *New Zealand Rulers and Statesmen* (London 1897), 176.
22 Sinclair, K. *Maori Wars*, 100–101.
23 *AJHR* 1860, F3, 8–12.
24 McLean to Judge [Johnstone], 3 Nov 1860, McLean Papers, MS 1323.
25 Sewell to McLean, 27 Oct 1860, McLean Papers, MS 32/568.
26 Gisborne, *New Zealand Rulers and Statesmen*, 164–66.
27 Featherston to McLean.
28 McLean to W. S. Grahame, 3 Oct 1860. McLean Papers, MS 32/723.
29 Denison to Gore Browne, *AJHR* 1861, E3B.

Chapter 13

1 Gore Browne to Fortescue, 3 Nov 1860, Gore Browne Letter Book, MS 284.
2 McLean to Governor, 8 Nov 1860, McLean Papers, MS 1323.
3 Gore Browne to McLean, 30 Nov 1860, McLean Papers, MS 1323.
4 Ibid.
5 McLean to Gore Browne, 1 Dec 1860, McLean Papers, MS 1323.
6 McLean to Gore Browne, 16 Mar 1861, McLean Papers, MS 1324.
7 Gore Browne to McLean from Hobart, 6 Sep 1862, McLean Papers, MS 32/184.
8 McLean to Sinclair, 6 Mar 1861, McLean Papers, MS 1324.
9 Weld to McLean, 21 May 1861, McLean Papers, MS 32/628.
10 McLean to Governor, 22 Mar 1861, McLean Papers, MS 1299.
11 McLean to Gore Browne, 22 Mar 1861, McLean Papers, MS 1299.
12 Ibid.
13 Gore Browne to McLean, 22 Apr 1861, McLean Papers, MS 1324.
14 McLean to Strang, 6 May 1861, McLean Papers, MS 32/999.
15 Evelyn Stokes, *Wiremu Tamihana: Rangatira* (Wellington, 2002) 203.
16 J. A. Wilson to McLean, 18 Jul 1861, McLean Papers, MS 1325.
17 Gore Browne to Morgan, 21 Oct 1861. Gore Browne Letter Books, MS 284.
18 Executive Council Minutes, 29 May 1861. NA.
19 McLean and Smith to Executive Council, Memo, 23 May 1861, McLean Papers, MS32/14.
20 Executive Council Minutes, 29 May 1861, 369.
21 Ibid.
22 McLean to Strang, 6 June 1861, McLean Papers, MS 32/999.
23 Cooper to McLean, 9 Jul 1862, McLean Papers, MS 1325.
24 Parris to McLean, 23 Sep 1862, McLean Papers, MS 32/494.
25 McLean to Strang, 6 Dec 1861, McLean Papers, MS 32/999.
26 McLean to Strang, 6 Sep 1862, McLean Papers, MS 32/999.
27 F. E. Maning to McLean, 10 Aug 1861, McLean Papers, MS 1325.
28 McLean, Diary, 16 Jul 1861, McLean Papers, MS 1250.

Chapter 14

1 Parr, 'The McLean Estates', 9.
2 Ibid., 16.
3 M. Fitzgerald to McLean, 19 Dec 1853, McLean Papers, MS 1316.
4 Donald to Alexander McLean, 11 Jan 1857, McLean Papers, MS 1318.
5 Cooper to McLean, 16 Nov 1856, McLean Papers, MS 1318.
6 Donald to Alexander McLean, 13 Jul 1859, McLean Papers, MS 32/947.
7 Donald to Alexander McLean, 27 Jan 1860, McLean Papers, MS 32/947.
8 Ibid., 15 Mar 1860.
9 Featherston to McLean, 19 Mar 1860, McLean Papers, MS 1322.
10 Campbell, 'Hawkes Bay Landed Society', 73.
11 Ibid.
12 Donald to Revd D. McColl, 4 Aug 1853, McLean Papers, MS 32/405.
13 Extract from despatch of Duke of Newcastle, 18 Oct 1857, McLean Papers, MS 32/16.
14 Donald to Alexander McLean, 1846, McLean Papers, MS 32/947.
15 Donald to Archibald McLean, 31 Aug 1858, McLean Papers, MS 32/967.
16 Ibid.
17 Ibid., 11 Nov 1858.
18 Donald to Alexander, McLean Papers, MS 32/947.
19 Gore Browne to Newcastle, 9 Sep 1860, Gore Browne Letter Book, MS 284.
20 Donald to Alexander McLean, 11 Jan 1859, McLean Papers, MS 32/951.
21 Donald to Archibald McLean, 27 Jan 1859, McLean Papers, MS 32/967.
22 McLean, Diary, 14 and 16 Oct 1850, McLean Papers, MS 1286.
23 Donald to Annabella McLean, 17 Jun 1859, McLean Papers, MS 32/963.
24 Ibid., 20 Jan 1860.
25 Donald to Catherine McLean, 15 May 1858, McLean Papers, MS 32/974.
26 Ibid., 1 and 2 Feb 1859.
27 Donald to Douglas McLean, 24 Jun 1859, McLean Papers, MS 32/899.
28 Donald to Alexander McLean, 27 Oct 1860, McLean Papers, MS 32/947.
29 D. Hood to J. B. Gillies, 18 Feb 1861, McLean Papers, MS 32/776.
30 Donald to Alexander McLean, 2 Jul 1861, McLean Papers, MS 32/947.
31 Ibid., 3 Aug 1861.
32 Parr, 'The McLean Estates', 40.
33 Donald to Alexander McLean, 7 Jan 1861, McLean Papers, MS 32/947.
34 Donald to Archibald McLean, 16 May 1861, MS 32/697.
35 McLean to W. S. Grahame, 5 Aug 1862, Letter Book, McLean Papers, MS 1196.
36 Ibid.
37 McLean to Gore Browne, 26 May 1862, in Parr, 'The McLean Estates', 38.
38 McLean to Gore Browne, 29 Oct 1862, qMS 0615, ATL.
39 Donald McLean to Alexander, 24 Apr 1867, McLean Papers, MS 32/948.
40 Parr, 'The McLean Estates', 224.
41 Ibid., 39
42 Ibid., 40
43 McLean to Strang, 3 Aug 1861, McLean Papers, MS 32/999.
44 Donald to Catherine McLean, 9 Jun 1861, McLean Papers, MS 32/974.
45 McLean to Catherine, 5 Aug 1862, McLean Papers, MS 32/974.
46 Ibid.

47 Ibid.
48 Annabella to Donald, 5 Feb, McLean Papers, MS 32/816.
49 McLean to Strang, 9 May 1863, McLean Papers, MS 32/999.
50 Donald to Douglas, 17 May 1862, McLean Papers, MS 32/899.
51 Donald to Alexander McLean, 27 Oct 1860, McLean Papers, MS 32/947.
52 Ibid.
53 Donald to Douglas, 26 Mar 1864, McLean Papers, MS 32/899.
54 Ibid., 5 Oct 1864.
55 Donald McLean to Donald McColl, 27 Oct 1860, McLean Papers, MS 32/899.
56 McLean to Annabella, 3 Feb 1870, McLean Papers, MS 32/963.
57 Douglas to Donald, 4 Aug 1870, McLean Papers, MS 32/820.
58 Ibid., 11 Oct 1871.
59 F. E. Hamlin, to Native Minister, 20 Sep 1869, OP A/2, quoted in Parr, 'The McLean Estates', 87.
60 Ormond to McLean, 8 Nov 1870, McLean Papers, MS 32/483.
61 Parr, 'The McLean Estates', 94.
62 W. K. McLean to Donald McLean, cited in Parr, 'The McLean Estates', 84.
63 Condie to McLean, 28 Dec 1862, McLean Papers, Hawkes Bay Museum.

Chapter 15

1 Ormond to McLean, 12 Dec 1862, McLean Papers, MS 1235.
2 McLean to Strang, 18 Dec 1862, McLean Papers, MS 32/999.
3 Parr, 'The McLean Estates', 40.
4 McLean to Strang, 8 Apr 1863, McLean Papers, MS 32/999.
5 Ibid., 17 Apr 1862.
6 Ibid., 5 Jul 1864.
7 13 Oct 1866, Hawkes Bay Provincial Council Proceedings.
8 Rolleston, *The Master*, 100.
9 McLean to Colonial Secretary, 23 Nov 1863, McLean Papers, MS 1300.
10 Ibid., 24 Nov 1863.
11 Ibid., 2 Dec 1863.
12 Donald to Alexander, McLean Papers, MS 32/948.
13 Donald to Alexander, 22 Nov 1864, McLean Papers, MS 32/948.
14 McLean, 1865, McLean Papers, MS 1287.
15 Superintendent's Opening Address to H. B. Provincial Council, 13 June 1865, NA.
16 McLean to Colonial Secretary, 28 Jun 1864, Hawkes Bay Provincial Council Proceedings, NA.
17 McLean to Richmond, 30 May 1865, McLean Papers, MS 32/128.
18 FitzGerald to McLean, 28 Jul 1867, McLean Papers, MS 1301.
19 *NZPD* 1867, 336.
20 In cases involving Maori only, the magistrate had two Maori assessors whose assent was necessary before judgement was executed
21 Donald to Douglas, 30 Apr 1868, McLean Papers, MS 32/899.
22 *NZPD* 1867, 336.
23 McLean to Stafford, 27 Nov 1867, McLean Papers, MS 32/584.
24 *AJHR* 1866 F11A, 4.

25 Vincent O'Malley, 'Report for the Crown Forest Rental Trust on the East Coast Confiscation Legislation and its Implementation', 60–79.
26 Ormond to McLean, 9 Oct 1869, McLean Papers, MS 32/483.

Chapter 16

1 Dalton, *War and Politics*, 207–208.
2 Belich, *The New Zealand Wars*, 204–205, 208.
3 Weld to McLean, 15 Mar 1865, AGG/HB 1/1/1, NA.
4 Weld to McLean, 26 Apr 1865, McLean Papers, MS 1301.
5 Ormond to McLean, 26 Apr 1865, McLean Papers, MS 1301.
6 McLean to Harris, 30 Mar 1865, McLean Papers, MS 32/18.
7 W. Oliver, *Challenge and Response*, 86–87.
8 McLean to Weld, 5 May 1865, McLean Papers, MS 32/19.
9 McLean to Native Minister, 14 Sep 1865, McLean Papers, MS 32/19.
10 McLean, Diary, 15 Jul 1865, McLean Papers, MS 1287.
11 McLean to Richmond, 7 Sep 1865, McLean Papers, MS 32/19.
12 McLean to Williams, 13 Sep 1865, McLean Papers, MS 32/19.
13 Weld to McLean, 10 Nov 1865, McLean Papers, MS 1301.
14 Stafford to McLean, 1 Nov 1865, quoted in Waitangi Tribunal, *Turanga Tangata, Turanga Whenua: The Report on the Turanganui-a-Kiwa Claims* (Wellington, 2004), 879–80.
15 FitzGerald to McLean, 28 Nov 1865, McLean Papers, MS 1301.
16 Judith Binney, *Redemption Songs: A Life of Te Kooti Arikirangi Te Turuki* (Auckland 1995), 50–60.
17 Ibid., 62.
18 Ibid.
19 McLean to Grey, 21 Jan 1866, McLean Papers, MS 32/19.
20 Stafford to McLean, 7 Nov 1865, McLean Papers, MS 32/584.
21 McLean to Stafford, 16 Dec 1865, McLean Papers, MS 32/19.
22 Stafford to McLean, 4 Jan 1866, McLean Papers, MS 1301.
23 McLean to Stafford, 19 Jan 1866, McLean Papers, MS 1203.
24 O'Malley, *A Tangled Web*, 266–70.
25 *NZPD* 10 Sep 1867, 859.
26 The *Mohaka ki Ahuriri Report* of the Waitangi Tribunal gives a detailed account of subsequent events.
27 McLean Papers, MS 1301.
28 Stafford to McLean, 17 Oct 1866, McLean Papers, MS 32/584.

Chapter 17

1 Ormond to McLean, 7 Nov 1867, McLean Papers, MS 32/482.
2 Richmond to McLean, 18 Nov 1867, McLean Papers, MS 32/534.
3 Binney, *Redemption Songs*, 93.
4 Belich, *The New Zealand Wars*, 225.

5 *NZPD*, 16 Sep 1868, 374–78.
6 Ibid., 378–83.
7 Donald to Douglas McLean, 8 Oct 1868, McLean Papers, MS 32/899.
8 McLean to Ministers, Memo, 10 Oct 1868. McLean Papers, MS 32/26.
9 Richmond to McLean, 12 Oct 1868, McLean Papers, MS 32/20.
10 Richmond to McLean, 13 Oct 1868, McLean Papers, MS 32/534.
11 Ibid., 12 Oct 1868.
12 Biggs to McLean, 9 Nov 1868, McLean Papers, MS 32/162.
13 Binney, *Redemption Songs*, 121.
14 Belich, *The New Zealand Wars*, 231.
15 Ibid., 3 Jan 1869.
16 Featherston to McLean, 11 Dec 1868. McLean Papers, MS 1337.
17 McLean to Whitmore, 14 and 24 Oct 1866. Whitmore Papers, Hawkes Bay Museum.
18 Belich, *The New Zealand Wars*, 220.
19 Westrupp to McLean, Confidential, 9 Dec 1868, McLean Papers, MS 1302.
20 Westrupp to McLean, 27 Nov 1868, McLean Papers, MS 1337.
21 Richmond to Stafford, 13 Aug 1869, Stafford Papers, MS 28/42, Alexander Turnbull Library.
22 McLean to Richmond, 12 Dec 1868, McLean Papers, MS 32/22.
23 Richmond to Stafford, 26 Dec 1868, Stafford Papers, Folder 28, ATL.
24 McLean to Richmond, 15 Nov 1868, McLean Papers, MS 32/21.
25 Lambert to McLean, 14 Nov 1868, McLean Papers, MS 1337.
26 Deighton to McLean, 17 Nov 1868, McLean Papers, MS 1337.
27 Richmond to McLean, 14 Nov 1868, McLean Papers, MS 32/534.
28 McLean to Richmond, Nov 1868, McLean Papers, MS 32/21.
29 Ibid., 23 Nov 1868.
30 McLean to Carlyon, 18 Feb 1869, McLean Papers, MS 32/23.
31 Rogan to McLean, 24 Feb 1869, McLean Papers, MS 1328.
32 McLean to Defence Minister, 2 Mar 1869, McLean Papers, MS 32/23.
33 *AJHR* 1869 A4.
34 McLean to Haultain, 10 Mar 1869, McLean Papers, MS 32/23.
35 McLean to Ministers, 12 Mar 1869, McLean Papers, MS 32/23.
36 Stafford to McLean, 18 Mar 1869, *AJHR* 1869 A4.
37 Vogel to McLean, Private, 19 Mar 1869, McLean Papers, MS 1302.
38 It is hereby notified that the New Zealand Government has withdrawn from the Honourable Donald McLean Esq. the authority he has held as its Agent on the East Coast. 13 March 1869, *NZ Gazette*.
39 McLean to Dillon Bell, Mar 1869, McLean Papers, MS 1302.
40 G. Preece to McLean, 27 Mar 1869, McLean Papers, MS 1338.
41 *NZPD* 1869, 240–42
42 McLean to Haultain, 10 Mar 1869, McLean Papers, MS 32/23.
43 Hawkes Bay Provincial Council Proceedings, 24 Sep 1869, NAW.

Chapter 18

1 McLean, Journal, 1 Jan 1870, McLean Papers, MS 1287.
2 McLean to Annabella, 1870, McLean Papers, MS 32/967.

3 Sinclair, *Maori Wars*, 57.
4 Ormond to McLean, 9 Oct 1869, McLean Papers, MS 32/483.
5 McLean to H. C. Clarke, 19 Feb 1870, McLean Papers, MS 1303. Cf. Belich, *New Zealand Wars*, 285.
6 Firth to Defence Minister, 12 Oct 1870, McLean Papers, MS 32/45.
7 Binney, *Redemption Songs*, 552.
8 Land Purchases under Public Works and Immigration Act, McLean Papers, MS 32/36.
9 Fox to McLean, 26 May 1871, McLean Papers, MS 32/279.
10 Ward, *A Show of Justice*, 237.
11 Fox to McLean, 31 Oct 1869, McLean Papers, MS 32/278.
12 Fox to McLean, 20 Sep 1869, McLean Papers, MS 32/279.
13 Fox, Memo for Cabinet, 14 Apr 1871, McLean Papers, MS 1304.
14 Gisborne, *New Zealand Rulers and Statesmen*, 163–68.
15 Fox to McLean, 30 Dec 1871, McLean Papers, MS 32/279.
16 Vogel to McLean, 2 May 1872, McLean Papers, MS 32/615.
17 McLean, Journal, 9 Nov 1869, McLean Papers, MS 1287.
18 *AJHR* 1870 A12.
19 Ibid.
20 McLean to FitzGerald, 16 Nov 1869, McLean Papers, MS 1201.
21 McLean, Diary, 20 Nov 1869, McLean Papers.
22 *AJHR* 1870 A12.
23 McLean to Searancke, 3 Dec 1869, McLean Papers, MS 1201.
24 McLean to Ngai Te Rangi, November 1869, McLean Papers, MS 32/43.
25 Ward, *A Show of Justice*, 236.
26 Martin to Native Minister, 21 Feb 1870, McLean Papers, MS 32/30.
27 Fox to Ministers, Feb 1870, McLean Papers, MS 32/30.
28 McLean, Cabinet Paper, 16 Sep 1870, McLean Papers, MS 32/30.
29 McLean to Ormond, 27 Oct 1869, AGG-HB 1/1 NO 246 NA.
30 Ward, *A Show of Justice*, 247.
31 Ibid., 229–30.
32 *NZPD* 22 Oct 1872, 894–95.
33 McLean to Vogel, 15 Oct 1870, McLean Papers, MS 32/615.
34 Ormond to McLean, 4 May 1872, McLean Papers, MS 1304.
35 McLean to Governor, 5 Jan 1872, McLean Papers, MS 32/33.
36 McLean to Ministers, 10 Sep 1872, McLean Papers, MS 32/33.
37 McLean to Governor, 2 Oct 1872, McLean Papers, MS 32/33.
38 Waterhouse to McLean, Telegram, 27 Feb 1873, McLean Papers, MS 32/80.
39 Ward, *A Show of Justice*, 248–49.
40 Ibid., 250.
41 *NZPD* 1870, vol. 9, 564.
42 Richard Boast, *Maori Land Law* (Wellington 1999), 67–68.
43 *AJHR* 1891 G1 47.
44 *AJHR* 1873 vol. 14, 604–606.
45 Ibid., 611.
46 *NZPD* 1874, 939
47 Ibid.
48 Boast, *Maori Land Law*, 68.
49 *NZPD* 1876, vol. 22, 239.

Chapter 19

1 McLean to Kemp, Telegram, 27–28 Dec 1872, McLean Papers, MS 32/63.
2 McLean to Ormond, Telegram.
3 Brissenden to Native Minister, 3 Jan 1874, McLean Papers, MS 32/33.
4 W. K. McLean to Donald McLean, 5 Mar 1872, McLean Papers, MS 32/435.
5 Ibid., 8 June 1872.
6 J. Hall to Premier, 23 Nov 1872, McLean Papers, MS 32/31.
7 William Reynolds, Re Worgan's Commission, 6 Dec 1872, McLean Papers, MS 32/31.
8 Worgan to McLean, 2 Jan 1873, McLean Papers, MS 1350.
9 Fox to McLean, 15 Jun 1873, McLean Papers, MS 1350.
10 Ibid., 31 May 1873.
11 Gisborne, *New Zealand Rulers and Statesmen*, 166–67.
12 Ormond to McLean, 13 May and 4 Jun 1875, McLean Papers, MS 32/485.
13 McLean, Diary, 14 Sep 1859, McLean Papers.
14 Russell to McLean, 16 Sep 1863, McLean Papers, MS 32/552.
15 Ibid., 28 Mar 1866.
16 Ormond to McLean, 4 May 1872, McLean Papers, MS 1364.
17 Ormond to McLean, Aug 1869, McLean Papers, MS 32/483.
18 McLean to Kinross, 8 Aug 1870, McLean Papers, MS 32/379.
19 Ibid., 18 Oct 1870.
20 *Hawke's Bay Times*, 7 Mar 1870.
21 Ormond to McLean, 7 Mar 1870, McLean Papers, MS 32/483.
22 Supreme Court hearing between Karaitiana and Frederick Sutton, Paora Torotoro, Ahera Te Koara, Nikera Whitingara, Eureti Ngamu, Samuel Locke and Sir Donald McLean. McLean Papers, Hawkes Bay Museum.
23 *NZPD* 1871 vol. 10, 270– 71.
24 Ibid., 1872, 24 Jul, 75–77
25 Ormond to McLean, 26 Mar 1872, McLean Papers, MS 32/485.
26 Locke to Native Minister, 4 Jun 1872, McLean Papers, MS 32/35B.
27 Ormond to McLean, 10 Jun 1872, McLean Papers, MS 32/485.
28 *NZPD* 1872, 768–69.
29 Donald to Alexander McLean, 1 Nov 1871, McLean Papers, MS 32/951.
30 Ormond to McLean, 4 May 1872, McLean Papers, MS 32/485.
31 W. K. McLean to Donald McLean, 5 Mar 1873, McLean Papers, MS 32/435.
32 Ibid., 5 Apr 1873.
33 Sinclair, *Kinds of Peace*, 118.
34 *AJHR* 1873 vol. 3 G7, 48.
35 Cowie, *Hawkes Bay*, 69.
36 Ibid., 82.
37 Maning to McLean, 6 Dec 1873, McLean Papers, MS 1351.
38 Fenton to McLean, 16 May 1873, MS 1350.
39 M. P. K. Sorrenson, *The Maori and New Zealand Politics*, 40.
40 McLean to Atkinson, 23 Jan 1873, McLean Papers, MS 32/34.
41 Of 1,200,000 acres confiscated in Taranaki, 21,866 acres were set aside as reserves for returned 'rebels', 91,663 acres were given as compensation for 'friendly natives' and

180,000 acres were given back to the owners. Hazel Riseborough, *Days of Darkness Taranaki 1878–1884* (Wellington, 1989), 12.

42 *NZPD* 8 Oct 1875, 339–42.

43 Ibid., 5 Oct 1875, 207–24.

44 *NZPD* 11 Aug 1876, vol. 21, 250–56; also McLean Papers, MS 32/122B.

45 *NZPD* 1876.

46 McLean to Premier, 27 Oct 1876, McLean Papers, MS 32/22B.

Chapter 20

1 Donald to Annabella, Nov 1873, McLean Papers, MS 32/963.

2 McLean to Premier, 30 Nov 1876, McLean Papers, MS 32/32b.

3 Parr, 'The McLean Estates', 144.

4 Parr, 'The McLean Estates', 134–35.

5 Ormond to McLean, 25 Nov 1876, McLean Papers, MS 332/486.

6 *Hawke's Bay Herald*, 9 Jan 1877, McLean Papers, MS 32/732.

7 Ibid., 19 Jan 1877.

8 Memorial Service, 14 Jan 1877, McLean Papers, MS 32/732.

Appendices

1 George Clarke to McLean, 2 Aug 1844, Protector's Office, McLean Papers, MS 32/1.

2 Extract From Native Secretary's Memo to Governor, 23 September 1859, McLean Papers, MS 32/9.

3 Goldsmith, *Wairarapa*.

4 Extracted from Cowie, *Hawkes Bay*.

Bibliography

Primary Sources

MANUSCRIPT

Alexander Turnbull Library
- Gore Browne Letter Books
- McLean Papers
- Richard Taylor Journals
- Richmond Papers
- Sinclair Papers
- Stafford Papers

National Archives
- Colonial Secretary's Office
- Governors
- Native Affairs

Auckland Public Library

Hawkes Bay Museum
- Whitmore Papers

Hocken Library

Taranaki Museum

OFFICIAL RECORDS

Appendix to the Journal of the House of Representatives
Journals of the House of Representatives
Votes and Proceedings of the House of Representatives
New Zealand Parliamentary Debates
Great Britain Parliamentary Papers
Turton, H. H., ed., *Maori Deeds of Land Purchases in the North Island of New Zealand*. 2 vols. Government Printer Wellington 1877, 1878

REPORTS

Anderson, Robyn and Keith Pickens, *Rangahaua Whanui District 12: Wellington District: Port Nicholson, Hutt Valley, Porirua, Rangitikei, and Manawatu* Wellington, 1996.
Cowie, Dean, *Rangahaua Whanui District 11B: Hawkes Bay*, Wellington, 1996.
Goldsmith, Paul, *Rangahaua Whanui District 11A: Wairarapa*, Wellington, 1996.

Phillipson, G. A., *Rangahaua Whanui District 13: The Northern South Island.* Wellington, 1996.
O'Malley, Vincent, Report for the Crown Forestry Rental Trust on the East Coast Legislation and its Implementation, 1994.
——, The Ahuriri Purchase: An Overview Report, Research report commissioned by the Crown Forestry Rental Trust, 1995.
——, 'An Entangled Web: Te Aitanga a Mahaki Land and Politics, 1840–1873, Report Commissioned by the Te Aitanga a Mahaki Claims Committee, 2000.
Rigby, Barry, and John Koning, Muriwhenua Land Claim (Wai-45): A Preliminary Report on Historical Evidence, Waitangi Tribunal 1989
Waitangi Tribunal, *Muriwhenua Land Report*, Wellington, 1997.
——, *Te Whanganui-a-Orotu Report*, Wellington, 1995.
——, *The Taranaki Report: Kaupapa Tuatahi*, Wellington, 1996.
——, *The Mohaka ki Ahuriri Report*, Wellington, 2004.
——, *Turanga Tangata, Turanga Whenua: the report on the Turanganui-a-Kiwa claims*, Wellington, 2004.
Ward, Alan, *Rangahaua Whanui National Overview Report* Vol. 2, Wellington, 1997.

NEWSPAPERS

Hawke's Bay Herald
Independent
Southern Cross
Spectator

Secondary Sources

BOOKS, MAGAZINES, ARTICLES

Altick, Richard D., *Victorian People and Ideas*, London, 1973.
Bagnall, A. G., *Wairarapa: An Historical Excursion*, Masterton, 1976.
Ballara, Angela, *Iwi: The Dynamics of Maori Tribal Organisation from c.1769 to c.1945*, Wellington, 1998.
Battersby, H., *The One Day War: The Battle of Omarunui 1866*, Auckland, 2000.
Belich, James, *The New Zealand Wars and the Victorian Interpretation of Racial Conflict*, Auckland, 1986.
——, *Making Peoples: A History of the New Zealanders from Polynesian Settlement to the End of the Nineteenth Century*, Auckland, 1996.
Binney, Judith, *Redemption Songs: A Life of Te Kooti Arikirangi Te Turuki*, Auckland, 1995.
Binney, Judith and Deborah Montgomerie ed., *Koha: Essays in Honour of M. P. K. Sorrenson, New Zealand Journal of History* April 1997.
Boast, Richard, *Maori Land Law*, Wellington, 1999.
Bohan, Edmond, *Edward Stafford: New Zealand's First Statesman*, Christchurch, 1994.
——, *'Blest Madman': Fitzgerald of Canterbury*, Christchurch, 1998.
Bolt, Christine, *Victorian Attitudes to Race*, London, 1971.
Boyd, Mary, *City of the Plains: A History of Hastings*, Wellington, 1984.
Burns, Patricia, *Fatal Success: A History of the New Zealand Company*, Auckland, 1989.

Cage, R. A., *The Scots Abroad: Labour, Capital, Enterprise 1750–1914*, London, 1985.
Cain, P. J. and A. G. Hopkins, *British Imperialism: Innovation and Expansion 1688–1914*, London 1993.
Colley, Linda, *Britons: Forging the Nation 1707–1837*, London, 1996.
Cowan, James, *Sir Donald Maclean*, Dunedin, 1940.
Dalton, B. J., *War and Politics in New Zealand 1855–1870*, Sydney, 1967.
Dalziel, Raewyn, '*"Making us one": Courtship and Marriage in Colonial New Zealand*', *The Turnbull Library Record*, Vol.19 No.1 May 1986.
Dieffenbach, Earnest, *Travels In New Zealand*, London, 1843.
Evison, H., *Te Wai Pounamu: The Greenstone Island*, Wellington, 1993.
Francis, Mark, *Governors and Settlers: Images of Authority in the British Colonies 1820–1860*, London, 1992.
Gaskell, Philip, *Morven Transformed: A Highland Parish in the Nineteenth Century*, Cambridge, 1968.
Gisborne, W., *New Zealand Rulers and Statesmen*, London, 1897.
Gore Browne, Harriet Louisa, *Narrative of the Waitara Purchase and The Taranaki War*, ed. W. P. Morrell, Dunedin 1965.
Gorst, J. E., *The Maori King*, ed. Keith Sinclair, London, 1959.
Graham, Jeanine, *Frederick Weld*, Auckland, 1983.
Hancock, W. K., *Survey of British Commonwealth Affairs*, vol. 2 Part 1. London, 1940.
——, *Argument of Empire*, London, 1943.
Harrop, A. J., *England and the Maori Wars*, London, 1937.
Hill, Richard S., *Policing the Colonial Frontier: The Theory and Practice of Coercive Social and Racial Control in New Zealand 1767–1867*, Wellington, 1986.
Hilton, Boyd, *The Age of Atonement*, Oxford, 1988.
Ignatieff, Michael, *The Warrior's Honour*, London, 1998.
Kiernan, V. G., *The Lords of Human Kind*, London, 1969.
——, *Imperialism And Its Contradictions*, ed. Harvey J. Kaye, London, 1995.
Lethbridge, Christopher, *The Wounded Lion: Octavius Hadfield 1814–1904*, Christchurch, 1993.
Lugard, F. D., *The Rise of Our African Empire*, Edinburgh, 1893.
McIntyre, William D and W. J. Gardner (eds), *Speeches and Documents on New Zealand History*, Oxford, 1971.
McLean Sinclair, Rev. A., *Clarsach Na Coille–The Harp of the Wood; The McLean Songster*, Glasgow 2nd. ed. 1928.
Macleod, John, *Highlanders: A History of the Gaels*, Great Britain, 1997.
McLintock, A. H., *Crown Colony Government In New Zealand*, Wellington, 1958.
Macmorran, Barbara, *Octavius Hadfield*, Wellington, 1971.
Martin, Sir W., *The Taranaki Question*, Auckland, 1860.
Miller, Harold, *Race Conflict in New Zealand*, Auckland, 1966.
Miller, John, *Early Victorian New Zealand: A Study of Racial Tensions and Social Attitudes*, London, 1958.
Morrell, W. P., *British Colonial Policy in the Age of Peel and Russell*, Oxford, 1966.
——, *British Colonial Policy in the Mid-Victorian Age*, Oxford, 1969.
Oliver, W. H., ed. *The Dictionary of New Zealand Biography*, vol.1, Wellington, 1990.
Oliver, W. H. and Jane M. Thomson, *Challenge and Response: A Study of the Development of the East Coast Region*, Gisborne, 1971.
Orange, Claudia, 'The Covenant of Kohimarama', *New Zealand Journal of History*, April, 1980.
——, *The Treaty of Waitangi*, Wellington, 1987.
Pocock, J. G. A., ed., *The Maori and New Zealand Politics*, Auckland, 1965.

Renwick, William, ed. *Sovereignty and Indigenous Rights: The Treaty of Waitangi in International Contexts*, Wellington, 1991.

Reynolds, Henry, *Frontier*, Sydney, 1987.

Rice, G. W., *Oxford History of New Zealand*, 2nd. ed., Auckland, 1992.

Rickard, L. S., *Tamihana: The Kingmaker*, Wellington, 1963.

Rolleston, Rosemary and Ormond Wilson, *The Master: J. D. Ormond of Wallingford*, Wellington, 1980.

Ross, W. Hugh, *Te Kooti*, Auckland, 1996.

Rusden, G. W., *History of New Zealand*, 3 vols, London, 1883.

Rutherford, J. *Sir George Grey K.C.B. 1812–1898: A study in Colonial Government*, London,1961.

Said, Edward W., *Culture and Imperialism*, London, 1994.

Sewell, Henry, *The Journal of, 1853–7*, vols 1 and 2 ed. W. David McIntyre, Christchurch, 1980.

Sinclair, Keith, *The Origins of the Maori Wars*, Auckland, 1952.

——, *The Penguin History of New Zealand*, Auckland 1980.

——, ed., *The Oxford Illustrated History of New Zealand*, Auckland 1990.

——, *Te Tikanga Pakeke: The Maori Anti-Landselling Movements In Taranaki*, in *The Feel of Truth* ed. Peter Munz, Wellington, 1969.

Smout, T. C., *A History of the Scottish People 1560–1830*, London, 1972.

——, *A Century of the Scottish People 1830–1950*, London, 1986.

Sorrenson, M. P. K., *Maori Origins and Migrations*, Auckland ,1979.

——, *The Maori King Movement 1858–1885*, in *Studies of a Small Democracy* ed. Robert Chapman and Keith Sinclair, Auckland, 1963.

Stanley, B., *The Bible and The Flag: Protestant Mission and British Imperialism in the 19th and 20th Centuries*, 1990.

Stokes, Evelyn, *Wiremu Tamihana: Rangatira*, Wellington, 2002.

Stone, R. C. J., *Young Logan Campbell*, Auckland, 1982.

I. L. G. Sutherland, ed., *The Maori People Today*, Christchurch, 1940.

Ward, Alan, *A Show of Justice: Racial 'Amalgamation' in Nineteenth Century New Zealand*, Auckland, 1973.

——, *An Unsettled History*, Wellington, 1999.

Wards, Ian, *The Shadow Of The Land*, Wellington, 1968.

Weber, Max, *The Protestant Ethic and the Spirit of Capitalism*, London, 1930.

Williams, David V., *'Te Kooti Tango Whenua': The Native Land Court 1864–1909*, Wellington, 1999.

J. C. Wilson, *Early Rangitikei*, Christchurch, 1976.

Wilson, J. G., ed. *Centennial History of Hawke's Bay*, Dunedin, 1939.

Wright, Matthew, *Hawkes Bay: The History of a Province*, Palmerston North, 1994.

Young, David, *Woven By Water*, Wellington, 1998.

UNPUBLISHED THESES

Campbell, M. D. N., 'The Evolution of Hawke's Bay Landed Society 1850–1914', PhD thesis, Victoria University of Wellington, 1973.

Fargher, R. W. S., 'Donald McLean, Chief Land Purchase Agent 1846–1861 and Native Secretary 1856–1861', MA thesis, University of Auckland, 1947.

Goldsmith, P. J., 'Aspects Of The Life Of William Colenso', MA thesis, University of Auckland, 1995.

McKirdy, A., 'Maori–Pakeha Land Transactions in Hawkes Bay, 1848–1864', MA thesis, Victoria University of Wellington, 1994.

McNicholas, P., 'The Interaction between Pakeha Social History and Maori–Pakeha Relations at New Plymouth, 1840s-1860s', MA thesis, Victoria University of Wellington, 1996.

Parr, B. C., 'The McLean Estates: a study of pastoral finance and estate management in New Zealand 1853–1891', MA thesis, University of Auckland, 1970.

Parsonson, Ann R., 'He Whenua Te Utu (The Payment Will Be Land)' PhD thesis, University of Canterbury, 1978.

Turnbull, M., 'An Enquiry into the Conduct of the East Coast War 1865–1869', MA Thesis, 1947.

Index

DM refers to Donald McLean.